1 MONTH OF
FREE
READING

at

www.ForgottenBooks.com

By purchasing this book you are eligible for one month membership to ForgottenBooks.com, giving you unlimited access to our entire collection of over 1,000,000 titles via our web site and mobile apps.

To claim your free month visit:

www.forgottenbooks.com/free559624

ISBN 978-0-265-96766-9
PIBN 10559624

This book is a reproduction of an important historical work. Forgotten Books uses state-of-the-art technology to digitally reconstruct the work, preserving the original format whilst repairing imperfections present in the aged copy. In rare cases, an imperfection in the original, such as a blemish or missing page, may be replicated in our edition. We do, however, repair the vast majority of imperfections successfully; any imperfections that remain are intentionally left to preserve the state of such historical works.

THE ROMAN REPUBLIC

AND

THE FOUNDER OF THE EMPIRE

BY

hower Edward

T. RICE HOLMES

HON. LITT.D. (DUBLIN.) ; HON. D.LITT. (OXON.) ;
HONORARY MEMBER OF THE ISTITVTO
PER LA STORIA DI ROMA ANTICA

VOLUME II
(58-50 B.C.)

OXFORD
AT THE CLARENDON PRESS
1923

CONTENTS

OF THE SECOND VOLUME

PART I

CHAPTER VII

GAUL BEFORE THE ROMAN CONQUEST

CHAPTER VIII

CAESAR'S FIRST TWO CAMPAIGNS IN GAUL

2592·2

27452

CHAPTER IX

ANNEXATION OF CYPRUS.—THE HUMILIATION OF POMPEY,
THE RECALL OF CICERO, AND THE CONFERENCE AT LUCA

CHAPTER X

CAMPAIGNS AGAINST THE MARITIME TRIBES AND THE
AQUITANI.—RESULTS OF THE CONFERENCE AT LUCA.—
MASSACRE OF THE USIPETES AND TENCTERI.—CAESAR'S
INVASIONS OF BRITAIN.—THE DISASTER AT ATUATUCA
AND ITS RESULTS

CHAPTER XI

THE DISSOLUTION OF THE TRIUMVIRATE

CHAPTER XII

THE REBELLION OF VERCINGETORIX.—COMPLETION OF THE CONQUEST OF GAUL

CHAPTER XIII

THE GATHERING OF THE STORM

PART II

LIST OF ILLUSTRATIONS

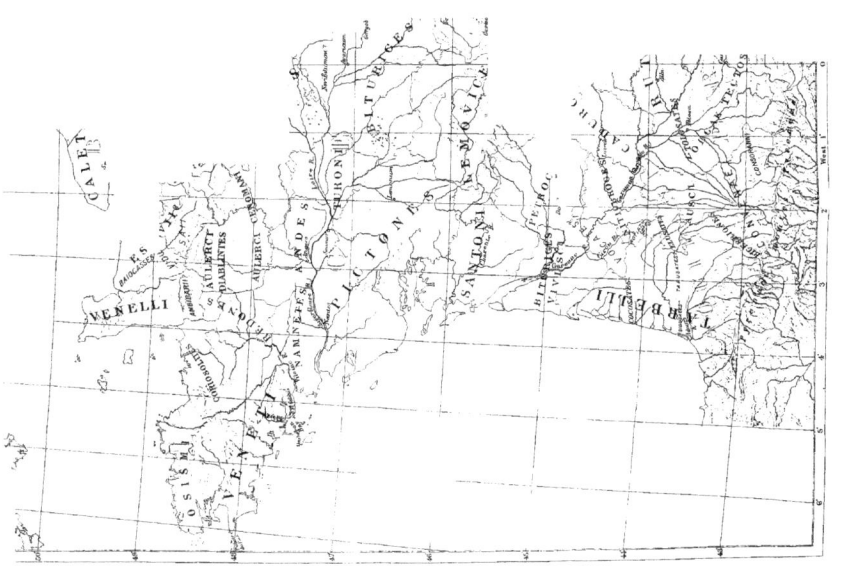

CHAPTER VII

GAUL BEFORE THE ROMAN CONQUEST

THE Roman province of Transalpine Gaul, bounded The Pro-vince. originally by the Maritime Alps and the Rhône, had been extended westward until the frontier ran along the Cevennes and the river Tarn to the centre of the Pyrenees. The Gallic tribes were obliged to pay tribute and to furnish troops ; and although, in accordance with Roman principles, they were permitted to retain their forms of government, their subjection was assured by the con-struction of roads and fortresses. The heavy exactions of the conquerors provoked frequent insurrections ; but year by year the Provincials became steadily Romanized. Roman nobles acquired estates in the Province, and sent their stewards to manage them. Roman merchants built warehouses and counting-houses in the towns ; and the language and civilization of Rome began to take root. Narbo with its spacious harbour was not only a powerful military station, but in commerce the rival of Massilia. Nor was the activity of the Romans confined to the Province itself. Catamantaloedis, King of the Sequani, received from the Senate the title of Friend ; and the same honour was bestowed upon an Aquitanian noble [1] and upon Ollovico, King of the Nitiobroges, who ruled the upper valley of the Garonne. For what services these distinctions were conferred, we do not know ; but events were paving the way for the conquest of the country that stretched beyond the Rhône and the Cevennes to the Rhine and the Atlantic Ocean.

The aspect of this region was very different from that Gaul and its inhabitants. of the beautiful France with which we are familiar. The land of gay cities, of picturesque old towns dominated by

---

[1] One of his grandsons, who served as a cavalry officer under Caesar, bore the Roman name Piso (*B. G.*, iv, 12, 4).

awful cathedrals, of cornfields and vineyards and sunny hamlets and smiling châteaux, was then covered in many places by dreary swamps and darkened by huge forests. Gaul extended far beyond modern France, including a large part of Switzerland, the Rhenish Provinces, Belgium, and Southern Holland. The people were divided into three groups, differing, so Caesar tells us, in race, language, manners, and institutions. Between the Garonne and the Pyrenees were the Aquitani. North-east of the Seine and the Marne, in the plains of Picardy, Artois, and Champagne, on the mist-laden flats of the Scheldt and the lower Rhine and in the vast forest of the Ardennes, dwelt the Belgae, who may have partially mixed and were continually at war with their German neighbours. The lowlands of Switzerland, Alsace, Lorraine, and part of the Rhenish Provinces, the great plains and the uplands of central France, and the Atlantic seaboard, were occupied by the Celtae.

Modern science, however, has established a more precise classification. The Celts, represented in all three groups, were the latest invaders ; and their life was profoundly influenced by the Ligurians, the Iberians, and the nameless tribes who, during countless centuries, had dwelt in Gaul before them. There is evidence that the Neolithic, which followed the incalculably long Palaeolithic Age, set in nearly ten millenniums before our era ; the Bronze Age, which succeeded it, began about 2000 B.C. ; and it was not until more than a thousand years had passed that the culture which derives its name from the Tyrolese settlement of Hallstatt, and in which bronze, as material for tools and weapons, gradually gave place to iron, spread westward across the Rhine.

Ligurians and Iberians.

The earliest inhabitants of Gaul about whom history has anything to tell were the Ligurians and Iberians, neither of whom are mentioned by Caesar. According to the ancient geographers, the land that originally belonged to the Ligurians was the mountainous tract between the Rhône, the Durance, and the Cottian and Maritime Alps : but by the fifth century before Christ they were mingled with Iberians on the west of the Rhône; and from the evidence of certain geographical names as well as of archaeology, it would seem that they once possessed the whole of Eastern Gaul as far north as the Marne. The Iberians, when they came under the notice of the Greeks, occupied the eastern part of Spain as well as the country between the Pyrenees and the Rhône; and there are signs that they had settled in Aquitania as well as on the Mediterranean coast. There is little doubt that in the land which belonged to them, in Spain as well as in Southern Gaul, there once existed, besides Celtic, at least two forms of speech,—Basque and a language or languages, still undeciphered, in which were engraved the so-called Iberian inscriptions.[1] But if the Iberians were homogeneous, the bulk of them were small and dark and not unlike the neolithic people of the Mediterranean race.[2] It was about the seventh century before the Christian Celts. era that the tall fair Celts began to cross the Rhine,[3] accompanied doubtless by the descendants of aliens who had joined them during their long sojourn in Germany. Successive swarms spread over the land, partly subduing and mingling with the descendants of the palaeolithic peoples and of their neolithic conquerors, partly perhaps driving them into the mountainous tracts. Physically they resembled the Germans whom Caesar and Tacitus describe; but they differed from them in character and customs as well as in speech.[4] The Belgic Celts were the latest comers; and, if Caesar was rightly informed, the languages of the Belgae and the Celtae were distinct. Of the modern Celtic dialects Gaelic, which is spoken in the Highlands of Scotland, Manx, and Erse, which is spoken by a diminishing remnant in the west of Ireland, are descended from an old language called Goidelic; while

---

[1] The well-known Basque scholar, H. Schuchardt (*Mitt. d. anthr. Gesellsch. in Wien*, xlv, 1915, pp. 109–24) holds that Basque was an Iberian dialect. Cf. *Caesar's Conquest of Gaul*[2], 1911, pp. 287–302.

[2] See vol. i, p. 2.

[3] *Anc. Britain*, pp. 432–3; *Caesar's Conquest of Gaul*[2], p. 274. See p. 271, *infra*.

[4] *Caesar's Conquest of Gaul*[2], pp. 325–37.

Welsh and Breton are traceable to the British language called Brythonic, which was closely akin to Gaulish. The difference between the languages of the Belgae and the Celtae was probably slight ; for if a Goidelic dialect was spoken anywhere in Gaul, the vestiges of Gallic that remain belong, for the most part, to the Brythonic branch of the Celtic tongue.[1] In Aquitania the natives remained comparatively pure, and formed a separate group, which, in Caesar's time, stood politically apart from the Celtae as well as from the Belgae. They are generally spoken of as an Iberian people ; but the name is misleading. The conquering Celts, as we may infer from proper names, had advanced, though probably in small numbers, beyond the Garonne ; and evidence supplied by measurements of living inhabitants seems to show that in certain parts of Aquitania an old broadheaded element was considerable. But the Celtic language was not generally spoken in Aquitania ; and the Iberian type was sufficiently conspicuous to give some support to the popular theory.

Thus when Caesar entered Gaul, the groups whom he called Belgae, Celtae, and Aquitani were each a medley of different races. The Belgae were the purest and the least civilized ; and both in Belgic and in Celtican Gaul the Celtic conquerors had imposed their language upon the conquered peoples. Even politically the Belgae and the Celtae were not separated by a determinate line ; the Celtican Carnutes were among the dependants of the Belgic Remi, while the Celtican Aedui claimed supremacy over the Belgic Bellovaci. But, if not scientifically complete, the grouping adopted by Caesar was sufficient for his narrative. Just as a modern conqueror, without troubling himself about questions of ethnology, might say that the people of Great Britain were composed of Englishmen, Scotsmen, and Welsh, so Caesar divided the people of Gaul into Belgae, Celtae, and Aquitani. The Civiliza-tion of the notices which he and other writers have left of their Gauls. civilization have been supplemented by archaeology. Five centuries before the birth of Christ the culture of

[1] *Caesar's Conquest of Gaul*[2], pp. 281-2, 319-21.

Hallstatt had given place to that which takes its name from the village of La Tène, at the northern end of the Lake of Neuchâtel, where, some seventy years ago, was discovered a precious series of antiquities. The art, essentially Celtic, characterized by the tasteful use of curves, which was practised in the design and decoration of these objects, was in part an outgrowth of that of Hallstatt, but also owed much to classical and even to Oriental influences.[1] Imported into Britain by the Brythonic invaders, it there shook itself free from all trammels, and attained a yet higher level than in Gaul, - culminating in the graceful and exquisitely decorated shield of bronze and red enamel which adorns the Central Saloon of our National Museum. Specialists have determined three periods, known as La Tène I, II, and III, of which the last began about forty years before the proconsulship of Caesar. By that time the Gallic peoples had all risen far above the condition of barbarians ; while the Celticans of the interior had attained a certain degree of civilization and even of luxury. Their trousers, from which the Province took its name of Gallia Braccata, and their many-coloured tartan shirts and cloaks excited the astonishment of their conquerors. The chiefs wore rings and bracelets and collars of gold ; and when those tall fair-haired warriors rode forth to battle with their helmets wrought in the shape of some fierce beast's head and surmounted by nodding plumes, their chain armour, their long bucklers, and their clanking swords, they made a splendid show. From graves of the department of the Marne, belonging to an earlier generation, bronze horse-trappings of most delicate open-work, and bronze flagons, which had come from Greece, have been unearthed. Walled towns or large villages, the strongholds of the various tribes, were conspicuous on numerous hills. The plains were dotted by scores of hamlets. The houses, built of timber and wattle-work, were large and well

[1] Up to 1914 no antiquities of the period of La Tène had been discovered in Western France south of Brittany ; but exploration may reveal them. See J. Déchelette, *Manuel d'archéol.*, &c., ii. 3, 1914, p. 1061.

thatched. Tweezers and ornamental mirrors of bronze lay on the tables of Gallic dames. Painted pottery, decorated with spirals, symmetrical curves, and other geometrical patterns, was used everywhere, except, apparently, in the remote north-western peninsula.[1] The fields in summer were yellow with corn. Though the vine was not yet cultivated, the merchants of Massilia imported wine from Italy ; and wealthy Gauls would eagerly barter a slave for a jar. Roads, suitable for wheeled traffic, ran from town to town. Wooden bridges spanned the rivers ; and barges, laden with merchandise, floated along them. Ships larger than many that were seen on the Mediterranean, braved the storms of the Bay of Biscay and carried cargoes between the ports of Brittany and of Southern Britain. Tolls were levied on the goods which were transported on the great waterways ; and it was from the farming of these dues that the nobles derived a large part of their wealth. The Aeduans were familiar with the art of enamelling. The miners of Aquitaine, of Auvergne, and of the Berri were celebrated for their skill. Every tribe had its coinage ; and the knowledge of writing was not confined to the priests. Caesar, after he had defeated the Helvetii, found in their encampment a schedule, on which were recorded in Greek characters the names of individuals, the number of emigrants capable of bearing arms, and the numbers of old men, women, and children. It would seem, indeed, that some tincture of Latin had penetrated even to the rudest tribe of the Belgae ; and there were natives, at least in the Province, who acquired a smattering of Greek. Rich enthusiasts resorted to Massilia as a school of learning, and became so enamoured of Hellenic culture that they wrote their contracts in the language of their teachers. Indeed in all that belonged to outward prosperity the peoples of Gaul had made great strides since their kinsmen first came in contact with Rome, and the fortunes which Caesar and his staff amassed are evidence of their wealth.

[1] Compare with *Caesar's Conquest of Gaul*[2], p. 16, n. 6, Déchelette, *op. cit.*, pp. 1467-74, 1488-94.

∴ The coins require special notice ; for none of the antiquities of the Later Iron Age have thrown more light
upon the culture of the Gauls. The oldest were copied
from gold staters of Philip, the father of Alexander the
Great, which had been introduced through Massilia.
About the middle of the following century—more than
a hundred years before the same change was made in our
island—their derivatives begin to be stamped with the
names of the rulers by whom they were issued, among
whom are to be recognized some who have been com-
memorated by Caesar—notably Vercingetorix, whose
coins are worth about fifty times their weight in gold.[1]
Many Roman coins must have been circulated in Gaul
after the colonization of Narbo ; and Roman influence
is apparent on many Gallic coins,[2] for example in a figure
of Pegasus, which appears on one that bears the name of
Tasgetius, King of the Carnutes. For many years gold
coins were the only medium of exchange ; but, as commercial needs increased, silver and bronze came gradually
into use,[3] the coins of the latter metal being imitated not
only from those of Massilia, but, in the case of certain
Belgic specimens, even from those of Campania. The
coins indeed illustrate not only the commerce of the Gauls,
but also their inter-tribal relations, their manners and
customs, and perhaps occasionally their religion. Thus,
while the extreme rarity of Arvernian coins in the great
mart of Bibracte may perhaps be explained by the
traditional enmity between the Arverni and the Aedui,
the discoveries of British coins in Gaul and of Gallic coins
in Britain attest the maritime trade which Caesar notices ;
coins of Central Europe found as far west as Saintonge
and Gallic coins found in the Bohemian stronghold of
Stradonič prove that·the Gauls had intercourse with the
valley of the Danube ; Massilian coins found in many

[1] Or were in 1905, when A. Blanchet published his *Traité des monn. gaul.*
(ii, 621).

[2] Dr. G. Macdonald (*Coin Types*, 1905, p. 222) remarks that many of the
types of Gallic coins were directly borrowed from Roman *denarii*.

[3] With *Caesar's Conquest of Gaul²*, p. 18, n. 6, cf. *Rev. belge de numism.*,
xix, 1913, pp. 296–9, and Déchelette, *op. cit.*, p. 1566.

parts of Gaul bear witness to the enterprise of the Greek
colony ; and numerous hoards of silver coins of one type,
all of which have been found in the basin of the Garonne,
confirm the impression which we derive from the *Commentaries* that the relations of Aquitania were mainly
with Spain. Again, when we notice that horses and swine
are figured on Gallic coins more frequently than any other
animals, we are reminded of the passage in which Caesar [1]
observes that the Gauls imported well-bred horses at
great cost, and of that in which Strabo [2] speaks of the
hams which the Sequani exported to Italy. Shields and
trumpets recall Diodorus's [3] description of Gallic arms ;
and the lyre portrayed on certain coins may represent
the instrument with which the bards accompanied their
songs.[4] It is remarkable that all the coins [5] that have been
found in the great strongholds are of late date—not earlier
than about a hundred years before the Christian era—
which tends to show that none had been founded more
than half a century before Caesar entered Gaul. Probably
Avaricum, Bibracte, Lutecia, and the other towns which
he mentions were fortified during the invasion of the
Cimbri and Teutoni, which devastated Gaul a few years
before his birth.

Bibracte. Of all these towns the one best known to us was Bibracte,
described by Caesar [6] as ' by far the wealthiest and most
important town of the Aedui ', which stood upon Mont
Beuvray, a few miles west of Autun. Like most of the
other fortresses,[7] it was a hive of industry ; and if Cicero
had visited it, he might have spoken [8] with less dis-
dain of the urban life of the Gauls. Streets, workshops,
ramparts have been revealed by excavation. Nearly
sixteen hundred coins, nine-tenths of which belonged to
the period of independence, testify to the manifold
commercial relations of the inhabitants. The houses

---

[1] *B. G.*, iv, 2, 2.   [2] iv, 3, 2 ; 4, 3.
[3] v, 30, 2–4.   [4] *Ib.*, 31, 2.
[5] See, besides the references in *Caesar's Conquest of Gaul*[2], p. 19, n. 5, *Rev
belge de numism.*, lxix, pp. 302, 305–6.
[6] *B. G.*, i, 23, 1.   [7] Déchelette. *op. cit.*, p. 958.
[8] *De prov. cons.*, 12, 29.

provided with iron keys, show that the round conical wooden huts which Strabo described were only the more primitive productions of Gaulish domestic architecture. Like them, indeed, the houses of Bibracte were partly subterranean, this form having been adopted as a precaution against cold on such a high altitude, and probably, like the modern cottages of the Morvan, they were thatched with straw ; but their shape was rectangular, many were built of stone compacted with clay, and they were entered by an interior staircase. A large one, covering over twelve hundred square yards, was doubtless the residence of a wealthy Aeduan. The crucibles, moulds, and polishing-stones of enamel-workers, broken tools, brooches, and pottery, all belong, like the coins, to the latest period of the Celtic Iron Age. Besides these relics of native workmanship were painted vases, imported from Italy, which Gallic artificers soon learned to imitate.[1]

But material prosperity had not been matched by national progress.[2] The Aquitani, indeed, the maritime tribes, and the Belgae were untouched by foreign influences ; but the Celticans of the interior had been enfeebled by contact with Roman culture. The Gauls had lost the strength of barbarism, and had not gained the strength of civilization. They had once, as Caesar remarked,[3] been more than a match for the Germans ; but, enervated by imported luxury and cowed by successive defeats, they no longer pretended to be able to cope with them. *Gallic decadence.*

Their constitution was based upon the tribe, if that word may be applied to the political unit which Caesar called a *civitas*. The tribe was generally an aggregate, more or less compact, of communities to which he gave the name of *pagi*, the members of which had originally been related by blood or by near neighbourhood ; but *Political and social organization.*

---

[1] *Caesar's Conquest of Gaul²*, p. 20, n. 1. Cf. Déchelette, *op. cit.*, pp. 952–5, 1390. Gallic sculptures, found in Southern Gaul and inspired by Greek prototypes, have been described by the same writer (pp 1531–9).

[2] Moreover, as Déchelette observes (p. 1512), ' A La Tène III, la décadence politique des Celtes eut sa répercussion inévitable sur leur prospérité industrielle.'   [3] *B. G.*, vi, 24, 5–6.

it would seem that some of the smaller tribes consisted each of one *pagus* only. Each *pagus*, under its own magistrate, appears to have enjoyed a certain measure of independence, and to have contributed its separate contingent to the tribal host. Each tribe had its council of elders, and had once had its king ; but in certain tribes the king was now superseded by an annually elected president, while in others perhaps the council kept the government to itself. A rule which prevailed among the Aedui illustrates the jealousy which was felt of monarchical power. In that state the chief magistrate, who was called the Vergobret, was forbidden to stir beyond the frontier, from which it may be inferred that it was not lawful for him to command the host.[1] The executive was generally weak. Some of the smaller communities of which a tribe was composed occasionally acted on their own account, in opposition to the rest or to the policy of the tribal authorities. Like the Anglo-Saxon thanes and the Norman barons, the nobles surrounded themselves with retainers,—loyal followers or enslaved debtors ; and none but those who became their dependants could be sure of protection. On the other hand, none but those who were strong enough to protect could be sure of obedience. The oligarchies were no more secure than the kings whom they had supplanted. These men or their descendants plotted for the restoration of their dynasties, and, reckless of the common weal, they were ready to grasp the hand even of a foreign conqueror, and to reign as his nominees. Here and there some wealthy noble, like Pisistratus in Athens, armed his retainers, hired a band of mercenaries, won the support of the populace by eloquence and largess, and, overthrowing the feeble oligarchy, usurped supreme power. Thus the oligarchies lived in perpetual unrest : if no one noble was conspicuously strong, there was intestine strife ; if one could make himself supreme, the government was overthrown. The populace were perhaps beginning to have some glimmering of their own latent strength ; but there is no evidence that anywhere they

[1] *B. G.*, vii. 33, 2.

had any definite political rights. The Druids and the nobles, or, as Caesar called them, the knights, enjoyed a monopoly of power and consideration : the bulk of the poorer freemen, ground down by taxation and strangled with debt, had no choice but to become serfs.

And if in individual tribes there was anarchy, want of unity was the bane of them all. It is of course true that disunion is the normal condition of half-civilized peoples. The old English tribes showed no genius for combination : it was the strong hand of an Egbert, an Edgar, an Athel-stan, that laid the foundations of the English kingdom. Moreover, the circumstances of the Gauls were peculiarly unfortunate. Their patriotism, if it was latent, was real : they were proud of what their fathers had achieved in war ; and the sense of nationality was stirring in their hearts. Caesar himself allows that some of the tribes were comparatively well governed ; and his readers know that even clientship, which menaced our own government until Henry the Seventh stamped it out, had its noble side. Who does not respect the ' six hundred devoted followers ' of Adiatunnus,[1] the four squires whom neither fear nor favour could induce to betray Ambiorix,[2] and those attendants of Litaviccus who remembered that ' Gallic custom brands it as shameful for retainers to desert their lords even when all is lost ' ? [3] If the Gauls had been unmolested or had been exposed to attack only from a single enemy, it seems probable that in the fullness of time a Vercingetorix would have welded them into a united nation. But menaced as they were by the Germans on one hand and by the Romans on the other, their tendency to disunion was increased. Much glib generalization has been published about the defects of the Celtic character ; but only a very rash or a very discerning historian would undertake to say how far the evil was due to circumstances, how far to an inherited strain. Organism and environment are for ever acting and reacting upon one another. While, however, it is foolish to pass sweeping judgements upon a people of

---

[1] *Ib.*, iii, 22. [2] *Ib.*, vi, 43, 6. [3] *Ib.*, vii, 40, 7.

whom, except during the few years that preceded the loss of their independence, we have only the scantiest know-ledge, it would be a mistake to leap to the conclusion that, in political capacity, one race is as good as another. The important fact is, explain it as we may, that the tribal rulers of Gaul had not achieved even that initial step towards unity which the kings of Wessex, Mercia, and Northumberland achieved when they swallowed up the petty kingdoms of the heptarchic period. Or rather it would be more true to say that when the Romans first established themselves beyond the Alps, the Arvernian king had achieved that step ; but that first his defeat, and afterwards the revolution which subverted royal power, had broken the supremacy of his house and dealt a fatal blow to the political development of Gaul. There, as in Latium, the downfall of the monarch weakened the tribe which had overthrown him ; and the oligarchies, if they had the strength, were not granted the time to work out their own salvation. Individual tribes, such as the Aedui and the Arverni, did indeed attain some sort of supremacy over their weaker neighbours ; and in certain cases two tribes, for example the Senones and the Parisii, formed one state. There were leagues of the Belgae, the Aquitani, and the maritime tribes. But supremacy had not hardened into sovereignty ; and the leagues were loose, occasional, and uncertain. If some powerful baron, stimulated by ambition or impressed by the evils of dis-union, succeeded in clutching the power of a Bretwalda, he was forthwith suspected by his brother nobles of a design to revive the monarchy, and was lucky if he escaped the stake. The country swarmed with outlawed criminals, who had fled from justice, and exiled adventurers, who had failed to execute *coups d'état*. Nobles and their clients lived sword in hand ; and hardly a year passed without some petty war. Every tribe, every hamlet, nay every household was riven by faction. One was for the Romans and another for the Helvetii ; one for the Aedui and another for the Arverni ; one for the constitu-tional oligarchy and another for the lawless adventurer.

All, in short, were for a party; and none was for the state.
" 'Απωλόμεθα ἄν," said Themistocles, " εἰ μὴ ἀπωλόμεθα " : [1]
like the English, whom the Normans chastened, the Gauls
needed the discipline of foreign conquest.

Yet, besides the memory of their glorious past, which, Unifying
as Caesar remarked,[2] both saddened the Gauls and spurred influences.
them to desperate enterprises, there were influences which
tended to make every man feel that he and his fellows
belonged to one nation. That favoured land was formed by
Nature to tone down distinctions of race and to foster the
growth of nationality. If the French are the most united
of all nations, they owe this fortune to their country,
whose unifying tendency has ever been the same. France,
says Vidal de la Blache, is a country whose regions are
naturally connected, and whose inhabitants learned early
to mingle with and to know one another. No country of
equal extent comprises such diversities ; but they pass off
into each other by insensible gradations. ' There is ', says
this writer, ' a beneficent force—a *genius loci*—which has
guided our national life,—an indefinable power which,
without obliterating varieties, has blended them in a
harmonious whole.' The wayfarer who roams from the
sand-hills of the Channel to the mountains of Auvergne,
from the uplands of the Morvan to the plain of the Berri,
conversing with peasant and townsman in turn, who is
touched by the spirit of prehistoric life wafted from the
rude stone monuments of Brittany and by the spirit of
imperial Rome which broods over the mediaeval glories
of Bourges and over that ancient town which has been
revealed by the excavator on Mont Auxois—who feels
how one influenced the other and both survive in our
Mechanical Age—will comprehend what the geographer
means ; and for him the tale which Caesar told will
become real.

And in Gaul, as in England before the Norman Conquest, Religion.
there was another unifying influence,—community of religious ideas, controlled by one ecclesiastical organization.

---

[1] ' We should have been undone if we had not been undone ' (Plut.,
Themistocles, 29, 9).   [2] *B. G.*, v, 54, 5.

Local cults of course abounded : but the great gods whom Caesar noticed,[1] however variously they may have been conceived by various tribes, were common to Gaul ; while every rite and every sacrifice was regulated by the Druids.

Druidism. The question of the origin and affinities of Druidism has given rise to superabundant speculation, which has led to no certain result. Caesar was informed that the system was believed to have been imported from Britain. At all events there is no evidence that it was known to the Celts of Cisalpine Gaul ; and the Germans, with whom the Celts were long in contact and to whom they were ethnically akin, had no Druids. If, then, Druidism originated in Gaul, it probably did not appear until after the Celtic invasion of Italy ; and yet in Britain, the civilization of which was more backward than that of Gaul, it was apparently of long standing. The prevalent opinion is that the Celtic conquerors of both Gaul and Britain found it existing, and that it was strong enough to secure terms and finally to make itself supreme. Caesar's words are sometimes explained in the sense that in his time Druidism was more vigorous in Britain than in Gaul, and that Gallic Druids travelled to Britain in order to be initiated into its mysteries : but no sufficient reason can be given for not accepting them in their literal sense ; and if they are true, the Celtic invaders of Britain did not create Druidism, and, neolithic or not, it was at all events pre-Celtic.[2] The Druids formed a corporation, admission to which was eagerly sought : they jealously guarded the secrecy of their lore ; and full membership was only obtainable after a long novitiate. They were ruled by a pope, who held office for life ; and sometimes the succession to this dignity was disputed by force of arms. They were exempt from taxation[3] and from service in war. The ignorance and superstition of

[1] B. G., vi, 17, 1–3 ; 18, 1. For a detailed account of the religion of the Gauls see Caesar's Conquest of Gaul², pp. 26–32, with which cf. Anc. Britain, pp. 271–86.

[2] See Caesar's Conquest of Gaul², pp. 523–5.

[3] Cf. ib.; p. 33, n. 2, with H. Meusel's edition of B. G., 1920, note on vi. 14, 1.

the populace, their own organization and submission to
one head, gave them a tremendous power. The educa-
tion of the aristocracy was in their hands. The doctrine
which they most strenuously inculcated, if Caesar was not
misinformed, was that of the transmigration of souls.
' This belief ', he said, ' they regard as a powerful incentive
to valour, because it inspires a contempt for death.' [1]
They claimed the right of deciding questions of peace
and war ; but it is doubtful whether, at least in Caesar's
time, they concerned themselves, as a corporation, with
political affairs.[2] Among the Aedui, if not among other
peoples, at all events in certain circumstances, they
appointed the chief magistrate.[3] They laid hands on
criminals and, in their default, even on the innocent,
imprisoned them in monstrous idols of wickerwork, and
burned them alive as a sacrifice to the gods. They
immolated captives in order to discover the divine will
in the flow of their blood or their palpitating entrails ; they
lent their ministrations to men prostrated by sickness or
going forth to battle, who trusted that heaven would
spare their lives if human victims were offered in their
stead ; and one form of sacrifice which they appear to
have countenanced—the slaughter of a child at the
foundation of a monument, a fortress, or a bridge—has
left traces in European folklore and been practised in
Africa, Asia, and Polynesia in modern times. They
practically monopolized both the civil and the criminal
jurisdiction ; and if this jurisdiction was irregular, if they
had no legal power of enforcing their judgements, they
were none the less obeyed. Every year they met to
dispense justice in the great plain above which now soar
the spires of Chartres cathedral.[4] Those who disobeyed
their decrees were excommunicated ; and excommunica-
tion meant exclusion from the civil community as well as
from religious rites. Nor did their power extend only to

---

[1] *B. G.*, vi, 14, 5. Cf. *Caesar's Conquest of Gaul*[2], pp. 34–5.

[2] See *ib.*, pp. 527–8, and *Class. Rev.*, xxv, 1911, p. 257.

[3] *B. G.*, vii, 33, 4.

[4] The disputes of humble litigants were probably settled by their lords.
See *Caesar's Conquest of Gaul*[2], p. 34, n. 3.

individuals : contumacious states were laid under an interdict—a warning that they had forfeited the protection of their gods. In fine it was Druidism that formed one of the strongest ties between Gauls and Britons and between the warring tribes of Gaul.

The German peril.

But though religion might foster the idea, it could not supply the instant need of political union. Over the vast plains of Germany fierce hordes were roaming, looking with hungry eyes to the rich prize that lay beyond the Rhine. Moreover, the danger of Gaul was the danger of Italy. The invader who had been attracted by 'the pleasant land of France' would soon look southward over the cornfields, the vineyards, and the olive-groves of Lombardy. When Caesar was entering public life, men who were not yet old could remember the terror that had been inspired by the Cimbri and Teutoni ; and though this danger had been averted, the movements of other German peoples might well cause anxiety. Ariovistus, secure in the enjoyment of the title which Caesar had procured for him, was soon to be reinforced ; the Helvetii, whose raids had alarmed the Senate while Caesar was still in Spain, fearing, it would seem, that Ariovistus would sever them from their Celtic kinsmen, were even then planning the migration which led Caesar to set out from Rome.

Projected invasion of the Helvetii.

The design was originated by Orgetorix, the head of the Helvetian baronage. He persuaded his brother nobles that they would be able to win the mastery of Gaul, and undertook a diplomatic mission to the leading Transalpine states. Two chiefs were ready to listen to him, Casticus, whose father had been the last king of the Sequani, and Dumnorix, brother of Diviciacus, who was at that time the most powerful chieftain of the Aedui. If Diviciacus saw the salvation of his country in dependence upon Rome, his brother regarded the connexion with abhorrence. He was able, ambitious, and rich ; and the common people worshipped him. Orgetorix urged him and Casticus to seize the royal power in their respective states, as he intended to do in his, and promised them armed support. The three entered into a compact for the conquest and partition of Gaul ; and, if they had any aim beyond their own aggrandizement, they may have hoped that their success would not only checkmate Ariovistus, but stop the anarchy which paralysed their country and avert the encroachments of Rome. But they had still to reckon with the Helvetian government, who, learning that their envoy had betrayed his trust, recalled him to answer for his conduct. He knew that if he were found guilty, he would be burned alive ; and accordingly, when he appeared before his judges, he was followed by his retainers and slaves, numbering over ten thousand men. The magistrates, determined to bring him to justice, called the militia to arms ; but meantime the adventurer died, perhaps by his own hand.

Thus the scheme of the triumvirate was destroyed ; and perhaps Cicero was thinking of the death of Orgetorix when he wrote to Atticus that tranquillity was restored in Gaul. But the Helvetii had no intention of abandoning their enterprise, nor Dumnorix of abandoning his. He had married a daughter of Orgetorix ; and he was ready to help them if they would make it worth his while. They resolved to spend two years in preparing for their emigration ; bought up wagons and draught cattle ; and laid in large supplies of corn. Three neighbouring tribes, the Rauraci, the Tulingi, and the Latobrigi, and also the Boi, who had long ago migrated into Germany, were induced to join them ; they had sufficient food to last three months ; and, to stimulate their resolution and enterprise, they cut themselves off from all prospect of return by burning their homes.

Such was the situation with which Caesar had to deal. The inten-
It can hardly be doubted that he dreamed of adding a new tions of Caesar.
province to the empire, which should round off its frontier and augment its wealth. But whether he had definitely resolved to attempt a conquest of such magnitude, or merely intended to follow, as they appeared, the indications of fortune, it would be idle to conjecture. The greatest statesman is, in a sense, an opportunist. When Caesar should find himself in Gaul, he would know best how to shape his ends.

CHAPTER VIII

CAESAR'S FIRST TWO CAMPAIGNS IN GAUL

58 B. C. IT is time to relate how Caesar acted after he set out from Rome. The Helvetii, it will be remembered, had March 24 (Julian). fixed the 28th of March for their muster on the banks of the Rhône. Travelling ninety miles a day, Caesar crossed the Alps, took command of the legion quartered in the Province, ordered a fresh levy, and, on arriving at Geneva, immediately destroyed the bridge by which the Helvetii Helvetian envoys ask Caesar's leave to pass through the Province. intended to cross the river. They sent ambassadors to say that they only wished to march through the Province, and would promise to do no harm. Would Caesar give them permission ? Caesar had of course no intention of granting their request ; but, as he wished to gain time for his levies to assemble, he, told the ambassadors that he would think over what they had said and give them an Apr. 9. answer on the 13th of April. The levies arrived in time He promises to reply in a fortnight, and meanwhile fortifies the left bank of the Rhône. to join the legion in executing the design which he had formed. It would seem that the Helvetii had not yet assembled in full force. Along the southern bank of the Rhône, between the lake and the Pas de l'Écluse— a distance of about seventeen miles—Caesar erected earthworks in the places where the banks were not so steep as to form a natural rampart ;[1] and troops were posted in redoubts behind. When the ambassadors returned, Caesar plainly told them that he would not He prevents the Helvetii from crossing. allow the Helvetii to pass through the Province. Undeterred by this rebuff, the emigrants made several attempts to force the passage of the river ; but the Romans, rapidly concentrating at the threatened points, repulsed every assault.

Only one route now remained,—the road that winded along the right bank of the Rhône, beneath the rocky

---

[1] See *Caesar's Conquest of Gaul*[2], 1911. pp. 614–5.

steeps of the Jura, through the Pas de l'Écluse. The 58 B. c
emigrants might perhaps have made their way into Gaul
by Pontarlier or one of the other passes ; but either
because they shrank from encountering Ariovistus, or for
some reason of which Caesar took no account, these
routes were out of the question. The road that led through
the Pas de l'Écluse was so narrow that there was barely
room for a single line of wagons : beyond the pass it led
into the territory of the Sequani ; and if they offered
any opposition, it would be hopeless to attempt to get
through. They refused at first to grant a safe-conduct ; The
but Dumnorix, who had established his influence with Sequani
them by wholesale bribery, succeeded, after a little allow
negotiation, in procuring for his allies the favour which them to
they sought. The Helvetian leaders undertook to restrain march
their people from plundering ; and hostages were ex- through
changed for the fulfilment of the compact. Caesar learned the Pas de
that the ultimate object of the emigrants was to settle in l'Écluse.
western Gaul, in the fertile basin of the Charente, with the
inhabitants of which they were already on friendly terms.[1]
Thence they would be able to make raids upon the open
corn-growing districts of the Province ; and their mere
presence, with Dumnorix in the background, would be
a standing menace to Roman interests in Gaul. But first
they would have to make their way along the valley of
the Rhône, across the plain of Ambérieu, and over the
plateau of Dombes to the Saône ; and Caesar calculated Caesar
that while their huge unwieldy column was crawling along fetches re-
the muddy tracks, he would have time to reinforce his ments
little army. Leaving Labienus to guard the entrench- from Cis-
ments on the Rhône, he hastened back to Cisalpine Gaul ; Gaul.
formed two new legions from the recruits whom he had [The 11th
ordered to assemble ; withdrew the other three from their and 12th.]
winter-quarters ; and marched back by the road leading
along the valley of the Dora Riparia and over Mont
Genèvre. The mountain tribes, who doubtless hoped to
plunder his baggage-train, attempted to delay his advance ;
but, repelling their desultory attacks, he descended into

[1] See *Sitzungsber. d. Königl. Preuss. Akad. d. Wiss.*, 1896. p. 453.

the valley of the Durance, pushed on through the highlands of Dauphiny, past Briançon, Embrun, and Gap,[1] crossed the Isère and the Rhône, and encamped on the heights of Sathonay, near the point where the rushing current is swelled by the sluggish waters of the Saône.

The Aedui solicit his aid against the Helvetii.

He was only just in time. The bulk of the Helvetii, after ravaging the outlying settlements of the Allobroges, had crossed the Saône and descended, like a swarm of locusts, upon the cornfields and homesteads of the Aedui. If their leaders wished to spare the partisans of Dumnorix, they could not restrain the predatory host. But the appointment of Caesar had wrought a change in Aeduan politics. Liscus, who belonged to the Romanizing party, had been elected Vergobret ; and Diviciacus had regained his prestige. Envoys came to beg Caesar to help them to get rid of the invaders, and Liscus undertook to feed his army. Labienus with his legion had already rejoined him. The rearguard of the Helvetii, numbering about a fourth of the entire host, were gathered on the eastern side of the river, in the valley of the Formans, eleven miles to the north.[2] Caesar left his camp soon after midnight, marched up the valley of the Saône over ground which

He defeats the Helvetian rearguard,

masked his approach, and launched his legions upon the unsuspecting multitude as they were crowding into their boats. Those who escaped the slaughter vanished in the surrounding forests. They and their slain kinsfolk belonged to a tribe called the Tigurini, by which, fifty years before, a Roman army, under the consul Lucius Cassius, had been defeated and compelled to pass under the yoke.

and crosses the Saône.

Within twenty-four hours Caesar had thrown a bridge of boats over the river, and transported his entire army

The Helvetii attempt to negotiate, but reject his terms.

to the right bank. Impressed by his celerity, the Helvetii, who had taken three weeks over the passage, sent an embassy to meet him. The principal envoy, an aged chief named Divico, who in his youth had commanded the host that defeated Cassius, said that his countrymen were

---

[1] *Caesar's Conquest of Gaul*[2], pp. 615–6.   [2] *Ib.*, p. 617–9.

willing to settle wherever Caesar pleased, provided that 58 B.C.
he would leave them unmolested. But if he was bent
upon war, they were ready ; and he would do well to
remember that they had already overthrown a Roman
army. Caesar replied that he remembered the treacherous
exploit of which they boasted, and remembered it with
indignation. Moreover, even if he were inclined to
condone the past, he could not overlook the outrages of
which they had just been guilty. They must compensate
the Aedui and the Allobroges for the damage which they
had done, and give hostages for their future good behaviour :
on that condition he was willing to make peace. Divico
retorted that the Helvetii, as the Romans had the best
of reasons to know, were accustomed to receive hostages,
not to give them.

Next day the emigrants broke up their encampment. They
To reach the valley of the Charente, it was necessary to march
cross the Loire. The direct line intersected that river near ward,
Roanne ; but the rugged country between the basins of followed
the Saône and the Loire presented difficulties to wagons by Caesar.
drawn by oxen, and beyond Roanne the mountains of Le
Forez barred the way. If Divico had intended to take
this route, Caesar could head him off ; and the only
course was to move up the valley between the Saône and
the hills of Beaujolais until a practicable road could be
found. Caesar sent on his cavalry, four thousand strong,
to watch the enemy's movements. They were composed
of levies from the Province and from the Aedui ; and
the Aeduan contingent was commanded by Dumnorix.
Caesar, if he was already acquainted with his character
and aims, probably did not think it expedient to challenge
his appointment ; indeed he may have welcomed the
opportunity of keeping him under his eye. The cavalry
ventured too near the Helvetian rearguard, and lost a few
men in a skirmish. As the victors were only five hundred,
Caesar must have suspected that something was amiss.
For a fortnight the two armies continued to advance,
northward and then north-westward, never more than
five miles apart. The Helvetii turned off from the Saône

58 B. C.

Caesar pressed for supplies, owing to the intrigues of Dumnorix.

near Mâcon, and moved up the valley of the Petit Grosne,[1] along the line of the road which leads from Mâcon to Autun ; near Mont St. Vincent they struck westward in the direction of Toulon-sur-Arroux.[2] Elated by their recent success, they occasionally faced about and challenged their pursuers ; but Caesar would not allow his men to be drawn into a combat. He was looking for an opportunity to fight a decisive battle ; but for the time he had enough to do in trying to prevent the enemy from plundering his allies. Nor was this his only anxiety. Day followed day, and the supplies which Liscus had promised did not come. The Aeduan notables in Caesar's camp promised, protested, and poured forth excuses, till he lost all patience and accused them of deliberate breach of faith. Liscus, who shrank from committing himself before his brother chiefs, admitted in a private interview that Dumnorix had exerted his influence over the people to prevent them from sending supplies, telling them that if the Romans succeeded in defeating the Helvetii, they would use their victory to enslave the Aedui as well as the other tribes. Dumnorix had amassed great wealth, and had spent it lavishly in buying popular support ; he had acquired great influence with divers Gallic tribes by arranging marriages between the women of his family and powerful chieftains ; and not only was he politically connected with the Helvetii, but he personally detested Caesar, because Caesar had set him aside and restored his brother Diviciacus to power. If the Helvetii succeeded, they would help him to mount the throne ; if they failed, he would be worse off than before. He had kept them regularly supplied with information ; and in the cavalry skirmish a few days before he had set the example of flight.

Caesar hardly knew how to act. He could not afford to overlook such flagrant hostility ; but he was afraid of offending Diviciacus, whom he particularly desired to conciliate. Perhaps the astute Druid had no great love for his brother ; but it would not do to exasperate the whole

[1] *Caesar's Conquest of Gaul²*, pp. 620–1.   [2] *Ib.*, pp. 620–1, 624–7.

patriotic party. Caesar summoned him to his tent, and, 58 B.C.
addressing him through the medium of Gaius Valerius
Troucillus, a distinguished Provincial, his principal
interpreter and a trusted friend, earnestly pressed him to
consent to his punishing Dumnorix. Diviciacus, with
a burst of tears, begged him not to be too hard upon his
brother ; for it would be said that it was he who had
advised the infliction of the punishment, and public
opinion would brand him as a monster. Pressing his hand
kindly and bidding him dismiss his fears, Caesar assured
him that out of regard for his friendship he would condone
the insult which had been offered to his Government and
the provocation which he had himself received. The
truth was that he had no choice. He had not yet won
the prestige that would only come from victory ; and with
powerful enemies before him and doubtful allies around
him, upon whose goodwill he depended for subsistence,
it would be folly to raise a hornet's nest about his ears.
He contented himself therefore with sending for Dumnorix,
and giving him a severe rebuke and a stern warning.
This once, he said, for his brother's sake, his conduct
should be overlooked. At the same time he gave secret
orders that Dumnorix should be watched and his movements reported.

Next morning Caesar made an attempt to surprise the His
enemy, who had encamped at the foot of a hill eight miles abortive
distant, probably Sanvigne, about six miles east of the attempt
river Arroux. He intended to attack them in front while to surprise
Labienus, who ascended the hill from behind, swooped the Hel-
down upon their rear ; but through a blunder of the vetii.
officer commanding his patrols, who reported that the
enemy, not Labienus, occupied the height, the plan
miscarried. The legions moved on in the afternoon and
encamped about three miles in the rear of the Helvetii,
near the site of Toulon-sur-Arroux.[1] The day after, as no
corn-carts had appeared and only two days' rations were
left, Caesar, knowing that he could soon overtake his
slowly moving enemy, struck off to the right, and marched

[1] *Ib.*, pp. 625-7.

DEFEAT OF THE HELVETII*
(after Col. Stoffel)

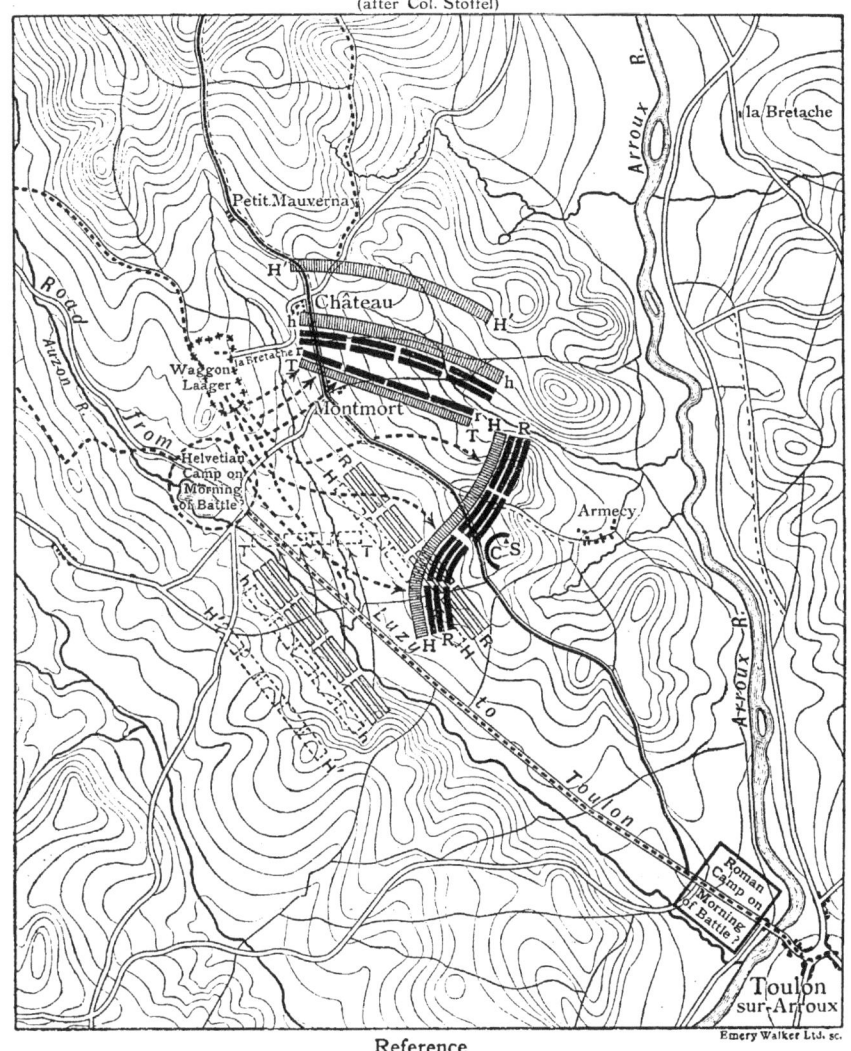

la Bretache

Petit Mauvernay

Road

Château

Auzon R.

from

Waggon Laager

Montmort

Helvetian Camp on Morning of Battle?

Armecy

Luzy to Toulon

Arroux R.

Roman Camp on Morning of Battle?

Toulon sur-Arroux

Emery Walker Ltd. sc.

Reference

S Summit of hill of Armecy	**H H** Helvetii
C Entrenchment for protection of baggage	**H'H'** Helvetii forced to retreat to a hill
R R 4 legions in line of battle	**T T** Boi(i) & Tulingi
r r Roman 3rd. line facing Boi(i) & Tulingi	**h h** Helvetii renewing attack
Roman line of march ▬▬▬	Helvetian line of march •••••••

The contours denote intervals in altitude of 10 metres

* Col. Bircher's modifications of Stoffel's theory, which are adopted
by the author and by M. Jullian, are shown thus:•.... .Romans ▭▭▭ Helvetii ⌐_⌐_⌐

Scale, 1:56,000
Kilometres

0   1   2   3   4

58 B. C.

for Bibracte, about sixteen miles to the north, where he knew that he would find granaries stored with corn. The route ran along the watershed between the Arroux and one of its affluents, a rivulet called the Auzon. The Helvetii were far on their way, the head of the column having passed Luzy and turned westward down the valley of the Alène, when some deserters from Caesar's army brought them the news. Fancying that he was afraid of them, or hoping to prevent him from reaching Bibracte,[1] they turned likewise, marched back rapidly, and attacked his rearguard near the hill of Armecy, about three miles north of Toulon. Caesar sent his cavalry to retard their advance, while he ordered the infantry to retrace their steps and ascend the slopes of Armecy. Half-way up, the four veteran legions were ranged in three lines of cohorts, the soldiers' packs being collected on the top under the protection of the auxiliaries and the two newly-raised legions, who were ordered to entrench the position. The baggage-train may either have been parked on the ridge along which it was moving or have continued its march towards Bibracte. Caesar was about to fight his first pitched battle; and he knew that for him and his army defeat would be destruction. He therefore dismounted and made his staff do the same, so that the men might see that their officers shared their dangers; and then, in accordance with custom, he harangued the expectant troops. The wagons of the Helvetii were laagered, as they came up, on rising ground to the left of the road; and about one o'clock in the afternoon the entire host, congregated in compact masses, drove back Caesar's horsemen, and with shields closely locked pressed up the hill against the Roman line. When the phalanx was within a few yards, the centurions gave the word; the legionaries in the front ranks hurled their javelins; and the mass began to break. The blades of the javelins, composed of soft iron, had bent as the points penetrated the shields. Sword in hand the cohorts charged: many of the Helvetii, finding their shields pinned together by the javelins, which,

[1] See pp. 280-1.

pull and wrench as they might, were not to be torn out, flung them away, and parried the thrusts as best they could ; but they were soon overborne, and fell back to a hill about a mile south-west of Armecy on the further side of the road by which they had marched. One may perhaps suspect that their first attack had been a feint, designed to entice Caesar from his strong position ; for the Romans were following when the Boi and Tulingi, who had just arrived upon the field, rushed upon their right flank and rear. The Helvetii instantly returned to the attack, and while the first two lines of the Romans closed with them the third faced about and confronted their fresh assailants.

Defeat of the Helvetii   Long and fiercely the battle was fought out. In due time the men of the rear ranks relieved those in front, advancing between the files as the latter withdrew ; and again the men who had been relieved, relieved in turn their comrades ; the cohorts of the second line reinforced those of the first, and the groups thus formed an unbroken whole.[1] Gradually the Helvetii were forced further up the hill, while the Boi and Tulingi retreated to their baggage. Standing behind the wall of wagons, they hurled down stones and darts upon the advancing Romans, and thrust at them between the wheels with pikes when they attempted to storm the laager.[2] Even the women and children joined in the defence.[3] The struggle was prolonged far into the night ; and meanwhile the Helvetii, covered by the resistance of their allies, were making good their retreat. At length the legionaries burst through the barrier ; women and children who could not escape were slaughtered ; and the flying remnant of the invading host disappeared in the darkness of night.[4]

---

[1] *Caesar's Conquest of Gaul*, pp. 588–98.
[2] See my edition of the *Commentaries*, p. 436.
[3] Plut., *Caes.*, 18, 2.
[4] A comment made by A. Klotz (*Neue Jahrb. f. d. klass. Altertum*, xxxv, 1915, p. 632) will appeal to the English (and, I hope, to the German) reader's sense of humour. Remarking that an objection raised against the credibility of Caesar's statement of the number of the Helvetii—that he could not with four legions have beaten 70,000 men—has been stultified by recent events,

Caesar was unable to pursue, for his troops were 58 в. с.
exhausted, his cavalry were untrustworthy, he had to Caesar's
give the wounded time to recover and to bury the teeming treatment of the
corpses, and supplies had to be fetched from Bibracte ; [1] fugitives.
but he sent mounted messengers to warn the Lingones,
through whose country the fugitives would have to pass,
to give them no help. The Lingones occupied the country
round Tonnerre and Bar-sur-Aube, as well as the plateau
of Langres and the neighbourhood of Dijon. At the end
of three days Caesar started in pursuit. On the way he
was met by envoys, whom the Helvetii, now faced with
utter destitution, had sent to sue for terms. He bade
them tell their countrymen to halt and await his arrival :
when he overtook them he required them to give hostages
and to surrender their arms and the slaves who had
escaped to them.[2] Six thousand Helvetians slipped away
in the night and took the road towards the Rhine : but
Caesar sent orders to the inhabitants to hunt them down
and bring them back ; and on their return they were
' treated as enemies '.[3] The Boi were allowed, at the
request of the Aedui, who appreciated their martial
qualities, to settle in Aeduan territory ; the Helvetii and
the other tribes, who would be useful as a barrier between
the Germans and the Province, were sent back to their own
land, and the Allobroges were directed to supply them
with grain.[4] .

and particularly by the battle of Tannenberg, ' Und ', he adds, ' Caesar
verliert nicht, wenn wir ihn mit Hindenburg vergleichen ' (Caesar loses nothing
by comparison with Hindenburg).

[1] Caesar does not mention the necessity of procuring supplies; but it is
obviously to be inferred from *B. G.*, i, 23, 1.

[2] Oberleutnant H. Giehrl (*Mil.-Wochenbl.*, Feb. 6, 1912. col. 414) assumes
that the slaves had deserted during the battle.

[3] *B. G.*, i, 28, 1. Whether the 6,000 fugitives were put to death (cf. Cic.,
Verr., v, 25, 64 ; 28, 73 ; *In Cat.*, iii, 10, 25) or sold to the traders who accompanied the enemy, is uncertain.

[4] Mommsen (*Hermes*, xvi, 1880, pp. 447–8 ; *C. I. L.*, xiii, pars 2, p. 5)
infers from the passage in which Cicero (*Pro Balbo*, 14, 32) spoke of a treaty
(*foedus*) as existing between Rome and the Helvetii that they were already
(56 в.с.) included within the Roman Province. Cicero's historical statements
were so loose, and he was notoriously so ignorant of Gallic affairs that I am
inclined to think that he was referring to a treaty which had been made before
Caesar went to Gaul. In his speech on the consular provinces (8, 19), delivered

58 B. C.
Gallic
envoys
solicit
his aid
against
Ario-
vistus.

The news of the victory produced its effect upon a people among whom Roman influence had already begun to permeate. The success of the Helvetii would have been a calamity to all except Dumnorix and his following; and this calamity Caesar had averted. He appeared as the conqueror, not of Gaul, but of the invaders of Gaul ; the oligarchies who dreaded ambitious upstarts welcomed his support ; and the Aedui might expect that their old pre-eminence would be restored. At the worst, his rule would be preferable to the tyranny of Ariovistus ; and he would doubtless be glad to aid in expelling his rival. Chieftains came from all parts of central Gaul to congratulate the victor and to solicit his support. Diviciacus, who spoke for them, gave a moving account of the invasion of Ariovistus, his barbarity, his rapacity, and his insolence. The Sequani, whom he had already robbed of a third part of their territory, would soon be forced to give up another third, for a fresh horde, the Harudes, had recently crossed the Rhine ; and if Caesar would not help his hapless victims, they must all go forth, like the Helvetii, and seek some new home.

Failure of
his at-
tempts to
negotiate
with Ario-
vistus.

Caesar assured the chiefs that they might rely upon his support. Like the Cimbri and Teutoni, these fierce German hordes might soon, if they were not checked, overrun the whole of Gaul, and thence pour into Italy ; and the interest as well as the honour of Rome required that she should protect her allies. And there was another reason why Caesar should interfere. He could not stand still : he must either advance or retreat. Unless he espoused the cause of the Gauls, he would lose the credit which his victory had won, and perhaps force them to make common cause with Ariovistus against him : if he

shortly before the speech pro Balbo, he said that Caesar's victories had not yet been legally consolidated (domitae sunt a Caesare maximae nationes, sed nondum legibus, nondum iure certo, nondum satis firma pace devinctae). Would he have said this if a treaty had already been concluded with the Helvetii ? When Mommsen adds, citing Pliny (Nat. Hist., iv, 17 [31], 106), that along with the Helvetii the Remi also undoubtedly received a treaty of alliance from Caesar, he apparently forgets that the date of the foedus which Pliny mentions is uncertain.

boldly confronted their oppressor, he himself would 58 B. C.
become the arbiter of Gaul. Peaceful methods, however,
might be tried first. The Roman army was still comparatively weak. Ariovistus was master of a formidable host ;
and it would be foolhardy to attack him without absolute
need. Besides. it would be impolitic for the proconsul to
levy war against the King and Friend upon whom those
titles had been conferred with his sanction, without
preliminary diplomacy, which he must so conduct as to
justify himself before his countrymen. Ariovistus was
then probably in the plain of Upper Alsace, and Caesar
sent envoys to invite him to name some intermediate
spot for a conference. Ariovistus told them to say that
if their master wanted anything from him he must take
the trouble to come to him in person ; and meanwhile he
would like to know what business Caesar had in a country
which the Germans had won by their own swords. Caesar
now assumed a more peremptory tone. Ariovistus had
rejected his invitation. Then these were his terms. No
German must thenceforth set foot across the Rhine : the
hostages of the Aedui must be restored ; and Ariovistus
must cease to molest that people or their allies. The
Senate had decreed that the Governor of Gaul for the time
being should protect the Aedui and the other allies of the
Republic ; and that decree he intended to obey. Ariovistus replied that he was a conqueror ; and, as a conqueror, he had a right to treat his subjects as he pleased.
The Romans invariably acted on the same principle. He
did not interfere with them : what right, then, had they
to interfere with him ? He would not molest the Aedui
so long as they paid their tribute : but most certainly he
would not give up the hostages ; and if the Aedui did not
pay, much good would their alliance with the Romans do
them ! For Caesar's threats he cared nothing. No man
had ever withstood Ariovistus and escaped destruction.
Let Caesar choose his own time for fighting. He would
soon find out what mettle there was in the unbeaten
warriors of Germany.

With this message came the news that a host of Suebi

58 B. C. had appeared on the further bank of the Rhine, and that the Harudes were actually harrying the lands of the Aedui. Not a moment was to be lost if these new-comers were to be prevented from reinforcing Ariovistus. With all possible speed Caesar made arrangements with the Aedui, the Sequani, and the Lingones for the forwarding of supplies, and immediately put his army in motion. Three days later he heard that Ariovistus was hurrying to seize Vesontio, now Besançon, the chief town of the Sequani, a strong place, nearly encircled by the Doubs and stored with all munitions of war. Marching night and day at his utmost speed to anticipate him, he encamped on the outskirts of the town.

He marches against Ariovistus and seizes Vesontio.

While Caesar was collecting the first instalment of the supplies, his soldiers had plenty of opportunities for gossiping. The people of Vesontio, and especially the traders, whose business had brought them into contact with the Germans, told sensational stories of their great strength and superhuman valour—one could not bear even to look them in the face, so terrible was the glare of their piercing eyes. The Roman soldiers were very credulous ; they remembered their struggle with the Helvetii ; and the idle chatter of their new acquaintances completely demoralized them. The mischief began with the tribunes, the officers of the auxiliary corps, and others who formed the personal following of the General. Like every other Roman Governor, Caesar had been obliged, for political reasons, to find places in his army for fashion-able idlers and disappointed professional men, who had had no experience of war, and simply wanted to mend their fortunes by looting.[1] Now that there was a prospect of desperate fighting they began to tremble. They whispered that the campaign was not authorized by the Senate, but undertaken simply to gratify Caesar's ambition[2] ; and some were not ashamed to invent excuses for asking leave of absence. Gradually even centurions and seasoned veterans were infected by the general alarm.

Panic in the Roman army.

[1] B. G., i, 39, 2. See also Cicero, Fam., vii. 5–6. 8, 10. 18 ; Q. fr., ii. 13, 3.
[2] Dio, xxxviii. 35, 2.

Some of them, indeed, made an effort to disguise their
fears. They told each other that it was not the enemy
that they dreaded, but only the forests between them and
the enemy and the probable failure of supplies. All over
the camp men were making their wills ; and Caesar was
actually warned that when he gave the order to march
the men would refuse to obey.

He immediately sent for the tribunes and centurions, How
and gave them a severe lecture. What business had they Caesar
restored
to ask where he intended to march ? It was most unlikely confi-
that Ariovistus would be mad enough to fight ; but dence.
supposing that he did, what was there to be afraid of ?
Had they lost all confidence in themselves, all faith in
their General ? What had these terrible Germans ever
really done ? The crushing defeats which Marius had
inflicted upon the Cimbri and the Teutoni, the defeats
which had been inflicted on the gladiators, trained though
they were in Roman discipline, in the recent Servile War,
gave the measure of their prowess. Even the Helvetii
had often beaten them ; and the Helvetii had gone down
before the legions. No doubt Ariovistus had defeated the
Gauls ; but what of that ? He had tired them out by
avoiding a battle for months, and then attacked them
when they had dispersed and were off their guard. This
did not mean that Germans were braver than Gauls ; and
Ariovistus himself must know that Roman armies were
not to be trapped by such transparent devices. To talk
about the difficulty of the country or the difficulty of
getting supplies was downright impertinence. Supplies
were coming up to the front from the friendly tribes ; and
the croakers would soon see that their alarm about the
forests was absurd. As for the story that the army was
going to mutiny, he did not believe it ; for armies did not
mutiny unless generals were incapable or dishonest.[1]
Anyhow, on the very next night he intended to march ;
and if nobody else would follow him, he would go on with
the 10th legion alone ; for it, at all events, was faithful
to its commander.

[1] Caesar (*B. G.*, i, 40, 12) was probably thinking of generals who, as Cicero
said (*De imp. Cn. Pompei*, 13, 37), sold the office of centurion.

This vigorous little speech had a marvellous effect upon the troops. From despair their spirits bounded to the highest pitch of confidence ; and they were only impatient to cross swords with the enemy. The men of the 10th, flattered by Caesar's trust in them, sent him a message of thanks through their officers ; while the other legions asked theirs to tell him that they were sorry for what had occurred. At the hour which he had fixed Caesar struck his camp. He left a detachment to hold Vesontio. Before him all was unknown ; but Diviciacus undertook to be his guide. To avoid the broken wooded country between Besançon and Montbéliard, he made a circuit northward and eastward of about fifty miles, and then, threading the pass of Belfort, debouched into the plain of the Rhine, and pushed on rapidly past the eastern slopes of the Vosges till he reached a point within twenty-two miles of the German camp. He has not told us where he formed his own : probably it was on the river Fecht, between Ostheim and Gemar.[1] Ariovistus, who was on the north, sent messengers to say that, as Caesar had come nearer, he had no objection to meeting him. Caesar accepted his proposal ; and the conference was fixed for the fifth day following. Ariovistus, who knew that Caesar's cavalry were weak, pretended to be afraid of treachery from the legions, and insisted that they should each bring with them a cavalry escort only. Caesar was unwilling to raise difficulties ; but as all his cavalry were Gauls, and he did not care to trust his safety to them, he mounted the 10th on their horses. The place of meeting was a knoll,[2] rising above the plain, nearly equidistant from the Roman and the German camp. Caesar stationed the bulk of his escort about three hundred yards off : Ariovistus did likewise ; and each rode up with ten horsemen to the knoll. Caesar began by reminding Ariovistus of the honours which the Senate had conferred upon him, and afterwards repeated the demands which he had already made through his envoys on behalf of the Aedui. Ariovistus replied that

He resumes his march against Ariovistus.

His conference with Ariovistus.

---

[1] See *Caesar's Conquest of Gaul*[2], pp. 648–52, and p. 282, *infra*.

[2] Or perhaps an earthen mound (*Caesar's Conquest of Gaul*[2], pp. 639–40).

he had crossed the Rhine in response to Gallic appeals. The country which he occupied in Gaul had been formally ceded to him by Gauls : it was not he who had attacked them, but they who had attacked him. He had over-thrown their entire host in battle ; and, if they wished to repeat the experiment, he was ready to fight them again. As for the friendship of the Romans, it was only fair that he should get some solid advantage out of it ; and if he could only retain it by giving up the tribute which he received from his subjects, he would fling it aside as readily as he had asked for it. He had entered Gaul before the Romans. Caesar was the first Roman Governor who had ever passed beyond the frontier of the Province. What did he mean by invading his dominions ? That part of the country belonged to him just as much as the Province belonged to Rome. Caesar talked a great deal of the titles which the Senate had bestowed upon the Aedui ; but he knew too much of the world to be imposed upon by such shams. The Aedui had not helped the Romans in the war with the Allobroges ; and the Romans had not stirred a finger to help their ' Brethren ' against himself. He had good grounds for suspecting that the friendship which Caesar professed for him was another sham—a mere blind under cover of which Caesar was plotting to ruin him. He happened to know what was going on in Rome ; and there were prominent men there who would be glad to hear of Caesar's death. If Caesar did not withdraw from his country, he would expel him by force of arms ; but if he would only go away and leave him in peace, he would show his gratitude. Caesar answered that it was impossible for him to break his word or to forsake the allies of his country ; and, he added, if history were to be appealed to, the claim of the Romans to supremacy in Gaul was better founded than that of the Germans. He was still speaking when a soldier rode up and warned him that a number of Germans were edging up towards the knoll and stoning his escort. Riding back to his men, he withdrew them without attempting to retaliate ; for, though he was confident that his favourite

58 B. C. legion could easily beat the Germans, he was determined not to give them any pretext for accusing him of foul play. On the following day Ariovistus requested Caesar to meet him again, or else to send one of his generals. Caesar saw no reason for further discussion, and did not care to expose his lieutenants to the caprice of a treacherous barbarian ; but he sent a trustworthy provincial, Valerius

Mission of Procillus and Metius.

Procillus,[1] whom, as he believed, there could be no motive for injuring, and a man called Metius, who was on friendly terms with Ariovistus. They were instructed to hear what he had to say, and bring back word. The moment he saw them Ariovistus shouted, ' Why have you come here ? to play the spy ? ' and when they attempted to explain, he cut them short and put them under arrest.

Ariovistus cuts Caesar's line of communication.

On the same day he made a long march southward, and halted about six miles north of Caesar's camp, at the very foot of the Vosges. Next morning his column ascended the lower slopes, marched securely along them past the Roman army, and took up a position two miles south of Caesar's camp. As he watched the long train of wagons winding leisurely by, Caesar saw that he was being out-manœuvred : to send the legions up the hill-side would be to court destruction ; and he could only wait, a passive spectator, while Ariovistus was cutting his communications and barring the road by which he expected his supplies.

How Caesar regained command of it.

Next day Caesar, intending perhaps to strengthen the morale of his veterans and to hearten the recruits, formed up his army immediately in front of the camp, under the protection of his artillery. If Ariovistus attacked, he would do so at his peril ; if he declined the challenge, the legionaries would be assured that the Germans were not invincible. Ariovistus remained where he was. On each of the four following days Caesar offered battle ; but the enemy would not be provoked into leaving their encampment. Cavalry skirmishes, indeed, took place daily, but without any decisive result. The Germans had light-armed active footmen, who accompanied the cavalry into action,

[1] See p. 337.

each one of them selected by the rider whom he attended : they were trained to run by the horses' sides, holding on to their manes ; and if the troopers were forced to retreat they supported them and protected the wounded. As the infantry remained obstinately within their laager, and it was necessary for Caesar to win back communication with his convoys, he resolved to take the initiative. Forming his legions in three parallel columns, prepared, at a moment's notice, to face into line of battle, he marched back to a point about a thousand yards south of the German position, and there marked out a site for a camp. One column fell to work with their picks, while the other two formed in two lines to protect them. Ariovistus sent a detachment to stop the work, but it was too late : the fighting legions kept their assailants at bay, and the camp was made. Two legions with a corps of auxiliaries were left to hold it ; and the other four returned to the larger camp. Next day Caesar led them into the open, but not far from the rampart, and again offered battle. Ariovistus again declined the challenge ; but as soon as the legions had returned to their entrenchments he made a determined attempt to storm the smaller camp, and did not withdraw his force till sunset. The Romans had suffered as heavily as the Germans ; but Caesar now learned from prisoners that the enemy had been warned by their wise women, whose divinations they accepted with superstitious awe, that they could not gain the victory unless they postponed the battle until after the new moon.[1]

The Germans from superstition delay to fight a pitched battle.

Sept. 26 (Sept. 18 [1])

Caesar saw his opportunity. He waited till the following morning, and then, leaving detachments to guard his camps, he formed his six legions, as usual, in three lines, and marched against the enemy. They had no choice but to defend themselves. Their wagons stood in a semicircle, closing their flanks and rear ; and, as they tramped out, their women stretched forth their hands and piteously begged them not to suffer their wives to be made slaves.

Caesar attacks them.

[1] The Germans doubtless intended to postpone the battle until the date (Sept. 20 of the Julian calendar) when the crescent might be expected to be visible. See vol. i, pp. 339–40.

The host was formed in seven distinct groups, each composed of the warriors of a single tribe. Two of the legions—the 11th and the 12th—had never fought in a pitched battle ; and as the whole were numerically inferior to their opponents, the auxiliaries were drawn up in front of the smaller camp, to make a show of strength. Caesar commanded the right wing in person, and, noticing that the enemy's left was comparatively weak, directed against it his principal attack, in the hope of overwhelming it speedily and thus disconcerting the rest of the force ; but before the front ranks could poise their javelins the Germans were upon them, and they had barely a moment to draw their swords. Quickly stiffening into compact masses, the Germans locked their shields to receive the thrusts : but some of the Romans flung themselves right on to the phalanxes ; they tore the shields from the grasp of their foes, and dug their swords down into them ; and, after a close struggle, they broke the formation, and their weapons got freer play. The unwieldy masses, unable to manœuvre or to deploy, reeled backward, dis-solved, and fled. But the Roman left, overpowered by numbers, was giving ground. Young Publius Crassus, who was in command of the cavalry outside the battle, saw the crisis, and promptly sent the third line to the

They are defeated and expelled from Gaul. rescue. The victory was won, and the whole beaten multitude fled towards the Rhine. Many fell under the lances of the cavalry ; only a few, among whom was Ariovistus, were lucky enough to swim the river or find boats. Caesar, in the course of the pursuit, came upon his interpreter, who was being dragged along in chains by his captors, and had only escaped death by the accident that, on drawing lots, they had decided to postpone his execution. There is nothing in Caesar's memoirs more full of human interest than the passage in which, breaking his habitual reserve, he tells us of the joy he felt on seeing this man, for whom he had the greatest respect and regard, alive and unhurt. It gave him, he says, a pleasure as great as he had felt in gaining the victory.[1]

[1] *B. G.*, i, 53, 6.

The victory was decisive. Caesar had saved Gaul from 58 B. C. German domination and Italy from a long-standing peril. What use was he to make of his success ? Having once transgressed the frontier of the Roman Province, he knew that it would be fatal to withdraw. That would be to invite the German to attempt a new invasion, to confess weakness to the Gaul. For the present he must return to the Cisalpine province, to discharge the civil duties of his government and to watch the politics of Italy ; but leaving his legions under the command of Labienus, he quartered them for the winter in the strong- Caesar hold of Vesontio.[1] To all who had eyes to see and ears to quarters his legions hear he had made it evident that his purpose was nothing at Veson- less than the conquest of Gaul. tio.

While Caesar was holding the assizes he doubtless Events communicated with his two confederates and with his in Italy other supporters in Italy ; but nothing is known of what passed between them. Cicero was still languishing in exile ; Crassus was apparently inactive ; Pompey was unable to maintain his pre-eminence against the impish attacks of Clodius ; Cato had been compelled to withdraw for a time from the political arena. Before the close of The Bel- winter Caesar heard rumours, presently confirmed by gae con- spire dispatches from Labienus, that the warlike Belgae were against conspiring. They were fearful that Caesar would first Caesar. conquer the other tribes and then conquer them ; and they were egged on to fight by influential chiefs from Central Gaul. The motives of these counsellors were various. Some simply desired to make their country free. It was all very well, they argued, to have expelled the Germans, but these new intruders were not a whit more welcome : the legions had settled down in the country, and they evidently intended to make the country support them. Others, merely because they were Celts, longed, above all things, for revolution. Then there were princely adventurers, who were plotting to seize royal power, and who foresaw that if Gaul became a Roman province they would be obliged to submit to law, and

[1] *Caesar's Conquest of Gaul*[2], p. 68, n. 1.

57 B. C.   would no longer be allowed to hire troops for the gratifica-
tion of their ambition.

He
marches
against
them.

On his own responsibility and, provisionally, at his own
cost, Caesar raised two new legions [1] in Cisalpine Gaul,
and sent them in the early spring to join Labienus. As
soon as the herbage was sufficiently forward to subsist
the mules and horses he crossed the Alps and rejoined his
army at Vesontio. The tribes nearest to the Belgae,
whom he charged with the duty of collecting information,
reported that they were busily raising and concentrating
levies. Having arranged for supplies of corn, Caesar
pushed on and, after another fortnight's marching,
appeared on the northern bank of the Marne.

The Remi
submit,
and help
him.

The Belgae were taken completely by surprise ; but
one tribe, the Remi, who occupied the country round
Reims, Laon, and Châlons, were shrewd enough to
perceive that the patronage of Caesar would assure their
own position. They were subject to the overlordship of
their neighbours, the Suessiones, and saw an opportunity
of supplanting them. Two of their leading men, Iccius
and Andebrogius, presented themselves in Caesar's camp,
and not only submitted on behalf of the tribe, but
promised to render him every assistance. Seeing that it
would be easy to establish in the heart of Belgium a power
as devoted to his interests as the Aedui in Central Gaul,
he gave them a gracious welcome, stipulating, however,
that the Reman council should present themselves before
him, and that the sons of the leading men should be
delivered up as hostages. The envoys reported that
Galba, the King of the Suessiones, who had been unanimously elected commander-in-chief, was prepared to put
nearly three hundred thousand men into the field. The
estimate was certainly exaggerated : [2] but Caesar could

He sends
Diviciacus
to ravage
the lands
of the
Bellovaci,

muster little more than forty thousand ; and his enemies
were the stoutest and most stubborn of all the warriors
of Gaul. Perceiving that his only chance of success was
to force the huge host to divide, he requested Diviciacus

---

[1] The 13th and 14th.
[2] See *Caesar's Conquest of Gaul*[2], pp. 241-2.

to raise a levy of Aeduans and ravage the lands of the 57 B. C.
Bellovaci, which lay beyond the Oise. The entire Belgic *marches against*
force was now marching down the road which led from *the ad-*
La Fère past Laon to Reims.[1] Moving rapidly northward, *vancing host,*
Caesar crossed the Aisne by a bridge and encamped on *crosses*
rising ground—either the plateau of Pontavert or the *the Aisne, and en-*
slope of Mauchamp near Berry-au-Bac [2]—between that *camps near the*
river and a small morass. At the northern end of the *bank.*
bridge he established a *tête de pont*; and to guard its
further extremity, he left a detachment about three
thousand strong under one of his generals, Titurius
Sabinus. Towards midnight a messenger came into his
camp with the news that the Belgae were making a furious *The Bel-*
onslaught upon Bibrax, or Vieux-Laon, a Reman strong- *gae at-*
hold about seven miles to the north, and that Iccius, who *Bibrax.*
commanded the garrison, despaired of being able to hold
out unless he were promptly reinforced. Caesar instantly *Caesar*
dispatched his archers, light-armed Numidians, and *sends his*
Balearic slingers to the rescue.[3] The Gauls knew nothing *ries to the*
of the methods by which the Romans captured fortified *rescue.*
towns. When their numbers were sufficiently great, they
used to drive the defenders from the rampart by showers
of missiles, and then, locking their shields over their heads,
to demolish a portion of the wall. But Bibrax was protected on the south by impregnable escarpments : it
would seem that Galba had neglected to invest this side ;
and when Caesar's troops appeared, the impatient and
undisciplined host abandoned their attempt,[4] only linger-
ing long enough to ravage the lands and fire the hamlets
within reach. On the following night the sudden blaze *The*
of a line of watch-fires, extending some seven miles in *Belgae*
length beyond the further side of the morass, revealed to *opposite*
Caesar their encampment. *Caesar.*

The position which he had himself chosen may be *Caesar*
described in his own words. ' The hill on which the camp *makes his*
stood, rising gradually from the plain, extended, facing *impreg-*
nable.

[1] *Ib.,* pp. 658-9.
[2] *Ib.,* pp. 659-66. Cf. p. 337, *infra.*   [3] See p. 282.
[4] *Caesar's Conquest of Gaul²,* p. 241, n. 6, and pp. 399-400.

the enemy, over the exact space which the line of battle would occupy : on either flank its sides descended rapidly ; while in front it gradually merged in the plain by a gentle slope.'[1] The legions were protected in front by the morass ; but the vast numbers of the enemy might outflank them. To prevent this, Caesar made his men dig two trenches, each about three furlongs in length, transversely on either side of the hill ; and at the extremity of each trench he caused forts to be erected and armed with catapults. Along the whole length of the hill, in front of the camp, he drew up his six veteran legions in battle array, while the other two remained to guard the camp. Each of the two armies waited for the other to cross the morass, and meanwhile Caesar's cavalry were scattering the Belgic squadrons. At length, as the enemy were too wary to attack, he withdrew his legions into camp. There was a ford on the Aisne, about two miles from the *tête de pont*, which he had either failed to notice or had not thought it necessary to guard. Presently an orderly came from Sabinus, who reported that a division of the enemy were moving down to the bank, evidently intending to cross over, assault his camp, and destroy the

The Belgae attempt to cut his communications, but are defeated.

bridge. Even if they failed, the cornfields of the Remi would be exposed, and the Roman convoys would be cut off. Taking his cavalry, Numidians, archers, and slingers, Caesar hurried down the hill, crossed the bridge, and pushed along the bank towards the ford. There were the enemy, splashing through the water. The archers and slingers attacked them and shot them down in scores. The survivors clambered over the fallen bodies and staggered on, but were beaten back by showers of stones and arrows ; while the leading division, who had crossed already, were surrounded by the cavalry and cut to pieces.

They disperse

The Belgae were thoroughly disheartened. They had no organized commissariat, and their supplies were running out. Galba had not the genius to control a vast multitude made up of hordes without discipline, with conflicting interests, and distracted by mutual jealousies.

[1] *B. G.*, ii, 8, 3.

Caesar's position was impregnable ; and he evidently had 57 B. C.
no intention of quitting it. His allies would soon be
swarming over the frontier of the Bellovaci, and the chiefs
of that tribe insisted on returning to defend their homes.
It was decided therefore that each tribe should go back
to its own country, and that, whatever district the
Romans might invade, all should rally to its defence. In
the night the whole multitude poured out of their encampment with great uproar and confusion, each man struggling
to get in front of his fellows. Caesar at first suspected
that this movement was a ruse ; but at daybreak his
outposts reported that the enemy had really gone, and Caesar's
he immediately sent his cavalry, supported by three cavalry
pursue
legions under Labienus, in pursuit. The rear ranks, when them.
they were overtaken, stood at bay, and resisted resolutely ;
but those in front, hearing the shouts of the combatants,
made haste to escape. As long as daylight lasted the
Romans hung on the rearguard, slaying, pursuing, and
slaying again ; and at sunset they returned to camp.
Caesar left the disorganized host no time to rally.[1] The He re-
Suessiones, Bellovaci, and Ambiani had diverged from ceives the
submis-
their natural route, in order to fetch their baggage ; and sion of
by a great effort he might be able to surprise their forts.[2] the Suessiones,
Next morning he pushed on westward down the valley Bellovaci,
of the Aisne. In a single forced march he reached Novio- and
Ambiani.
dunum, the chief stronghold of the Suessiones, not far [Pom-
west of Soissons, and at once attempted an assault ; but miers.]
though the garrison was weak, the moat was so wide and
the wall so high that his troops were repulsed. In spite
of their fatigue, however, they proceeded to fortify their
camp and to make preparations for a siege. Sappers' huts
were constructed for protecting the workers : earth and
fascines were shot into the moat ; and movable towers
were erected to carry the artillery which was to play upon
the defenders of the wall. During the night the whole
host of the fugitive Suessiones thronged into the town ;
but they were so confounded by the appearance of the

---

[1] See my edition of the *Commentaries*, note on p. 80.
[2] *Caesar's Conquest of Gaul*[2], p. 670.

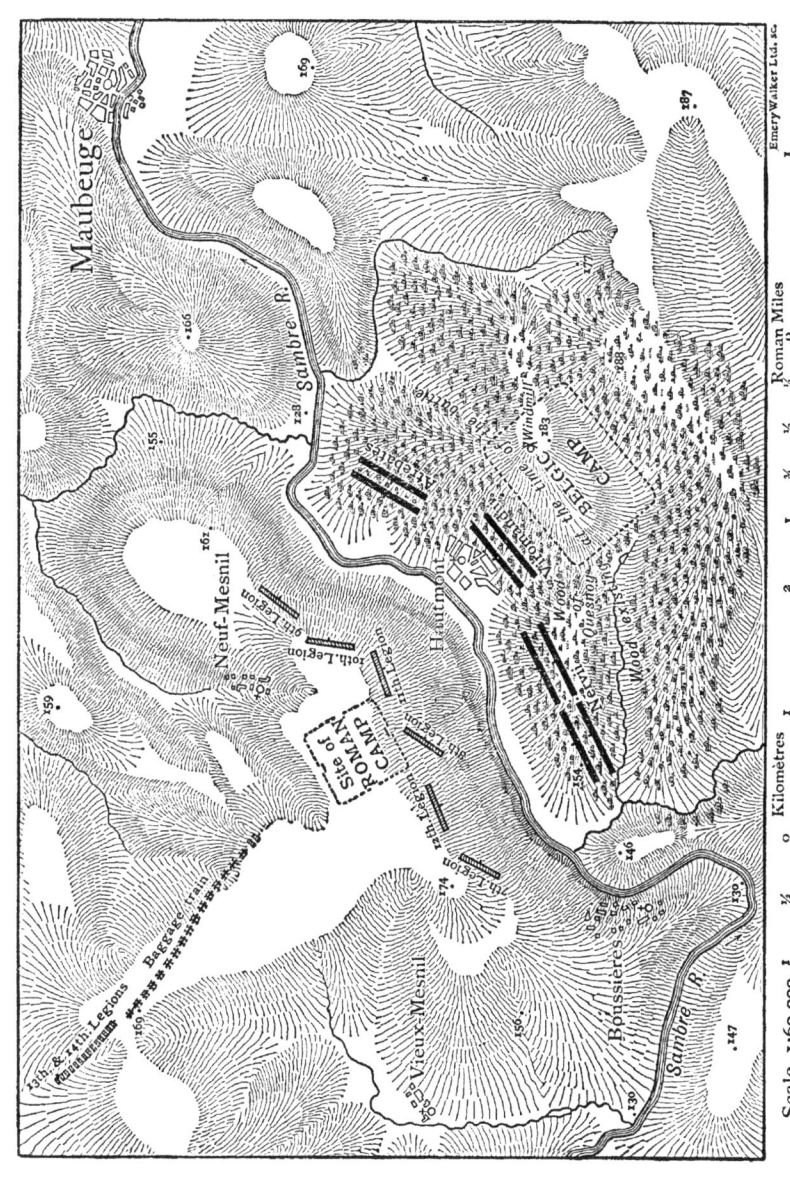

Scale, 1:60,000

Kilomètres
Roman Miles

THE BATTLE OF NEUF-MESNIL.

The numbers denote the heights in metres above the level of the sea

Emery Walker Ltd. sc.

siege works that they surrendered without striking a blow. 57 B. C.
Marching on westward, Caesar crossed the Oise. Bratuspantium, the chief town of the Bellovaci, opened its gates
on his approach ; and when he drew near Samarobriva,
where now rises the cathedral of Amiens, the Ambiani
likewise tendered their submission. Caesar punished no
one ; but he disarmed the garrisons of Noviodunum and
Bratuspantium, and required the surrender of hostages
of noble birth. But now he learned that his progress was
about to be disputed. On the north-east, among the
forests of the Sambre and the marshes of the Scheldt,
dwelt a tribe whose primitive virtues had not yet been
enfeebled by contact with civilization. No traders were
suffered to cross their frontier, for fear the luxuries of
which the rude warriors were still ignorant might sap
their manhood.[1] Bitterly taunting their neighbour tribes   The Ner-
for having so tamely surrendered, they vowed that for   vii resolve
their part they would accept no terms of peace. This   to resist.
people, of whom Caesar wrote with one of those rare
touches of enthusiasm that here and there relieve the
severity of his narrative, and whom Shakespeare deemed
worthy of remembrance, were the Nervii.

A couple of marches brought the legions to the Nervian   Caesar
frontier. The road led through Hainaut, past the site of   marches
the modern Cambrai. Three days later Caesar ascertained   against
them.
from peasants, who had been taken prisoners, that the
warriors of the tribe were encamped only nine miles off,
on the further bank of the Sambre, with their allies, the
Viromandui and the Atrebates ; and that another tribe,
the Atuatuci, were marching from the east to join them.
They were waiting for him near Maubeuge, where they
expected that he would cross the river.[2] He immediately
sent on a party of centurions and pioneers to choose
a camping ground. It happened that some of his

---

[1] B. G., ii, 15, 4. Salomon Reinach (Rev. arch., 3ᵉ sér., xxxix, 1901, p. 370)
says that the Nervii feared, with good reason, the Roman traders, who were
preparing [by peaceful penetration] the conquest of Gaul. Has he any
evidence that the traders were Italians and not Massilians, and would he assign
the same reason for the prohibition by the Suebi of the importation of wine
(B. G., iv, 2, 6) ?   [2] Caesar's Conquest of Gaul², p. 675.

prisoners had escaped to the enemy in the night. They told them that each of the Roman legions was separated on the march from the one that followed it by a long baggage-train ; and that when the foremost legion, encumbered with their heavy packs, reached the camping ground, it would be easy to overwhelm them and plunder the baggage before the others could come to the rescue. The centurions selected for the site of the camp the heights of Neuf-Mesnil, about three miles south-west of Maubeuge. The ground sloped evenly and gently towards the left bank of the Sambre ; but from a point opposite the front of the camp to the bend of the river at Boussières, nearly a mile and a half further up, the slope terminated near the water's edge in a steep escarpment. The depth of the river was not more than three feet. From the opposite bank an open meadow, over which were scattered a few cavalry piquets, rose into a hill covered with woods. The space for the camp was measured and marked out. Meanwhile the army was toiling up from behind, its progress being delayed by thick hedges, which the inhabitants had planted long before to check the raids of their neighbours' cavalry. The formation was different from that which had been described to the Nervii ; for when an enemy was near Caesar always changed his order of march. In front came six legions in column : then followed the entire baggage-train, protected by the two newly-raised legions, which closed the rear. The cavalry, who had gone on in front, crossed the shallow stream and, supported by archers and slingers, engaged the enemy's piquets. The piquets fell back into the wood, whither the cavalry dared not follow them ; and there leisurely re-forming, they charged again and again. As the infantry arrived upon the ground, some began to dig the trenches for the camp, while others scattered over the country to cut down wood. Caesar neglected to take the precaution of keeping a part of his force under arms.[1] At length

---

[1] As he had done when constructing his smaller camp in presence of the hostile force of Ariovistus. The great Napoleon (*Précis des guerres de César*, 1836, p 45) blames him for having allowed himself to be surprised.

the head of the baggage-train appeared. Ambushed 57 B. C. among the trees, the Gauls caught sight of it. Suddenly they darted forth from the wood and came pouring down the meadow ; their rush swept away the terrified cavalry ; now they were across the river and racing up the slope, and now they fell upon the half-formed line.

The confusion was overwhelming. From the moment Battle of when the onrushing host was seen there were hardly ten Neuf-Mesnil. minutes for preparation. The legionaries flung aside their tools. Caesar had to give all his orders in a breath. The red battle-ensign was quickly hoisted over his tent. The blast of the trumpet recalled the men who were working at the further side of the camp, while messengers ran to fetch those who had scattered far afield. They had not a moment even to cram on their helmets or pull the coverings off their shields. The generals were obliged to act without waiting for orders ; and Caesar was glad that he had forbidden them to leave their respective legions while the camp was being made. He could not direct them ; for the hedges which crossed the field obstructed his view. Want of time as well as the nature of the ground prevented them from forming a regular line of battle : along the brow of the hill isolated combats were beginning ; and all that could be done was to make each legion face its immediate assailants. Disciplined, and self-reliant from the experience which they had gained, the soldiers instinctively grasped the situation : they did not trouble themselves to join their respective companies, but one after another, as they hastened up, they fell into the ranks by the standards nearest them. Hurrying down at haphazard to cheer them on, Caesar found himself close to the left of the line. There was the 10th,—his favourite legion. 'Keep cool, men,' he cried, ' and remember the honour of the legion. Stand up against that rush ! ' He had no time to say more ; for the enemy were within a javelin's cast, and, as he passed along, both sides were engaged.

Hurling their javelins, the 10th and, on their left, the 9th charged the Atrebates, who, panting from their headlong rush, soon gave way. Hunted down the slope, they plunged into the stream, but the Romans dashed after, sword in hand, and when the survivors clambered up the further bank and tried to rally, fell upon them again and chased them up the hill. At the same time the 11th and 8th drove the Viromandui from the front of the camp right down to the water's edge. But the very success of these four legions was disastrous to their comrades—the 12th and the 7th—on their right. The left and front of the camp were exposed; Boduognatus, the commander-in-chief, seized his opportunity; and the Nervii, compacted in one mighty column, climbed the steep bluff, swarmed up the heights, and while some outflanked the two legions on their right, the rest pressed on for the defenceless camp. The beaten cavalry came full upon them and again took to flight : the officers' servants, who had gone out to plunder, looked back, and ran for their lives : the baggage-drivers, who were coming up, scattered in all directions, shrieking with terror ; and a body of horse from the Treveri, who formed part of the auxiliary force, rode off homewards to announce Caesar's defeat.

Caesar saw it all as he made his way from the left to the right wing. The men of the 12th were huddled together so closely that they could hardly use their swords ; and nearly every officer was either killed or wounded. The standard-bearer of the 4th cohort had fallen : the standard —to Roman soldiers a holy emblem—was lost. Sextius Baculus, the chief centurion of the legion, was so weakened by loss of blood that he could no longer stand. From the rear ranks men were slinking away to escape the showers of missiles. There were no reserves ; and the numbers of the enemy were inexhaustible. Fresh swarms kept pressing up the hill and closing in on either flank. Seizing a shield from a man in the rearmost rank, Caesar pushed his way through to the front ; he called to his centurions by name ; he told the men to open up their ranks—so they would be able to use their swords better—and charge. But the 7th also, on their right, were hard pressed. Caesar

told the tribunes to bring the two legions gradually closer
together, and form them up so as to face the enemy on
every side.[1] And now, as the men were relieved from the
dread of being attacked in the rear, they fought with
renewed confidence. The two legions that guarded the
baggage were marching up at their utmost speed. Suddenly above the ridge of Neuf-Mesnil they appeared ;
and presently the 10th, dispatched by Labienus, recrossed
the river, hurried up the hill-side, and threw themselves
upon the enemy's rear. The effect of their appearance
was electrical. Even the wounded leaned on their shields,
and plied their swords ; the scattered camp-followers
plucked up courage and turned upon the enemy, while the
cavalry did all they could to expiate their flight. The
Nervii in their turn were hemmed in ; but they made good
their boast. Man by man, beneath the javelin and the
thrust of the short sword, their front ranks fell : higher
rose the heap of prostrate bodies ; and leaping on to
them, the survivors snatched up the fallen javelins and
flung them back, till they too fell, and all was still.[2]

The old men of the Nervian tribe, with the women and
children, had gathered before the battle in the midst of the
marshes formed by the estuary of the Scheldt ; and
within a few days a deputation came from them to ask
an audience of the conqueror. Wishing to establish   Caesar
a reputation for clemency, Caesar permitted the survivors   treats the
                                                            survivors
to retain their lands and even their fortified villages, and   with
warned the neighbouring tribes to refrain from molesting   clemency.
them. He then marched eastward against the Atuatuci,
who, on hearing of the defeat of their allies, had returned
home and concentrated in one town of great strength,
situated on Mont Falhize,[3] opposite the modern fortress
of Huy. The Meuse, winding in the shape of a horse-
shoe, flowed through the meadows beneath the southern
slopes of the hill ; and the town, perched above its rocky

---

[1] *Caesar's Conquest of Gaul*[2], pp. 676–7.

[2] Caesar's narrative (*B. G.*, ii, 27, 3–5 ; 28, 1–2) implies that a few of the
Nervian contingent escaped ; but whether they left the fighting line or had
not come into action at all, he does not say.

[3] *Caesar's Conquest of Gaul*[2], pp. 387–93.

He
besieges
the
strong-
hold of
the Atua-
tuci.

heights, seemed unassailable, save by one gentle ascent
on the north-east, where there was a deep moat, backed by
a double wall. At first the garrison made a succession of
sorties : but Caesar threw up a rampart from one reach
- of the river, round the north of the hill, to the other ;
and a terrace, composed of a core of earth and timber,
supported by logs piled crosswise, was built up at right
angles to the wall. On the level surface was erected one
of the wooden towers from the stories of which archers,
slingers, and artillery used to shower missiles among the
defenders of a besieged town ; and it was intended that,
as soon as the terrace approached the wall, a battering-
ram should be employed to effect a breach. The garrison,
confident in the strength of their fortress, and jeering at
the Romans for their small stature, watched these operations with ignorant contempt ; but when they saw the
tower actually moving on its rollers and steadily nearing
the wall, they fancied that there must be some super-
natural power at work, and sent out envoys to sue for
terms. They would surrender, the envoys said ; only
they entreated to be allowed to keep their arms, without
which they could not defend themselves against their
neighbours. Caesar insisted on unconditional surrender :
he would take care that their neighbours did not molest

They sur-
render,

them. The chiefs could only submit ; and swords, spears,
and shields were pitched down into the moat until the
heap almost reached the top of the wall. Towards sunset
all the Roman soldiers who had gone into the town were
withdrawn, for fear they might commit any excesses. The
garrison had kept about a third of their weapons in
reserve, and had improvised shields of bark and wattle-

but after-
wards
make a
treacher-
ous at-
tack.

work, covered with skins. Fancying that the Romans
would be off their guard, they sallied forth at midnight,
and advanced to attack the contravallation. But Caesar
had provided against the chance of treachery. Piles of
wood, all ready laid, were set ablaze ; and, warned by the
signal, the troops came streaming from the nearest
redoubts. The Gauls fought with the courage of despair ;
but missiles rained down upon them from the rampart

and from the towers which had been erected upon it ; and
they were driven back with heavy loss into the town.
Next day the gates were burst open, and the Romans
rushed in. Fifty-three thousand of the Atuatuci—all who
were found within the walls—were sold as slaves.

The campaign was over. The prestige which it had
won for Caesar was so great that more than one German
tribe sent envoys across the Rhine to offer submission.
One partial failure alone marred the general success. On
his way back to Italy, Caesar sent one of his generals,
Servius Galba, to open up the road leading from the
Valais over the Great St. Bernard into Italy, which
traders had only been able to use hitherto at great risk
and by the payment of heavy tolls. Galba's force consisted only of the 12th legion, which had suffered so
severely in the battle with the Nervii, and a contingent of
cavalry. Skirting the northern shore of the Lake of
Geneva, the little column entered the broad valley of the
upper Rhône, walled in on right and left by wooded
mountains. Having inflicted several defeats upon the
mountaineers, captured several of their strongholds, and
compelled the chiefs to surrender their sons as hostages,
he posted two cohorts in the neighbourhood of St. Maurice,
and took up his own quarters in Octodurus, near the
confluence of the Dranse and the Rhône. The Dranse,
which then flowed in a different channel, down the middle
of the valley, divided the village into two parts, the
eastern of which he allowed the inhabitants to occupy,
while he reserved the vacant quarter for the legion and
proceeded to fortify it. The encampment thus formed was
between Martigny-la-Ville and the more southerly Mar-
tigny Bourg. Besides the cohorts which he had detached,
Galba was obliged to send out a number of small parties
for supplies ; and the force that remained was insufficient
to protect the camp. The mountaineers, who resented the
deprivation of their children, and believed that the
Romans intended to annex their country, occupied the
heights that bordered the valley, and attacked the
entrenchment, which was still incomplete. For six hours

the Romans fought at bay, till their stock of missiles was
nearly spent : then, as the enemy were on the point of
breaking in, Galba, acting on the advice of Sextius
Baculus, who had fought so gallantly on the Sambre,
and of a tribune named Gaius Volusenus, ordered a sortie.
Suddenly, at a given signal, four compact little columns
dashed out from all four gates, cut their way through the
loose ranks of the astounded mountaineers, and chased
them over the hills. But Galba's position was plainly
untenable, for it appeared impossible to procure supplies ;
and, after burning all the houses in the village, he returned
to spend the winter in the Roman Province.

The other legions had already been distributed in their
winter-quarters. One, under Publius Crassus, whose
promptitude had contributed so much to the defeat of
Ariovistus, had been sent, after the battle with the
The tribes Nervii, to receive the submission of the maritime tribes
of Brit-
tany and of Normandy and Brittany. This legion and certain
Nor- others were cantoned along the valley of the Loire, from
mandy
submit. Angers to Orléans ; while the rest were quartered near
the theatre of the recent Belgic campaign. In Italy the
Rejoicings news of Caesar's victories was received with enthusiasm.[1]
at Rome. Men felt that he had avenged the disaster of the Allia ;
and even the Senate gave expression to the popular
sentiment. After his dispatches had been read, it was
decided to hold a thanksgiving service of fifteen days—
an honour which no Roman citizen had received before.

Delusive   The political outlook seemed everywhere favourable.
prospects
of peace. The barbarian invaders of Gaul had been destroyed or
driven back ; the Belgae had been chastised ; and many
of the other states had proffered their submission. The
Aedui and the Remi were still friendly ; and the countenance of Caesar had greatly increased their renown, and
therefore the influence which they were able to exert on
his behalf. Confident in the prospect of tranquillity, he
set out on a tour to Illyricum, the most distant quarter
[The   of·his province. But he was soon undeceived. The legion
country
of the under Publius Crassus had been quartered in the northern
Andes.]   [1] Plut., Caes., 21, 1.

part of Anjou. The most considerable of the neighbouring 56 B. C.
tribes were the Veneti, who dwelt in the tract of western
Brittany which comprises the department of the Morbihan
and the southern part of the department of Finistère.
Like the modern Bretons, they were the most skilful
seamen in Gaul ; they had a powerful fleet of large
vessels ; and their prosperity depended upon the carrying
trade with Britain, of which, at least in the western region,
they possessed the monopoly. They, however, as well as
the more distant tribes of Brittany and Normandy, professed to submit ; and Crassus sent officers to arrange with
them for a supply of corn. But the chiefs of the Veneti, Rebellion
besides their natural impatience of foreign ascendancy, of the
had a business-like motive for resistance : they had heard Corioso-
that Caesar was contemplating an invasion of Britain, lites, and
and they were determined to prevent him from interfering Esuvii.
with their trade.[1] The rumour which had reached them
was true. The subjection of the Veneti was a necessary
prelude to the invasion of Britain ; for Caesar could not
safely embark his army unless he had command of the
Channel, and at the time when he planned the invasion
the masters of the Channel were the Veneti.[2] Hoping to
induce Crassus to restore their hostages, they detained as
prisoners the officers who had come to them. The tribes [The
of the Côtes-du-Nord and the Orne followed their example : lites and
presently the whole north-western seaboard was sworn to Esuvii.]
resist the encroachments of Rome ; and an embassy was
sent to Crassus, to demand the restoration of the hostages.
    Messengers were soon posting with dispatches for Caesar
Caesar, who was still in Illyricum. He had studied the for a naval
character of the Gauls ; and he knew that, if they soon war.
lost heart, their blood was up on the slightest stimulus.
Unless he made an instant example of the Veneti, the
other tribes of Gaul would fancy that they might defy
him with impunity. The Belgae indeed were only half
subdued ; and they were said to have solicited the support
of the Germans. Accordingly Caesar sent instructions to

[1] Strabo, iv, 4, 1.
[2] *Anc. Britain and the Invasions of Julius Caesar*, pp. 301-3.

his officers to have a fleet built in the ports at the mouth of the Loire, to raise oarsmen from the Province, and to collect as many pilots and seamen as they could. But not long afterwards he learned that the acts of his consulship were about to be impugned,[1] that one of his enemies, Domitius Ahenobarbus, was threatening to deprive him of his army,[1] and that even Pompey was not to be relied upon. If his work in Gaul was not to be prematurely ended, he must devise some means of securing the fidelity of his confederates and checkmating the machinations of his foes.

[1] Suet., *Div. Iul.*, 24, 1. See p. 74

CHAPTER IX

ANNEXATION OF CYPRUS.—THE HUMILIATION OF POMPEY, THE RECALL OF CICERO, AND THE CONFERENCE AT LUCA

CICERO had hardly fled from Rome when Clodius proceeded to remove the inflexible Republican who might agitate for his restoration and thwart the schemes of the triumvirs. At that time the island of Cyprus was ruled by Ptolemy, a brother of the Egyptian king who a few months before had purchased the recognition of his sovereignty from Caesar ; but the Cyprian had not effected the same insurance for the security of his realm. Clodius proposed a bill, which was accepted by the popular assembly, for confiscating the royal treasures, annexing the island, and dispatching Cato to execute the details. The official pretext was that Ptolemy had aided the pirates who still, though in greatly diminished numbers, infested the Levant, and Clodius, who some time before had himself been kidnapped, had a personal grudge against the King because he had made only a small contribution to his ransom ; but it is safe to assume that the annexation, which would round off the bequest of Cyrene and the conquest of Crete, of Cilicia, and of Syria, had been prearranged, and doubtless Caesar as well as Clodius desired to get rid of Cato.[1] Before Cicero departed Clodius had invited Cato to accept the mission, and, as he refused, had told him that, willing or unwilling, he must go. Why Cato yielded, it would be vain to guess ; but we may doubt whether he approved the apology of Cicero—

---

[1] Mr. Strachan-Davidson (*Cicero*, 1894, pp. 235–6) asserts that Clodius acted in obedience to Caesar. This is the general opinion, and it is supported by the fact that Clodius acted with the approval of Caesar in forcing Cicero to go into exile ; but there is no direct evidence except the alleged assertion of Clodius (Cic., *De domo*, 9, 22) that Caesar had congratulated him on having got rid of Cato.

58 B. C. that he saw that the crime was unavoidable and believed
that he could best secure whatever good might come out
of evil.[1] Since his entire staff consisted of two clerks,
and not a single soldier followed him, we must suppose
either that the Cyprians were apathetic or that they were
in no condition to attempt resistance. Ptolemy, as soon
as he heard that he was to be deprived of his treasures,
committed suicide : Cato, who was sent in the first
instance on business to Byzantium (for Clodius intended
to keep him employed as long as possible), commissioned
his nephew Marcus Brutus to represent him and take
charge of the dead King's property, and when he himself
arrived, sold it for nearly seven thousand talents. Cyprus
itself was annexed to the province of Cilicia.[2]

But the virtual banishment of Cato did not in fact
serve the purpose either of Clodius or of his master ; and
Clodius himself, without knowing it, was the mainspring
of the movement for the restoration of Cicero. His lust
destroys for vengeance was not satiated by Cicero's exile. Immedi-
Cicero's
house and ately after Cicero had gone his villas near Tusculum and
villas, Formiae were destroyed ; his house on the Palatine was
plundered and afterwards burned by the gang of roughs
who attended Clodius ; and Clodius himself, who intended
to build a mansion on the site, dedicated a part of it
and erected thereon a temple, in order to prevent the
property from ever being restored to his enemy.[3] Nor
and flouts was he satisfied with injuring Cicero. Although Pompey
Pompey. had helped to make him a tribune, he did not hesitate
to attack him also. Tigranes, the son of the King of

---

[1] *Pro Sest.*, 29, 62–3.

[2] Livy, *Epit.*, 104 ; Pliny, *Nat. Hist.*, xxix, 4 (30), 96 ; xxxiv, 8 (19), 92 ;
Val. Max., ix, 4, 3 ; Vell., ii, 45, 4–5 ; Plut., *Cato min.*, 34–8 ; *Brut.*, 3, 1 ;
Flor., i, 44 ; App. (who dates Cato's mission six years too late), *B. C.*, ii, 23,
85–6 ; Ps. Victor, *De vir. ill.*, 80, 2 ; Rufus Festus, 13, 1. The insinuations,
qualified by the repeated use of the word 'perhaps', which Tyrrell (*The
Correspondence of Cicero*, iii, 1890, p. xxvi) made against Cato's honesty are
hardly worth noticing. Dio (xxxix, 22–3), who admits that, 'according to
some writers', Caesar made accusations against Cato, nevertheless affirms
his innocence.

[3] *Pro Sest.*, 24, 54 ; *In Pis.*, 11, 26 ; Plut., *Cic.*, 33, 1 ; App., ii, 15, 58 ;
Dio, xxxviii, 17, 6.

Armenia, who had figured in Pompey's triumph, was 58 B. C. detained at Rome in the custody of the praetor Lucius Flavius. Clodius, bribed by the King, contrived by trickery to get possession of him, and refused to produce him even when Pompey demanded his surrender. The praetor attempted to recover. his prisoner forcibly ; but he and his attendants were worsted by the Clodian bravoes, and Tigranes, it would seem, escaped.[1] Cicero's friends believed that Clodius had acted with the approval of Caesar, and that the result would be a rupture between Caesar and Pompey, which might lead to Cicero's recall. Cicero was soon undeceived. Writing to Atticus on the 29th of May, he remarked, ' I cannot see, as you do—or May 24. perhaps you only suggest it to console me—that a move-ment in politics is impending. For as the case of Tigranes was ignored, all hope of a breach is gone '.[2] But, what was more important, Pompey was estranged from Clodius ; and even Gabinius, who, having secured his province, had no longer anything to fear, now turned against him. The consul actually condescended to fight the tribune with his own weapons. He too hired a gang of rowdies, and the rival bands encountered each other daily in the streets.[3] On the 1st of June Ninnius, the tribune who May 27. had stood by Cicero early in the year, proposed at the instance of Pompey in the Senate that Cicero should be recalled. A full house accepted the proposal, but another tribune, Aelius Ligur, vetoed it.[4] Popular feeling, however, was setting strongly in Cicero's favour. In the course of the month his brother Quintus returned to Rome from his government of Asia, and was received with demonstrations of sympathy.[5] Pompey determined to Pompey do his utmost to recall the orator whom he had betrayed, works for
Cicero's but whose eloquence would now be useful. As early as recall. July Terentius Varro assured Atticus, who promptly communicated the news to Cicero, that Pompey was well-

[1] Ascon., ed. Clark, p. 47, ll. 12–26 (ed. Stangl., pp. 40–1) ; Plut., *Pomp.*, 48, 6 ; Dio, xxxviii, 30, 1–2.   [2] *Att.*, iii, 8, 3. Cf. 13, 1.
[3] Cic., *In Pis.*, 12, 27 (cf. *De domo*, 47, 124) ; Dio, xxxviii, 30, 3.
[4] Cic., *Pro Sest.*, 31, 68 ; Dio, xxxviii, 30, 3.
[5] *Pro Sest.*, 31, 68. Cf. *Att.*, iii, 9, 1.

disposed towards him and that as soon as he received a letter from Caesar to signify his approval, he would commission some magistrate to carry out the necessary formalities.[1] But Clodius was determined to baffle
Pompey. On the 11th of August Pompey, on entering the Senate House, was informed that a slave had been ordered by Clodius to assassinate him. He returned home immediately,[2] resolved to avoid coming into collision with Clodius so long as he remained in office, and took no further part in public affairs during the year, spending his time in his country houses with his young wife Julia ;[3] but he adhered to his purpose of recalling Cicero,[4] and doubtless it was with his consent or at his instance that Publius Sestius, one of the newly elected tribunes, travelled to Gaul with the aim of obtaining the consent of Caesar.[5] The elections had turned out as Pompey wished : one of the consuls designate, Lentulus Spinther, was not only a friend of his but also an intimate friend of Cicero ; the other, Metellus Nepos, was impelled by a sense of justice or induced by Pompey to forget his long-standing quarrel.[6] Eight of the tribunes were
equally well disposed ; and on the 29th of October they promulgated a bill for Cicero's recall, which, though it was opposed by the consuls Piso and Gabinius and vetoed by the tribune Ligur,[7] was useful as a declaration of opinion.

Meanwhile Cicero was anxiously awaiting events. His friends persuaded him to remain at Thessalonica, although it was within the prescribed limit of five hundred miles,[8] assuring him that the movement for his restoration was impending.[9] He could not distract his attention from his miseries by work, for apparently he had access to no library ;[10] he blamed himself for the blunder which

---

[1] *Att.*, iii, 15, 1 ; 18, 1.
[2] Ascon., ed. Clark, p. 46, ll. 21–6 (ed. Stangl, p. 40).
[3] Plut., *Pomp.*, 48, 5 ; 49, 2.   [4] *Att.*, iii, 22, 2.
[5] *Pro Sest.*, 33, 71.   [6] *Att.*, iii, 22, 2 ; 23, 1.
[7] *Ib.*, §§ 1–3. Cf. *Q. fr.*, i, 4, 3.   [8] See vol. i, p. 335.
[9] *Q. fr.*, i, 4, 2.   [10] *Att.*, iii, 15, 2.

he had committed in leaving Rome,[1] and cursed the well-
wishers who had counselled him to go ;[2] and although
he was grateful to Atticus, who had given him a sum
equivalent to two thousand five hundred pounds to provide
for his necessities,[3] and who was not only doing everything
that he could to smooth the way for his return, but also
looking after the interests of his family,[4] he could not
refrain from occasionally reproaching even this devoted
friend. It was a ground of complaint that Atticus and
others had dissuaded him from suicide. ' You,' he wrote,
' all of you who are responsible for my survival, have
brought me to this pass.'[5] But, ashamed perhaps of
such outbursts, he tried to make amends : ' Your consideration for me has been on a higher plane than mine
for you.'[6] ' My honoured consulship,' he told his
brother, ' has robbed me of you, of children, country,
fortune . . . I know not how far Hortensius can be trusted.
With the most elaborate pretence of affection and the
closest daily intimacy he treated me basely and treacherously '.[7] 'Blind that I was ', he cried, ' to discard my
senator's dress and entreat the people ; it was a fatal
step to take when I had not been attacked by name.'[8]
Atticus told him plainly that his lamentations were
unmanly, and he smarted under the rebuke : ' You
upbraid me often sternly and say that I am weak. I ask
you, is there any misery, however great, not included in
my calamity ? Did any one ever fall from such a great
position, in so good a cause, so endowed with genius,
wisdom, popularity, with such support from all loyal
men ? Can I forget what I was ? Can I help feeling
what I am ? '[9] Towards the end of the year he was constrained to quit Thessalonica, for the incoming Governor,
Piso, had already shown himself unfriendly ;. and, moreover, he was anxious to be near Italy in order that he
might get timely news of what his friends at Rome were

[1] Q. fr., i, 4, 4 ; Att., iii, 15, 5. 7.
[2] Q. fr., i, 3, 8 ; Att., iii, 13, 2 ; 15, 2 ; Fam., xiv, 1, 2.
[3] Nepos, Att., 4, 4.   [4] Att., iii, 15, 4 ; 20, 2–3 ; iv, 1, 1.
[5] Ib., iii, 9, 1.   [6] Ib., 20, 3.   [7] Q. fr., i, 3, 1. 8.
[8] Att., iii, 15, 5.   [9] Ib., 10, 2. Cf. 13, 2 ; 15, 1.

58 B. C.   doing. He therefore proceeded to Dyrrachium, a free
city in which he would be secure from molestation and
where he had many friends. ' I am now ', he wrote
Nov. 16.   thence on the 25th of November, ' awaiting some definite
step, or else blank despair.' [1] Early in the new year he
heard good news from Quintus ; [2] but a few weeks later
he wrote to Atticus, ' I see from your letter and from the
bald facts that I am an utterly ruined man '.[3]

Dec. 20,   On the 1st of January the consul Lentulus proposed
58 B. C.   in the Senate that Cicero should be recalled. Metellus
made no objection : Appius Claudius, the brother of
Clodius, the only praetor opposed to Cicero, was silent ;
eight of the ten tribunes were on Cicero's side. Cotta,
who had been consul eight years before, insisted that it
was the duty of the Senate not only to recall Cicero, but
also to honour him : Pompey assented, only adding that
in the interest of Cicero the resolution of the Senate
ought to be confirmed by a popular vote. The senators
were about to pass the resolution when Atilius Serranus,
one of the two hostile tribunes, who, if Cicero was not
misinformed, had been bribed by Clodius, asked to be
allowed one night for consideration. The request was
received with vehement expressions of dissent : some of
the members begged Atilius to withdraw his opposition,
and his own father-in-law actually knelt at his feet.
Atilius promised to raise no objection on the morrow ;
and the meeting was adjourned. But Atilius did not keep
his word. On every available day during the remainder
of the month the Senate continued the discussion ; but,
Jan. 13,   doubtless through the machinations of the hostile tribunes,
57 B. C.   the resolution was delayed. The 25th was fixed for the
decision of the people. Quintus Fabricius, the tribune
who had undertaken to propose the bill, entered the
Forum before dawn, but found it occupied by a posse
of armed men. He and his supporters were attacked ;
several were killed or wounded ; and when Quintus
Cicero mounted the platform to address the assembly

[1] Att., iii, 22, 1. 4 ; Fam., xiv, 3, 4.
[2] Att., iii, 26.   [3] Ib., 27.

on behalf of his brother, he was thrown down and only made his escape by the aid of his slaves and freedmen, who carried him away under cover of the darkness. The blood that stained the Forum was swabbed up with sponges, and the corpses were pitched into the Tiber. It was the news of this slaughter, the like of which had not been perpetrated since the days of Cinna,[1] that, after Cicero had been encouraged by the assurances of Quintus, led him to despair.

Further affrays followed. Sestius, who staunchly supported Cicero, was attacked in the temple of Castor, to which, trusting in the sanctity of his office, he had come unprotected, by the ruffians of Clodius, and severely wounded, but was able to escape because they thought that he was killed.[2] His assailants were brought before the Senate, where they confessed their guilt, and imprisoned by the tribune Milo; but Atilius released them, and they went unpunished.[3] Sestius in his turn raised a band, which protected him against renewed attacks;[4] while Milo attempted to bring Clodius to trial for violent crime. Clodius thereupon offered himself as a candidate for the aedileship, knowing that if he were successful, he could not be tried except for bribery. The quaestors, whose duty it was to appoint the jurors, had not yet been elected, and Metellus forbade the praetor to hear any prosecution before the jurors were duly chosen.[5] Thus balked, Milo collected a troop of gladiators

---

[1] *Cum senatui*, &c., 3–4; *Pro Sest.*, 34–5; *In Pis.*, 15, 34–5; *Fam.*, i, 9, 16; Plut., *Cic.*, 33, 2; Dio, xxxix, 7, 2.

[2] *Q. fr.*, ii, 3, 6; *Pro Sest.*, 37–8, §§ 79–81.

[3] *Ib.*, 39, 85.

[4] *Ib.*, § 84; 42, 90.

[5] *Pro Sest.*, 41, 89, explained by Dio, xxxix, 7, 4 (cf. G. Long, *Decline of the Roman Republic*, iv, 1872, p. 87); *Pro Milone*, 13, 35; 15, 40. E. Meyer (*Caesars Monarchie*[2], 1919, pp. 109–112, note) thinks that Dio misunderstood the passage in *Pro Sestio,* and therefore wrongly connected the events which I have described in the text with Milo's first attempt to bring Clodius to trial; for, he argues, if Dio is right, we must assume that no aediles or quaestors were elected throughout the year, an anomaly which, if it had happened, would have been expressly mentioned. I fail to understand this reasoning. If, as Meyer holds, no quaestors had been elected by Dec. 5, why should we disbelieve Dio when he says that none had been elected early in the year?

57 B. C. and prepared to repel force with force.[1] But the day of Cicero's deliverance was not far off. The Senate resolved on the motion of Lentulus to thank Plancius for having entertained Cicero at Thessalonica, to commend Cicero to the protection of provincial governors, and to summon citizens from all parts of Italy to come and vote for his recall. Senators who entered the theatre after this session were received with loud applause ; the audience, weeping with joy, rose with one accord to welcome Lentulus ; and Clodius, who ventured to appear, was assailed with abuse and threats.[2] Caesar, it would seem, had stipulated for a pledge, which Quintus Cicero had consented to give, that Marcus, in return for his restoration, should support the triumvirs.[3] Pompey, now assured of Caesar's consent, not only harangued the populace in the Forum, but went from town to town to speak on Cicero's behalf, and affirmed in the House that he was the saviour of his country ; [4] and on the next day the Senate, on his motion, passed a resolution that if any man hindered Cicero's return, he should be deemed a public enemy.[5] The

July 19. 4th of August was fixed for taking the popular vote. Citizens who could afford the expenses of the journey

Despite the violence of Clodius a bill is passed for Cicero's recall. had poured into Rome from every district ; shops were shut as if on a public holiday ; and the Field of Mars, where the voting was to take place, was densely thronged. Lentulus proposed the bill. Milo was there with his troop to intimidate Clodius ; and the bill was passed.[6]

Clodius was not elected aedile till the 20th of January in the following year (Cic., *Q. fr.*, ii, 1, 3, compared with ii, 2, 2).   [1] Dio, xxxix, 8, 1. ·
[2] *Pro Sest.*, 54–6, §§ 116-7, 120, and *Schol. Bob.*, ed. Stangl, p. 136 (ed. Orelli, p. 305) ; *In Pis.*, 15, 34 ; *Pro Planc.*, 32, 78.   [3] Cic., *Fam.*, i, 9, 9.
[4] *Pro Sest.*, 61, 129 ; *De prov. cons.*, 18, 43 ; *In Pis.*, 32, 80.
[5] *Ib.*, 15, 34 ; *Pro Sest.*, 61, 129. The Senate decreed that no one should 'observe the sky' or delay the proceedings (*ne quis de caelo servaret, ne quis moram ullam afferret*). This decree was not general, but made for a particular purpose. Was the law of Clodius which forbade any one to 'observe the sky' similarly restricted ? If it was general, it may have been so drafted that the Senate feared that some enemy of Cicero might find a loophole for evasion. At all events, if it was not obsolete, it was violated by Milo and by Clodius himself.
[6] *Att.*, iv, 1, 4 ; *De domo*, 33, 90 ; Vell., ii, 45, 3 ; Plut., *Cic.*, 33, 2 ; Dio, xxxix, 8, 2-3.

Quintus instantly dispatched a courier with the glad
tidings to his brother, who embarked at Dyrrachium on
the same day, landed on the morrow at Brundisium,
and there on the 8th of August received the letter.[1] On
the 4th of September he was in Rome, and as soon as
he could engage a messenger wrote to Atticus. ' Of this
I can sincerely assure you, that in my great joy, amid
congratulations that fulfilled my heart's desire, the one
thing wanting to complete my happiness was to see you,
or rather to clasp you to my bosom . . . I reached Brundisium on the 5th of August. My little Tullia was there
to meet me, on her own birthday, which happened also
to be the anniversary of the foundation of the colony of
Brundisium and of the temple of Salvation, near your
house. The coincidence was noticed by the people of
Brundisium and hailed with great rejoicing . . . After
receiving high honour from the principal Brundisians,
I could not pursue my journey without deputations
from every quarter meeting me with congratulations,
and when I approached the city not a soul of any rank
known to my attendant failed to come and meet me,
except those enemies who could neither dissemble nor
deny their enmity. On my arrival at the Capuan Gate
the steps of the temples were thronged from top to
bottom by the populace, who expressed their congratulations by loud applause ; a like throng and like applause
accompanied me right up to the Capitol, and in the Forum
and on the Capitol itself the crowd was prodigious.
Next day, the 5th of September, I returned thanks to
the senators in the House.' [2]

An opportunity had already presented itself to Cicero
of showing his especial gratitude to Pompey, perhaps
also of attempting again to realize his cherished dream
of enlisting him on the side of the constitution and making
him its champion. On the day of his arrival the price of
corn suddenly rose ; for while politicians had carried

Marginal notes:
57 B. C.

July 23.

Aug. 17.

Cicero re-
turns in
triumph.

July 20.

Aug. 18.

Pompey
entrusted
with con-
trol of the
corn
supply.

---

[1] See vol. iii, p. 376, n. 9.
[2] *Att.*, iv, 1, 2. 4. 5 (cf. *Pro Sest.*, 63, 131 ; *In Pis.*, 22) ; Livy, *Epit.*, 104 ;
Vell., ii, 45, 3 ; Plut., *Cic.*, 33, 3 ; App., ii, 16, 60.

corn laws for their own purposes, no statesman had
contrived a plan for ensuring a constant and sufficient
supply.[1] Crowds, instigated by Clodius, thronged to
the theatre and afterwards to the Senate House, shouting
that Cicero, whose coming had occasioned an unusual
influx into Rome, was responsible for the scarcity. On
the 5th and 6th of September the Senate deliberated on
the question. In the streets and in the mansions of the
rich it was the common topic, and the general feeling
was that Pompey should be called upon to administer
the supply ; it was known that he desired the commission,
and Cicero was urged to speak in favour of his appointment. On the 6th [2] Cicero carried a motion that Pompey
should be invited to undertake the duty, and that a law
to that effect should be proposed to the assembly. The
decree of the Senate was read in the Forum ; the mention
of Cicero's name was received with applause ; and he
proceeded to address the people. Pompey intimated
that he should require fifteen lieutenants, above all
Cicero, to assist him : the Senate assented ; and the
consuls drafted a bill by which absolute control of the
corn-supply throughout the Roman world was to be
given to Pompey for five years. But it would seem that
what Pompey really wanted was a military command
which would counterbalance that of Caesar. Another
bill was introduced by a tribune, Gaius Messius, which
was more than equivalent to the Gabinian law of ten
years before. Messius proposed that Pompey should

---

[1] It must be remembered that corn was distributed gratis to citizens only,
not to aliens, women, or children.

[2] Cicero (*Att.*, iv, 1, 6), immediately after describing his arrival in Rome
and the speech which he made next day (Sept. 5), says that *eo biduo* he carried
the motion which I have mentioned in the text, the Senate having deliberated
' during those [two] days ' (*per eos dies*). The question is whether he spoke
on Sept. 5 (as L. Lange holds [*Röm. Alt.*, iii, 1871, p. 307]) or 6 or 7. G. Rauschen (*Eph. Tull.*, 1886, pp. 31-2) argues that *eo biduo* can only mean ' two
days after ' Sept. 5 : H. Meusel, who agrees that that is the meaning in this
context, remarks in a note on Caesar's *B. C.*, i, 41, 1, that the words sometimes
mean what Lange thinks that they mean here,—' within those two days '.
I incline to agree with Meusel, but with this reservation : I believe that Cicero
reckoned inclusively (see p. 166, n. 2), and therefore that he spoke on
Sept. 6.

have power to draw at his discretion upon the treasury ; 57 B. C.
that a fleet and an army should be assigned to him ;
and that he should be vested with authority, superior
to that of the provincial governors, in every province of
the empire.[1] ' After that ', wrote Cicero, ' our consular
law seems quite moderate ; that of Messius is intolerable.
Pompey says he prefers the former, but really, his friends
think, wants the latter.   The ex-consuls, led by Favonius,
grumble ; I hold my tongue, the more so ', he significantly
added, ' that the pontiffs have as yet given no answer
about my house.   If they annul the consecration, I shall
have a splendid site.'[2]   Despite certain disagreements
with his wife,[3] he was full of hope.   ' I am on the threshold ',
he told his old friend, ' of a new life.'[4]   Whatever may
have been the effect of his silence in the Senate, the bill
of Messius was either abandoned or rejected ; the consular
bill was passed ;[5] and Pompey's lieutenants started soon
afterwards for the various provinces which supplied
Rome with grain.   Pompey himself for the present
remained behind, perhaps because he saw a prospect
of obtaining a fresh appointment which would give him
not only employment but also power.

Meanwhile Cicero was engaged in personal affairs which,
however unimportant they may seem, had their influence
in determining his political career.   On the last day of Sept. 11.
September he addressed the college of pontiffs, with the
aim of persuading them to annul the act by which
Clodius had consecrated the area of his house.   They
virtually decided that the consecration was illegal.[6] Two Sept. 13.
days later the Senate passed a resolution, proposed by
Marcellinus, one of the consuls designate, that Cicero's
house should be restored to him ; and the consuls Compen-
resolved to pay him by way of compensation sums sation
awarded
equivalent to twenty thousand pounds for the house, to Cicero.

[1] *Att.*, iv, 1, 6–7.   Was the clause relating to the provincial governors
inspired by Pompey's recollection of how he had been flouted by Metellus
in the affair of Crete (vol. i, p. 175) ?
[2] *Ib.*, § 7.   [3] *Ib.*, § 8 ; 2, 8.   [4] *Ib*, 1, 8.
[5] *Ib.*, § 7 ; Livy, *Epit.*, 104 ; Plut., *Pomp.*, 49, 4 ; Dio, xxxix, 9, 2–3.
[6] *Att.*, iv, 2, 2–3 ; Dio, xxxix 11, 1.

57 B. C. five thousand for his Tusculan villa, and two thousand five hundred for the one near Formiae. He privately complained that the compensation was inadequate, and put it down to jealousy : 'My dear Pomponius, I tell you, the very same men—you know them as well as I do—who clipped my wings are unwilling that they should grow again. But they are growing already, so I hope.' [1] Clodius, however, was not disposed to

Oct. 15. acquiesce in the pontifical decision. On the 3rd of

Renewed violence of Clodius. November the masons who were rebuilding Cicero's house were scattered by a gang of rowdies, and his brother's, which adjoined it, was set on fire. [2] The Senate, which might have empowered the consuls to reduce Clodius to submission, remained passive : evidently he had powerful friends, while Cicero had comparatively few ; the majority had had sufficient sense of justice to vote for his recall, but they were not sorry to see his

Oct. 23. persecution. [3] On the 11th he was walking down the Sacred Way, accompanied fortunately by a bodyguard, when Clodius followed him with his gang. Stones were thrown and swords were drawn ; but Cicero took refuge in the vestibule of a house, and his escort prevented Clodius and his roughs from getting in. Cicero assured Atticus that Clodius himself had been at his mercy, but that he had shrunk from permitting his attendants to

Nov. 12 (Oct. 24). dispatch him. On the very next day Clodius was attempting in broad daylight to set fire to Milo's house on the Palatine when an armed band rushed out from another house which also belonged to him, killed many of the Clodian gang, and chased Clodius into the house of his

Milo intends to bring him to trial. friend Publius Sulla. Clodius, knowing that Milo was still bent upon bringing him to trial, was anxiously looking forward to the aedileship as a means of escape, and threatened to wreck the city if the elections were put off ; but Milo gave notice that on every day on which they might lawfully be held he would watch the sky

Oct. 31. and bring the proceedings to a standstill. On the 19th

---

[1] *Att.*, iv, 2, 4–5 ; *Fam.*, i, 9, 5 ; *In Pis.*, 22, 52 ; Dio, xxxix, 11, 3.
[2] *Att.*, iv, 3, 2.   [3] *Fam.*, i, 9, 5. Cf. G. Long, *op. cit.*, p. 99.

he occupied the Field of Mars with his armed followers, 57 B. C.
and Clodius did not venture to appear. Thereupon
Metellus, who, though he had acquiesced in Cicero's
recall, was still his political opponent, challenged Milo
to serve his obstructive notice on the following day.
Milo entered the Forum before dawn : Metellus, hoping
to outwit him, hurried stealthily at daybreak to the Field
of Mars to take the votes ; but Milo caught him up in
time and served his notice. ' I don't think the election Nov. 23
will come off,' wrote Cicero : ' I think Publius will be (Nov. 4).
brought to trial by Milo—unless he is killed first. If he
once puts himself in his way in a disturbance, I foresee
that Milo himself will kill him. Milo has no scruples and
avows his aim. . . . In spirit at any rate I am as vigorous
as in my prime, or even more.' [1] What happened during
the next fortnight is unknown ; but neither the elections
nor the trial were held, and on the 10th of December Nov. 20.
Milo and his fellow tribunes of course went out of office.
About the middle of the month [2] the Senate met, and Stormy
Rutilius Lupus, one of the new tribunes, made a speech, debate in
in which, with the approval of Cicero, whose arguments Senate.
he repeated,[3] he attacked Caesar's legislation on the
Campanian land. He was listened to in silence ; but
when he was about to dismiss the House Marcellinus
rose and said, ' Don't infer from our silence, Lupus, what
we approve at the moment or disapprove. As far as I
am concerned, and I think it is the same with the rest,
I am silent only because I do not think it right that the
case of the Campanian land should be debated in Pompey's
absence '. Immediately afterwards another tribune,
Racilius, reopened the burning question whether the trial
of Clodius or the elections should be held first. Marcellinus
proposed that Clodius should be brought to trial instantly,
and the other consul designate, Philippus, agreed with
him : two of the tribunes, Gaius Cato, who in the previous
year had denounced Pompey as ' an unofficial dictator ',

---

[1] Att., iv, 3, 3–5.   [2] Long, op. cit., p. 101.
[3] See vol. i, p. 305. Meyer (op. cit., pp. 125–6) thinks that Lupus was encouraged by Pompey's unfriendly attitude towards Caesar. See pp. 72–3, infra.

57 B. C.

and Gaius Cassius, who was destined to become famous, supported Clodius. Cicero thundered against the murderous violence of his enemy. ' I impeached him ', he boasted, ' as though he were on his trial, amidst frequent murmurs of approbation from the entire House.' The senators were crossing the floor, to vote for the priority of the trial, when Clodius was called upon. Intending to talk out the sitting, he inveighed furiously against Racilius : his rowdies, congregated on the steps of the building, raised a menacing shout ; and the indignant

Clodius escapes prosecution.

senators dispersed in alarm.[1] Clodius was not brought to trial, and on the 20th of January he was elected curule aedile.[2]

Dec. 29, 57 B. C.

Meanwhile Quintus Cicero, who had taken his brother's place as Pompey's first lieutenant, was negotiating in Sardinia for a supply of grain, and Pompey himself was considering how he might strengthen his position.

Ptolemy Auletes, expelled from Egypt, seeks Pompey's support.

Ptolemy Auletes, only a few months after he bought from Caesar and Pompey the recognition of his sovereignty, had been expelled by his own subjects, exasperated by the taxes which he imposed in order to repay the Italian financiers who had advanced the purchase-money and indignant at his acquiescing in the seizure of his brother's kingdom.[3] Leaving Alexandria with the aim of inducing Pompey to re-establish him on his throne, he called at Rhodes, and there met Cato, who advised him not to go to Rome, where he would be fleeced by money-lenders, but to return and be reconciled with his people. Disregarding this advice, Ptolemy proceeded to Rome, and was entertained by Pompey, who openly supported him. Cato's prophecy was of course fulfilled. Rabirius Postumus, a capitalist who had already lent Ptolemy large sums, now made fresh advances, which were required for bribery.[3] The Alexandrians, as soon as they heard

[1] Q. fr., ii 1.
[2] Ib., 2, 2. Cf. Dio, xxxix, 18, 1.
[3] Cic., Pro Rab. Post., 2, 4–5 ; Livy, Epit., 104 ; Plut., Cato min., 35, 2–3 ; Dio, xxxv, 12. Cicero (op. cit., 3, 6), as an advocate, of course denied that the money lent by Rabirius was required for bribery ; but see Fam., i, 1, 1.

that the King had arrived at Rome, sent a deputation 57 B. C.
to the Senate, to rebut the charges which he had made
against his subjects and to formulate complaints against
him ; but he contrived to have many of the deputies
murdered and purchased the silence of the rest. The
Senate, instigated by Favonius, summoned the head of
the deputation to appear before them and give evidence ;
but a bribe prevented his appearance.[1] Towards the end
of the year the Senate decreed, on the motion of Lentulus
Spinther, that the Governor of Cilicia should be entrusted
with the duty of restoring the King.[2] Lentulus was
himself the Governor elect. It was generally believed,
however, that Pompey coveted the office and, moreover,
that he wished to obtain an army for the purpose ;[3]
and his bitter enemy Gaius Cato determined to checkmate
him. On the 10th of December Cato became a tribune, Nov. 20.
and soon afterwards it was announced by the keepers of
the Sibylline Books that if the King of Egypt should
solicit the assistance of the Romans, they must not
refuse him friendship, but neither must they help him
with an army ; otherwise they would be exposed to peril.
Thereupon, on the motion of Cato, the Senate annulled
their decree [4] and passed another, declaring it dangerous
to the Republic that the King should be restored with
an army.[5] The question, however, was not dropped.
Perhaps, after the publication of the oracle, Pompey was Intrigues
less anxious to obtain the office ; but his friends, who to obtain
believed that he still wanted it, used their influence in tion of
his favour.[6] 'The Senate', wrote Cicero to Lentulus, him.
'supports the trumped-up religious cavil, not from any Jan. 13,
respect to religion, but from ill-feeling towards him and 698
(Dec. 22,
disgust at the King's bribery. I lose no opportunity of 57 B. C.)
exhorting and imploring Pompey—even expostulating
with him frankly and admonishing him—to avoid such

<hr />

[1] Dio, xxxix, 13 ; 14, 1-3. Strabo (xvii, 1, 11) makes the incredible
statement that Pompey procured the murder of the deputies.
[2] Cic., *Fam.*, i, 1, 3 ; Dio, xxxix, 12, 3.
[3] *Fam.*, i, 1, 3-4 ; 2, 3 ; 4, 2 ; *Q. fr.*, ii, 2, 3 ; 3, 2.
[4] Dio, xxxix, 15, 1-3.   [5] *Q. fr.*, ii, 2, 3.   [6] *Fam.*, i, 1, 3.

57 B. C. a discreditable imputation.'[1] Proposals were made in the Senate on behalf of Pompey, Lentulus, and others ; and Cicero kept Lentulus informed of the debates.

Dec. 24. ' I happened ', he wrote on the 15th of January, ' to be dining with Pompey yesterday . . . and in the course of conversation I think I said enough to induce him to abandon every other idea and to support your claims. Indeed, when I hear him talk, I acquit him entirely of all suspicion of self-seeking ; but when I mark the bearing of his intimates of every rank, I perceive, what is no secret to anybody, that the whole business has been arranged long ago by the jobbery of a certain clique, with the

Jan. 18, connivance of the King and his advisers.'[2] Writing to
698 his brother, who was still in Sardinia, he remarked that
(Dec. 27,
57 B. C.) in the Senate he had fully discharged his obligations to Lentulus, while at the same time fulfilling Pompey's wishes. ' I cannot make out ', he added, ' what Pompey really wants. What his *entourage* desire everybody sees. The people who are financing the King are openly advancing money to baffle Lentulus. There seems no doubt that he has been deprived of the commission— to my great regret.'[3] For some time, however, nothing was definitely settled.[4]

Clodius Clodius was meantime preparing to use his newly
attempts acquired power by prosecuting Milo for violent crime—in
to prose-
cute Milo. other words, for having employed armed men to resist

Jan. 14, the attacks of Clodius.[5] On the 7th of February Milo
56 B. C. duly presented himself in the Forum. Pompey had come to support him. Cicero was there also ; and a letter which he wrote soon afterwards to his brother contains

Typically the classic description of a Roman public meeting in the
violent dying Republic. ' Pompey spoke, or rather meant to, for
scene in
the as soon as he got up the Clodian rowdies raised a shout,
Forum. and all through his speech he was interrupted, not only by hostile cries, but by personal abuse and insults. When he had finished—for I must admit that in the circumstances

---

[1] *Fam.*, i, 1, 1-2. Cf. 4, 2.   [2] *Ib.*, 2, 2-3.
[3] *Q. fr.*, ii, 2, 3. Cf. *Fam.*, i, 5, 3.
[4] Cf. *ib.*, 7, 4.   [5] Dio, xxxix, 18.

he showed great courage ; he was not cowed, he said all
he had to say, and had at times by his commanding
presence even enforced silence—well, when he had
finished, up got Clodius. On our side there was such
a yell—for we had determined to pay him out—that he
lost all presence of mind, and could not control his voice
or his countenance. This went on up to two o'clock
(Pompey had hardly finished speaking at noon), people
shouting every kind of abuse and finally the most obscene
doggerel against Clodius and his sister. Furious and white
with rage, Clodius, in the midst of the shouting, kept
putting questions to his claque : " Who is starving the
people to death ? " His rowdies answered, " Pompey ".
" Who wants to go to Alexandria ? " " Pompey ", they
answered. "Whom do you wish to go ? " They answered,
" Crassus ". The latter was present with no friendly
feelings to Milo. About three, as though at a given signal,
the Clodians began spitting at our men. This made one's
blood boil. They made a push and tried to hustle us
out of the ground, when our men charged and the ruffians
fled. Clodius was shoved off the platform ; and then
I too made my escape for fear of anything happening
in the riot. The Senate was summoned. Pompey went
home. I did not enter the House myself, not wishing to
remain silent in such a crisis or to give offence to good
patriots by defending Pompey, who was being attacked.' [1]
The prosecution of Milo was repeatedly adjourned ; [2]
but on the 9th, when the Senate passed a resolution that Jan. 16.
the proceedings of the 7th were against the public interest,
Gaius Cato fiercely attacked Pompey, who, said Cicero, Pompey
' answered him boldly, and said plainly, evidently hints in
alluding to Crassus, that he intended to protect himself the Senate
against assassination. . . . He tells me confidentially that Crassus
plots are being formed against his life, that Gaius Cato is plotting against
is backed up by Crassus and some one is finding money his life.
for Clodius, that both are being egged on not only by
him, but also by Curio, Bibulus, and the rest of his
detractors. . . . So he is getting ready and sending for

_____
[1] *Q. fr.*, ii, 3, 1-2.   [2] *Ib.* ; 5, 4.

53 B. C.

men from the country, while Clodius is reinforcing his gang of roughs '.[1] But the quarrel was not decided by force of arms, for Clodius kept quiet and ultimately dropped his prosecution. Notwithstanding these stormy scenes, Cicero was in high spirits. ' My position ', he assured his brother, ' is what you used to tell me, though I hardly could believe it, that it would be—one of dignity and influence '.[2] But Pompey, despite the bold stand which he had made against Gaius Cato, was depressed by the signs of his waning popularity : ' he appeared to me ', wrote Cicero to Lentulus, ' to be very much upset. Accordingly he seems to me to have quite given up the Alexandrian business, which, as far as we are concerned, remains exactly where it was '.[3]

Cicero defends Sestius.

Balked in his attempt to dispose of Milo, Clodius suborned one of his adherents to bring an action for riot against Sestius, who had been so severely wounded by his ruffians in Cicero's cause. Cicero of course defended him, for, though he found him difficult to deal with and cross-grained,[4] he owed much to his courageous championship. In accordance with Roman procedure, the witnesses were called after the speeches for the defence, and Vatinius, who had acted for Caesar three years before, gave evidence against Sestius, remarking that Cicero had courted Caesar because Caesar was successful. Cicero punished him by inveighing against the unconstitutional methods by which he had supported Caesar and gibing at his personal appearance with all the licence which Roman custom allowed. If Caesar's measures had been somewhat irregular, he had made full atonement by his services in Gaul ; but a scoundrel like Vatinius must not claim the indulgence that was accorded to a great man.[5] Cicero was highly delighted at the result. ' Our friend Sestius ', he wrote to his brother, ' was acquitted unanimously . . . I made mince meat of Vatinius, who was openly attacking him, just as I pleased, with the applause

His elation.

[1] *Q. fr.*, ii, 3, 3–4.
[2] *Ib.*, § 7.   [3] *Fam.*, i, 5 B, 1.   [4] *Q. fr.*, ii, 4, 1.
[5] *In Vat.*, 2, 4 ; 6, 15 ; 9, 21–2 ; 12, 29 ; 14, 33 ; 15, 35 ; 16, 38–9.

of gods and men. . . . Our friend Pompey', he continued, 56 B. C.
'is severely condemned for the way he has behaved His criti-cism of
towards Publius Lentulus. He is not the man he was. Pompey.
The fact is that to the lowest dregs of the populace
his support of Milo gives some offence, while the Conservatives expect much from him which he does not do,
and find fault with much that he does. My only complaint
against Marcellinus is that he is too hard upon him,
though the Senate has no objection to that. This makes
me glad to withdraw from the House and from politics
altogether. In the courts I am as strong as ever : never
was my house more crowded.' [1]   Yet, if not at this
moment, a few days later Cicero was contemplating
a political *coup*, by which, as he afterwards said, he
' assaulted the citadel of Caesar's policy ' [2]—a *coup* the
motives of which must be explained, if they can be
explained at all, by considering the significance of the
events which this chapter has detailed.

The reader who is struck by the contrast between the Signifi-cance of
results which Caesar had achieved in Gaul and the scenes the fore-
that were simultaneously disgracing Rome may be going
inclined to endorse the remark of Mommsen,[3] that it narrative.
would be hopeless to attempt ' to write the history of
this political witches' revel '. But history can by no
means dispense with narrative. The revellers, no less
than the great proconsul, were instruments of the power
that was determining the destinies of the Roman world.
The historian is not excused from recording the course of
events fraught with momentous issues because they
consist of or are bound up with ' miserable quarrels ' and
appear to him ' disgusting ' and ' barren of all instruction ' : [4] the essay that professes to interpret, often by
conjecture that will not bear investigation, the phenomena which it disdains to describe, cannot be profitably
studied except by those who have traced the sequence
and reflected upon the connexion of the facts. From the

[1] *Q. fr.*, ii, 4, 1 ; 6, 5–6.   [2] *Fam.*, i, 9, 8
[3] *Röm. Gesch.*, iii⁸, 1889, p. 308 (Eng. tr., v, 1908, p. 111).
[4] Long, *op. cit.*, pp. 71, 103.

story of the two years that followed the exile of Cicero and the departure of Caesar certain broad conclusions emerge. Pompey, the most illustrious member of the coalition, whose function it was to superintend affairs in the capital, failed to maintain tolerable order.[1] It is true that the uproar, the murders, and the incendiarism in the Forum and its neighbourhood affected only a small part of the life even of Rome itself : in outlying streets and slums business went on as usual ; artisans and slaves, except when they left their work to listen to the harangues of politicians, toiled unmolested ; while over the length and breadth of the peninsula people took little heed of what was happening in Rome. But Caesar must have gathered from the reports that reached him that the heart of the empire was like to fail. While he remained in Rome the coalition had been omnipotent : when he had gone his influence could not even secure the election of those candidates whom he preferred. The coalition itself was virtually dissolved. Pompey and Crassus were mutually hostile : Pompey himself, though he could hardly have intended to break with Caesar, was looking for a power which would make him independent, but which the Senate, unable to discern that he might be made the bulwark of their authority and the mainstay of the tottering Republic, were determined that he should not have.

March 13.
Cicero
purposes
to attack
Caesar's
agrarian
laws.
Apr. 21.

On the 5th of April Cicero appeared in the House and moved that the question of the Campanian land, which had been raised in December by the tribune Lupus, should be referred to a full meeting of the Senate on the 15th of the following month. The proposal made a deep impression.[2] Those senators who were not in Cicero's confidence must have been astounded at his audacity. He was evidently elated by forensic triumphs, and doubtless he was aware that Pompey had become estranged from Caesar ;[3] but were not Pompey's interests

---

[1] Meyer (*op. cit.*, p. 114) contrasts the feebleness of the Senate in dealing with Clodius with the vigorous action which it had taken against the Gracchi and Saturninus.   [2] *Fam.*, i, 9, 8.   [3] See p. 299.

as well as those of Caesar bound up with the maintenance 56 B. C. of Caesar's law ? It has been suggested, indeed, that the agrarian law which provided for Pompey's veterans had nothing to do with the Campanian land, but was that which authorized the purchase of allotments from private owners ; [1] but it is difficult to accept this theory in view of the facts that Marcellinus had lately refused to discuss the Campanian question in the absence of Pompey,[2] and that seven years later Pompeian veterans were actually settled in Campania.[3] Had Cicero forgotten the pledge which his brother had given on his behalf, and in consideration of which Caesar had consented to Pompey's procuring his recall ? ' To assault the citadel of Caesar's power ' was a forlorn hope, which no politician in his senses would have attempted unless he could reckon upon the support of Caesar's confederate and rival. Cicero may perhaps have had reasons, of which we are ignorant, for such confidence ; and, idealist as he was, he may still have hoped that even then, at the eleventh hour, Pompey might unite with him to form a party for the defence of the constitution against the dreaded schemes of Caesar. At all events he believed that Pompey was not offended by his motion.[4] After an animated debate, which, as he told his brother, was ' almost as uproarious as a public meeting ',[5] the motion was adopted.[6] Two days later Cicero, on the eve of Apr. 7 leaving Rome for a tour in Latium, went after dinner to (March visit Pompey, who told him that he intended to start on 15). the 11th for Sardinia, embarking at Leghorn or Pisa, to look after the supply of corn. He showed not the slightest sign of displeasure, and indeed genially promised to allow Quintus to rejoin his family immediately.[7] Did it occur to Cicero that if Sardinia was Pompey's immediate destination, Leghorn and Pisa were far out of his way, whereas both were close to Caesar's province ?

[1] See vol. i, p. 478.   [2] See p. 65, *supra*.
[3] *B. C.*, i, 14, 4.
[4] *Fam.*, i, 9, 9.   [5] *Q. fr.*, ii, 5, 1.   [6] *Fam.*, i, 9, 8.
[7] *Q. fr.*, ii, 5, 3 ; *Fam.*, i, 9, 9.

Meanwhile Crassus was posting to Ravenna, where he met Caesar and informed him of what Cicero had done.[1] Caesar had to secure time for completing his work in Gaul : the rebellion of the Veneti required his immediate presence ; he knew that Domitius, who was canvassing for the consulship, was determined to bring about his recall ; and he instantly made up his mind that the coalition must be at once reconstructed and that Cicero must again be reduced to submission. From Ravenna he travelled to Luca, the southernmost town in his Cisalpine province. Pompey, if he had really intended to sail for Sardinia, was doubtless met by a messenger About from Caesar and requested to confer with him : anyhow
he too went to Luca, full of the indignation which he had concealed from Cicero. The little town was presently thronged by place-hunters and persons of every class who had anything to gain from Caesar. More than two hundred senators were counted, besides proconsuls, pro-praetors, and one hundred and twenty lictors. The
Caesar
thereupon
meets
Pompey
and
Crassus at
Luca and
reconstructs the
coalition. triumvirs met in secret, and Caesar, now master of eight legions, made a tempting offer. It was agreed that he should exert his influence to secure the consulship for Pompey and Crassus for the ensuing year, and that Pompey should have the provinces of Nearer and Further Spain and Crassus Syria, for five years : in return Pompey and Crassus undertook to procure the enactment of a bill by which Caesar's governorship should be pro-longed for a second quinquennial period, and to arrange that a grant for the payment of the legions which he had raised should be made to him from the treasury.[3] More-over, as we shall afterwards see,[4] there is reason to believe that Caesar stipulated that the question of appointing
his successor should not be raised before the 1st of March, 704 (50 B. C.) and that he should be enabled to pass direct from his province to a second consul-

[1] Fam., i, 9, 9.
[2] See pp. 292–5.
[3] Fam., i, 9, 9 ; Plut., Cras., 14, 4–5 ; Pomp., 51, 2–3 ; Caes., 21, 2–3 ; Suet., 24, 1 ; App., ii, 17, 62–3.
[4] See pp. 301–2.

ship.   Pompey undertook to bring Cicero to a docile 56 B.C.
frame of mind.

Thus the coalition was not merely reconstructed, but
made far stronger than before.   Pompey proceeded to About
Sardinia, to remind Quintus Cicero of his pledge : Caesar Apr. 20 [1]
(March
returned to Gaul to suppress the rebellion of the 28).
Veneti.

[1] See p. 295.

CHAPTER X

CAMPAIGNS AGAINST THE MARITIME TRIBES OF GAUL AND
THE AQUITANI.—RESULTS OF THE CONFERENCE AT
LUCA.—MASSACRE OF THE USIPETES AND TENCTERI.—
CAESAR'S INVASIONS OF BRITAIN.—THE DISASTER AT
ATUATUCA AND ITS RESULTS

56 b. c.

[The
territory
of the
Treveri.]

[The
Lexovii,
Venelli,
and
Corioso-
lites.]

Prepara-
tions of
the
Veneti.

CAESAR'S first care, when he returned to Gaul, was to take measures for restricting the rebellion. Labienus was sent to the neighbourhood of Trèves, to watch the movements of the Belgae and to prevent the Germans, whose aid they were said to have solicited, from crossing the Rhine. Sabinus was directed to disperse the allies of the Veneti in the Calvados, the Cotentin, and the Côtes-du-Nord ; while Crassus marched for Aquitania. It is unlikely that the Aquitanians intended to take up arms on behalf of their alien neighbours ; but Caesar may not have been aware of the want of sympathy between the two peoples, and, with or without provocation, he determined to compel the tribes which in the Sertorian War had defeated two Roman generals [1] to acknowledge the supremacy of Rome. Meanwhile the Veneti and their allies, who saw that they had irretrievably committed themselves, repaired and provisioned their fortresses, assembled their ships in the Venetian ports, and even sent across the Channel to ask for help. But more significant of the alarm which Caesar's designs had aroused was that they succeeded in securing the alliance of the Morini and the Menapii,—two Belgic tribes whose territory was four hundred miles from their own, but who commanded the north-eastern coast, from which he would have to embark for Britain. The Veneti counted much upon the peculiar features of their country. The coast of the Morbihan was pierced by long estuaries and broken

[1] See vol. i, pp. 140, 380.

by numerous inlets, which would greatly hinder the progress of an invading army. Little corn was grown in those parts ; and the granaries had been emptied to supply the forts. Want of food therefore must soon force the Romans to retreat ; and if the worst came to the worst, those born sailors knew that they could take to the stout ships which had weathered so many storms, while the frail Roman vessels would run aground among the shoals or founder in the tempestuous seas that buffeted the rock-bound shore.

The Roman fleet, which included ships impressed from the tribes between the Loire and the Garonne, was soon assembled, under Decimus Brutus, in the estuary of the Loire ; but the weather was too stormy for it to put to sea. Meanwhile Caesar crossed the Vilaine and entered the Morbihan, hoping by the time the gales moderated, to get possession of the enemy's strongholds. This, however, as he soon found, was a work of extreme difficulty. The forts were situated at the ends of promontories, connected with the mainland by shoals, which, at high tide, were completely submerged. Caesar constructed dykes across the shoals, along which the troops advanced ; but before they could deliver the assault the garrison took to their ships, and sailed away to the nearest fort. The greater part of the summer was frittered away in these tedious sieges ; and Caesar was obliged to confess that all his labour had been expended in vain. Accordingly he resolved to wait for his fleet, and encamped on the heights of St. Gildas, south-east of Quiberon Bay. Hard by, in the river Auray, which discharges itself into the bay, the Venetian armada was assembled.[1]

At length the wind moderated ; and one morning the long-looked-for fleet was descried in the offing. Forthwith, gliding out from the mouth of the Auray, appeared the hostile squadrons, numbering two hundred and twenty sail. They stood out of the water like floating castles. Clustering on the cliffs, the legionaries had a good view of the two fleets as they approached one another. Brutus

The Roman fleet weatherbound in the Loire.

Caesar's fruitless campaign against the Veneti.

Sea-fight between the Veneti and D. Brutus.

[1] *Caesar's Conquest of Gaul*², 1911, pp. 679–85.

and his officers were aware that the rams of their light galleys would fail to make any impression on those huge hulls ; and though the deck-turrets were run up, even then the Romans were overtopped by the lofty poops, and could not throw their javelins with effect. But the Veneti had neglected to provide themselves with missiles,[1] and the Roman engineers had prepared an ingenious device. Two or more galleys rowed up close to one of the enemy's ships. Then, with sharp hooks fixed to the ends of long poles, the Romans caught hold of the halyards, and pulled them taut : the rowers plied their oars with might and main ; and the sudden strain snapped the ropes. Down fell the yards : the troops clambered on to the helpless hulk ; and the struggle was soon ended by the short sword. When several ships had been thus captured, the rest prepared to escape. But they had hardly been put before the wind when there was a dead calm ; and as they had no oars, they could not stir. The galleys ran in and out among them, and captured them one after another. When the evening breeze sprang up, a few slipped away in the dusk and made for the shore ; but all the rest were taken.

Punishment of the Veneti.

This battle decided the war. All the chiefs and all the warriors of western Brittany had taken part in it ; and the surviving population, deprived of their ships, had no means of defending their forts. There was nothing for them therefore but unconditional surrender. Caesar determined to teach the Gauls that 'the rights of envoys' must be respected in future. As the Venetian council were responsible for the act of violence that had led to the war, every man of them was put to death ; and all the tribesmen who failed to escape were sold into slavery.

[The Lexovii and the Aulerci Eburovices.]

About the same time dispatches arrived from Sabinus, who had encountered the northern allies of the Veneti in the peninsula of the Cotentin. The tribes of the Calvados and the Eure, in their feverish eagerness for war, had massacred their senators, simply because they counselled peace ; and desperadoes from every part of Gaul flocked

[1] Dio, xxxix, 43, 1.

to join the host. Sabinus encamped on a hill, and devised
a plan for seducing them to attack him at a disadvantage.
He bribed a native belonging to his auxiliary corps to go
over to the enemy in the guise of a deserter, and tell them
that Caesar was in great straits, and that he himself was
on the point of going to his assistance. The man had
a ready wit and a glib tongue, and played his part well.
The Gauls eagerly swallowed the tale, and clamoured to
to be led to the attack. Their commissariat had, as
usual, been neglected ; they were impatient to finish the
war at a blow ; and their leaders were obliged to let
them have their way. They ran up the hill at the top
of their speed, carrying armfuls of brushwood to fill up
the trench and hoping to fall upon the Romans before
they had time to man the ramparts ; but the disciplined
cohorts, sallying from the right and the left gate, fell
upon the flanks of the panting multitude, and sent them
flying. The cavalry allowed few to escape. No second
blow was needed. The league fell to pieces at once. As
inconstant as they had been impetuous, the tribes abandoned the struggle, and laid down their arms.

Meanwhile Crassus was carrying all before him in
Aquitania. Caesar had only been able to spare him
twelve cohorts, or about five thousand men ; but he had
a powerful body of cavalry, which he strengthened by
fresh levies ; and he also raised auxiliaries and summoned
Roman veterans who had settled in provincial towns to
join him. Crossing the Garonne, he defeated the Sotiates
near the source of the Ciron, and captured their stronghold, the site of which is now occupied by the town of
Sos. Thence he penetrated into the basin of the Adour.
The Aquitanians, in great alarm, obtained reinforcements
from their kinsmen, the Iberians of the Pyrenees. The
leaders, who had learned the art of war under Sertorius,
selected a strong position for their camp, and fortified it
in the orthodox fashion, neglecting, however, to secure
the hinder gate. Relying on their numbers, they hoped
to gain a bloodless victory by cutting off the invader's
supplies, and harassing his rear as soon as he should be

56 B. C. obliged to retreat. Crassus could not spare a man to look after his supplies, but, knowing that his troops were emboldened by the enemy's inaction, he offered battle, and when they declined the challenge did not hesitate to assault their camp. They resisted stoutly and threw their javelins from the rampart with great effect ; but some fresh cohorts managed to get round by a circuitous way, break down the feeble defences in the rear, and steal in unobserved while the battle was raging at the opposite end. The Aquitanians and Spaniards rushed pell-mell out of the entrenchment, and made a desperate effort to escape ; but the country was one vast open plain, and they were ridden down and slaughtered in thousands. Forthwith all except the remoter tribes tendered their submission, and voluntarily sent hostages.

Fruitless campaign of Caesar against the Morini. The conquest of the maritime peoples was all but complete. The Morini and the Menapii—those Belgic tribes who had formed an alliance with the Veneti—alone refused to submit. Their country, which extended from the neighbourhood of Étaples to the lower Rhine, comprised the northern parts of the Pas-de-Calais and the Nord, Flanders, Zeeland, and North Brabant. Caesar had over four hundred miles to march, and the summer was nearly at an end ; but he felt confident that he would be able to subdue the recalcitrant tribes in one brief campaign. He traversed Brittany and Normandy, joining Sabinus on the way ; crossed the Seine and the Somme ; and then pushed northward through Artois. Taught by the experience of their impetuous countrymen to avoid a battle, the Morini sought refuge, on the approach of the legions, in their vast forests. While the Romans were fortifying their camp, the enemy, who had not yet been seen, suddenly dashed out of the woods and attacked them ; and although they were driven back with heavy loss, a few of their pursuers, who advanced too far, were cut off and killed. This mishap made the legionaries more careful. They spent some days in cutting down the trees, piling them up on both flanks, as they advanced, to guard against surprise. The enemy's cattle

and part of their baggage fell into their hands. But now 56 B. C.
the wind blew and the rain fell with such violence that
the work of felling the trees had to be stopped : the
troops could no longer live safely in tents ; and it was
necessary to abandon the campaign. The cultivated
lands of the Morini were harried and their hamlets burned ;
and the legions returned to winter in the newly conquered
districts between the Seine and the Loire.

By this time Caesar must have been informed that the Cicero's
conference at Luca was producing satisfactory results. recantation.
From Luca Pompey travelled to Sardinia, and had an
interview with Quintus Cicero :—' You ', he exclaimed,
' are the very man I want to see . . . you went bail for
your brother Marcus ; [1] unless you speak strongly to
him, you'll have to pay up.' He complained seriously of
the step which Marcus had taken in reopening the question
of the Campanian land ; dilated on the service which he
had rendered him in the previous year ; reminded Quintus
that his brother was indebted for his recall from exile to
the consent of Caesar ; and urged him to dissuade his
brother from attacking Caesar's policy if he could not
actively support it.[2]   Quintus of course reported the
interview to Marcus, and Pompey sent Vibullius Rufus,
who had served on his staff in Asia, to request him not
to commit himself about the Campanian land until he
himself returned to Italy. Cicero must have seen that
to persist would involve his ruin. He remembered with
indignation that leading Conservatives, with whom he
had hoped to act, had, as he expressed it, petted his
enemy Clodius. Unlike Cato, he was no martyr, and had
the wit to see that martyrdom would not prolong the
life of the Republic. He persuaded, or tried to persuade,
himself that he would be justified in supporting Pompey,
who was an enemy of his enemy, and therefore also
Caesar, who, if the acts of his consulship had been irregular, had atoned for them by his services in Gaul. Above
all, he could not refuse to abide by his brother's pledge.[3]

[1] See p. 60.   [2] Cic., Fam., i, 9, 9.
[3] Ib., §§ 10-12.

56 B. C.   Accordingly he wrote a letter to Pompey,[1] which unhappily has not been preserved, to make his amends.
Apr. 21.   The 15th of May came ; but the promised debate on the
Campanian land did not take place : 'In this matter',
he wrote to Quintus, 'I am in a fix. But I have said
more than I intended : we'll talk about it when we
meet.'[2]   Even in his agitation, however, he was thinking
of the glory of his consulship. 'I am burning', he wrote
to Lucceius, who was a historian as well as a politician,
'to have my name mentioned conspicuously in your
writings . . . without disguise I do earnestly beg you to
praise my administration more warmly perhaps than you
really think of it, so far disregarding the canons of history.
. . . I am all agog that in my life-time men should know
me from your books and I have the full enjoyment of
my little renown.'[3]   Meanwhile Atticus had heard of the
letter which he had written to Pompey, and was rather
sore because he had not let him see it before it was
dispatched. 'What!' Cicero replied, 'Do you really
think that I would rather have what I write read and
approved by any one than by you ?   Why, then, did
I send it first to any one else ?   Because I was pressed
by the man to whom I sent it, and had no copy. And—
well !   I am nibbling at the pill, but I must after all
swallow it—my recantation did seem to me rather ignominious ! . . . The treachery of the leading Conservatives
is incredible . . . and yet I did intend to stick by them
in politics. . . . At last I have hearkened to you, and my
eyes have been opened. You will say that your advice
only extended to action, not to writing. The truth is
that I wanted to bind myself to this new coalition that
I might have no excuse for slipping back to those who,
even when I deserve their sympathy, are still jealous of
me. . . . Since those who have no power will not care for
me, let me take care to win the regard of those who have.
You will say, " I wish you had done so before ". I know
you wished it, and that I have been a downright ass.'[4]

[1] See pp. 292-7.   [2] Q. fr., ii, 6, 2.
[3] Fam., v, 12, 1. 3. 9. Cf. Att., iv, 6, 4.   [4] Att., iv, 5.

But, notwithstanding his excuses, and although he was meditating a speech in which he intended to proclaim his adhesion to the triumvirs, he was not quite happy in his new connexion. A little later he wrote to Atticus again : ' What could be more degrading than the life we are leading, especially mine ? . . . Am I to be a ranker after declining to be a general ? [1] . . . in my present retirement I am thinking how to express my rejection of the old policy, and when we are together you will keep me up to the mark.' ' It is not ', he added, referring to a friend who had lately died, ' he who is to be pitied, but we who are fast bound in misery and iron.' [2]

The conference of Luca was still a secret ; but the influence of the reunited trio was already felt. About this time, perhaps while Cicero was preparing his contemplated speech, the Senate, at his instance, decreed that the thanksgiving service which I have already mentioned should be held in honour of Caesar's victories, and that the grant which he required for his troops should be allowed.[3] ' This state of affairs ', he wrote to Lentulus, without mentioning his own part in it, ' gives me no pleasure.' [4] Early in June [5] the Senate met again to consider what provinces should be assigned to the consuls who would hold office in the ensuing year. One proposal was that Caesar's two provinces should be given to them ; another that one of his provinces should be reserved for one consul and Syria or Macedonia for the other.[6] Cicero, who desired to gratify Caesar, but was not afraid to press for the recall of Caesar's father-in-law, Piso, and of Gabinius, Pompey's creature, urged that the provinces should be Macedonia and Syria, which they respectively held. Inveighing against the misgovernment of his enemies and eulogizing the services which Caesar had rendered to his country by vanquishing the Helvetii and by freeing Italy from the peril of barbarian invasion, he declared that thenceforward the Alps would be no longer

The Senate honours Caesar and grants pay for his troops.

Cicero's speech on the consular provinces.

---

[1] See vol. i, p. 328.   [2] *Att.*, iv, 6, 1–2.
[3] *Fam.*, i, 7, 10 ; *De prov. cons.*, 11, 28 ; *Pro Balbo*, 27, 61.
[4] *Fam.*, i, 7, 10.   [5] See pp. 295–9.   [6] *De prov. cons.*, 7, 17; 15, 36.

56 B. C.

needed as a rampart, and pleaded that Caesar should be left unhindered to complete his work.[1] For the present neither Gabinius nor Piso was superseded ; but the plea on behalf of Caesar was successful : ' no difficulty ', wrote Cicero to Lentulus, ' has been made in deferring the appointment, required by the Sempronian law, of his successor '.[2] Thus the way was prepared for the bill which Pompey and Crassus had secretly pledged themselves to pass ; and Clodius, admonished perhaps by Caesar, for the time left Rome in peace.

.Pompey and Crassus intrigue to postpone the consular elections,

But Pompey and Crassus were aware that their candidature would be opposed, and, partly perhaps because they desired to await the arrival of the soldiers whom Caesar had promised to send to their assistance, they intrigued to prevent the elections from being held before the new year. For this purpose they approached the tribune Gaius Cato, who during the past three years had been a bitter enemy of Pompey, but now consented, in return, as we may suppose, for a substantial bribe, to stop the elections by his veto. It was generally suspected that Pompey and Crassus had gone to Luca for some purpose that boded ill to the Republic, and when Cato exercised his power the senators, despite his protests, assumed mourning to show that they deemed his interference a national calamity.[3] Towards the end of the year Marcellinus asked Pompey and Crassus in the popular assembly whether it was true that they desired to be consuls. Pompey replied that perhaps he might stand, perhaps not ; but, being pressed, he admitted that he intended to be a candidate, because there were disloyal citizens about. Crassus merely answered that he would act in the interest of the State.[4] The year passed away

---

[1] De prov. cons., 3–6, §§ 5–14 ; 13–4, §§ 32–5.   [2] Fam., i, 7, 10.

[3] Livy, Epit., 105 ; Plut., Cras., 15, 1 ; Dio, xxxix, 27, 3 ; 28.

[4] Plut., Cras., 15, 2 ; Pomp., 51, 4 ; Dio, xxxix, 30. Plutarch variously says that Marcellinus interrogated Pompey in the Senate and before the people, agreeing in the latter case with Dio. Perhaps the question was asked in both places. The answer which Plutarch attributes to Pompey differs from that given by Dio, which I have reproduced, but is not absolutely inconsistent with it.

without any elections ; and accordingly on the 1st of January, 699, an interrex was appointed.[1] The consular election was to be held that month.[2] Except Pompey and Crassus, no candidate at first came forward, for the Conservatives were apparently cowed ; but Marcus Cato urged Domitius to stand, warning him that Pompey and Crassus were scheming to establish tyranny. Publius Crassus was in Rome with soldiers whom he had brought from Gaul, and who, whether they had votes or not,[3] might overawe the opponents of his father and of Pompey. Before dawn on the day of the election Domitius and Cato, preceded by a linkman, came down with their friends to the Field of Mars, but were instantly attacked. The linkman was killed ; Cato and others were wounded. Domitius, disregarding the remonstrances of Cato, who urged him to remain and fight, fled to his house ; and the confederates were of course elected.[4] Cicero, without noticing the violence by which the election had been won, spoke of the political situation to Lentulus in a tone of resignation : ' Affairs are unmistakably in the power of our friends, so much so that it seems unlikely that this generation will see a change . . . you cannot fail to see how hard it is to discard one's political convictions, especially when they are right and fully justified. However, I conform myself to the wishes of him from whom I cannot dissent with dignity ; and this not, as perhaps some may think, from insincerity, for principle and, I assure you, affection for Pompey have such weight with me that everything which promotes his interest and which he wishes appears to me both right and reasonable.' Then, remarking that he intended thenceforth to devote

Margin notes: Nov. 28, 56 B. C. / and secure their own election by violence. / Cicero comments on the political situation.

---

[1] Dio, xxxix, 31, 1.

[2] Or perhaps early in February. The consuls were in office before the 11th of that month (Cic., *Q. fr.*, ii, 7, 3).

[3] See p. 320, n. 4. P. Crassus was in Rome before Feb. 11 (*Q. fr.*, ii, 7, 2).

[4] Vell., ii, 46, 1 ; Plut., *Cras.*, 15, 4-7 ; *Pomp.*, 52, 1-2 ; *Cato min.*, 41, 2-3 ; Dio, xxxix, 31. Cf. Cic., *Att.*, iv, 8 B, 2. Long (*Decline of the Roman Republic*, iv, 1872, p. 175) finds it ' very difficult to believe ' the statement of Dio that P. Crassus brought soldiers to Rome to influence the election. Why ? He was about to take Gallic troopers to serve under his father in the East.

55 B. C.

himself to literature, he explained that without loss of self-respect it was no longer possible to take part in senatorial debates :—' we have either to assent to a small clique, with the sacrifice of all dignity, or to dissent in vain. . . . The whole status of the Senate, the law courts, indeed the entire constitution, has completely changed. All we can hope for is tranquillity '. This state of affairs he attributed to the obstinacy of the extreme Con-servatives—men like Lucullus and Marcus Cato—who had alienated the knights and Pompey from the Senate.[1]

How Pompey and Crassus obtained magistra-cies for their friends.

Following up their victory, the consuls determined to secure for their supporters as many of the other magis-tracies as they could. With this aim they suddenly summoned the Senate without giving notice to many of the members ; and Afranius, Pompey's tool, moved a resolution, the nature of which is not certain, with regard to bribery. The resolution was carried, but, to the loudly expressed indignation of the House, the consuls refused to consider a rider, proposed by certain senators who had assented to it, that the new praetors should remain private citizens for sixty days after their election. ' That day ', wrote Cicero, when he reported the incident to his brother, ' they simply threw Cato overboard. In short, their power is unlimited, and they mean all the world to know it.' [2] What Cicero meant is unmistakable. Pompey and Crassus intended to prevent the praetors whose election

---

[1] *Fam.*, i, 8, 1–4.

[2] *Q. fr.*, ii, 7, 3, with which cf. Plut., *Cato min.*, 42, 2. Tyrrell (*The Corre-spondence of Cicero*, ii, 81–2) remarks that the *sententia* of Afranius (which Cicero did not explain because his brother already knew what it was) ' seems to have been a motion actually exempting the newly elected praetors from the penalties of bribery ' : accordingly he holds that Plutarch reversed the order of events and that the motion was made after Cato had been defeated at the poll. He seems to have forgotten that the senators who proposed the rider had already assented to the motion. Besides, Cicero's words (consules non sunt persecuti eorum sententias qui, Afranio cum essent adsensi, addiderunt ut) *praetores ita crearentur* (ut dies LX privati essent) surely prove that the election had not yet been held. [I find that in the 2nd edition (p. 91), in which Tyrrell had the benefit of Purser's collaboration, his note is corrected. Meyer (*op. cit.*, p. 155, n. 1) holds that Afranius's motion was for strengthening the law against bribery, which, he says, citing Dio, xxxix, 37, 1, Pompey certainly did.]

they desired to secure from being prosecuted for bribery 55 B. C. and unseated. They distributed bribes themselves and stood by while the voting was in progress ; but, not-withstanding all their efforts, it became evident that Cato was likely to be returned. Thereupon Pompey announced that he had heard thunder,[1] and the voting was sum-marily stopped. On a later day Vatinius was elected by means of bribery and violence ; but Cato was escorted to his house by a crowd of sympathizers greater than that which attended the successful candidates. At the election of the curule aediles several persons were killed, and Pompey, who was present, was splashed with blood ; but the official candidates were returned, and of the new tribunes all but two were on the side of Pompey.[2]

It remained to give effect to the secret agreement about the consular provinces, which the Senate, probably cajoled or overawed by the two consuls, had not determined according to the Sempronian law. One of the tribunes, The Tre-Gaius Trebonius, proposed to the popular assembly that bonian the provinces should be Syria, Nearer and Further Spain, law. that their tenure should be for five years, and that the proconsuls should have the right of making war or peace at their discretion. Favonius and Marcus Cato spoke against the bill. Cato persisted in speaking after the two hours allotted to him had elapsed, and was therefore removed by an attendant from the platform. As he would not stop even then, he was expelled from the Forum altogether, but presently returning, ascended the platform again, and called upon the citizens to support him. Trebonius, losing patience, ordered him to be con-veyed to prison, whither he was followed by a crowd, whom he continued to harangue ; and Trebonius, thinking it unwise to allow him the honour of martyrdom, ordered his release. During the next few days there were further riots, in the course of which Cato, Favonius, and the two anti-Pompeian tribunes, Aquillius Gallus and Ateius,

---

[1] See p. 60, n. 5 and vol. i, p. 330.
[2] Livy, *Epit.*, 105 ; Plut., *Pomp.*, 52, 3 ; 53, 3 ; *Cato min.*, 42, 3-4 ; Dio, xxxix, 32. Cf. Val. Max., vii, 5, 6.

55 B. C. endeavoured to obstruct the bill ; several lives were lost, Gallus, despite the sanctity of his office, was wounded, and Crassus, forgetting consular decorum, struck a hostile senator in the face : but the bill was ultimately passed.[1]

Pompey and Crassus prolong Caesar's government for five years. Having secured what they wanted for themselves, Pompey and Crassus carried a bill, which even Cato was too prudent to oppose, though he warned Pompey that the results would be calamitous, prolonging Caesar's tenure for five years and containing the stipulated clause which forbade the appointment of his successor to be discussed

50 B. C. before the 1st of March, 704.[2] Thus in the consulship of Pompey, as in the consulship of Caesar and in the cases of the Gabinian and the Manilian law, not the Senate but the popular assembly was the instrument of legislation.

When Cicero exhorted the Senate to leave Caesar free to complete his work, he did not foresee how long a time it would require. Since he spoke, indeed, the maritime tribes and the Aquitanians had been, for the most part, subdued ; but a fresh incursion of hungry Germans had

The Usi-petes and Tencteri invade Gaul. already begun. Though the defeat of Ariovistus had alarmed the Teutonic races, it had not stilled the inward throes by which they had so long been convulsed. Dis-possessed by the powerful Suebi, the lesser tribes of the Usipetes and Tencteri crossed the lower Rhine near Emmerich, despite the opposition of the Menapii, and for the rest of the winter lived at free quarters in their land.

The news reached Caesar in Cisalpine Gaul, while he was discharging the civil duties of his government. He knew the character of the Gauls—the frivolity and the craving for excitement that impelled them to rush blindly into new connexions without counting the cost. Belgians had courted German aid a year before ; and it was not

[1] Livy, *Epit.*, 105; Vell., ii, 46, 2; Plut., *Cras.*, 15, 7; *Niciae cum Crasso comp.*, 2, 2; *Pomp.*, 52, 4; *Cato min.*, 43, 1-3; App., ii, 18, 65; Dio, xxxix, 33-6. Plutarch (*Pomp.*, 52, 4; *Cato min.*, 43, 1) and Appian incorrectly say that Africa as well as Spain was assigned to Pompey.

[2] Hirt., *B. G.*, viii, 53, 1; Vell, ii, 46, 2; Plut., *Cras.*, 15, 7; *Cato min.*, 43, 4; Suet., *Div. Iul.*, 24, 1; App., ii, 18, 65; Dio, xxxix, 36, 2. Plutarch (*Pomp.*, 52, 4) wrongly says that Caesar's government was prolonged by a law carried by Trebonius; and Long (*op. cit.*, iv, 178) repeats the mistake. See p. 301.

unlikely that some of the tribes might be impelled by
jealousy of their rivals or hostility to the Romans to
welcome the new-comers. Determined to prevent such
a coalition or to crush it in the making, Caesar returned
to Gaul earlier than usual, and proceeded to join the
legions, which had concentrated at some point near the
lower Seine, probably in the neighbourhood of Évreux.
His apprehensions were justified. Certain tribes had
entered into negotiations with the Germans, who had by
this time moved as far southward as the territories of
the Eburones, including portions of the provinces of
Limbourg and Liège, and of the Condrusi, who inhabited
Condroz, between the Meuse and the Ourthe. Caesar
summoned the Gallic chiefs, including those who had
committed themselves to a council ; and, pretending to
be ignorant of the negotiations, told them that he was
going to make war upon the common enemy, and called
upon them to furnish their regular contingents of cavalry.
As soon as they arrived, he made a selection from the
whole number and advanced towards the distant country
in which he heard that the Germans were encamped.
When he was still some days' march from their position,
their envoys met him. The Germans, they said, had no
desire to fight ; but if Caesar attacked them, they would
not flinch. All they asked was that he should assign
them lands, or at all events leave them to enjoy those
which their swords had won. Caesar replied that he
could make no terms with them while they remained in
Gaul, but that they were welcome, if they cared to recross
the Rhine, to settle in the country of the Ubii, who had
just put themselves under the protection of Rome. The
territory of this people—the only German tribe which
had definitely submitted to Caesar [1]—extended from the
neighbourhood of Coblenz to the neighbourhood of Bonn.
The envoys said that they would refer Caesar's proposal

Margin notes:
55 B. C.

Caesar returns, and summons a Gallic council.

He marches against the Usipetes and Tencteri;

and negotiates with their envoys.

---

[1] No doubt the Ubii were one of the tribes that had sent envoys to Caesar
two years before (see p. 49 and *B. G.*, ii, 35, 1). As he was on the point
of starting for Italy, he had then ordered the embassies to return in the
following spring ; but apparently the Ubii alone had obeyed.

to their principals, and come back with an answer in three days : till then they hoped that he would advance no further. This request he rejected ; for he felt sure that it was simply a pretext to gain time for the German cavalry, which had crossed the Meuse in quest of corn and plunder, to return.

Marching on steadily, he was only eleven miles from the German camp when the envoys returned. Again they begged him to halt ; and again he refused They then asked for three days' grace, to arrange terms with the Ubii. What they really wanted, as Caesar saw, was to gain more time. He meant to do the same. He promised, however, not to advance that day beyond a river, four miles distant, where he intended to water, and told them to come back again on the morrow, that he might decide on their request, and to bring with them as many of their leaders as could come. What he desired was to get those leaders into his power, so that their formidable host might be helpless in his hands. Perhaps he knew that his offer to let the Germans settle in the country of the Ubii was impracticable : perhaps indeed he had only made it in order to gain time and to put the Germans off their guard : certainly he believed that they were trying to outwit him, and he was determined to outwit them— determined, by hook or by crook, to secure the object of ridding himself and Gaul of these dangerous immi- grants, and to secure it at the least possible cost to his own army. Meanwhile, at the urgent entreaty of the envoys, he sent orders to his Gallic cavalry, who had gone on in advance, to refrain from provoking a combat.

Their cavalry, violating a truce, attack his. The envoys took their leave. The cavalry, five thousand strong, were riding quietly along, on the faith of the truce, when, without a moment's warning, a band of horsemen swept down, and scattered them right and left. As they tried to rally, the enemy leaped to the ground, and stabbed their horses in the belly. An Aquitanian noble, named Piso, did his best to save the honour of the Gallic cavalry, hazarding his life to rescue his brother, and when he was himself unhorsed, fighting against

desperate odds till he fell. His brother, who had escaped,
would not survive him, and spurred back into the press
to die. But their example was wasted The Gauls were
six to one, but they were thoroughly unnerved ; and
while many lay dead, the rest galloped away and never
drew rein till they came within sight of the Roman
column.

Caesar made up his mind. Those Germans were He re-
treacherous savages ; and he saw no reason why he solves to
should make any terms with them. Besides, this paltry them at
triumph they had stolen would make them heroes to the once :
feather-pated Gauls. To wait until they were reinforced
would be sheer madness. Next morning the German
chiefs came to his camp—to apologize, as they said, for
the unauthorized attack by their cavalry. Caesar was
delighted. He determined to end the business by a single
blow, bloodlessly—for his own men. Believing, or pro- arrests
fessing to believe, that the chiefs only wanted to cajole chiefs,
him into granting an extension of the truce, refusing to who had
hear what they had to say, he ordered them to be put ostensibly
under arrest, and then, placing his demoralized cavalry to ex-
in the rear, marched on rapidly against the Germans. plain ;
They were taking their ease among their wagons, with
their wives and children, when the legions appeared.
Confounded by the sight, not knowing what had become
of their leaders, they lost all presence of mind and, crying
aloud in their terror, ran hither and thither about the
camp. The infuriated Romans burst in. The few Ger- and vir-
mans who were quick enough to seize their weapons tually
clustered behind the wagons and tried to resist : but, lates the
distracted by piercing shrieks, they turned and saw their host.
wives and children flying before the emboldened cavalry ;
and flinging aside their arms, they rushed pell-mell to
overtake them. Many were slain in the pursuit : others
scattered over the country and escaped. At length the
panting remnant reached the confluence of the Moselle
and the Rhine.[1] Worn out and desperate, they plunged
in ; and the swift current swept them away.

[1] *Caesar's Conquest of Gaul*[2], pp. 691-706. Cf. pp. 282-3.

The conduct of Caesar was fiercely condemned by Cato and others in the Roman Senate. The refusal to listen to the explanation of the German chiefs ; their detention, contrary, as it appeared, to the law of nations ; and then the virtual extermination of an entire people—these things perhaps shocked sensitive consciences, and certainly gave a handle to political opponents. Cato actually proposed that the perfidious Governor should be given up to the Germans.[1] Caesar pursued his course unmoved, and emphasized in his narrative the comprehensiveness of the massacre :—' the host of women and children began to flee in all directions ; and Caesar sent his cavalry to hunt them down '. The object for which their blood was spilt was gained. Thoroughly cowed, the Germans thenceforward ceased to disturb the tranquillity of Gaul.

But Caesar determined to make assurance doubly sure. As the Germans were so ready to cross the Rhine, he would cross it too, and teach them that invaders might in their turn be liable to invasion. Besides, it was neces- sary to chastise the Sugambri, the northern neighbours of the Ubii, in whose country the cavalry of the Usipetes and Tencteri had just found refuge. When he sent to demand their surrender, the Sugambrian chiefs asked with what face he, who complained so loudly of the Germans' crossing the Rhine, could claim the right to dictate to the Germans in their own country. The Ubii, on the other hand, besought him to come and help them against the Suebi : his renown, they said, was such that the mere appearance of his army would be enough to secure them from attack ; and they would gladly undertake to find boats to cross the stream. But Caesar did not think it safe to trust to boats ; and he intended to make the passage in a way that would produce a greater moral effect. Broad, deep, and swift as the river was, he would throw a bridge across it, to teach the Germans what Roman science could effect. He selected for the spot a site between Coblenz and Andernach, opposite the

[1] Plut., Caes., 22, 3 ; Cato min., 51, 1 ; Suet., 24, 3.

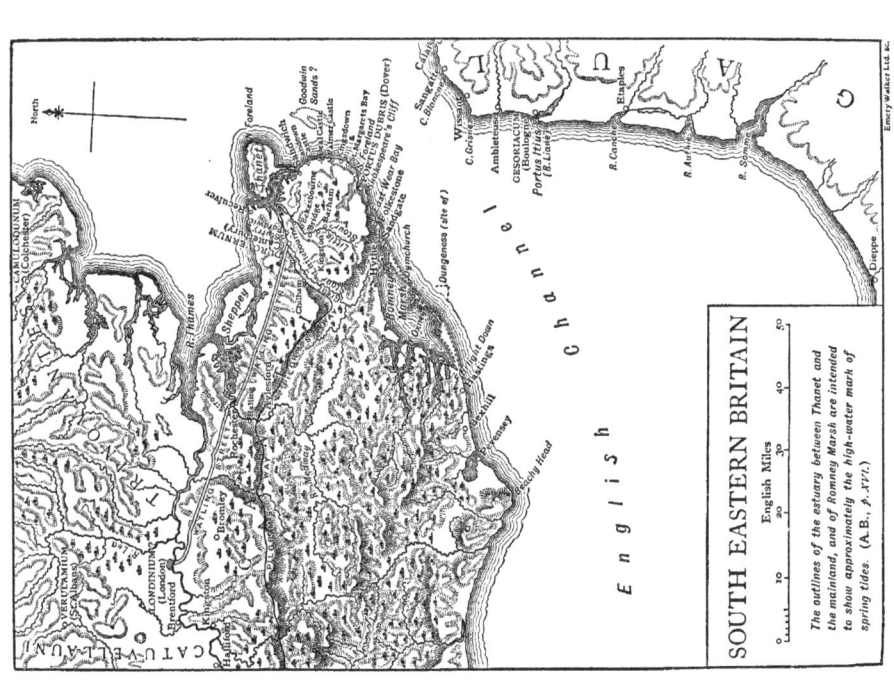

SOUTH EASTERN BRITAIN

English Miles

0   10   20   30   40   50

The outlines of the estuary between Thanet and
the mainland, and of Romney Marsh are intended
to show approximately the high-water mark of
spring tides. (A.B., p. xvi.)

Emery Walker Ltd. sc.

territory of the Ubii.[1] Within ten days from the time 55 B.C.
when the first tree was felled, the great river was spanned
by a firm bridge of piles, buttressed to withstand the
force of the flood ; and the legions were encamped on
the German bank. Leaving a strong guard at either end,
Caesar marched rapidly northward against the Sugambri.
Envoys from various tribes, who met him on the way
and solicited his friendship, were courteously received and
directed to bring hostages to his camp : but the Sugambri
had taken refuge in the outlying woods ; and, after
burning their villages and cutting their corn, he returned
to the country of the Ubii. The Suebi had sent their
wives and children into the secure recesses of the vast
forest of Central Germany, and were banded together
somewhere in the heart of their country, ready for battle.
Caesar had neither the force nor the inclination to attack
them. Having accomplished every object for which he
had entered the country—punished his enemies, reassured
his friends, and made the name of Rome respected—he
recrossed the Rhine and destroyed his bridge.

Caesar's attention was now diverted from the affairs He deter-
of Gaul. The time had come for him to make his long- mines to
planned expedition to Britain, the avowed object of which Britain.
was to obtain information about the island and its inhabitants, and to punish the southern tribes, who had helped
their kinsmen in Gaul to resist him. Marching westward
into the country of the Morini, he selected for his port
of departure the mouth of the Liane, on whose right bank
stood Gesoriacum, the village whose site is now covered
by Boulogne. Gallic merchants sailed from the port to
the harbours of Kent, and at a later period it was the
naval station of the Roman Channel Fleet. The estuary,
longer, wider, and deeper than it is now, was protected
from every gale by the bold bluff of land which on the
west throws out the promontory of Alprech, and which
then projected northward considerably beyond its present
limit.[2] Shipyards lined its banks ; roads connected it

[1] *Caesar's Conquest of Gaul*[2], pp. 706-10.
[2] *Anc. Britain*, p. 572 and n. 2.

55 B. C.   with the interior ; and timber in abundance could be
floated down the river from the forest of Boulogne.
Caesar gave orders that vessels should be collected
from the adjacent coasts, and assemble in the harbour
along with the galleys which had been docked after the
Venetian war.

He at-   The summer was now far advanced, and Caesar saw
tempts to   that his first expedition must be a mere reconnaissance ;
obtain
informa-   but, as he tells us, ' he thought that it would be well
tion from
Gallic   worth while merely to visit the island, to see what the
traders.   people were like, and to make himself acquainted with
the features of the country, the harbours, and the landing-
places '.[1] Though on a clear day he could see beyond the
straits those ' astonishing masses of cliff ' which haunted
the imagination of Cicero,[2] he was about to venture into
an unknown land. The Italians of that time knew hardly
anything of Britain, which they vaguely regarded as the
end of the inhabited world, except that it produced tin,
some of which found its way to the markets of the
Mediterranean. Caesar sent for traders from all parts
of north-eastern Gaul, and questioned them about the
island :—How large was it ? What tribes inhabited it ?
What were their methods of fighting, their manners and
customs ? What ports were capable of accommodating
a large fleet ? He failed to obtain the information which
he required : ' the traders ', he explained, ' know nothing
of Britain except the coast and the parts opposite the
various regions of Gaul '.[3] Still, they could have given
valuable information about the Kentish coast ; and the
passage in which Strabo accounts for the hostility of the
Veneti suggests that they kept silence from interested
motives. They could not foresee that Caesar's expedi·

Volusenus tions would stimulate British trade. Thrown back upon
sent to   his own resources, he sent Gaius Volusenus, who had
recon-
noitre the distinguished himself in Galba's campaign against the
opposite
coast.   mountaineers of the upper Rhône, to reconnoitre the
opposite coast.

All this time trade was going on as usual between Gaul

[1] *B. G.*, iv, 20, 2.   [2] *Att.*, iv, 16, 7.   [3] *B. G.*, iv, 20, 3.

and Britain ; and Gallic merchants had informed their
clients in Kent that the long-expected invasion was about
to take place. While Volusenus was cruising in the
Straits of Dover envoys from various British tribes arrived
at Gesoriacum. Presenting themselves in Caesar's camp,
they announced that their principals were prepared to
submit to the Roman People and to give hostages. Caesar
received them courteously, exhorted them to adhere to
their resolve, and dismissed them. But they were not
to return alone. The tribes of South-Eastern Britain were
divided into antagonistic groups, headed respectively by
the Catuvellauni, whose territory extended on the northern
bank of the Thames, west of the river Lea, and the
Trinovantes, who occupied Essex. Cassivellaunus, the
King of the Catuvellauni, was the ablest and most aggres-
sive of the British princes ; but his opponents were supported by the influence of Commius, a chieftain of the
Belgic Atrebates, who possessed portions of the depart-
ments of Pas-de-Calais and Nord and were connected with
a British tribe of the same name. Two years before
Caesar had gained over Commius, whose connexion with
Britain he had perhaps already ascertained, and, in accordance with the policy which he often followed, had
established him as king over his tribe. He had doubtless
learned much from him about British politics, and had
concluded that, just as in Gaul he had found it useful to
support the Aedui and the Remi against their rivals, so
in Britain his best course would be to side with the
Trinovantes against the Catuvellauni. Accordingly he
charged Commius to approach all the British chieftains
with whom he had any influence, engage them on the
side of Rome, and inform them that he himself would
shortly visit the island. Commius took with him a troop
of cavalry, composed of thirty of his retainers.

Meanwhile Volusenus had been carrying out Caesar's
instructions. Probably his voyage did not extend beyond
Lympne on one side and the North Foreland on the
other ; for within those limits the port and the alternative landing-place of which he was in search were to

55 B.C.
Envoys
from
British
tribes
promise
submis-
sion.

Caesar
commis-
sions
Commius
to return
with them
and gain
over
tribes.

Volu-
senus's
voyage.

55 B. C.   be found, and, moreover, he knew that Caesar intended to cross the Channel in its narrowest part. While he was still some miles from the British coast he could see the precipitous chalk cliffs, backed by a commanding range of heights, that hem in the rock-strewn shore of East Wear Bay : the inlet of Folkestone was plainly too small to shelter the Roman fleet ; and the first sight of the hills that guarded the coast from Folkestone to Hythe and of the wooded uplands that overlooked the tide-washed flat which is now Romney Marsh, must have warned him not to advise his chief to land beneath them. The hills behind Hythe were, indeed, pierced by three valleys : but it was evident that they ascended to high, broken, and wooded ground, where cavalry would be useless and an invading army would be encompassed by manifold perils. Eastward of Shakespeare's Cliff Volusenus saw that he must look for the place of disembarkation. There, sheltered in the valley between the cliffs, was old Dover harbour, in which we may suppose that Gallic merchants used to discharge their freight.[1] But even this haven would be useless if the landing were to be opposed ; and it was necessary to search for some broad expanse of open beach which would give easy access to the interior. The galley ran on under the Castle Cliff, round the Foreland, and past the coomb within which lies St Margaret's Bay, past the cliffs, still precipitous but diminishing in height, which end at Kingsdown. About a hundred yards further on the ground was seen rising again ; and the tribune observed a low rampart of cliff gradually sinking towards the north till it terminated just south of the spot where Walmer Castle rises amid embowering trees. Stretching northward for several miles from this place he saw the open beach for which he had been looking. Not a trace of high ground was visible. Once the legions had succeeded in forcing their way on to dry land, they would find no difficulty in following up their advantage ; and the cavalry would be able to ride down the beaten enemy. The slope upon

[1] Anc. Britain, pp. 530-1.

which Walmer Church now stands would afford a suitable 55 B. C.
site for the camp. But it was impossible to see far
inland ; and as Volusenus could not venture to disembark
and run the risk of being captured by the natives, he was
unable to find out all that he wished to know. But
Caesar had chosen him because he was the fittest man
whom he could find ; and we may assume that he did
not neglect precautions which any competent officer
would have taken, and that he did not overlook what
no observant man could have failed to perceive. We may
be sure that he bore in mind that the beach was of
shingle ; that he took soundings all along the coast
between Walmer and Deal as close inshore as he could
venture ; and that he noted the phenomena which twice
daily obtruded themselves upon his attention,—the rise
and fall of the tide and the movement up and down the
Channel of the tidal stream. One other feature, if it
then existed, cannot have escaped his scrutiny,—the
Goodwin Sands, perhaps only half formed, or the long
low bank of London Clay which, as some geologists
believe, may then have occupied their place. On the
fourth day following that of his departure he returned,
and presented his report to Caesar.

The preparations for the expedition were nearly com- Certain
plete ; but the base of operations was still insecure. The clans of the
Morini had hardly felt the weight of Caesar's hand, and Morini
might give trouble to the garrison which he intended to spontane-
leave for the protection of his communications ; but the mise to
summer was fast waning, and he had no time to reduce submit.
the tribe to submission. Fortune, however, befriended
him. The various communities of the Morini were accustomed to act independently. Envoys from some of them
appeared in Caesar's camp, and excused themselves for
having resisted the Romans in the two previous years.
He of course accepted their excuses, but ordered them
to give a large number of hostages, who were promptly
brought to the camp. Caesar's

And now all was ready. The expeditionary force con- expedi-
sisted of two legions—the 10th and the 7th—besides tionary force,

2592.2   H

Balearic slingers, Numidian and Cretan archers, and about five hundred cavalry. A small squadron of galleys and about eighty transports were assembled in the harbour ; and on the 11th of September the legionaries embarked on the transports while the galleys were assigned to the archers, slingers, and artillerymen. The transports had not been designed for disembarking troops on an enemy's coast ; and in case it should prove necessary to land on an open beach, the troops whom they carried would find themselves, on entering the water, almost out of their depth. The fleet included some small fast-sailing vessels of light draught, which were commonly used for reconnoitring, and would now be called scouts. Eighteen other transports were lying in the harbour of Ambleteuse, between five and six miles to the north, having been prevented by contrary winds from reaching the Liane ; and, as the weather was now favourable for the voyage, Caesar sent his cavalry by road with orders to embark on these vessels and follow him. As the expedition was to be of such short duration, no heavy baggage was taken, and only sufficient supplies to last for a few days. An adequate force remained to guard the camp and the harbour ; while Titurius Sabinus and a young officer, Aurunculeius Cotta, were directed to march with the remaining legions against those clans of the Morini which had not submitted and their neighbours, the Menapii.

Sabinus and Cotta sent to punish the recalcitrant Morini and the Menapii.

Caesar's voyage.

It was just five days before the full moon. Soon after midnight the order was given to sail. As the ships passed Ambleteuse there was no sign that the cavalry transports had yet got under way. At some period of the voyage the wind must have shifted to an unfavourable quarter ; for it was not until about nine o'clock in the morning that the galleys approached the Dover cliffs, and at that time the transports, which were slower sailers and had no oars, were far behind. Above the white precipices, ranged on the undulating downs behind, Caesar descried an armed force of the enemy. To attempt a landing in the harbour or below the cliffs on either side of it was

[1] *Anc. Britain*, pp. 600-3.

out of the question ; and Caesar determined to remain
at anchor until the rest of the fleet should arrive. Sum- He an-
moning his generals and tribunes to board his galley, he chors off
communicated to them the report which he had received cliffs.
from Volusenus, and instructed them how to handle
their ships and troops when the landing-place should be
reached, warning them to be prepared to obey all orders
on the instant. Between three and four in the afternoon
the infantry transports arrived ; and although Caesar
does not expressly say so, it seems reasonable to assume
that he communicated with their officers as well. Between
four and five the stream, which for about six hours had
been running down the Channel, turned towards the east,
and, as the wind was now favourable, Caesar gave the
signal to weigh anchor.[1] A few minutes later galleys, Late in
transports, and smaller craft, with all sail set, were running the after-
in an extended line past the Foreland, while the British sails on to
chariots and cavalry, followed by their infantry, were Walmer-
hurrying across country to intercept them. In about an Deal.
hour the armada was off the coast between Walmer and
Deal, heading for the shore ; and while the galleys were held
ready for emergencies, the transports were run aground.

Caesar now saw crowding upon him the troubles that The
were due to insufficient preparation. All along the beach landing
a multitude of painted warriors with long moustaches and resisted.
hair streaming over their shoulders were drawn up ready
for action. The transports were immovable in water so
deep that the men, crowding in the bows, shrank from
plunging in ; and when some of them overcame their
hesitation, they found themselves staggering and slipping,
over-weighted by their armour and encumbered by the
shields on their left arms and the javelins which they
grasped in their right hands ; while the Britons, standing
securely on the beach, and the charioteers, driving their
trained horses into the sea, harassed them with missiles
to which they could not reply. Old soldiers as they
were, they felt unnerved by difficulties which they
had never encountered before. Caesar promptly sent

[1] *Ib.*, pp. 610-1, 647-9.

H 2

the galleys to the rescue. Driven through the water at
their utmost speed, they were ranged on the right flank
of the enemy, who, alarmed by the long low rakish hulls,
the like of which they had never seen, and distracted by
the measured stroke of the oars, suddenly found themselves assailed by archers and slingers, and enfiladed by
strange artillery. Unable to use their shields unless they
changed front, they ceased to press their attack, stood
still, and presently gave ground. But few of the legionaries had yet ventured into the water ; and the rest still
hesitated to take advantage of the respite. Then the
standard-bearer of the 10th legion, invoking the gods,
turned to his comrades and cried, ' Leap down, men,
unless you wish to abandon the eagle to the enemy. I, at
all events, shall have done my duty to my country and
my general.' Springing overboard, he advanced alone,
holding the eagle above his head. The men plucked up
courage, and, calling upon one another not to bring the
10th to shame, leaped all together from the bows. Encouraged by their example, the men in the nearest vessels
followed ; and the fight became general.

But the advantage was still with the defenders. The
galleys could not be everywhere at once. The Romans,
though they could not get firm foothold, tried hard to
keep their ranks and follow their respective standard-
bearers ; but they soon lost all formation. As men entered the sea from one ship or another, they attached
themselves in bewilderment to any standard they came
across ; and the enemy on the shore, whenever they saw
a few legionaries dropping one by one into the water,
drove their horses in and surrounded and attacked them
before they could join their comrades ; while others
planted themselves on the exposed flank of a disordered
unsupported group, and showered missiles into their
midst. Caesar now manned his scouts and the boats
belonging to the galleys, and sent them in various
directions to assist all who were overmatched. Gradually
the foremost bodies of legionaries fought their way on to
the beach : the rest followed quickly in support ; and

now, closing their ranks and drawing their swords, they charged the enemy with exultant cries and put them to the rout. Want of cavalry, however, made it impossible to complete the victory.

It would seem that the resistance which the Britons had opposed to the disembarkation was purely local, and that no defensive league had been formed. The men of East Kent were disheartened by failure, and on the next day sent envoys to sue for peace. Some days before, when Commius had just landed and was formally communicating Caesar's mandate to the chiefs, he had been arrested and imprisoned. The envoys, who brought him with them, begged Caesar to pardon this outrage, for which, they said, the ignorant rabble were responsible. He replied that their countrymen had made an unprovoked attack upon his army although they had spontaneously sent an embassy to Gaul to proffer their submission ; but he promised to accept their excuses on condition of their giving hostages. Part of the required number were handed over there and then, the envoys promising that the rest, who would have to be fetched from considerable distances, should be brought within a few days. The Britons who had fought at Walmer were ordered by their leaders to return home ; and within the next few days tribal chiefs arrived from various districts and formally surrendered.

On the morning of the 16th of September the long-looked for cavalry transports were descried ; but as they were approaching Caesar's camp, a sudden storm prevented them from keeping on their course. Some, swept down past the Foreland and the Dover cliffs, scudded before the north-easterly gale, and anchored close inshore off the southern coast ; but, as they were becoming waterlogged, they were forced towards nightfall to stand out to sea and make for the continent. The rest hauled back across the Channel ; and once they had got past Cape Gris-Nez into comparatively sheltered water, they were able to stand in for the shore and fetch the port of Ambleteuse.

But on the shores of East Kent the gale was still raging ; and the moon that shone out that night through the fleeting clouds was at the full. It was high water about an hour before midnight ; and the seas that came rushing over the shingle before the north-east wind rose as high as a spring tide. The galleys, which had been hauled up, as Caesar supposed, above high-water mark, were swept by the billows ; the transports were driven ashore. Several vessels were totally wrecked ; and the rest lost their anchors, cables, and other tackle. No provision had been made against the chance of such a disaster ; and the tools and materials that were needed for repairs were on the other side of the Channel. The whole army was seized with panic. Men asked one another how they were to subsist when they had no grain, and how they were to get back to Gaul when there were no ships to carry them.

The
British
chiefs
prepare to
renew hos-
tilities.

The British chiefs who were still in the Roman camp saw their opportunity. They knew that Caesar had no supplies ; and although they did not know exactly the strength of his force, they saw that his camp was small, and concluded that his troops were correspondingly few. Besides, his want of cavalry would place him at a disadvantage. Accordingly they determined to recall their tribesmen, to prevent the Romans from getting corn, and to harass them by irregular warfare, in the hope that they would be able to starve them out, or at any rate to prevent them from re-embarking until wintry weather should have set in. One by one they moved away from the camp without attracting observation.

Meanwhile Caesar was doing his best to retrieve the disaster ; and although the chiefs managed to keep their plans secret, he suspected that they meant michief. Moreover, the hostages who were still due did not arrive. The crops were ripe ; and troops were detailed every day to get corn. A galley was sent back to Gaul to fetch everything that was required for repairing the ships. Twelve of them were so badly damaged that it was impossible to patch them up even for one voyage ; but their timbers and bronze were utilized for the repair of

the rest. All the legionaries who had any knowledge of
carpentry or metal-working were employed as shipwrights, and worked with such goodwill that within a few
days the fleet had been made tolerably seaworthy.

All this time natives were daily passing in and out of The 7th
the camp ; and no one in the Roman army suspected that legion
attacked
trouble was brewing. At a considerable distance from while
Walmer there was a wood, close to which was a field of cutting
corn.
standing corn. Everywhere else the crops had been
already cut ; and to this spot the 7th legion was dispatched. The officer who commanded it neglected to
send out scouts ; and the troops laid aside their arms, and
went to work securely with their sickles. It would seem
that even the ordinary precaution of keeping some of the
cohorts under arms was neglected.[1] Suddenly the
enemy's chariots and cavalry emerged from the wood,
and swept down upon the unarmed and scattered reapers.
Meanwhile two cohorts were on guard, as usual, outside
the gates of the camp ; and some of their number reported
to Caesar that an unusual amount of dust was visible in
the direction in which the 7th had gone. Ordering the
two cohorts to accompany him, two others to take their
places, and the remaining cohorts to leave their work,
arm, and follow him immediately, he marched towards the
corn-field. He had advanced some little distance before
he came in sight of the legionaries. Huddled together in
a small space with ranks disordered, they were surrounded
by cavalry and charioteers, missiles flying into them from
every side. Caesar was just in time. When the enemy
saw reinforcements approaching, they suspended their
attack, and the 7th recovered from their panic. But if
the enemy had no mind to renew the combat, Caesar
did not feel able to strike an effective blow. Accordingly
he contented himself with maintaining his ground, and,
after a short interval, withdrew both legions into camp. Military
operations
During the next few days stormy weather kept both suspended
sides inactive. Caesar would not attack a mobile enemy owing to
bad
whom it was difficult to bring to battle, but preferred to weather.

[1] *Anc. Britain*, p. 321, n. 1.

wait until they should attack him on his own ground, before his impregnable camp : on the other hand the ground was so miry that their chariots could not act. Reinforcements, however, summoned by the chiefs, speedily assembled, and advanced towards the coast. If they had been commanded by a skilful leader, and had adhered to the simple plan of harassing the Romans when they were endeavouring to embark, they might have achieved something ; but they were a mere aggregate of tribal levies, and greed and impatience worked their ruin.

The Britons are defeated with heavy loss. They made a wild attack upon the camp ; and the legions, which were drawn up outside, of course scattered them. Commius's horse were of some slight service in the pursuit, while the legionaries, who exerted themselves to the utmost, killed many of the fugitives and burned all the buildings which they had time to reach.

Caesar compelled by the approach of the equinox to return. This success came just in time to enable Caesar to leave Britain with some show of credit.. His departure could not be postponed ; for the dreaded equinox was near, and, with his unsound ships, he would need a fine night for the voyage.. He must therefore have been relieved when, on the very day of their defeat, the chiefs sent envoys to sue for peace. He ordered them to find twice as many hostages as he had before demanded ; and, as he could not wait for them, the chiefs were to send them in their own or the merchants' vessels to the continent. Before he embarked, he may have himself reconnoitred the coast north of Walmer : anyhow he decided that when he returned in the following year, his best landing-place would be the sandy flats between Sandown and Sandwich, where the anchorage was better, and the seaward slope was gentler than that of the Walmer shingle. But otherwise the objects for which he had undertaken the expedition had not been attained. The troops were embarked without opposition ; but two of the transports, which perhaps were in worse condition than the rest, failed to make the mouth of the Liane and drifted a few miles further down the coast. The soldiers who had disembarked from them, numbering about three hundred, were marching north-

Two transports fail to make the harbour :

ward to join their comrades when they were intercepted
by a band of the Morini, who belonged to one of the clans the troops
which had submitted a few weeks before. As the Romans they
were considerably outnumbered, they were obliged to carried
form in a square ; and, hearing the shouts of the com-by the
batants, large numbers flocked to join in the attack. Morini.
The three hundred defended themselves with vigour ;
and four hours later, when Caesar's cavalry came to the
rescue, they were still unbeaten. The assailants speedily Punish-
dispersed ; but next day Labienus marched against them ment of
with the two legions which had just returned from Britain, Morini
and almost all were taken prisoners. Titurius and Cotta, and
with the other legions, had been punishing the Menapii. Menapii.
Finding that they had taken refuge in their forests, they
mercilessly ravaged the open country, cutting the corn
and burning the hamlets. Thus, when the legions went
into winter-quarters in the country of the Belgae, Caesar
might feel that in the ensuing summer his base of operations would be secure. 'Thither', he wrote dryly, 'two
British tribes and no more sent hostages : the rest
neglected to do so.' [1]

Caesar had learned the lessons which failure had taught Caesar
him. Before he left Belgium for Cisalpine Gaul he ordered builds a
his generals to employ the legions in repairing the old a second
ships and building a new fleet for the second expedition, expedi-
and drew up minute instructions for their guidance. The tion.
ships were to be comparatively shallow, in order to
facilitate the work of loading and to enable them to be
hauled up on shore : on the other hand, to make room
for troops and freight, they were to be rather broad in
the beam. Their low freeboard would admit of their
being constructed for rowing as well as sailing. The cost
of the expedition would be very heavy ; but Caesar hoped
to do more in Britain than recover his expenses.[2]

News of these preparations must of course have flown
swiftly across the Channel ; but the British chieftains
did not take advantage of the time that was given them
to mature a scheme of defence. Cassivellaunus was still

---

[1] *B. G.*, iv, 38, 4.   [2] *Anc. Britain*, p. 327.

55 B. C.
Mandubracius
flees from Britain
and takes refuge with Caesar.

Caesar winters in Cisalpine Gaul and Illyricum.

Cicero's correspondence with Caesar and Quintus.

intent on self-aggrandizement ; and in the struggle with the Trinovantes he slew their king, whose son, Mandubracius, contrived to escape, took ship for Gaul, and presented himself in Caesar's camp.

Caesar did not start for Italy until the beginning of the new year ; and after he had fulfilled his civil duties in Cisalpine Gaul he was obliged to travel to the further shore of the Adriatic in order to punish a tribe which had been making raids upon Illyricum. In the early spring he was again in Cisalpine Gaul, clearing off arrears of work and preparing to recross the Alps. He was of course beset with letters of recommendation written by public men on behalf of friends who hoped to acquire riches in Gaul or Britain ; and Cicero wrote one, as he alone knew how to write, begging him to do something for a young lawyer named Trebatius, who was destined to achieve distinction as a jurist. Caesar, however pressed with business he might be, received such applications, when they came from men whom he cared to conciliate, with good humour. ' Just as I was speaking ', wrote Cicero, ' to our friend Balbus . . . a letter from you was handed to me, at the end of which you say : " Rufus, whom you recommend to me, I will make King of Gaul. . . . Send me some one else to provide for ! " . . . I therefore send you Trebatius.' [1] The confiding lawyer wanted to make a fortune without having to work for it ; but Cicero banteringly told him to moderate his expectations. ' I hear ', he wrote, ' there is no gold or silver in Britain. If so, I advise you to capture a war-chariot and come back in it as soon as you can.' [2] But Caesar had gained another adherent who, though his temper was blustering [3] and he wasted time in writing worthless tragedies,[4] turned out a real soldier. Quintus Cicero had consented to serve on his staff ; and a few words from a letter in which this consent is alluded to illustrate the gracious tact which was one of Caesar's gifts. ' Caesar ', wrote Marcus Cicero to his brother, ' has written to Balbus that the little bundle of letters in which

[1] *Fam.*, vii, 5, 2.
[2] *Ib.*, 7, 1.
[3] *Q. fr.*, i, 1, 37–9 ; 2, 5–7.
[4] *Ib.*, iii, 6, 7.

mine and Balbus's were packed was so saturated with 54 b. c.
rain when it was delivered to him that he was not even
aware that there was one from me. However, he had
made out a few words of Balbus's, to which he replied as
follows : " I see you have written something about Cicero,
which I have not deciphered ; but as far as I could guess,
it was of a kind that I might wish, but hardly hope to be
true ".' [1] Marcus was not slow to respond to this friendly
overture. He suspected that political troubles were
impending, and he determined to cultivate Caesar's
friendship.[2] Stimulated by sage counsel from his brother,[3]
who hoped to make enough money in Gaul to extricate
himself from debt,[4] he indulged the fancy that Caesar's
exploits would furnish him with a theme for an heroic
poem. ' Only give me Britain ', he wrote to Quintus, ' to
paint in colours supplied by you, but with my own
brush.' [5]   But he must have soon received discourag- His
ing tidings ; for early in July he wrote to Atticus, ' The anxiety
                                                            about the
result of the British expedition is a source of anxiety. second
For it is notorious that the approaches to the island are tion.
ramparted by astonishing masses of cliff ; and besides,
it is now known that there isn't a pennyweight of silver
in the island, nor any hope of loot except from slaves ;
and I don't suppose you expect any of them to be a
scholar or a musician.' [6]   He went on to impart a piece
of news which shows that Caesar, in the midst of preparations for the invasion, was devising plans for beautify-
ing Rome. ' Caesar's friends (I mean myself and Oppius,
though it may make you furious) have thought nothing
of sixty million sesterces . . . in order to open up the [£600,000].
Forum. . . . It was impossible to settle private claims for
less. We shall make it a glorious success. In the Field of

---

[1] *Ib.*, ii, 10, 4.

[2] *Ib.*, iii, 8, 1 ; *Att.*, viii, 3, 2. Cicero's admission in this letter confirms
the impression, which I derived from his correspondence in 54 B.C., that
his sudden outburst of cordiality towards Caesar was not disinterested.
Though he was touched by the evidences of Caesar's goodwill, he seems to
have tried to lash himself into friendship. Cf. *Q. fr.*, ii, 13, 1–2 ; iii, 1, 9 ;
5–6, 4 ; *Fam.*, i, 9, 21 ; *Att.*, iv, 19, 2.

[3] *Q. fr.*, iii, 5–6, 4.   [4] *Ib.*, ii, 14, 2–3 ; iii, 8, 1.
[5] *Ib.*, ii, 13, 2.   [6] *Att.*, iv, 16, 7.

Mars we mean to erect a marble-roofed enclosure for the
Assembly of the Tribes and to surround it with a lofty
colonnade, a mile from end to end.'[1] Caesar's design,
the execution of which he had entrusted to his friends,
was to build a new basilica for the accommodation of the
courts, to enlarge the Forum, which was too small for the
crowds who transacted business there, to transfer the
Assembly of the Tribes to the projected voting-hall, and
to facilitate communication between the Forum and the
Field of Mars. Old buildings had to be demolished and
land, the most valuable in the city, to be bought ; and
the owners were in a position to dictate their terms.[2]

Caesar
returns to
Gaul.
By this time Caesar and Quintus Cicero, having posted
across Gaul at the rate of fifty miles a day or more,[3] must
have reached the country of the Belgae. Caesar had
occupied himself during the passage of the Alps in writing
a dissertation, which he dedicated to Marcus as the great
master of oratory, and in which, while he endeavoured to
determine the true forms of divers words, he deprecated
the use of new-fangled terms.[4] On arriving at the coast
he proceeded to inspect the shipyards, near which the
troops were encamped, and gave orders that the ships—
six hundred new transports and twenty-eight galleys—
should all assemble, as soon as they were ready for sea,

He is
obliged to
march to
the coun-
try of the
Treveri.
in a harbour which he called the Portus Itius.[5] Meanwhile his presence was urgently required in the country
of the Treveri. Since the battle with the Nervii, when
their cavalry had deserted him, they had refused to send
representatives to attend the councils of Gallic magnates
which he annually convened ; and he was now informed
that they were intriguing with the Germans. Accordingly
he marched against them with a strong force to re-
establish his authority. Fortunately for him the Treveri
were not unanimous. Two chiefs, Indutiomarus and

---

[1] *Att.* iv, 16, 8. Cf. Pliny, *Nat. Hist.*, xxxvi, 15 (24), 103, and Suet.,
26, 2.

[2] Ch. Huelsen, *Forum Rom.*², 1905, pp. 14–6 (Eng. tr. by J. B. Carter,
pp. 16–7) ; *Quart. Rev.*, ccix, 1908, pp. 109, 112.

[3] *Anc. Britain*, pp. 329, 727.   [4] See pp. 310–1.

[5] Whether it was at Boulogne or Wissant is still disputed. See p. 283.

Cingetorix, were struggling for supremacy. Cingetorix at once presented himself before Caesar, promised fidelity, and give full information of all that was going on. Indutiomarus collected levies, and prepared to resist ; but, finding that most of his fellow chieftains were going over to the stronger side, he endeavoured to explain away his conduct. Caesar, who had no time to spare, feigned to accept his excuses, and contented himself with taking hostages for his good behaviour. At the same time he of course did everything to strengthen the influence of Cingetorix ; and Indutiomarus smarted under the feeling that his credit with his countrymen was gone.

About the 6th of July Caesar returned to the Portus Itius. More than eight hundred vessels were assembled, including numerous small craft, built by rich officers who desired to make the voyage in comfort, by merchants who had dealings with the troops, or by adventurers who had been attracted by stories of the wealth of Britain ; but sixty of Caesar's ships had encountered contrary winds, and failed to arrive. The entire Roman army, comprising eight legions—probably about thirty-five thousand men—besides slingers, archers, and four thousand Gallic cavalry, was on the spot ; and the notables from all the tribes had also repaired thither in obedience to Caesar's summons. He knew that there was much smouldering discontent among them, and he intended to take all but the few on whose fidelity he could depend, as hostages across the Channel. Among them was the notorious Dumnorix, who was as popular with the masses and as determined an enemy of Rome as when he had been detected in his intrigues with the Helvetii. Quite recently he had caused great alarm and indignation to the Aeduan council by giving out that Caesar intended to make him king. Perhaps he had received a hint that if he proved himself loyal he would be rewarded ; [1] at all events Caesar was provoked by the indiscreet or malicious utterance. Dumnorix, who doubtless saw that he might never again have such an opportunity as Caesar's absence

54 B. C.

June 11. Returning to the Portus Itius,

he resolves to take chiefs of doubtful fidelity as hostages to Britain.

Dumnorix resolves not to go.

[1] *Caesar's Conquest of Gaul²*, p. 102, n. 1.

54 B. C. afforded of furthering his schemes, determined that to Britain he would not go. He began by imploring Caesar to allow him to remain behind, pleading that he was not accustomed to the sea and dreaded it, and insisting that he was debarred by religious obligations from leaving the continent. Finding Caesar obdurate, he approached his brother chieftains, and exhorted them to join him in refusing to go, assuring them that Caesar only wanted to get them out of Gaul in order that he might safely put them all to death. Caesar kept himself informed of his intrigues, and did his best to prevent him from rushing

The fleet weather-bound. on his doom. All this time the fleet was weather-bound ; but at length the wind shifted, and infantry and cavalry began to embark. Suddenly, while every man in the force had his thoughts concentrated on the work in hand, Caesar was informed that Dumnorix and his troopers had gone. Instantly he stopped the embarkation ; and a strong detachment of cavalry was soon riding in pursuit with orders to bring Dumnorix back, or, if he resisted, to

The fate of Dumnorix. kill him on the spot. Adjuring his retainers to be true to him, he fought desperately ; but he was surrounded and slain, passionately crying with his last breath that he was a free man and a citizen of a free state.

July 6. Caesar sails, leaving Labienus in charge of Gaul. It was about the 31st of July, probably the day after this episode, when the embarkation took place. Commius accompanied the expedition, as well as Mandubracius, the Trinovantian prince who had put himself under Caesar's protection. Caesar hoped, if all went well, to winter in Britain, and thus to find time not merely to deter the Britons from combining with the Gauls but to conquer the south-eastern part of the country.[1] Labienus therefore remained in charge of the camp and port with three legions and two thousand cavalry. Towards sunset the hawsers were cast off. By midnight the leading division of the fleet was not far off the South Foreland ; but it is probable that the steersmen had not made sufficient allowance for the eastward current, and that the shallow flat-bottomed vessels had already sagged to leeward away from their true course. And now the wind, which had been gradually

---

[1] See *Anc. Britain*, p. 334, and *B.G.*, v. 22, 4.

dying down, almost entirely dropped. Borne along by 54 B. C.
a rapid flood, the armada drifted into the North Sea ; and *The fleet drifts*
about a quarter past three, when day broke, Caesar *out of its*
descried the white cliffs of Kingsdown and the South *course.*
Foreland, receding on the port quarter. Presently the
stream ceased to run up the Channel, and, after a few
minutes' slack water, the ebb set in. The soldiers on board *The land-*
the transports got out their oars. About noon the whole *ing place reached*
fleet had reached the landing-place ; but no enemy was to *by row-*
be seen, and in the course of the day a galley was speeding *ing.*
back across the Channel with one of Caesar's couriers on
board, who carried, besides other dispatches, a letter in
which Quintus Cicero informed his brother that all was well.

While the troops and baggage were being disembarked, *Leaving*
Caesar chose a site for his camp, perhaps on the slight *the fleet at anchor*
eminence near the village of Worth. Some prisoners, who *in charge*
were brought in by the cavalry, stated that their country- *of a brigade,*
men had assembled in large numbers to oppose the landing, *Caesar*
but that, on observing the huge size of the armada, they *marches against*
had retreated to higher ground inland. Caesar determined *the Britons,*
to march against them that very night, and accordingly
took the risk of not beaching his ships, an operation which
would have consumed valuable time. He had not forgotten the disaster of the previous year ; but, as the shore
where he now left the ships at anchor was not only
perfectly open, but sloped very gently seaward, he felt
little anxiety for their safety. Moreover, the storm which
had wrought such havoc before had occurred on the night
of a full moon : the moon was now new ; and it may be
doubted whether he had studied the writings of the
Greek astronomers or consulted the pilots, from whom
he would have learned that the tides at new and at full
moon are virtually the same. Ten cohorts selected from
the various legions and three hundred cavalry were left
under the command of an officer named Quintus Atrius
to protect the fleet. Soon after midnight Caesar set out
against the enemy, who were posted on the hills over-
looking Durovernum, a village which stood upon the site
of Canterbury. He had advanced about eleven miles
when, in the early morning, he descried cavalry and

54 b. c.   charioteers descending towards the left bank of the Stour. The spot where he encountered them must have been somewhere between Sturry, on the east of Canterbury, and Thanington on the west ; and military experts who know the country will probably conclude that it was near the

forces the   latter.[1] Caesar may have sent a detachment to turn their

passage of   flank : anyhow they were driven from the banks after
the Stour

near Can-   a combat which he recorded in a single sentence. Retreat-

terbury,   ing to the higher ground, they took up their position in a stronghold situated in the midst of woods,—probably the earthwork, about a mile and a half west of Canterbury, through which runs the Pilgrim's Way.[2] The legions, pressing after them, found the entrances blocked by *abatis*, and when they attempted to force their way in, the Britons, issuing from the woods in small groups, met them with showers of missiles. The 7th legion was selected for the assault. Advancing in a dense column with shields close-locked over their heads, they shot earth or fascines into the ditch so as to form a causeway flush with the top of the rampart ; and it may be conjectured that the work was performed by men who advanced between the files under their comrades' uplifted shields.[3]

and   In this way the entrenchment, which, like all the British

storms a   forts that Caesar saw, was far weaker than those of Gaul,
fort, to

which   was speedily captured with small loss ; and the Britons

they had   were expelled from the woods. Caesar soon stopped the
retreated.

pursuit, for he was afraid to incur the risk of letting his troops get entangled in a wooded country, of the intricacies of which he was ignorant ; and, as it was late in the afternoon, he was obliged to utilize the remaining hours of daylight for the construction of his camp.

He sends   Early next morning he dispatched his cavalry in three

columns   columns, each supported by a strong body of infantry, to
in pur-

suit,   hunt down the fugitives. The pursuers had advanced a considerable distance from the camp when some troopers rode up to Caesar with a note from Atrius. A storm had

---

[1] *Anc. Britain*, pp. 682–5.

[2] *Ib.*, pp. 253, 337.

[3] A. von Göler, *Gall. Krieg*², 1880, p. 149, n. 5.

arisen on the previous night : the ships had parted from
their anchors, collided with one another, and almost all
been dashed ashore. Caesar sent gallopers to recall the but is
pursuing columns, and started in person for the scene of forced to
the wreck. When he arrived he found that the report them by
was accurate : about forty ships were totally destroyed ; many
but after inspecting the rest, he saw that it would be ships had
possible to repair them. In the course of the day the wrecked.
legions returned. The men who had enlisted as skilled
artisans were segregated and set to work, and galleys were
sent to Labienus with a letter in which he was ordered to
dispatch gangs of shipwrights from his three legions and
to employ the rest of the men in building new vessels.
Caesar reluctantly concluded that the only way of prevent- He
ing another disaster was to have all the ships hauled up constructs
out of reach of the highest spring tides, and then, in order camp, and
to secure them against attack, to throw up an earthwork damage.
behind them and connect it with the existing camp. The
labour which these operations entailed was enormous ; but
by employing the troops in relays all day and all night he
was able to complete the task in about ten days.

This second shipwreck was a calamity of which the Results
mere loss in ships formed the smallest part. Why had not disaster.
Caesar restrained his eagerness to close with the enemy,
and employed every available man in beaching the
vessels which he had constructed with that very aim ?
Nobody knew better how necessary it is, especially in
making war upon a half-barbarous people, to complete all
preparations, even at the cost of delay, before opening
the campaign, so as to lose not a moment in following up
an initial success and to give fugitives no time to recover
from their demoralization. Less than two days after he
set foot in Britain he had dealt the enemy a succession of
heavy blows, and the game was in his hands—when all that
he had done was undone by his own carelessness. Britons
saw Romans in full retreat, and concluded that they were
not invincible.

It was near the end of the second week in August when
Caesar was able to renew his campaign. The Britons had

Cassivel-
launus
elected
comman-
der-in-
chief.

Caesar
again
marches
towards
Canter-
bury.

made good use of their respite. The tribes had suspended
their feuds : Cassivellaunus had been appointed commander-in-chief with full powers ; and a large force,
composed of contingents from all, or almost all, the
cantons of the south-eastern district, had marched to join
the men of East Kent. We may doubt whether the
Trinovantes had not held aloof ; but if they had been
forced to join the league, they were half-hearted. Caesar
left the same force as before—ten cohorts and three
hundred cavalry—to protect the camp, and marched once
more in the direction of Canterbury. As he was approaching the valley of the Stour, the enemy's cavalry and
charioteers commenced a running fight with his Gallic
cavalry ; but they were beaten back and driven to take
refuge on the heights near the river. The Gallic cavalry,
however, over-eager to pursue, and getting entangled in
ground which was unknown to them, suffered considerable
loss ; and soon afterwards, while the legionaries were
engaged in entrenching their camp, the enemy suddenly
swooped down upon the cohort on guard and began to
overpower it. Caesar had not yet learned due respect
for the Britons ; otherwise he would have kept a much
more powerful force, as he had done on a like occasion in
Gaul, to protect the working parties. He sent two
cohorts, however, to support the struggling guard and to
cut off the retreat of the assailants. These reinforcements
were separated from one another by a narrow interval :
the men who composed them and who had not served in
the preceding year, were unnerved by the novel tactics
of the charioteers ; and the enemy boldly rushed through
the interval, and got back to the main body unhurt.
Several additional cohorts, accompanied by cavalry, were
sent to retrieve the situation. The combat was clearly
visible from the camp ; and Caesar saw that his troops,
who had so often routed their continental enemies, were
at a serious disadvantage. The Britons fought not in
close order but in small groups, separated by wide intervals ; and when these were tired, their places were taken
by reserves. Whenever a group was hard pressed by the

legionaries, the men who composed it ran away : the 54 B. C
Romans, weighted by their heavy armour, were ineffective
in pursuit ; and, accustomed as they were to fight in
compact masses, they and their officers failed to adapt
themselves to new conditions. Again, when the Gallic
cavalry charged the charioteers, the latter drove rapidly
away ; and as soon as they had withdrawn their assailants
from the support of the legions, the warriors leaped to the
ground, and, supported by their own cavalry, fought as
infantry with the odds in their favour. At length, however, the reinforcements which Caesar sent up succeeded
in deterring the Britons for the moment from renewing
their attack.

All this time Caesar was doubtless fighting to gain the
line of the trackway by which he would have to march
westward into the interior and invade the dominions of
Cassivellaunus. But it was out of the question to begin
his march until he had inflicted a crushing defeat upon
the allies ; and, as he saw now, their game was to avoid
a pitched battle. On the following day, however, a
chance presented itself. In the morning the enemy, who
had taken up a position on the heights at some distance
from the Roman camp, moved down, as before, in
scattered groups, and began to assail the cavalry outposts,
but with somewhat diminished vigour. The outposts fell
back ; and presently the whole of the cavalry was sent
out, along with three of the legions, under Gaius Trebonius,
on a foraging expedition. Part of the force proceeded
to cut grass, while the rest was drawn up in support.
Suddenly the enemy rushed down from all points on the
foragers, and, made reckless by success, ' did not even
hesitate,' as Caesar said, ' to attack the ordered ranks of
the legions.' [1] The Romans charged them fiercely and   Trebonius
took ample revenge for the previous day. The Britons   routs the
were driven from the field, hotly pursued by Trebonius   Britons.
and his men, until the Gallic cavalry, relying upon the
support of the legions, which still followed as closely as
they could, hunted them in headlong rout, cutting them

[1] *B. G.*, v, 17, 2. See *Anc. Britain*, p. 692.

54 B. C.

The British infantry disperse.

down in numbers, and never giving them a chance to rally. Not even the charioteers could get a moment's respite, or dared to dismount and turn upon their pursuers. The tribal levies of foot at once dispersed to their homes ; and 'from that time ', wrote Caesar, 'the enemy never encountered us in a general action.' [1] It was perhaps at this juncture, after he had proved his superiority, that the Trinovantes sent envoys, promising submission and begging him to send Mandubracius back to them as their ruler and to protect him against Cassivellaunus. He allowed Mandubracius to depart, only stipulating that the Trinovantes should give him forty hostages and provide grain for his troops.

War-chariots *versus* Roman troops.

Cassivellaunus had learned the lesson which his kinsmen on the other side of the Channel were already taking to heart. He saw that his object was not to be obtained by regular warfare, and during a prolonged campaign he would have been unable to feed a large army. But he still had four thousand charioteers with the cavalry who supported them ; [2] and on them he determined to rely. The success with which he had already used them makes us wonder why the Continental Celts had abandoned the arm which their insular kinsmen wielded with such effect. The most satisfactory explanation is to be found in a passage of the *Commentaries*, from which we learn that the Gauls spent large sums in buying well-bred horses.[3] Evidently they discarded chariots for cavalry when they began to import from Southern Europe horses which were powerful enough to carry big men and charge with effect.[4] The German cavalry, it is true, had only small underbred cattle ; but they were virtually mounted infantry. The British may have been well or ill mounted ; but for the most part British horses were no bigger than ponies,[5] able

---

[1] *B. G.*, v, 17, 5.   [2] *Anc. Britain*, pp. 342, 675.   [3] *B. G.*, iv, 2. 2.

[4] W. Ridgeway, *Origin . . . of the Thoroughbred Horse*, 1905, pp. 94–5, 102–3.

[5] The late Lord Redesdale (*Memories*, ii, 1915, p. 711), ignorant of the statements of Arrian (*Ars tact.*, 19) and Dio (lxxvi, 12, 3) and of the archaeological discoveries which confirm them, asserted that the British chariot horses were big heavy animals ! See *Anc. Britain*, pp. 342–3, 676.

to draw a light car, but not to gallop fast with heavy
riders. Still, whoever calls to mind how in the last
Samnite War the Gallic chariots routed the Roman
cavalry will perhaps doubt whether the Gauls did well to
abandon chariots altogether in favour of mounted troops.

Nevertheless the reader who trusts to his first impressions of Caesar's narrative is prone to exaggerate the
successes of the British charioteers. Their object was to
break the formation of their opponents ; and this they
could only do when carelessness gave them an opening.
The punishment which they inflicted upon the 7th legion
was invited by the almost incredible negligence of its
commander : the check which Caesar himself suffered in
the following year befell an outpost of inadequate strength.
In irregular warfare chariots could cause serious trouble ;
but the difficulty which Caesar found in dealing with them
was partly due to the fact that his army, like all Roman
armies in this period, was weak in cavalry—and in cavalry
of the right kind.

Caesar now marched for the country of Cassivellaunus, *Caesar*
who, as he divined, intended thenceforward to wage *marches*
for the
a guerrilla warfare. What route he followed is an interest- *country of*
ing but perhaps insoluble question. It is, however, morally *Cassivel-*
launus,
certain that he went either by the trackway on the line
of which the Romans of a later period made the great road
called Watling Street, which crosses the Medway between
Rochester and Strood, or along the southern slope of the
chalk escarpment and across the Medway at Aylesford or
Halling, and we may reasonably believe that he chose the
route, leading through a fertile and populous country,
which his successors selected, diverged from it somewhere
near Rochester, and thence advanced by way of Bromley.[1]
During a great part of the march Cassivellaunus dogged *whose*
the Roman column. Caesar sent out parties of cavalry to *chariots*
harass his
devastate the country and despoil the inhabitants of their *cavalry.*
chief source of wealth,—their flocks and herds. But
Cassivellaunus soon taught him a lesson of caution. He
dispatched messengers to warn the inhabitants to drive

[1] *Anc. Britain*, p. 344. See also p. 285, *infra*

their cattle into the woods and to fly for refuge thither themselves. Knowing every yard of the country, and having the advantage of superior mobility, he would conceal his force in some wooded spot, and when he saw the Roman horsemen diverge from the column and ride forth to plunder, swoop down upon them and inflict heavy loss. Caesar was compelled to keep his cavalry, who were terrorized by these unforeseen attacks, in constant touch with the infantry, while the legionaries, whose powers of endurance were taxed to the uttermost, moved off the road from time to time, and burned and ravaged whatever they could reach.

Caesar crosses the Thames. Caesar had ascertained that the Thames, in that part of its course which formed the southern boundary of the territory of Cassivellaunus, was fordable at one spot only— perhaps near Brentford.[1] When the column descended into the valley he found that the further bank was fenced by a row of sharp stakes, behind which were massed the Catuvellauni ; and prisoners reported that similar stakes, concealed by the water, were planted in the bed of the river. He sent his cavalry behind cover to swim the stream close by ; and at the right moment the column of infantry plunged into the water and advanced to the attack. We may suppose that, while they were removing the stakes, the slingers and archers harassed the enemy.[2] ' The infantry ', wrote Caesar, ' advanced with such swiftness and dash, though they had only their heads above water, that the enemy, unable to withstand the combined onset of cavalry and infantry, abandoned the bank and fled.' [3]

Cassivellaunus orders the kings of Kent to attack the naval camp. But Cassivellaunus did not despair. Before Caesar crossed the Thames, he had sent mounted messengers to order the petty kings of Kent to raise all their tribesmen instantly and make a sudden attack upon the naval camp. Meanwhile Caesar was moving eastward into the country of the Trinovantes. Cassivellaunus still haunted

---

[1] *Anc. Britain*, pp. 692-8, 742. See also M. Sharpe, *Middlesex in Brit. . . . Times*, 1919, pp. 27-8, 33, 38.
[2] *Anc. Britain*, pp. 698-9.   [3] *B. G.*, v, 18, 5.

his line of march, and pursued the same harassing tactics ;
but the legionaries succeeded in doing considerable
damage. When, however, they crossed the Trinovantian
frontier, Caesar was careful to restrain them from committing any act of violence. The Trinovantes duly handed
over the hostages and delivered the grain which Caesar
had demanded ; and several other tribes [1] which had
joined the defensive league, seeing that they had been
rewarded for their submission, sent envoys to announce
their surrender. The envoys told Caesar that the stronghold of Cassivellaunus was not far off, and that a large
number of the inhabitants with their flocks and herds
had taken refuge in it. Possibly it was Verulamium, near
St. Albans,[2] which was in later times the capital of the son
and successor of Cassivellaunus : at any rate it was not
far west of the river Lea, which formed the boundary of
the Trinovantes. Caesar found that the stronghold was
protected by woods and marshes and fortified with
a rampart and trench ; but the legions, advancing on two
sides, speedily carried the place by assault : many of the
Britons, as they were endeavouring to escape, were killed ;
and all their cattle were taken.

Caesar enters the country of the Trino-vantes, who fur-nish hostages and grain. Five tribes submit.

Meanwhile the counter attack which Cassivellaunus
had ordered had been delivered. A chieftain named
Lugotorix was chosen to lead the assault upon the
naval camp ; but the garrison made a sortie, beat off
the Britons with considerable loss, and captured their
commander.

Attack on the naval camp repulsed.

It was perhaps just after this event that Caesar, accompanied by a flying column, made a journey to the coast, of
which he omits all mention in the *Commentaries*. On the
1st of September he wrote a letter from the naval camp
to Marcus Cicero. He had found time to write at least
once before ; and Quintus had sent a long series of letters
to his brother, whose allusions to them reveal something
of the inner history of the campaign.[3] In the last week
of August he replied to the one which had described the

Caesar's journey to the coast. Aug. 5.

---

[1] The Cenimagni, Segontiaci, Ancalites, Bibroci, and Cassi.
[2] *Anc. Britain*, pp. 699–702   [3] See pp. 285–6.

54 B. C.   safe arrival of the fleet : 'How I rejoiced at your letter from Britain. I was nervous about the sea and the coast of that island. I don't underrate what you have still to do ; but there is more ground for hope than fear.'[1]

Sept. 1.   On the 28th of September he dispatched a long letter, written in instalments, in which he acknowledged the receipt of four successive letters : ' I gather from yours ', he said, ' that we have no occasion either for fear or exultation.'[2]   The letter to which he here alludes—the

July 16.   first of the series—was written before the 10th of August, that is to say, while the construction of the naval camp was still in progress. Caesar's first letter was written in a spirit so friendly that it gave him the keenest pleasure, mingled with pain ; for he knew that Caesar could not long remain in ignorance of the death of his daughter Julia, the wife of Pompey. Towards the end of the letter of September 28 he says, ' Caesar wrote me a letter on the

Aug. 5, 31.   1st of September, which reached me on the 27th, satisfactory enough as regards affairs in Britain, in which, to prevent my wondering at not getting one from you, he tells me that you were not with him when he reached the coast.'[3]   Caesar did not, it would seem, write again until

Aug. 29.   the 25th, after which about a fortnight elapsed before he quitted the island ; and it is hardly credible that he should have spent more than five weeks inactive at the sea. The only conclusion is that he had some urgent motive for leaving the main body of his army, and that the journey was connected with the attack upon the camp. Perhaps he desired to see for himself that the defences were secure against any future attempt, to reinforce the garrison, and to ascertain what progress had been made in the repair of the fleet.[4]

Cassivel-launus sues for peace.   But Cassivellaunus had by this time begun to lose heart. His country had been mercilessly harried, his people had been dragged off by hundreds to be sold as slaves, and— what he valued most of all—his cattle had been taken from him. Discredited by reverses, he had not been able

---

[1] Q. fr., ii, 15 (16), 4.   [2] Ib., iii, 1, 10.
[3] Ib., § 25.   [4] Anc. Britain, pp. 672, 731-3.

to hold his ill-assorted confederates together; their 54 b. c
defection left him powerless to retrieve his fortunes, and
his last great stroke had failed. He therefore sent envoys
to the Roman camp to propose surrender, and requested
Commius to negotiate on his behalf.[1] Caesar, for his part,
was glad to be able to leave the island with a semblance
of success. Labienus had just warned him that the outlook in Gaul was threatening; the season for campaigning
was nearly over; and he was aware that Cassivellaunus
could still maintain a guerrilla warfare. He was obliged
therefore to content himself with demanding hostages,
fixing a sum which the tribes that had formed the
league were to pay annually as tribute, and admonishing
Cassivellaunus to leave the Trinovantes and their king
unmolested.

The hostages were handed over without delay; and Caesar
Caesar, with his army and his train of captives, marched and his
back to the coast.[2] He found all the ships which it had return
been possible to repair ready for sea; but as the prisoners to Gaul.
were very numerous, he determined to convey them in
two successive trips. He expected that when the empty
transports returned they would be accompanied by sixty
others, which had just been launched by Labienus; but
only a few either of the old or the new vessels arrived,
the rest having been driven back by contrary winds. Day
after day Caesar waited for them with increasing anxiety;
for the equinoctial gales might soon be expected. At
length he made up his mind that he could wait no longer.
The few available vessels were inconveniently crowded:
but the sea was perfectly smooth; and, leaving the
Kentish coast between nine and ten at night, the fleet
reached land at break of day. Although Caesar had
failed to achieve his aim, although the tribute which he
imposed was doubtless soon withheld, he had opened
a new world to his countrymen and directed the course
of British history into a new channel. Just as Roman
traders had prepared the way for his legions in Gaul, so

[1] *Ib.*, p. 349, n. 3.
[2] *Ib.*, p. 350 and n. 1.

Roman or Romanized traders prepared the way for the legions of Claudius in Britain.[1]

The Gallic nobles in a danger- ous mood. Labienus had not warned Caesar without reason. The fate of Dumnorix probably helped to kindle into a flame the discontent which had long been smouldering in the breasts of the Gauls. Not only were the constant presence of the legions and the endless requisitions of corn an intolerable burden,[2] but to the high-spirited Celtic knights the fact of subjection was more galling still. They had indeed partly themselves to blame. Weakness of purpose, mutual jealousy, petty ambition, had been their bane. They had not realized, or had not valued their national unity enough to make a united effort for its preservation. If the Nervii and the Veneti had fought like heroes, the states of the interior had acquiesced in the domination of Caesar without a blow, nay even without a protest. It would of course be uncritical to ignore the difficulties with which they had to contend. If Caesar was justified in the severity with which he described the infirmities of their national character, it would have been unreasonable to expect from a medley of tribes which had hardly had time to outgrow their political infancy, the harmonious action that could only have been the fruit of ages of discipline. They were attacked by a matured power while they were still in the stage through which every great people has been forced to travel before it could become a nation : they were heavily weighted by the selfishness or the astuteness, call it which one will, of the Aedui and the Remi ; and above all, no leader had appeared whose personality was sufficiently commanding to rally the patriots of every state round his standard. But the steady pressure of the conqueror was producing its natural effect upon a people who, notwithstanding their intestine quarrels, were animated by the recollection of ancient renown, who spoke one language, and who venerated one divine ancestor. The chiefs were in a dangerous mood ; and the populace were ready to back

---

[1] *Anc. Britain*, pp. 355-7.

[2] See *Caesar's Conquest of Gaul²*, p. 103, n. 2.

them. The harvest in Gaul this season was very scanty ; 54 B. C.
and Caesar was obliged, in order to ensure an adequate Distribu-tion of the
supply of grain, to distribute his legions for the winter legions
over a wide extent of territory. As the Belgic states for the winter.
appeared to be the most restless, he selected their country
for the occupation. One legion, under Gaius Fabius, was
quartered among the Morini ; another, under Quintus
Cicero, who was allowed to choose,[1] among the Nervii, in
the neighbourhood of Namur ; a third, under Labienus,
not improbably at Mouzon, some ten miles south-east of
Sedan, near the western frontier of the Treveri. Three,
under Trebonius, Marcus Crassus,[2] and Plancus respectively, were stationed close together at Samarobriva and [Amiens.]
in the plain round Beauvais. One, consisting entirely of
recruits, with five veteran cohorts, was sent to Atuatuca,
in the country of the Eburones. The site of this famous
camp has not been definitely fixed ; for, although it is
generally identified with Tongres, Caesar's narrative
seems to imply that it was east of the Meuse, and not
very far from Liège.[3] The garrison was commanded by
Sabinus and Aurunculeius Cotta, the former of whom, as
the senior officer, had the superior authority. One legion
only, under Roscius, was sent outside Belgic territory to
the country of the Esuvii in the Orne. The services of the
younger Crassus, who, except Labienus, had proved
himself the most capable of Caesar's lieutenants, were no
longer available ; for he was required to serve in Syria on
his father's staff. Caesar fixed his head-quarters at
Samarobriva ; and, in view of the prevailing discontent,
he determined not to leave Gaul for the winter until the
various camps were fortified.

About this time an incident occurred which Caesar may Assassina-
have regarded as a sign of a coming storm. In certain tion of King
states, where monarchy had been overthrown by oligarchy, Tasgetius,
he had elevated chiefs who had done him service to the Caesar's nominee,
thrones of their ancestors, his object doubtless being not by the Carnutes.

[1] Cic., Att., iv, 19, 2.
[2] Marcus Crassus was Caesar's quaestor and an elder brother of Publius.
[3] Caesar's Conquest of Gaul[2], pp. 371–84.

only to put a premium upon loyalty, but also to use the loyal as instruments for keeping the anti-Roman party in check. One of his nominees, Tasgetius, had, for three years, been King of the Carnutes, who dwelt in the country round Orleans and Chartres. How he used his power we are not told ; but soon after Caesar's return he was assassinated. Caesar instantly sent Plancus with his legion to arrest all who were concerned in the deed, and to terrorize intending rebels.

Intrigues of Indu-tiomarus,

All this time, Indutiomarus, whose pride Caesar had humbled, was busily intriguing against him. The isolation of the various camps gave him his opportunity. A few days after the legions had taken up their quarters he instigated Ambiorix and Catuvolcus, each of whom ruled one half of the country of the Eburones, to attack the camp of Sabinus and Cotta. Caesar was a hundred and fifty miles away : the nearest camp, that of Cicero, at least forty-five miles : at Atuatuca there were barely six thousand legionaries, and two-thirds of them were unseasoned men. Ambiorix and Catuvolcus, who had just taken their quota of corn to the generals, mustered their tribesmen in great force, surprised and overpowered a fatigue party, who were engaged in felling wood outside the camp, and then made a sudden onslaught upon the camp itself. But the camp was strongly fortified, and stood upon rising ground of great natural strength. The troops promptly manned the rampart : a squadron of Spanish horse made a successful sally ; and the assailants fell back in discomfiture. Their leaders shouted out that they would like some one to come and talk over matters, so that all disputes might be peaceably settled. Two deputies accordingly were sent out to hear what they had to say. Ambiorix had made himself useful as a political agent ; and, in acknowledgement of his services, Caesar had relieved him from the burden of paying tribute to the Atuatuci, and had restored to him his son and nephew, whom they had detained as hostages. Ambiorix began by speaking of Caesar's kindness, and said that he was most anxious to prove his gratitude. He protested that

The Eburones, under Ambiorix, make a futile attack on the ca mp of Sabinus and Cotta.

he had not attacked the camp of his own free will, but simply because he could not resist the pressure put upon him by his tribesmen ; nor would they have stirred if they had not been forced to join in the national movement. He was not such a fool as to imagine that his feeble levies could stand against the Romans ; but the leading powers of Gaul were banded together to recover their independence, and on that very day all the Roman camps were to be simultaneously attacked. He most earnestly entreated Sabinus to be on his guard. A host of German mercenaries had crossed the Rhine, and would be upon him in a couple of days. If the two generals would take his advice, they would abandon their camp at once, and make the best of their way to the quarters of Cicero or of Labienus. He would pledge his word that they should not be molested on the road. He would not merely be making some return for Caesar's kindness : it was to the interest of his people to be relieved from the burden of supplying the camp.

The deputies returned and reported what they had heard. Sabinus and Cotta agreed that whether Ambiorix were sincere or not in his professions of friendship, his warning was not to be despised ; for a single petty tribe like the Eburones would never have dared to pit itself against the power of Rome unless it had been strongly supported. The tribunes and the centurions of the first rank were summoned to attend a council of war. It took place in the middle of the camp, in full view of the soldiers. Cotta spoke first. He argued that without Caesar's express command they had no right to leave the camp. Behind its defences they could defy any force that could be brought against them ; they were not pressed for supplies ; and doubtless they would soon be relieved. Anyhow, nothing could be more unsoldierlike, more puerile, than to take a step fraught with the gravest issues by the advice of an enemy.

Most of the officers warmly supported this view. But Sabinus was only irritated by their unanimity. Speaking loudly and passionately, he insisted that it was not a question of being guided by the advice of an enemy, but by hard facts. Caesar had doubtless gone back to Italy, or the Eburones would never have attacked them; so they could not expect help from him. Both Germans and Gauls had many an old score to wipe out; and they were naturally burning for revenge. The course which he recommended was safe either way. If the whole thing turned out to be a false alarm, then they risked nothing by going to the nearest camp : if, on the other hand, Gauls and Germans were really leagued against them, their one chance of safety was to retreat at once. To follow Cotta's advice would involve, at the best, the miseries of famine and blockade.

The dispute waxed warm. In spite of all that Sabinus could say, Cotta and the centurions remained inflexible. Sabinus rapidly lost all patience. Raising his voice so that the men might hear, 'Have your own way,' he shouted, 'have your own way! Death has no terrors for me! These men will judge between us, and if any disaster happens, they'll call you to account for it. If you would only let them, they could reach the nearest camp the day after to-morrow, and join hands with their comrades.' The generals stood up. Their friends crowded round them, took them by the hand, and en-treated them not to quarrel. Go or stay, all would be well

Despite the pro-tests of Cotta, Sabinus decides to abandon the camp. if only they could agree. The strife of words was pro-longed till midnight. At length, overborne by the authority of his senior, Cotta gave way. All ranks were warned that they would have to quit the camp at dawn. The soldiers spent the small hours in looking over their belongings to see what they could carry away, and told each other that, after all, Sabinus was in the right. The drivers had enough to do in loading their cattle. Everybody was too agitated to think of sleep.

Meanwhile Ambiorix and his followers, hearing the hum of voices in the camp, concluded that the Romans had determined to follow their advice. Whether Sabinus intended to make for the camp of Labienus or for that of

Cicero, the first stage of his route would be the same.[1] 54 B. C.
Ambiorix prepared to execute his plan.

Just as day was breaking, the Romans marched out
in an extended column encumbered by a heavy baggage-
train. Sabinus had decided to make for the camp of
Cicero.[2] After advancing about two miles, the head of
the column plunged into a defile shut in between wooded
hills. Company after company tramped after. The last
was just entering the valley when, rushing from the woods,
the Gauls threw themselves upon the vanguard : the rear
was hustled forward : before, behind, to right, to left,
everywhere the enemy's masses were pouring down.
Sabinus hurried from place to place and feebly attempted
to make his dispositions. Cool and collected, Cotta did
his best to rally the men ; and, as the length of the
column made it unmanageable, he agreed with his colleague to abandon the baggage, and form in a square.[3] It
was perhaps the only course to adopt : yet the result
was that the Romans lost heart and the enemy were emboldened ; for both knew that such an expedient could
only have been resorted to by leaders who despaired.
Rough soldiers were actually weeping : confusion was worse
confounded ; and many contrived to slip away, and ran
to save their valuables in the baggage-train while there
was yet time. The Gauls, on the other hand, showed
extraordinary steadiness ; for their leaders told them
that they had only to win the battle, and they should
have plunder to their hearts' content. Still the square
remained unbroken. Now and again a cohort dashed
out ; and beneath their short swords many of the Gauls
sank down. Observing this, Ambiorix ordered his men
to fall back some paces, and hurl their missiles from a
safe distance. If the Romans charged, they were to
retreat : when the Romans attempted to return to the
square, they were to pursue. Maddened by the volleys
which they were powerless to return—for they had no
slingers and no archers—one cohort and then another

The Romans are sur- rounded by the Eburones,

---

[1] *Caesar's Conquest of Gaul²*, p. 373. [2] *Ib.* and n. 5.
[3] *Ib.*, p. 728. The term ' square ' is used loosely.

charged. Back darted the nimble Gauls. The right flank of the Romans was exposed, and missiles rained in on their unshielded bodies. The moment the baffled cohort retired, the enemy swarmed all round it ; and then followed a swift butchery. The rest stood shoulder to shoulder in the square, but now their courage was of no avail ; the enemy would not come to close quarters, and stones and arrows made havoc in the dense ranks. Yet, facing such fearful odds, after seven hours' fighting, they still held out ; and, as Caesar put it, throughout that trying time they did nothing unworthy of themselves. Quintus Lucanius, a centurion whom Caesar singled out for special mention, was killed in attempting to rescue his own son. Cotta himself was struck in the face as he was cheering on the men. The sun was sinking. The battle could only end in one way ; and Sabinus, catching sight of Ambiorix some way off haranguing his men, sent his interpreter to ask for quarter. Ambiorix replied that Sabinus might come and speak to him if he liked : he would answer for his personal safety, and he hoped that his men might be prevailed upon to be merciful. Sabinus asked Cotta to go with him ; but Cotta, true to Roman traditions, said that nothing would induce him to treat with an armed enemy. Accordingly Sabinus and a few tribunes and centurions went out alone. Sabinus was ordered to lay down his arms, and obeyed, bidding his officers to do the same. A parley followed ; and Ambiorix purposely spun out what he had to say. While he was speaking, a number of Gauls crept stealthily behind Sabinus ; and in a moment he fell dead. Then with a yell of triumph the Gauls rushed into the exhausted legion ; and Cotta and the bulk of his men were destroyed. The rest fled for the camp. The standard-bearer, Lucius Petrosidius, finding himself hotly pursued, flung his eagle inside the rampart, and died fighting like and virtu-a Roman soldier. His surviving comrades defended themally anni-hilated. selves till nightfall. Then, seeing that hope was gone, they fell upon each others' swords.

A few men, more fortunate than their comrades, had

managed to escape into the woods. They made their 54 B. C.
way to the camp of Labienus, and told him the whole
story.[1]

Ambiorix instantly followed up his victory. Bidding
his infantry follow, he rode off westward with the horsemen. All that night and the day after he sped over the
plateau of Herve and the plain of Hesbaye :[2] just
pausing to enlist the Atuatuci in the cause, he pressed on,
and next day crossed the frontier of the Nervii. This
people had not forgotten how their brethren had been
slaughtered, three years before, on the banks of the
Sambre. Ambiorix told the chiefs exultingly of his
success. Here was such a chance as they might never
have again. Cicero's camp was close by. Why should
they not do as he had done,—swoop down upon the
solitary legion, win back their independence for good,
and take a glorious revenge upon their persecutors ?
The chiefs caught at the suggestion. The small tribes
that owned their sway flocked to join them : the Eburones,
flushed with victory, were there to help ; and the united
host set out with eager confidence for the Roman camp.
Their horsemen, hurrying on ahead, cut off a party of
soldiers who were felling wood. Not the faintest rumour
of the late disaster had reached Cicero ; and the Gallic
hordes burst upon him like a bolt from the sky. Their
first onslaught was so violent that even the disciplined
courage of the Romans barely averted destruction.
Messengers were instantly dispatched to inform Caesar ;
and Cicero promised to reward them well if they succeeded in delivering his letters. Working all night with
incessant energy, the legionaries erected a large number
of wooden towers on the ramparts, and made good the
defects in the fortifications. The Gauls, who meanwhile
had been strongly reinforced, returned in the morning
to the attack. They succeeded in filling up the trench ;

Margin notes: Ambiorix persuades the Atuatuci and Nervii to join him in attacking Q. Cicero. Siege of Cicero's camp.

[1] Dr. K. Fr. Adami has argued that Caesar's narrative of the disaster
at Atuatuca was based upon a report probably written by one of the
delegates whom Sabinus sent to parley with Ambiorix (*Mitt. aus d. hist.
Litt.*, xxxii, 1904, pp. 5–6).

[2] Not if Atuatuca was on the site of Tongres.

but the garrison still managed to keep them at bay. Day after day the siege continued ; and night after night and all night long the Romans toiled to make ready for the morrow's struggle. The towers were furnished with stories and embattled breastworks of wattle-work ; sharp stakes, burnt and hardened at the ends, were prepared for hurling at the besiegers, and huge pikes for stopping their rush if they should attempt an assault. Even the sick and the wounded had to lend a hand. Cicero himself was in poor health : but he worked night and day ; and it was not until the men gathered round him and insisted on his sparing himself that he would take a little rest. Meanwhile the Nervian leaders, who had expected an easy triumph, were becoming impatient, and asked him to grant them an interview. They assailed him with the same arguments that Ambiorix had found so successful with Sabinus. They tried to frighten him by describing the massacre at Atuatuca, and assured him that it was idle to hope for relief. But they would not be hard upon him. All that they wanted was to stop the inveterate custom of quartering the legions for the winter in Gaul. If he and his army would only go, they might go in peace whithersoever they pleased. Cicero replied that Romans never accepted terms from an armed enemy. They must first lay down their arms : then he would intercede for them with Caesar, who would doubtless grant their petition.

The rebuff only stimulated the Gauls to redouble their exertions. From the experience of past campaigns they had got a rough idea of the nature of Roman siege works ; and now, with the quickness of their race, they proceeded to imitate them. Some prisoners, who had fallen into their hands, gave them hints. Having no proper tools, they were obliged to cut the turf with their swords, and to use their hands and even their cloaks in piling the sods ; but their numbers were so great that in three hours they had thrown up a rampart ten feet high and nearly three miles in extent.[1] They then proceeded, under

[1] *Caesar's Conquest of Gaul*[2], pp. 728-9.

the guidance of the prisoners, to erect towers, and to make
sappers' huts, ladders, and poles fitted with hooks for
tearing down the rampart of the camp. On the seventh
day of the siege there was a great gale. The besiegers
took advantage of it to fling blazing darts and white-hot
balls of clay,[1] which lighted on the straw thatch of the
men's huts ; and the wind-swept flames flew all over
the enclosure. With a yell of exultation the enemy
wheeled forward their towers and huts, and planted their
ladders : in another moment they were swarming up :
but all along the rampart, their dark figures outlined
against the fiery background, the Romans were standing,
ready to hurl them down : harassed by showers of missiles,
half scorched by the fierce heat, regardless of the havoc
that the flames were making in their property, every man
of them stood firm ; and hardly one so much as looked
behind. Their losses were heavier than on any previous
day ; but the Gauls too went down in scores, for those in
front could not retreat because of the masses that pressed
upon them from behind. In one spot a tower was wheeled
right up to the rampart. The centurions of the 3rd cohort
coolly withdrew their men, and with voice and gesture
dared the Gauls to come on : but none dared stir a step :
a shower of stones sent them flying ; and the deserted
tower was set on fire. Everywhere the result was the
same ; and at length, leaving their slain in heaps, the
assailants sullenly gave way.

Still the siege went on ; and to the wearied and
weakened legion its trials daily increased. Letters for
Caesar were sent out in more and more rapid succession.
Some of the messengers were caught in sight of the
garrison, and tortured to death. There was, however, in
the camp a Nervian named Vertico, who, just before the
siege, had thrown himself upon the protection of Cicero,
and had been steadfastly true to him. By lavish promises
he induced one of his slaves to face the dangers which to
the Romans had proved fatal. The letter which he had
to carry was fastened to a javelin and concealed by the

A messenger carries a dispatch to Caesar.

[1] *Ib.*, pp. 729-30.

lashing.[1] He passed his countrymen unnoticed, made his way safely to Samarobriva, and delivered his dispatch. None of the other messengers had arrived ; and so close was the sympathy between the peasants and the insurgents that Caesar had not heard a rumour of the siege.

Caesar marches to relieve Cicero. It was about four o'clock in the afternoon. Within a few minutes messengers were spurring to the camps in the surrounding country. Crassus was ordered to come in to Samarobriva at once, and take the General's place. Fabius was to join Caesar on the road. A letter went to Labienus, expressing the hope that he would be able to march direct to the relief of the besieged camp ; but this able officer was trusted to use his own discretion. Plancus and Roscius were too far off to be able to help. About nine o'clock next morning, hearing that Crassus was close at hand, Caesar set out with Trebonius's legion and about four hundred cavalry. No baggage-train accompanied the column : the men carried all that they required on their backs. The first march was more than eighteen miles. Fabius joined his chief on the way ; but Labienus did not appear. An express came from him instead, from which Caesar learned, for the first time, the fate of Sabinus and Cotta. Labienus explained that, as he was himself hard pressed by the Treveri, he thought it fool-hardy to leave his camp ; and Caesar approved his decision, though it left him with barely seven thousand men. Everything now depended upon speed. Passing through the Nervian territory, Caesar learned from some peasants who fell into his hands that Cicero's situation was all but desperate : immediately he wrote a letter in Greek characters, assuring him of speedy relief, and offered one of his Gallic horsemen a large reward to deliver it, telling him, in case he should not be able to get into the camp, to tie the letter to the thong of a javelin and throw it inside. Dreading the risk of apprehension, the man did as Caesar had directed ; but the javelin stuck in one of the towers, and remained unnoticed for two days.

[1] Or, perhaps, inserted in the hollowed shaft of a javelin. *Inligatas* (*B. G.*, v, 45, 4) does not necessarily mean ' lashed '. Cf. Cic., *Verr.*, iv, 24, 54.

A soldier then found it and took it to Cicero, who read the letter to his exhausted troops. As they gazed over the rampart, they saw clouds of smoke floating far away above the west horizon, and knew that Caesar was approaching and taking vengeance as he came.

That night Caesar received a dispatch from Cicero, warning him that the Gauls had raised the siege, and gone off to intercept him. Early in the morning, after a short march, the legions came to a rivulet, running through a broad valley, beyond which the enemy were encamped. Sending out scouts to look for a convenient place to cross, Caesar marked out his own camp on a slope, and constructed it on the smallest possible scale in the hope of seducing the enemy to attack him. But the enemy were expecting reinforcements and remained where they were. At dawn their horsemen ventured across the rivulet, and attacked his cavalry, who promptly retreated in obedience to orders. Sitting on their horses, the Gauls could see inside the camp. An attempt was apparently being made to increase the height of the rampart and to block the gateways. Caesar had told his men what to do ; and they were hurrying about the camp with a pretence of nervous trepidation. The enemy hesitated no longer ; and in a short time they were all across the stream. The gates of the camp looked too strong to be forced, though there was really only a mock barricade of sods, which could be knocked over in a moment. The Gallic infantry walked right up to the ditch, and began coolly filling it up, and actually tearing down the palisade [1] with their hands—when from right and left and front the cohorts charged ; there was a thunder of hoofs ; and reeling backward in amazement before the rush of cavalry, they flung away their arms and fled.

About three o'clock that afternoon the legions reached Cicero's camp without the loss of a man. Asking with keen interest for details of the siege, Caesar gazed with admiring wonder at the enemy's deserted works ; and when the little garrison was paraded, he found that not one man in ten had come off without a wound. Turning

The Gauls abandon the siege, and march to encounter him.

Defeat of the Gauls.

Caesar joins Cicero.

[1] *B. G.*, v, 51, 4. Cf. W. Fischer, *D. röm. Lager*, &c., 1914, p. 20.

to Cicero, he heartily thanked him for the magnificent stand which he had made, and then, calling out, one by one, the officers whom he mentioned as having shown conspicuous bravery, he addressed to them a few words of praise. From some prisoners who had served under Ambiorix he gleaned particulars of the massacre at Atuatuca. Next day he again assembled the men, and described to them what had befallen their comrades. The culpable rashness of a general officer had entailed a disaster ; but they must not be downhearted, for Providence and their own good swords had enabled them to repair the loss.

Immediate effects of his victory.

Meanwhile the news of the relief had spread like wildfire. Before midnight it was known near the camp of Labienus, more than fifty miles away. A number of loyal Remans hurried to congratulate the general ; and a shout of joy outside the gates told him what had occurred. Indutiomarus, who was on the point of attacking him, hastily withdrew. A large force from the maritime tribes of Brittany and Normandy was advancing against the camp of Roscius, when an express came to warn them of Caesar's victory, and they precipitately fled.

Many nobles continue to intrigue.

But even Caesar could not undo the effect of the annihilation of a Roman army. The Gauls had broken the spell of Roman success ; and, except among the Remi and the Aedui, there was hardly a chief who did not dream of similar victories. Nocturnal meetings were held in secluded places ; embassies passed from tribe to tribe ; and the state of affairs became so alarming that Caesar determined to break through his usual practice and spend the winter in Gaul. He sent for all the chiefs who were in any way compromised, and when he had thoroughly frightened them by letting them know that he was aware of their intrigues, he tried to convince them that it was their interest to keep the peace. The bulk of the tribes were thus deterred from actually rebelling ; but the Senones, a powerful people occupying the country round Sens and Montargis, were in grim earnest. Their council condemned to death Cavarinus, whom Caesar had set

over them as king, then, as he contrived to escape,
declared him an exile ; and when Caesar ordered them to
come to Samarobriva and answer for this outrage, they
flatly refused to obey. But of all the malcontents the
most daring and the most dangerous was Indutiomarus.
Rebuffed by the German chiefs, who replied to his appeals
for aid by reminding him of the fate of Ariovistus and the
Tencteri, he raised troops and drilled them, bought up
horses from the neighbouring peoples, and offered rewards
to all the outlaws and exiles in Gaul who would join his
standard. His prestige rapidly increased ; and all the
patriots began to look to him for guidance. Summoning
the warriors of his own tribe to muster in arms at a stated
place, he proclaimed his rival Cingetorix a public enemy
and confiscated his possessions. His plan was to make
a raid into the country of the Remi and punish them for
their desertion of the national cause ; then to join the
Carnutes and the Senones, and to raise a revolt in the
heart of Gaul. First of all, however, he determined to
make one more attempt against Labienus. But the
Roman general was too strongly posted to fear any attack ;
and he determined to make an end of Indutiomarus and
his schemes. He called upon the neighbouring tribes to
furnish him with cavalry, which were to arrive on a fixed
date ; and, like Caesar, he did his best to lure on the enemy
by a pretence of fear. Their horsemen rode up to the camp,
hurled missiles over the rampart, shouted every insulting
epithet at the Romans, and challenged them to come out
if they dared. Labienus would not allow his men to reply.
The cavalry which he had summoned arrived punctually ;
and in the night, thanks to the carelessness of the Treveran
sentries, they were admitted into the camp. Caesar
afterwards noted with admiration the extraordinary
precautions which Labienus had taken to prevent a single
man from going outside, lest the enemy should hear that
he had been reinforced. Next day, as usual, Indutiomarus
and his men spent their time in swaggering round the
rampart and abusing the Romans. In the evening, when
they were scattered and off their guard, two of the gates

were opened : the cavalry, supported by several cohorts, charged ; and the astounded Gauls fled. Labienus had given orders that every one should pursue Indutiomarus, and him alone ; and he promised a large reward to the man who should kill him. He was caught in the act of fording a river ; and his head was cut off. Forthwith the assembled bands of the Nervii and Eburones dispersed ; and for a time Gaul was comparatively still.

Only for a time however. Caesar had reason to believe that the chiefs were hatching a more formidable conspiracy ; and he saw that the best way to counteract it was to convince them that, whatever successes they might
gain, the fighting strength of Italy was inexhaustible. He accordingly raised two new legions—the 14th and 15th— in Cisalpine Gaul, and asked Pompey, with whom his relations were still amicable, to lend him a third. Pompey was at that time proconsul, charged with the government of Spain ; but, as Caesar explained with politic reticence, ' though vested with the command of an army, he remained on public grounds in the neighbourhood of the capital '.[1] Rome, whither Caesar must soon return, was convulsed by internal throes, and the civil war that was coming cast its shadow before ; but it was necessary that he should shut out from his mind all distracting thoughts, and perfect his work in Gaul.

Peace did not last out the winter. The Treveri, notwithstanding the death of Indutiomarus, succeeded in persuading, by promises of gold, some of the more distant tribes of Germany to aid them, and made a formal alliance with Ambiorix. The Nervii, the Atuatuci, the Menapii, and the Eburones were all in arms : the Senones and the Carnutes were still defiant. Leaving Samarobriva
with four legions, Caesar made a sudden raid into the country of the Nervii ; took numbers of prisoners before the bewildered tribesmen could either muster their forces or flee ; drove away their herds, ravaged their lands, and compelled the cowed chiefs to submit. When he convened his annual council at Samarobriva in the early spring,

[1] B. G., vi, 1, 2.

every Celtican tribe except the Senones, the Carnutes,
and the Treveri, sent its representatives. The contumacy
of the Treveri, who were always restless, was comparatively of little moment ; but Caesar has recorded what he
thought of the attitude of the other tribes :—' regarding
their absence as the first step in rebellion, he determined
to mark his sense of its paramount importance, and
accordingly transferred the council to Lutecia, a town
belonging to the Parisii.'[1] The Carnutes possessed the [Paris.]
great cornfield from which Caesar drew much of his
supply ; and the 'hallowed spot'[2] in their country
where the Druids held their annual synod was the religious
centre of Gaul. Immediately after the council adjourned
Caesar again took the field. A rapid march southward forces the
so disconcerted the Senones that they surrendered at Senones
once, and begged the Aedui to intercede for them. The and Car-
Carnutes, without waiting to be attacked, induced their submit;
overlords, the Remi, to do them a like service, and, as
time pressed, Caesar accepted, without inquiry, the
excuses of both peoples, took hostages for their good
behaviour, and, after dispatching the business of the
council, turned eastward to deal with the Treveri and the
Eburones. The exiled king of the Senones, with his
contingent of cavalry, accompanied the column ; for
Caesar did not venture to reinstate him, lest the odium
which he had incurred should provoke a fresh outbreak
and impede the legions in their punitive campaign. He and pre-
had not forgotten the shame and the suffering which pares to
Ambiorix had brought upon his soldiers ; and he was Ambiorix.
determined to inflict upon him a most signal and awful
retribution.

The first step was to deprive him of his allies, the As a pre-
Menapii, the Treveri, and the Germans. Caesar had liminary
ascertained that he did not intend to fight ; and the crushes
object was to bar against him every way of escape. The the
Menapii, alone of all the Gallic tribes, had never formally
surrendered to Rome. Sending all the heavy baggage to
Labienus and reinforcing him with two legions, Caesar

[1] *Ib.*, 3, 4.   [2] *Ib.*, 13, 10.

53 B. C.   marched against the recalcitrant tribe in overwhelming
force. Without attempting to resist, they again took
refuge in their forests and marshes ; but this time they
were not to escape. Caesar bridged the rivers, constructed causeways over the marshes, and launched
three separate columns into their country ; and when
their cattle were driven away, their villages ablaze, and
prisoners taken by scores, they were constrained to
surrender. Caesar left a body of horse to watch them
under Commius, and warning them, as they valued the
lives of their hostages, to give no refuge to Ambiorix or
his lieutenants, pushed southward to deal with the

Labienus   Treveri. Before he could arrive, however, Labienus
disperses   marched out to meet them, enticed them by a feigned
the Tre-
veri.   flight across a river, and then, suddenly wheeling round,
sent them flying into the woods. Their German allies,
who had not had time to join them, returned home ; and
within a few days the whole tribe submitted. Their
leaders fled the country ; and Caesar's adherent, Cingetorix, was appointed chief magistrate.

Caesar   About this time Caesar joined Labienus ; and with the
crosses   twofold object of punishing the Germans and preventing
the
Rhine,   Ambiorix from seeking an asylum in their country, he
and
threatens   built a second bridge across the Rhine, a little above the
the allies   site of the former one. Leaving a force to hold the Gallic
of Am-
biorix.   end and keep the Treveri in awe, he directed the Ubii to
inform him about the routes that led into the enemy's
country. A few days later he learned that the Suebi,
who had been active in sending mercenaries against
Labienus, were massing their warriors and warning their
dependent tribes to send in their contingents. He
immediately entrenched himself in a strong position, and
ordered the Ubii to remove their stores from the open
country into their strongholds, to drive in their cattle
from the pastures, and to send out scouts to watch the
enemy's movements. His hope was that, finding themselves short of supplies, they might be enticed to venture
a battle at a disadvantage ; but the scouts, after a few
days' absence, reported that the entire host had fallen

53 B. C. back to the outskirts of a huge forest near the mountains of Thuringia. To follow them thither through a wild country, where little or no corn was to be had, would simply be to court destruction. There was nothing for it but to return. But, in order to keep the Germans in constant fear of a fresh invasion, he only destroyed that part of the bridge which touched their bank of the Rhine ; erected a wooden tower for artillerymen on its extremity ; and detailed twelve cohorts to hold the other end.

And now, having made every preparation that fore-thought could suggest, Caesar bent all his energies to destroy Ambiorix. The road ran westward through the vast forest of the Ardennes. An officer named Minucius Basilus was sent on ahead with the cavalry. His orders were to march as rapidly as possible, so as to catch the Eburones unprepared, and on no account to allow any fires to be lighted in his camp, lest Ambiorix should be warned of his approach. Caesar followed with the infantry till he reached the deserted camp where, a few months before, the remnant of Cotta's force had died. There he left his heavy baggage and the newly raised 14th legion under the command of Cicero. He promised to return at the end of a week, and charged his lieutenant on no account to allow a single man to venture out of camp until then. The army was divided into three corps, each consisting of three legions, or, not counting auxiliaries, about eleven thousand men.[1] Labienus was sent to the northern part of the country of the Eburones, in the direction of the coast between the Scheldt and the Rhine ; Trebonius to the south-western, in the direction of Huy. They were to harry the enemy's country, to ascertain his designs, and to return, if possible at the end of a week, to concert measures with Caesar for a final campaign. Caesar himself marched towards the lower Scheldt, in the hope of catching Ambiorix, who was said to have retreated to the extremity of the Ardennes. Basilus and his cavalry, guided by some peasants whom they had caught in the fields, rode through a wood till

Returning unsuccessful, he marches against Ambiorix.

[1] Cf. *B. G.*, v, 49, 7.

53 B. C.

The Eburones keep up a guerrilla warfare.

they came to a cottage, in a small clearing, where he was said to be hiding ; but his retainers, taking advantage of the contracted space, gallantly flung themselves upon the Romans, while their chief threw himself on horseback and disappeared among the trees. Catuvolcus, the aged prince who had shared his counsels, was too infirm to bear the hardships of a hunted fugitive, and, invoking every curse upon the author of his ruin, committed suicide. The Eburones, less civilized than their neighbours, had no walled towns to retreat to ; and Ambiorix sent word over the country-side that every one must shift for himself. Many fled the country altogether : others dived into the recesses of the forest : others lurked in the marshes or the islets in the estuary of the Scheldt. Caesar found that there was no regular force to oppose him ; but every glen, every bog, every clump of trees held its nest of armed skulkers. Massed in their cohorts and companies, the legionaries were powerless against such foes : the only way to get at them was to send out small flying parties in every direction. But in those narrow woodland tracks it was not easy for even the smallest party to keep together. The enemy knew every inch of the ground, they were wary, and they were desperate ; and a few legionaries who strayed in search

Caesar invites the neighbouring tribes to harry them.

of plunder were cut off and killed. Wishing to spare his men as much as possible, Caesar invited the surrounding tribes to come and harry the Eburones and enrich themselves with plunder. He intended, as he tells us, ' that Gauls should risk their lives in the forests, and not his legionaries, and at the same time to surround the people with a mighty host, and, in requital for their signal villainy, to destroy them, root, branch, and name '.[1] Multitudes of eager plunderers were attracted by the prospect ; and Caesar's old enemies, the Sugambri, actually crossed the Rhine with two thousand horse in the hope of sharing in the spoil. The Eburones were captured by scores, and their cattle driven off. But the Sugambri were soon tempted by a richer prize. One of

[1] *B. G.*, vi, 34, 8.

their captives told them that Caesar was far away, and that they need not be afraid of him. Atuatuca was within a three hours' march. Why should they not pounce upon Cicero's camp, and carry off all the stores, the baggage, and the loot which it contained ?

It happened that on this very day Caesar was expected in the camp. But Cicero had heard nothing of or from him, and was beginning to fear that he would not be able to keep his promise. Hitherto he had carefully obeyed his instructions, and had not allowed a man to stir outside the rampart. But fresh rations were due : there were cornfields within three miles of the camp : it was absurd to suppose that the persecuted Eburones would venture an attack so near ; and besides it stung him to hear that the men were sneering at his caution. Accordingly he allowed half the legion, with three hundred convalescent veterans, who were under a separate command, two hundred cavalry, and a number of slaves, to go out and cut corn. They were hardly out of sight when a host of The horsemen broke from an outlying wood, swept down upon Sugambri the camp, and tried to burst in through the rear gate. Cicero. The dealers who accompanied the army were massacred in their tents outside the rampart ; and the cohort on duty barely sustained the first shock. The enemy spread round the camp, looking for an entrance ; and it was all that the guards could do to prevent them from breaking through the gates. Within all was confusion and panic ; and the superstitious recruits remembered with horror that, on the very spot where they stood, the soldiers of Cotta and Sabinus had perished. But it happened that there was in the camp an invalided centurion, whose deeds of daring Caesar was never tired of extolling,— Sextius Baculus. As he lay, ill and weak, in his tent, he heard the uproar, and walked out to see what was the matter. Without a moment's hesitation he snatched sword and shield from the men close by, and planted himself in the nearest gateway. The centurions on guard rallied round him ; and alone they kept the enemy at bay. Severely wounded, Sextius fell down in a faint, and was with difficulty rescued ; but his example shamed the trembling recruits into action, and the camp was saved.

Meanwhile the harvesters were on their way back. They heard the uproar. The cavalry rode on, and saw the enemy. The rest followed. The recruits had never seen a sword drawn in anger : there was no cover near : and in consternation they looked to their officers for orders. The Germans, descrying infantry and cavalry in the distance, took them for Caesar's legions and abandoned their attempt on the camp ; but presently, seeing how few they had to deal with, rode off to attack them. The slaves, who had rushed up a knoll for refuge, were speedily dislodged, and, flying pell-mell into the maniples, increased their alarm. A hurried consultation was held. The recruits, in spite of all warnings, ended by clustering together on a ridge, where they fancied that they might be safe. The three hundred veterans kept their presence of mind, and, followed by the cavalry and slaves, charged boldly through the enemy's loose array. The recruits stood watching them in helpless hesitation. At length they tried to reach the camp anyhow ; and two entire cohorts were surrounded and slain. Those who escaped owed their lives to their centurions, who threw themselves upon the enemy, for a moment forced them back, and died, fighting to the last man. The Germans rode away with the booty which they had left in the woods. Caesar's advanced guard reached the camp that night, and found the young soldiers almost beside themselves with panic. They were positive that the General himself and his army must have perished ; and nothing could quiet them till they actually saw him arrive. Reflecting that in war it is the unexpected that happens, he contented himself with telling Quintus that he ought to have followed his instructions to the letter, and not to have run the smallest risk ; but when he wrote to Marcus Cicero he animadverted sharply upon his brother's negligence.[1]

One more effort was made to catch Ambiorix. Fresh

---

[1] Charis., ed. H. Keil, 1857, p. 126,—*Caesar epistolarum ad Ciceronem* : ' Neque ', inquit, ' pro cauto ac diligente se castris continuit '.

plunderers from the surrounding tribes were hounded on
by Caesar to hunt down his people and to harry his land. Caesar
Every hamlet, every building was burned down ; every- ravages the
thing worth plundering was carried off ; and every ear country of the
of corn that was not sodden by the rain was devoured : Eburones.
for it was Caesar's deliberate intention that every man,
woman, and child who escaped the sword should perish
of hunger. The soldiers knew that he had set his heart
upon getting Ambiorix into his hands ; and they made
incredible exertions to win his favour. Cavalry in small
parties scoured the country in pursuit of the king. From
time to time they captured peasants, who declared that
he was hardly out of sight. But, in spite of the desperate Ambiorix
efforts of his exasperated pursuers, he was never caught. eludes pursuit.
With four retainers, who would have suffered anything
rather than betray him, he was lost in the dark recesses
of the Ardennes.

By this time Caesar must have heard the news that Caesar
brought such shame on Italy as had not been felt since hears of the death
the day of Cannae. Five-and-twenty thousand Roman of Crassus.
soldiers were lost to the Republic—fallen or held captive
in the East ; and Crassus and his gallant son were among
the slain. To Caesar the death of one of his confederates,
following the death of Julia, meant that the friendship
of the other was in jeopardy. He and Pompey were now
left alone ; and their aims must of necessity diverge. But
three years of his government remained ; and his work
in Gaul was not yet done.

The legions were distributed for the winter—two on the The
western frontier of the Treveri, two among the Lingones, legions distri-
the remaining six at Agedincum, now Sens, the chief buted
town of the Senones ; and the twelve cohorts, detached for the
from various legions, which had guarded the bridge over winter.
the Rhine, were doubtless now recalled. Caesar, before
he started for Italy, summoned a Gallic council to meet
at Durocortorum, the modern Reims. An inquiry was Execution
held regarding the rebellion, which at the time he had of Acco.
necessarily condoned, of the Carnutes and the Senones.
Acco, a Senonian chieftain, was convicted of having

53 B. C.   originated the movement ; and, in accordance with Roman custom, he was flogged to death.

' Gaul was now tranquillized ; and Caesar, in accordance with his determination, started for Italy to hold the assizes.' [1] So runs the first sentence of the book in which he narrated the events of the most momentous year of his command. But the stillness that lay upon Gaul was not peace ; and he had hardly turned his back when agitation was renewed. The fierceness with which the sporadic revolts of the last two years had been repressed was at length constraining tribes that were all embittered to combine ; and even in Central Gaul, which had submitted so tamely, the Senones and the Carnutes formed a nucleus of common action. The death of Acco was keenly discussed. Chieftains told each other that their own turn might come next, and that they must make a supreme effort to save their country. Even Commius was swept away on the wave of enthusiasm, and attempted to engage the Belgic tribes ; but Labienus heard of his intrigues, and sent Gaius Volusenus with a band of centurions to assassinate him. He escaped with a wound ; but for the time his plans had miscarried. His brother nobles, however, were more fortunate ; and early in the new year they were greatly heartened by a rumour, which ran through Gaul, that fire, rapine, and sedition were rife in Rome. Before we attempt to realize how they used their opportunity, we must follow the course of the events which had compelled the Senate to recognize Pompey as the saviour of society and the supreme ruler of the State.

Agitation renewed.

News of sedition in Rome reaches Gaul.

[1] *B. G.*, vii, 1, 1.

CHAPTER XI

THE DISSOLUTION OF THE TRIUMVIRATE

READERS who feel more interest in the significance than in the narrative of historical events will be on the watch, when they have seen how Pompey and Crassus fulfilled the bargain which they had made with Caesar, to learn whether the three confederates had other than self-regarding aims, whether the coalition had elements of stability, and what form of government could follow it in case it should be dissolved. Pompey, when his immediate objects had been attained, left the capital and spent much of his time in his country seats with Julia, to whom he was devotedly attached.[1] On the 20th of April Cicero visited him at his house near Cumae and, after hearing him discourse on the political situation, reported his impressions to his confidant : 'To judge from what he says—in his case one has to make that reservation—he is not pleased with himself at all.'[2] One may perhaps surmise that Pompey had an uneasy feeling that Caesar was now the predominant partner, and that he was slipping under Caesar's influence. But Cicero, who was taking no part in public life and busied with his treatise *On the Orator*,[3] had little of importance to relate about the second consulship of Pompey ; and one may gather from his silence that the political atmosphere, after its tempestuous dawn, was comparatively calm. We miss his pungent comments when we examine the legislation of the year ; for though he had something to say in a forensic speech [4] about a statute which Crassus framed, his private comments were probably more interesting. Crassus enacted a law to restrain candidates

---

[1] Plut., *Pomp.*, 53, 1–2.
[3] *Ib.*, 13, 2.
[2] *Att.*, iv, 10, 2 ; 9, 1.
[4] *Pro Plancio.*

2592.2

55 B. C.

Crassus's
law con-
cerning
election-
eering
clubs.
for office from using clubs, such as those which Clodius in his tribunate had legalized,[1] to secure their election by bribery or violence ; and the penalty which he fixed for convicted offenders is supposed to have been banishment for life.[2] Cynics, who reflected that Crassus and his colleague were qualified from their own practice and their own experience to gauge the evil which the law

was designed to check, may well have smiled. Connected, it would seem, in purpose with this measure was another by which Pompey modified the Aurelian law of his former consulship. Under the new enactment jurors were still to be selected from senators, knights, and ' tribunes of the treasury ', but only from the wealthier members of each class ; and one may suppose that the object was to lessen the temptation, to which so many jurors had succumbed in the trial of Clodius,[3] to sell their votes. But Pompey hoped that the favour of the populace might still be conciliated without breaking any law. In the early autumn the great theatre in the Field of Mars which he founded on returning from the East was formally dedicated. Built throughout of stone and decorated with statues, which had been arranged with the advice of Atticus, it was adjoined by a colonnade, adorned with paintings by Greek artists and containing a hall wherein

a statue of the founder stood. The dedication of the theatre and of a temple which Pompey had also built was signalized by manifold spectacles—dramatic, musical, gymnastic, gladiatorial combats, and fights between beasts and men. Ten thousand spectators assembled in the theatre ; and the entertainments lasted many days. In the play of *Clytemnestra* six hundred mules appeared upon the stage : five hundred lions and four hundred panthers were slaughtered in the circus ; twenty elephants fought with Gaetulian hunters and with criminals who

[1] *Pro Planc.*, 3, 8; 15, 36; *Schol. Bob.*, ed Stangl, pp. 152, 160 (ed. Orelli, pp. 253, 261); Dio, xxxix, 37, 1. Cf. Th. Mommsen, *De collegiis*, &c., 1843, pp. 61-73 ; *Paulys Real-Ency.*, iv, 408 ; Prof. R. W. Husband's articles in *Class. Weekly*, Oct. 9, 1916, pp. 11-4 ; Oct. 16, pp. 18-22 ; Oct. 23, pp. 26-30.

[2] *Ib.*, p. 26; Th. Mommsen, *Röm. Strafr.*, 1899, p. 874.

[3] See vol. i, p. 297.

had been condemned to death.[1] ' These things ', wrote 55 B. C.
Cicero to a friend, ' were the admiration of the populace,
but would have given you no pleasure. . . . The wild beast
baiting, lasting five days, was undeniably magnificent ;
but what pleasure can it be to a man of refined tastes
to see a feeble human being mangled by a powerful brute
or a splendid animal transfixed by a spear ? '[2] Even
the populace in some measure shared this sentiment ;
for when the elephants, finding escape impossible, trum-
peted in terror, they rose from their seats and uttered
imprecations against Pompey.[3]

If the consuls gained any popularity from the games,   Hostility
they incurred odium when they began to raise troops   of tribunes
                                                       to the
for their proconsular service.   Evidently few volunteers   consular
were attracted, for recourse was had to conscription.   levies of
                                                       troops
The hostile tribunes, Aquillius Gallus and Ateius Capito,
attempted to stop the levy ; but Pompey, ignoring their
opposition, sent his lieutenants to govern Spain with the
legions already quartered there, and resolved to remain
with the recruits in Italy, alleging that his presence was
required by the commission which he had received for
the superintendence of the corn-supply.[4] Altercations
had arisen in the Senate, perhaps on the question whether
the recent assignment of the provinces should be confirmed ;[5] but if that was the matter in dispute, the

[1] Cic., *Att.*, iv, 9, 1 ; Pliny, *Nat. Hist.*, viii, 7, 21 ; 16 (20), 53 ; 17 (24), 64 ;
xxxvi, 15 (24), 115 ; Ascon., ed. Clark, p. 2, ll. 1–3 (ed. Stangl, p. 11) ;
Plut., *Pomp.*, 52, 5 ; Dio, xxxix, 38, 1–3. According to Pliny, Pompey's
theatre could accommodate 40,000 spectators ; according to the *Notitia
urbis Romae*, 17,580. Ch. Huelsen, however, argues (*Bull. d. Comm. Archeol.
comun.*, 1894, pp. 319–24 ; *Topogr. d. Stadt Rom*, i, 3, 1907, p. 528) that the
figures denote, not the number of seats but the available space in Roman
feet, and that there was not room for more than 10,000 spectators.

[2] *Fam.*, vii, 1, 2–3. The view of Tyrrell (*The Correspondence of Cicero*,
ii, 1886, p. 94), that this letter ' must be regarded rather as a rhetorical
exercise on a theme suggested by his friend, than as the expression of the
writer's own opinion ', seems to me unwarranted by the sentence (§ 6)
on which it is based, where Cicero says, ' I have written you a longer letter
than usual . . . because . . . you asked me . . . to write you something to
prevent your feeling sorry that you missed the games '.

[3] Pliny, viii, 7, 21. Cf. Cicero, *Fam.*, vii, 1, 3, and Dio, xxxix, 38, 2–3.

[4] *Ib* , 39, 1–4 ; App., *B. C.*, ii, 18, 65.

[5] *Att.*, iv, 13, 1. Cf. Tyrrell, *op. cit.*, ii, 100.

opposition was overcome, and Crassus was preparing to set out. Before he started, he was reconciled, at the earnest desire of Pompey and of Caesar, to Cicero, whom he had offended, but who now entertained him at a farewell dinner.[1] ' What a rascal he is ! ' wrote Cicero

just afterwards to Atticus.[2] Every one knew that Crassus, although he had no decent pretext, purposed to wage war against the Parthians ;[3] and, hearing that Ateius intended to prevent his going, he induced Pompey to

escort him out of Rome. Awed by the presence of the illustrious general, the populace made way ; but Ateius ordered Crassus to be arrested, and when the other tribunes forbade this step, he placed a brazier, into which he cast incense and poured libations, at the Capuan Gate at the same time invoking dire curses upon the departing consul.[4] From a letter which Cicero wrote to him a few weeks later [5] it has been inferred that a motion in the Senate was made for his recall : at all events the new consuls as well as many consulars attacked him, and Cicero, evidently determined to convince Pompey and Caesar of the sincerity of his own conversion, vigorously replied. ' I have been so successful ', he told Crassus, ' that not only all your family, but the whole country knows that I am your warm friend.' [6] Readers who care for the personal element in history might like to know what the old ' rascal ' thought of this.

Gabinius, whom Crassus was about to succeed, had already settled the Egyptian question which engrossed pub-

lic interest after Cicero came back from exile. His own province, however, first required his attention. Pompey, when he quitted Asia, had taken with him as prisoners Aristobulus, the rival of Hyrcanus, and his sons Alexander and Antigonus. Alexander escaped on the journey,

---

[1] *Fam.*, i, 9, 20.   [2] *Att.*, iv, 13. 2.

[3] Plutarch (*Cras.*, 16, 3) implies and Dio (xl, 12, 1) affirms that Crassus had no authority to make war ; but the Trebonian law empowered him to do so at his own discretion.

[4] Cic., *De div.*, i, 16, 29–30 ; Vell., ii, 46, 3 ; Plut., *Cras.*, 16, 3–8 ; Flor. i, 46, 3 (inaccurate) ; App., ii, 18, 66 ; Dio, xxxix, 39, 5–7.

[5] *Fam.*, v, 8, 1.   [6] *Ib.*, § 2.

returned to Palestine, and, finding a faction ready to support him against Hyrcanus, attempted to rebuild the walls of Jerusalem, when he was attacked and defeated by Gabinius : Aristobulus, who escaped from 57 B. C. Rome, and who also raised rebellion, was speedily subdued and sent back to Italy. Gabinius then proceeded to reorganize the administration of Judaea. He rebuilt various cities, which had been destroyed in the wars of the Maccabees, restricted the authority of Hyrcanus to the custody of the Temple, divided the country into five cantons, each of which he placed under an aristocratic council, and restrained the exactions of the Roman tax-gatherers.[1] Cicero, who had reason to detest him, and supported the tax-gatherers on principle, denounced his administration as infamous : [2] Josephus, who was not partial to the oppressors of his countrymen, praised him as their benefactor. Gabinius was about to invade Parthia, in order to assist one of the sons of the late King Phraates, who had murdered their father, against his brother Orodes, when he received a letter from Pompey, enjoining him to restore Ptolemy to the throne of Egypt. The king promised ten thousand talents [3] to Gabinius, who, we may suppose, was to divide the money with the triumvirs.[4] However desirable it might be to put an He re-end to anarchy in Egypt, to leave his province on such stores an enterprise without authority from the Government Ptolemy to the was an act of treason, for which he would inevitably throne of be brought to trial ; but the influence of the ' unofficial Egypt. dictator ', his old commander, would doubtless save him

---

[1] Jos., *Ant.*, xiv, 5, 2–4 ; 6, 1–2 ; *Bell. Iud.*, i, 8, 2–7. See pp. 311–2.

[2] See p. 83, and cf. Dio, xxxix, 56, 1. ' There is no doubt ', says George Long (*Decline of the Roman Republic*, iv, 1872, p. 187), ' that Cicero received his information about Gabinius from the Publicani, who were knaves themselves and indignant that a greater knave should have authority over them.' According to Dio (xxxix, 55, 5), Gabinius amassed a fortune of more than 400,000,000 sesterces (£4,000,000) in his province ! At this rate he was richer than Crassus. Cf. Cic., *Pro Sest.*, 43, 93, *De prov. cons.*, 4, 9, *In Pis.*, 21, 48.

[3] £2,400,000.

[4] Cic., *Pro Rab. Post.*, 8, 21 ; 11, 30 ; *Schol. Bob.* (*Pro Planc.*, § 86), ed. Stangl, p. 168 (ed. Orelli, p. 271) ; Plut., *Ant.*, 3, 2. Cf. vol. i, p. 327.

55 B. C.

from condemnation. Ptolemy's daughter, Berenice, had usurped the throne. Antipater equipped the Roman army and induced the Jews of Pelusium, which guarded the eastern frontier of Egypt, to refrain from opposing the invasion. Mark Antony, who had done good service against Alexander, took part in the expedition and secured Pelusium for his chief. Gabinius defeated the troops of Berenice, restored Ptolemy, and left five hundred Gallic and German troopers to protect him and enable him to wring from his subjects the price of his restoration.

About Apr. 1 (?) [1] (March 19), 55 B. C.

Returning to his province, he finally subdued Alexander, who had taken advantage of his absence to raise a fresh rebellion, and, after settling the affairs of Jerusalem with the advice of Antipater, made a successful expedition against the Nabataean Arabs.[2] But, notwithstanding all that he had achieved, he was in no hurry to return to Rome, and omitted to report what he had done in Egypt to the Senate.[3] The Syrians complained that, in consequence of his desertion, they had been exposed to the attacks of pirates ; the tax-collectors added that these marauders had prevented them from collecting revenue ; [4] and doubtless the enemies of Gabinius recalled the fictitious oracle which forbade the Romans to restore Ptolemy with an army. Soon after the close of Pompey's consulship a deputation of the tax-gatherers appeared before the Senate to state their grievances, and various tribunes gave notice that they intended to prosecute Gabinius for treason.[5] It remained to be seen whether Pompey would be strong enough to shield him.

Complaints of his conduct in Syria.

Feb. 15 (Jan. 23), 54 B. C.

The triumvirs, notwithstanding their great power,

[1] Cic., *Att.*, iv, 10, 1. Cf. M. L. Strack, *D. Dynastie d. Ptolemäer*, 1897, p. 209, n. 42.

[2] Cic., *In Pis.*, 21, 49 ; *Pro Rab. Post.*, 10, 28 ; Caes., *B. C.*, iii, 4, 4 ; 103, 5 ; Strabo, xii, 3, 34 ; Jos., *Ant.*, xiv, 6, 2–4 ; *Bell. Iud.*, i, 8, 7 ; Plut., *Ant.*, 3 ; App., *Syr.*, 51 ; Dio, xxxix, 55, 1–3 ; 56–8 ; 60, 4. Josephus, our only authority, does not describe the nature of the settlement of Jerusalem ; but various guesses are noticed by G. F. Unger (*Sitzungsber. d. phil.-philol. u. d. hist. Cl. d. K. b. Akad. d. Wiss. zu München*, 1897, pp. 205-6).

[3] Dio, xxxix, 59, 1 ; 60, 4.   [4] *Ib.*, 59, 2-3.

[5] Cic., *Q. fr.*, ii, 11, 3. Cf. iii, 1, 15.

were unable to stifle criticism. One of the new consuls,
Domitius Ahenobarbus, who had failed the year before,
was still a bitter enemy of Caesar ; the other, Appius
Claudius, was no friend of Pompey ; and the confederates,
whose influence had not prevented their election, were
attacked by men of genius, whose weapon was the pen.
The conquest of Gaul coincided with a period of literary
activity. Lucretius, indeed, who awakened the poetical
spirit that was latent in materialism, who strove with
apostolic fervour to release men from the fear of death
by convincing them of its finality, but who yet communicated in one inspired passage [1] his sense of the sadness
with which they must await the end of intercourse with
those they loved, even though they would then be
insensible to pain ; who contemplated the myriad
activities of Nature with reverent awe, and whose
imaginative insight created anthropology, reconstructing
the life and the upward struggle of prehistoric man—
Lucretius was a recluse who took little heed of the
triumvirate. But two young writers, united by close friendship, were formidable assailants of Caesar and of Pompey,
though their enmity was rather personal than rooted in
political conviction. Gaius Licinius Calvus, orator and
poet, aimed scathing epigrams against Caesar, giving fresh
point to the persistent scandal about his connexion with
Nicomedes.[2] Gaius Valerius Catullus, whose lyrics were
inspired by his burning love for Clodia,[3] and then,
when he came to know her heartless profligacy, by the
hate which could not kill his love, who sung the awakening
fondness of an infant for his father with a tender sympathy
which was matched by Blake alone, directed two of his
most famous poems [4] against Caesar and his engineer
Mamurra, fastening upon them the charge of fellowship
in vice which it is better not to name. Caesar, whose
father-in-law Cicero might with impunity revile,[5] who

---

[1] iii, 894–977.

[2] Suet, *Div. Iul.*, 49, 1 ; 73 ; Seneca (the elder), *Controv.*, vii, 4, 7.

[3] For the identity of Catullus's Lesbia with Clodia see B. Schmidt, *Rhein. Mus.*, lxix, 1914, p. 267.

[4] 29 and 57.   [5] *In Pis., passim.*

54 B. C.   had treated the imputations of Bibulus with contempt, acknowledged that the poems of Catullus had branded an indelible mark upon his name.[1]   Catullus knew that he was angry, and defied him :   ' Naught care I if every line offend thee. . . . Unique commander, my innocent iambics shall make thee wroth again.'[2]   But Caesar, when the two poets afterwards apologized, freely forgave them both.[3]

Caesar indeed could afford to be forgiving ;   for mere obloquy did not affect his power.   The consuls could not, like the masters of legions, control the current of events. The object of Appius was to make a fortune, even before he proceeded to his province, by selling privileges to foreign dynasts and provincial deputations :[4]   Domitius candidly avowed that neither he nor his colleague had so much as the post of a military tribune to bestow,

Rumours of a coming dictatorship.   implying that all patronage belonged to Caesar.[5]   Early in June Cicero wrote to his brother, who was travelling to Gaul with the proconsul, that there were rumours of an approaching dictatorship.   ' There is profound calm ', he concluded, ' in the Forum ;   but the calm of decrepitude, not of content.   The opinions I express in the Senate are such as to win the assent of others rather than my own.'[6]

The internal history of Rome throughout the next two years is a record of corruption, intrigue, and violence, whose interest, apart from the light which it throws upon the capacity of the Republican Government, consists in helping us to trace the relations of Pompey to Caesar and to the Conservative party, with which, and not with any social movement, was involved the destiny of the Roman world.

---

[1] Suet., 73.   [2] 54.

[3] Suet., *l. c.* H. A. J. Munro (*Criticisms . . . of Catullus*[2], 1905, pp. 87-8) remarks that Suetonius, when he says (49, 1) that the only damaging charge of abnormal vice made against Caesar was that which related to his connexion with Nicomedes, proves that the lampoons of Catullus ' meant little or nothing '.   He goes on to show (pp. 88-90) the extreme improbability of the stories which that conscientious scandal-monger Suetonius collected about Nicomedes.

[4] Cic., *Q. fr.*, ii, 10, 2-3.

[5] *Ib.*, 13, 3. Cf. p. 153, n. 2.   [6] *Q. fr.*, ii, 13, 3. 5.

In July it became known that the consuls and the candidates for the consulship had been parties to a job of an unprecedented kind. The candidates were Gaius Memmius, to whom Lucretius had dedicated his poem, Domitius Calvinus, who had served two years before as praetor, Valerius Messalla a partisan of Caesar, and Pom- pey's former lieutenant, Aemilius Scaurus. The interests of the two chief triumvirs were now at variance. Pompey of course supported Scaurus : Memmius, who, like Messalla, was backed by Caesar and favoured by Caesar's veterans, relied also upon the influence of the Cisalpine colonies ; and it was generally expected that, failing this, some tribune would succeed in postponing the elections until Caesar recrossed the Alps.[1] The candidates offered sums equivalent to one hundred thousand pounds to the electors of whatever century should be the first to poll, whose vote the others would almost certainly repeat. To find the money they were obliged to borrow ; and the rate of interest rose from four to eight per cent. But the calculations of the quidnuncs were upset by a compact which Memmius and Domitius concluded with the consuls. Both were anxious, in case they should be elected, to proceed without delay after their term of office to the provinces in which they hoped to make their fortunes. To secure this end they bound themselves by a written and duly attested agreement, in return for the influence which the consuls were to exert on their behalf, to produce three augurs who should testify that full proconsular powers had been conferred upon them by the required law, and two ex-consuls who should affirm that they had helped to draft a decree for the equipment of the proconsuls and their staffs : in case of failure they were each to pay the consuls forty thousand sesterces—about four hundred pounds.[2] In the month of August violent debates,

[1] Cic., *Att.*, iv, 16, 6 ; 15, 7 ; *Q. fr.*, iii, 2, 3.

[2] *Ib.*, ii, 14, 4 ; iii, 1, 16 ; *Att.*, iv, 15, 7 ; 17, 2-3 ; App., ii, 19, 69. It is hardly necessary to say that law and decree would alike be fictitious. C. C. L. Lange (*Röm. Alt.*, iii, 1871. p. 336) conjectures that Memmius, who had attempted to bring Caesar after his consulship to trial, now purchased his

provoked by the outrageous bribery which the candidates had practised, took place in the Senate ; but nothing was yet officially known about the compact. Soon afterwards, however, Memmius, instigated by Pompey, determined to break faith with the consuls and his fellow candidate and to avow the compact in the Senate. Pompey apparently wished not only to prevent the success of Caesar's candidate, but to put off the elections in order that he might himself become dictator : Memmius doubtless expected that when Pompey gained his object, he would himself be recompensed. At all events he produced the document with the names of the augurs and ex-consuls blotted out, and read it aloud. The disclosure created a sensation. ' It has made no differ-ence ', wrote Cicero, ' to Appius—he had no character to lose ! His colleague was utterly bowled over.' [1] Memmius of course forfeited all chance of being elected, though he still hoped that the influence of Caesar, when he came back to Cisalpine Gaul, would ensure his return : Caesar, when he heard of the revelation, was displeased—perhaps with Pompey as much as Memmius.[2] The victory of Messalla and Domitius, who paid their bribes to the electors earlier than Scaurus, was now regarded as a certainty, and Scaurus was thrown overboard by Pompey ;[3] but the elections, repeatedly postponed by the device of announcing evil omens, were not held that year.[4] And now the event occurred by which, while the interests of Pompey and Caesar diverged on the question of the consulship, one of the ties that united them was severed.

Death of Julia. In the middle of September Julia, after giving birth to a daughter, died. When the funeral oration had been delivered the populace carried the body, which Pompey had intended to bury in his Alban property, to the Field of Mars, where, despite the protests of the consul Domitius,

support by undertaking to prevent Domitius Ahenobarbus from opposing him, and achieved this purpose by the agreement just described ; for Domitius, conscious of being a party to a discreditable bargain, was no longer a free agent. Cf. p. 152, n. 5.

[1] Q. fr., ii, 15, 2 ; Att., iv, 17, 2.　　[2] Ib., § 3 ; Q. fr., iii, 2, 3.
[3] Ib., 8, 3 ; Att., iv, 17, 4.　　[4] Ib. ; Q. fr., ii, 15, 3 ; iii, 3, 2.

it was cremated and interred.[1] The absence of Caesar 54 B.C.
had not weakened his hold upon the Roman people.

About this time Gabinius, whose enemies had already Hostile
announced their intention of bringing him to trial both reception
for treason and for having unlawfully accepted a bribe binius in
from Ptolemy, returned to Italy. On the 19th of Septem- Rome.
Aug. 23.
ber he reached the suburbs,[2] but lingered outside the city,
for he knew how he was about to be received. His old
commander, whose credit was at stake, determined to
prevent his condemnation and besought Cicero to defend
him.[3] ' Pompey ', wrote Cicero to his brother, ' is trying
hard to get me to be reconciled with him, but so far he
has not succeeded, nor will he, if I retain a particle of
liberty.' [4] On the 27th Gabinius entered the city in the Aug. 31
night, hoping to escape observation ; but on the next
day he was recognized, and hooted by a large crowd.[5]
He intended nevertheless to ask for a triumph, and
accordingly ten days after his arrival he ' slunk ', as
Cicero said, into the House, to make the necessary report
of his campaigns. Having done so, he was about to
leave when the consuls stopped him, and a deputation
of the aggrieved tax-collectors was introduced. Various
senators, including Cicero and Appius Claudius, inveighed
against him, and, stung by the taunts of his old enemy,
he cried in a voice trembling with anger, ' Exile ! '
Instantly the senators rose and with shouts of indignation
made a movement, followed by the tax-collectors, as if
to lay violent hands on Gabinius. ' No greater compliment ', wrote Cicero, ' was ever paid me.' [6] Cicero
longed to conduct the prosecution, but refrained, partly,
as he admitted, because he shrank from quarrelling with
Pompey, partly perhaps because he did not trust the jury.[7]
Pompey meanwhile was straining every nerve to save his
client, condescending even to solicit the jurors, who

---

[1] Livy, *Epit.*, 106 ; Val. Max., iv, 6, 4 ; Vell., ii, 47, 2 ; Plut., *Pomp.*,
53, 4-5 ; *Caes.*, 23, 4 ; Flor., ii, 13, 13 ; App., ii, 19, 68 ; Dio, xxxix, 64.
Cf. Cic., *Fam.*, vii, 9, 1   *Q. fr.*, iii, 1, 17 ; 8, 3.

[2] *Q. fr.*, iii, 1, 15.   [3] *Ib.*, 4, 3.
[4] *Ib.*, 1, 15.   [5] *Ib.*, § 24.
[6] *Ib.*, 2, 2.   [7] *Ib.*, §§ 2-3.

54 B; C.

had been empanelled, on his behalf.[1] The trial for high treason was the first. The prosecutor, Lucius Lentulus, who was known to be incompetent and was suspected of collusion,[2] made a feeble speech : ' Nothing ', remarked Cicero, who gave evidence against the defendant, ' could have been more absolutely puerile '. Many of the jurors had accepted bribes and were, moreover, influenced by a rumour that Pompey was about to become dictator. Nevertheless Gabinius only just escaped : thirty-two jurors out of seventy gave their votes against him. ' Republic, Senate, law courts are mere ciphers ; not one of us has any standing. . . . Domitius Calvinus voted for acquittal so openly that every one could see ' : [3] such was Cicero's comment on the verdict. When he was reproached by an acquaintance for having shirked the prosecution, he explained to Quintus that in the event of failure his reputation would have suffered ; moreover, he would have made an enemy of Pompey, who, since he regarded the trial as a contest in which his own position was at stake, would not have hesitated, despite his pro-consular position, to enter the city and force a quarrel on him. ' Now ', he asked, ' when the State is absolutely powerless, while he is absolutely supreme, was I to try a fall with him ? ' As for the alternative suggestion, that he should have defended Gabinius in deference to Pompey's wish, he scouted it : his friend had given him ' the alternative of a dangerous quarrel or eternal infamy ! ' [4] Pompey, however, who still hoped, in view of the impending prosecution, to secure his aid, showed unwonted consideration for his feelings, and admitted that he could not be expected to forgive Gabinius until he had atoned for his former conduct. Writing to Atticus about the recent verdict, Cicero remarked, as he had so often done, that the Republic was virtually dead : ' " Then you bear that philosophically ? " you will say. Precisely. For I recall how happy the country was for a little time,

Notwith-standing the support of Pompey he barely escapes conviction of treason.

Cicero's reflexions on the decadence of the Republic.

---

[1] Cic., *Q. fr.*, iii, 3, 3 ; 4, 1.

[2] *Ib.* ; *Att.*, iv, 18, 1. Dio (xxxix, 62, 2) wrongly says that Cicero prosecuted Gabinius.

[3] *Q.fr.*, iii, 4, 1 ; 9, 1 ; *Att.*, iv, 18, 1. 3.   [4] *Q. fr.*, iii, 4, 2–3.

while I was at the helm, and what gratitude has been 54 B. C.
shown to me! That one individual is all-powerful gives
me no pain.'[1] Nevertheless Cicero was a disappointed
man. 'It cuts me to the heart', he told his brother,
' that the object on which from boyhood I set my heart

"Far to excel, and tower above the crowd "[2]

is utterly gone.'[3]

One consolation remained. Although, at the pressing
request of Caesar, he had consented to defend Vatinius,
who had been prosecuted under the recent law of Crassus
for the bribery by which he gained the praetorship,[4] he
had found an opportunity of proving his gratitude
to Plancius, who befriended him in exile, by defending
him against a similar charge ; and, above all, he had not
yielded to the importunity of Pompey. ' If I had defended
Gabinius ', he told his brother, ' I should have been simply
ruined.'[5]

But Pompey was persistent, and Cicero could not long In defer-
continue to resist his pressure. Cato, now praetor, presided ence to
Pompey
at the trial ;[6] and, although on hot days he had shown he defends
Gabinius
his contempt for conventionality and his faith in the on the
Stoic maxim that what is natural is not indecent by charge of
corrup-
sitting in court barefooted and without a shirt under his tion.
toga,[7] his presence guaranteed that justice would be
upheld. A few months before, the tribunician candidates
had spontaneously bound themselves by oath to conduct
their canvass in obedience to his instructions, and had
each deposited with him five hundred thousand sesterces
on the understanding that any one whom he might
condemn should forfeit the money to the rest.[8] The speech
of Cicero has not survived, and probably, like his defence
of Vatinius, it was never published. As he told Atticus,[9]

---

[1] *Att.*, iv, 18, 1–2.   [2] Homer, *Il.*, vi, 208.
[3] *Q. fr.*, iii, 5 and 6, 4.
[4] *Pro Planc.*, 16, 40 ; *Q. fr.*, ii, 15, 3 ; *Fam.*, i, 9, 19 ; Ascon., ed. Clark,
p. 18, ll. 1–3 (ed. Stangl, p. 22).
[5] *Q. fr.*, iii, 5 and 6, 5.   [6] *Ib.*, 1, 15 ; 2, 1.
[7] Val. Max., iii, 6, 7 ; Ascon., ed. Clark, p. 29, ll. 7–9 (ed. Stangl, p. 29) ;
Plut., *Cato min.*, 44, 1.
[8] *Q. fr.*, ii, 14, 4 ; *Att.*, iv, 15, 8.   [9] *Ib.*, ii, 5, 1.

he kept in mind what posterity would say of him six centuries after his death, and doubtless he saw no reason why he should provide entertainment for cynics at the expense of his own fame. A communication from Pompey was read, in which he affirmed that Ptolemy had himself written to inform him that he had given no money to Gabinius except for purely military purposes,[1] and also a letter from Caesar, urging Pompey to see to it that Gabinius was saved. But neither this testimony nor the eloquence of Cicero availed. Gabinius was condemned, and forthwith went into exile.[2]

The result of this trial must have been a blow to Pompey, who had failed to save his client while Caesar's had escaped, and perhaps it stimulated his wish to become dictator. The consular elections, on one pretext or another, were still being postponed and postponed, though Milo was already pressing his canvass for the following year; and rumours about the dictatorship were still afloat.[3] Lucilius Hirrus, one of the tribunes designate, was active in Pompey's cause. 'The whole affair', wrote Cicero, before the second trial of Gabinius, 'is causing alarm and becoming unpopular. Pompey says distinctly that he doesn't wish it; but to me formerly he used not to disavow the wish. . . . Heavens, how fatuous he is! how in love with himself, without a rival! . . . whether he really wishes it or not, it is hard to tell. However, if Hirrus is the mover, he will fail to convince people that he does not. Nothing else is being talked about in politics just now.'[4] A little later Cicero reported that nothing had yet been settled : 'Hirrus is preparing for the move : many tribunes are counted on to veto it ; the people are indifferent, the leading men disinclined ; I do not stir.'[6] Soon afterwards Hirrus made the expected

[1] Cic., *Pro Rab. Post.*, 12, 34.

[2] Val. Max., iv, 2, 4 ; Dio, xxxix, 63, 4–5. Dio's statement (§ 2) that Gabinius was convicted because the jurors were afraid of popular indignation, and because Gabinius did not pay them enough, is negligible ; for he habitually invented motives.

[3] *Q. fr.*, iii, 8, 4. 6 ; 9, 2–3 ; *Fam.*, ii, 5, 2.   [4] *Q. fr.*, iii, 8, 4.

[5] L. Gurlitt (*Berl. philol. Woch.*, May 5, 1906, col. 575–6).

[6] *Q. fr.*, iii, 9, 3.

motion, which was opposed by Cato ; it would seem that 53 B. C.
Pompey ceased to impede the elections ; and at last in Consular
July, exactly a year after the normal time, Domitius elections
held after
Calvinus and Messalla, as Cicero had prophesied, were repeated
elected consuls.[1] Soon afterwards a sensational dispatch postpone-
ments.
arrived from Syria, but not from the proconsul.

The Parthian campaigns of Crassus are known to us Crassus in
from late compilations only, which were derived, not from the East.
the original sources, but from the work, no longer extant,
of a rhetorical historian.[2] When we tried to study the
operations of Sertorius, of Spartacus, of Lucullus, and of
Pompey, our materials were as defective, but they were
not overloaded with untrustworthy descriptions of tactical
details. Plutarch, our principal authority, gives a minute
account of the movements of Crassus, which presents
such difficulties that no critical historian would attempt
to found upon it a circumstantial narrative.[3] The cause
of the catastrophe is clear enough ; of the events that led
up to it only a sketch can be firmly drawn.

Early in 54 Crassus arrived in Syria, and in the spring
invaded Mesopotamia, apparently in order to prepare
for the grand campaign which he contemplated, with
the approval of Caesar,[4] against the Parthian king.[5]
The perfidy of Pompey towards Phraates[6] had given
occasion for a pretext which was not too shadowy to
serve : Orodes was attempting to recover from the
Armenians the territory which Pompey had assigned to
them.[7] Crossing the Euphrates at Zeugma,[8] Crassus
occupied several towns, the Greek inhabitants of which,

---

[1] Plut., *Pomp.*, 54, 2-3 ; App., ii, 19, 71 ; Dio, xl, 45, 1.

[2] Livy.

[3] *Cras.*, 17-33. Cf. Dio, xl, 12-27, and Flor., i, 46. The notices in the
other authorities—Livy, *Epit.*, 106 ; Val. Max., i, 6, 11 ; Vell., ii, 46, 4 ;
App., ii, 18, 66 ; Eutrop., vi, 18 ; Oros., vi, 13—are extremely cursory.
The difficulties are discussed on pp. 312-5.

[4] Plut., *Cras.*, 16, 3.

[5] Perhaps, as G. Ferrero suggests (*Grandezza e decadenza di Roma*, ii,
1902, p. 128 [Eng. tr., ii, 89]), Crassus hoped to seduce the Parthians into
approaching Syria, in order that he might be able to fight near his base.

[6] Vol. i, p. 209.　　　　　　　　　　　　[7] Justin., xlii, 2, 3-7 ; 4, 1-4.

[8] See *Klio*, vii, 1907, p. 365, n. 6.

54 B. C.   disliking Parthian rule, voluntarily surrendered ; pillaged
Zenodotium in punishment for treachery—an exploit
which his troops acknowledged, with perhaps unconscious
irony, by saluting him as Imperator—defeated the satrap
of the district near the fort of Ichnae ; and pushed on
to Nicephorium, by the confluence of the Euphrates and
the Belik. Ambassadors from Orodes presented themselves to ask on what pretext he was going to war ; and
then followed the dialogue which has been so often
recalled. Crassus replied that he would state his reasons
at Seleucia : the senior envoy, holding out the palm of
his left hand, retorted, ' Before you reach Seleucia hairs
will sprout upon this skin '.

Leaving seven thousand foot and one thousand horse
to garrison the surrendered towns, Crassus returned to
winter in his province. There he met his son Publius,
who had brought with him from Gaul a thousand horsemen ; and probably he raised more in Syria.[1] It appears
that he also demanded contingents of infantry, which he
did not need, from native communities and dynasts, but
dispensed with their services on payment of a stipulated
sum ; and we are told that he travelled to Jerusalem in
order to strip the Temple of the gold which Pompey had
forborne to touch.[2]

53 B. C.   In the following spring he set out once more towards
the east. His force comprised fifty-six cohorts—about
twenty-eight thousand men—four thousand light-armed
auxiliaries, and three thousand cavalry.[3] Before he
reached the Euphrates Artabazus, the Armenian king,
advised him to invade Parthia through Armenia, where
he would find abundant supplies, and the Parthian
cavalry, so formidable in the plains, would be unable
to attack him ; but Crassus, doubtless reflecting that if
he took this route, he would expose the garrisons in
Mesopotamia to assault and Syria to invasion, adhered
to his original design. While he was crossing the Euphrates

---

[1] See p. 312, n. 4.
[2] Jos., *Ant.*, xiv, 7, 1 ; *Bell. Iud.*, i, 8, 8 ; Oros., vi, 13, 1. Cf. Pliny,
xxxiii, 10 (47), 134.   [3] See pp. 313–4.

a dense mist lay upon the water ; a thunderstorm broke 53 B. C.
out ; and before the whole column reached the further
bank the bridge of boats was severed.. The superstitious
soldiers began to despond, and Crassus, who tried to
hearten them by announcing that he proposed to come
back through Armenia, unwittingly revived their fears
by adding that from the spot where they stood not one
of them should return. From the latitude of Zeugma
the army marched southward along the river to the
neighbourhood of Caeciliana, now Srēsat. The quaestor,
Gaius Cassius, urged his chief either to establish himself
in one of the towns which he had occupied until he got
certain information about the enemy, or else to keep on
following the river bank. The hostile cavalry would
then be unable to surround him, and he would remain
in touch with the barges that carried his supplies. Before
Crassus could make up his mind Abgarus of Osrhoene,
a sheikh with whom Pompey had had dealings, appeared
in his camp as a friend of Rome, and informed him that
Surenas, the Parthian general, was near, but that his
strength was still insignificant : if Crassus followed the
Euphrates, he would go far out of his way and lose
valuable time ; obviously his best course would be to
attack Surenas before he could assemble his whole force.
Crassus accordingly diverged from the Euphrates and
moved south-eastward across a fruitful plain, which,
as he approached the river Belik, merged into a sandy
desert.[1] Thirsty and weary of marching in the holding
sand, the troops became more and more dispirited ; and
meanwhile Abgarus informed Surenas of the Roman
plans. Near the river he departed, assuring Crassus that
he was going to circumvent the enemy. Soon afterwards
a few of the patrols returned, reporting that their comrades
had been cut off by the Parthians, who were advancing
in full force. Crassus was perplexed. Cassius advised
him to deploy his infantry as widely as he could, in order
to avoid a turning movement, and to post his cavalry
on the wings. He accepted the advice ; but after he had

[1] Cf. *Klio*, 1907, pp. 376 n. 2, 379 and n. 8.

given the order he changed his mind and determined to advance in a hollow square, assigning to each cohort a troop of cavalry. His son was to lead one wing and Cassius the other, while he himself took command of the centre. So runs the tale of his biographer ; but since a square has properly no wings, and three commanders only are named, soldiers may be inclined to conjecture that he was misinformed and to doubt whether the formation was completed. Not far south of Carrhae the army reached the Belik, where men and horses slaked their thirst. Most of the officers wished to encamp there, and, after ascertaining by reconnaissance the numbers and the formation of the enemy, to advance against them in the morning : but Crassus yielded to the importunity of his son, who was eager to lead his Gallic troopers into action ; [2] the troops wheeled to the right towards Ichnae ; and presently the Parthians—mail-clad cavalry and mounted archers—were descried swarming over the plain while the crash and clangour of kettledrums played them into action. The Roman cavalry, though they had been reinforced by the detachment left in the surrendered towns,[3] were, as often, far too few : the squadrons that were needed to turn the Parthians and force them within range of the javelins and on to the swords of the legions, were not there. The mail-clad cavalry with their lances attacked the Roman ranks in vain, but the auxiliaries were speedily driven to take shelter behind the infantry ; the mounted archers, riding leisurely round the legions, let fly their arrows again and again till their quivers were empty, and then replenished them from the reserves that were carried by camels behind the line. The cohorts, when they advanced in desperation, were as helpless as those of Cotta when they hurled themselves against the Eburones at Atuatuca : the Parthians cantered away, drew rein, and shot again. At length Crassus, seeing that

---

[1] See p. 315.

[2] According to Cicero (*Brut.*, 81, 282), Publius Crassus had a passion for military renown and longed to rival Alexander the Great.

[3] See p. 314, n. 4.

his son's division was in danger of being surrounded, ordered him to charge. Publius had three hundred horsemen besides his thousand Gauls, eight legionary cohorts, and five hundred bowmen. The Parthians at once gave way and never stopped until they had drawn their pursuers far from the main body. Then the heavy cavalry turned upon the Roman infantry ; the mounted archers plied their bows again from a safe distance ; and though the Gallic cavalry made some impression upon the mail-clad Parthians, the forlorn hope soon found its doom. Publius, who was urged by friends to make a dash for Ichnae, refused to leave his men and bade his armour-bearer kill him. Darkness suspended further slaughter : but many wounded men died where they lay ; ' many escaped worse sufferings by suicide ; many were butchered by the Parthians at break of day. Cassius, followed by the equivalent of two legions, escaped to Carrhae, where Crassus had left a garrison, and thence to Syria : ten thousand prisoners remained behind. Crassus, who also escaped with a few men to Carrhae, departed two days later in dread of capture, and sought refuge on a hill ; but, being invited to a colloquy by Surenas, who assured him that Orodes would treat him and his escort with humanity, he descended, though he was not deceived, in deference to the clamour of his men, and was forthwith put to death. When the tidings of the victory reached Orodes, the *Bacchae* of Euripides was being performed before the Parthian court. A tragedian appeared, bearing the head, not of Pentheus but of Crassus ; and the gory token evoked from the audience loud applause. But survivors related that the old proconsul had met the wreck of his ambition, the shame of defeat, and the bitterness of death with Roman fortitude.

When the report of these events reached Italy and Gaul, the surviving partners of Crassus must have reflected upon their future. Caesar was certainly anxious to maintain the alliance, for he had already proposed to Pompey a new matrimonial bond. The suggestion was that Pompey should marry Octavia, a grand-daughter of

Caesar's sister Julia, who was then the wife of a Marcellus, while Caesar should divorce Calpurnia and espouse the daughter of Pompey by his first wife, Mucia, though she was then betrothed to Faustus Sulla, a son of the dictator.[1]

Pompey rejects Caesar's proposal for a new matrimonial alliance.

But Pompey, though he readily granted Caesar's request for the loan of a legion,[2] declined the overture, and soon afterwards married Cornelia, the widow of Crassus, whose father, Caecilius Metellus Scipio, was canvassing for the consulship.[3] Caesar did not allow the rebuff to embitter their relations. In his consulship he had named Pompey as his heir, and three years were to elapse before he cancelled the bequest.[4] Pompey, however, if he did not yet contemplate a breach with Caesar, was pursuing aims which would lead him to become Caesar's rival rather than his colleague ; and, being constantly in touch with the Catonian party, even though he was not of it, he was insensibly drifting into a new connexion.

Cicero anxious to secure the consulship for Milo.

For the present his attention was fixed upon the contest for the consulship. Besides Milo and Scipio, the only candidate was Plautius Hypsaeus, who had served as Pompey's quaestor in the East.[5] If the consular authority was eclipsed by the power of Pompey and Caesar, success would still lead to the government of a province ; and Milo, if not yet Scipio, was overwhelmed with debt.[6] Pompey of course supported Scipio and Hypsaeus ; Cicero worked hard on behalf of Milo, who, if he judged correctly, was backed both by the Conservatives and by the populace, whose favour he had won in his aedileship by spending a million sesterces upon the games.[7] Caesar, we may be sure, exerted all his influence against the candidate who, if he were successful, would prove a redoubtable enemy.[8] Self-interest as well as gratitude

---

[1] Suet., 27, 1.   [2] See p. 136.

[3] Plutarch (*Pomp.*, 55, 1) incorrectly puts Pompey's marriage after his election as sole consul. Cf. Ascon. ed. Clark, p. 31, l. 9 (ed. Stangl, p. 30).

[4] Suet, 83, 1.

[5] Ascon., ed. Clark, p. 30, ll. 9–10 ; p. 35, ll. 17–8 (ed. Stangl, pp. 30, 33).

[6] Cic., *Pro Mil.*, 35, 95. According to Pliny (xxxvi, 15 [24], 104), Milo owed 70,000,000 sesterces (£700,000) !

[7] *Fam.*, ii, 6, 3. Cf. Ascon., ed. Clark, p. 31, ll. 4–8 (ed. Stangl, p. ·30) ; *Q. fr.*, iii, 9, 2.   [8] See *Fam.*, vii, 5, 3.

stimulated Cicero ; for Clodius was standing for the 53 B. C.
praetorship,[1] and since Scipio and Hypsaeus obeyed his
influence, their success and his would be a renewed
menace. Writing to his young friend Scribonius Curio,
Cicero urged him to come and give his aid :—' help me in
this anxiety, and devote your zeal to the rescue of my
honour or—to tell the truth—I may almost say my
safety.'[2] But the appeal was vain, for Curio and Clodius
were old friends. The struggle was unprecedently keen.
Not only were lavish bribes distributed, but violent
quarrels were frequent in the streets.[3] Clodius railed
against Milo in the Senate and against Cicero as his
supporter ; Cicero replied with scurrilous abuse.[4] Modern   Bloody
electioneering is not always bloodless ; but in Rome the   conflicts
between
leaders of parties were themselves promoters of sedition.   rival can-
The consuls were wounded in a riot :[5] in a fight which   didates.
took place in the Sacred Way between the armed bands
of Hypsaeus and Milo many of the latter were killed ;
and Cicero himself, if he told the truth, narrowly escaped
with his life.[6] In consequence of these affrays and of the
interference of Pompey, who, since he wished to become
dictator, was determined to prevent the success of Milo,
the elections were again repeatedly postponed ; and   The elec-
when the new year came there were neither consuls   tions postponed.
nor praetors at Rome.[7] Pompey, through the agency of   702 (53
a tribune, Munatius Plancus Bursa, prevented an interrex   B. C.).
from being appointed.[8] But the issue was soon to be
decided in an unexpected way.

On the afternoon of the 18th of January Milo, accom-   Dec. 8,
panied by his wife and followed by a train of gladiators   53 B. C.

---

[1] Ascon., ed. Clark, p. 30, ll. 18–20 (ed. Stangl., p. 30).

[2] Fam., ii, 6, 4. Cf. § 5.

[3] Ascon., ed. Clark, p. 30, ll. 9–10 (ed. Stangl, p. 30) ; Plut., Cato min.,
47, 1 ; Dio, xl, 46, 1. 3.

[4] Schol. Bob., ed. Stangl, p. 169 (ed. Orelli, p. 342).

[5] Dio, xl, 46, 3 ; Schol. Bob. (to fr. xiii of De aere alieno Milonis), ed.
Stangl, p. 172 (ed. Orelli, p. 343).

[6] Pro Mil., 14, 37 ; Ascon., ed. Clark, p. 48, ll. 4–15 (ed. Stangl., p. 41).

[7] Ascon., ed. Clark, p. 30, ll. 20–1 ; p. 31, ll. 1–2 (ed. Stangl, p. 30) ;
Plut., Cato min., 47, 1 ; App., ii, 20, 74 ; Dio, xl. 46.

[8] Ascon., ed. Clark, p. 31, ll. 9–12 (ed. Stangl, pp. 30–1).

53 B. C.
The murder of Clodius.

and slaves, was driving down the Appian Way to assist in a ceremony at Lanuvium, when, near Bovillae, some ten miles from Rome, he met Clodius, who with a few friends and about thirty armed slaves was riding towards Rome. After the two enemies had passed each other Milo's followers began to quarrel with those of Clodius. Hearing the uproar, Clodius turned to look and was instantly speared by one of Milo's gladiators. While the quarrel developed into a battle Clodius was carried into a tavern at Bovillae. Milo, learning that he had been wounded, sent some of his men to break into the house ; and Clodius was dragged out and killed. Then, leaving eleven of his rival's slaves dead upon the road, Milo continued his journey to Lanuvium. An hour or two later a senator, on his way to Rome, found the body of Clodius and conveyed it to the city, where, just after dark, it was laid in the hall of the dead man's mansion on the Palatine. Slaves and freemen of low degree thronged to see it, and the widow, Fulvia, inflamed their anger by exhibiting the wounds. Early next morning the house was again surrounded by a crowd, which, incited by Munatius Plancus and one of his colleagues, Pompeius Rufus, carried the corpse, still naked, to the Forum, and placed it on the Rostra. The two tribunes, joined by another, Sallust, who afterwards became famous as the historian of Catiline, harangued the populace, inveighing against Milo ; and the exasperated mob, carrying the body into the Senate House, made a funeral pile of benches, tables, and books, and set fire to it. The house and an adjoining hall were destroyed by the flames.[1]

Jan. 19, 702
(Dec. 9, 53 B. C.).

On the same day Marcus Aemilius Lepidus, a son of the consul who flouted Sulla, was appointed interrex.[2]

---

[1] Livy, *Epit.*, 107 ; Vell., ii, 47, 4 ; Ascon., ed. Clark, p. 31, ll. 12–26 ; p. 32 ; p. 33, ll. 1–9 ; p. 49, ll. 6–10 (ed. Stangl, pp. 31–2) ; App., ii, 20–1, 74–8 ; Dio, xl, 48, 2 ; 49, 1–2. Sallust had a personal grudge against Milo, who, having caught him in adultery with his wife, thrashed him soundly and forced him to pay for his release (Gell., xvii, 18).

[2] Ascon., ed. Clark, p. 43, ll. 3–4 (ed. Stangl, p. 38) ; Dio, xl, 49, 5. Comparison of the two texts shows that Asconius's *Post biduum* = *altero* or

The partisans of Scipio and Hypsaeus urged him to fix the day for the election, but as it was irregular for the first holder of the office, which was tenable for five days only, to do this, he refused. Thereupon they attacked his house and, though beaten off at first, returned, blockaded him during his official tenure, smashed in the door, and destroyed many of his belongings. When Milo's supporters also clamoured for the election, the besiegers came to blows with them, made an onslaught, which was repulsed, upon Milo's house, and finally thronging to Pompey's suburban residence, shouted that he must be made consul or dictator.[1] Being a proconsul, he could not yet enter the city; but he could well afford to wait, for the Conservatives would be compelled, sooner or later, to appeal to him to stop the growing anarchy.

Meanwhile Milo, who had returned to Rome on the day after the death of Clodius, was resuming his canvass and his bribery; for if he could become consul, he would escape prosecution for the murder. Marcus Caelius, now a tribune, presented him to the multitude in the Forum, and endeavoured to persuade them that Clodius had planned to murder Milo. While Milo was himself speaking, the hostile tribunes with their armed followers rushed into the Forum and attacked his party. He and Caelius managed to escape, but many of their supporters and even quiet citizens whose dress betokened affluence were killed; houses were broken into and plundered; and during several days, while Plancus, Sallust, and Pompeius Rufus daily incited the people against Milo, sedition, murder, pillage prevailed in Rome. Successive *interreges* being unable to hold the election, the Senate at last armed the interrex, the tribunes, and Pompey with extraordinary powers to save the commonwealth, and authorized Pompey to levy troops throughout the whole of Italy.[2]

53 B. C. Anarchy in Rome.

The 'ultimate decree'.

proximo die, that is, the day after—not two days after—the murder. Cf. the first note on *B. G.*, i, 47, 1 in my edition of Caesar.

[1] Ascon., ed. Clark, p. 33, ll. 10-5; p. 43, ll. 3-18 (ed. Stangl, pp. 32, 38); Dio, xl, 49, 3.

[2] Ascon., ed. Clark, p. 33, l. 25; p. 34, ll. 1-6; p. 51, ll. 8-11 (ed. Stangl, pp. 32, 43); Dio, xl, 50, 1. Cf. Caes., *B. G.*, vii, 1, 1. See p. 315.

52 B. C.   This last provision was doubtless made at the instance of Pompey or of his friends, for during the past three years he had had a strong force under arms.

Such was the state of affairs which encouraged the Gauls to rebel.

Pompey appointed sole consul.   Pompey at once proceeded to hold a levy ; but during his absence the rumours about a dictatorship increased, and the general opinion was that unless he were appointed, order could not be restored. The Conservatives, however, led by Cato, believed that it would be safer to adopt a middle course, and after some discussion a resolution was passed by the Senate, on the motion of Marcus Bibulus, that Pompey should be appointed consul without a colleague. Unconstitutional and illegal though the appointment was,[1] even Cato approved it as inevitable : any government, he remarked, was better than anarchy, and Pompey was the fittest man to govern. Pompey was appointed by the interrex, Servius Sulpicius Rufus.[2]

His legislation.   Two days later, in accordance with a senatorial resolution, he promulgated a couple of bills,—one relating to violent crime, with specific reference to the death of Clodius and the burning of the Senate House, the other to electioneering bribery. Under the latter Pompey announced that he intended to increase the existing penalties[3] and to bring to trial all who had offended since his own first consulship.[4] Cato, pointing out that such prosecutions

---

[1] Pompey was legally ineligible for the consulship, even with a colleague, before 45 B.C.

[2] Livy, *Epit.*, 107 ; Val. Max., viii, 15, 8 ; Vell., ii, 47, 3 ; Ascon., ed. Clark, p. 34, ll. 6–7 ; p. 35, ll. 25–6 ; p. 36, ll. 1–5 (ed. Stangl, pp. 32–4) ; Plut., *Pomp.*, 54, 3–5 ; *Cato min.*, 47, 2 ; Suet., 26, 1 ; App. (whose chronology is confused), ii, 23, 84–5 ; Dio, xl, 50, 3–4.

[3] Ascon., ed. Clark, p. 36, ll. 5–10 (ed. Stangl., p. 34).

[4] App., ii, 23, 87 (cf. Plut., *Cato min.*, 48, 2). Clark in his edition of *Pro Milone* (p xii) disbelieves this statement on the grounds that 'it is unlikely that Pompey would wish his own dirty linen to be washed in public' ; that such a measure would not have passed the Senate, which (Suet., 19, 1) was equally guilty ; that Asconius is silent ; and that no trial relating to a date earlier than 54 B.C. is recorded. I cannot, however, discard the circumstantial testimony of Plutarch. Perhaps Drumann (*Gesch. Roms*, ii, 1902, p. 294) was right in conjecturing that Pompey, in deference to the remonstrances of Cato, made his own second consulship (55 B.C.) the limit.

would be endless, and that it would be unjust to punish 52 B. C.
men under a law which they had not broken, urged Pompey, who had sought his advice, to let bygones be bygones ;[1] and, being no respecter of persons, he may well have added that Pompey himself would be liable to trial. When the bills were referred to the Senate, Hortensius urged that the existing laws against bribery were sufficient, and that Milo should be tried before one of the permanent courts ; but Plancus and Sallust interposed their veto,[2] and Pompey intended to adopt a procedure which would make it hopeless to bribe or intimidate the jury. When the bills were submitted to the popular assembly, Caelius insisted that the one which related to crimes of violence was really directed against an individual, Milo, and therefore illegal ; but his knowledge of law was unsound or his comment sophistical,[3] and Pompey declared that if he persisted in his opposition, he would defend the commonwealth by force. The threat was effective, and the bills were passed.[4]

The Clodian tribunes, however, did not abate their hostility to Milo. Determined to prejudice his trial, they attacked not only him, but also Cicero, who was preparing to defend him. Milo was to be prosecuted both for murder and for bribery, and the fourth of April was fixed March 14. for both the trials ; but the judge who was to preside at the latter consented to wait until the former had been Milo tried for murder. concluded. Pompey was careful to select jurors whose character he believed to be above suspicion. Three hundred and sixty were empanelled. The trial was to last four days, on the last of which the number of the jury was to be reduced to eighty-one : immediately before they voted five out of each class were to be rejected respectively by the prosecutors and the defendant ; and the verdict was to be given by the remaining fifty-one. It is perhaps superfluous to point out that the arrangement

[1] Plut., *Cato min.*, 48, 2.
[2] Ascon., ed. Clark, p. 44, ll. 13–21 ; p. 45, l. 1 (ed. Stangl, p. 39).
[3] See vol. i, p. 334, n. 4.
[4] Ascon., ed. Clark, p. 36, ll. 13–7 (ed. Stangl, p. 34).

52 B. C. made bribery virtually impossible. The ex-consul Domitius Ahenobarbus presided. Contrary to the usual practice, the evidence was to be taken on the first three days; and the prosecutors and the counsel for the defence were to address the jury on the last. The Forum, where the trial of course took place, was thronged by the partisans of Clodius. After the first witness for the prosecution had given evidence, Marcus Claudius Marcellus, a staunch Conservative, began to cross-examine him, but was so intimidated by the menaces of the Clodians that the judge allowed him to take refuge on the bench. Hearing the uproar, Pompey, who happened to be sitting in the treasury hard by, assured the judge that on the following day he would himself come to the court with an armed force; and during the next two days the rioters were overawed. On the third day, after the court adjourned, Plancus harangued the people in the Forum, exhorting them to close their shops on the morrow, assemble in their thousands, and let the jurors know that Milo must not be acquitted. Next day piquets were posted by Pompey in the Forum and at all the approaches; and by an edict which he had issued no unauthorized person was allowed to carry arms. He himself, protected by a bodyguard, remained just outside the treasury. Milo, knowing Cicero's temperament and foreseeing what he would have to face, had advised him to remain away until the last moment. During two hours—the allotted time [2]—the prosecutors spoke amid profound silence. Then Cicero rose. Shorthand writers were present, ready to take down his words.[3] The great orator was habitually nervous when he began to speak;[4] but this time he was tried by an ordeal which he had never experienced before, and he was suffering from a sleepless night.[5] Unrestrained by the

Apr. 6 (March 16).

Apr. 7 [1] (March 17).

Cicero breaks down.

---

[1] See pp. 315–6.

[2] Ascon., ed. Clark, p. 36, ll. 12–3 (ed. Stangl, p. 34). Milo's counsel was allowed three hours (ib. and Cic., Brut., 94, 324).

[3] Ascon., ed. Clark, p. 42, l. 2 (ed. Stangl, p. 37); Quint., Inst., iv, 3, 17.

[4] Cic., Div. in Caec., 13, 41; Pro Cluent., 18, 51; Pro Deiot., 1, 1.

[5] Plut., Cic., 35, 2.

presence of the soldiers, the Clodians raised so fierce an uproar that his courage failed : while his client remained impassive, he began to tremble and lost control over his voice. He tried to convince the jury that Clodius had laid an ambuscade for Milo, and that Milo had killed him in self-defence ; but his speech was comparatively a fiasco. Thirty-eight jurors voted against Milo, and only thirteen for his acquittal ; but among them was said to be Cato,[1] who believed that the death of Clodius was a blessing to the state. Milo went to Massilia in exile, and Cicero sent him a copy of the speech which he had consoled himself by writing after the event. The ironical reply is familiar to those who know little more of Roman history : Milo was glad that Cicero had not made that speech in court, or he would never have known the taste of the mullets of Massilia.[2]

Many other prosecutions followed under Pompey's Further laws. So intense was the hatred which Clodius had tions. inspired in the men of business from whom the bulk of the jurymen were taken that the leader of the gang which murdered him, who was defended by Cicero and Caelius, was acquitted, though only by a single vote. Most of those who were condemned belonged to the Clodian faction.[3] Hypsaeus, whose entreaties for protection Pompey contemptuously rejected, was convicted of bribery ;[4] and when Scaurus, who had served Pompey

---

[1] If the story is true, either Cato's voting tablet was seen by a fellow juror or he himself violated his oath ; for under the lex Acilia, l. 44 (C. G. Bruns, Fontes iur. Rom.⁶, 1893, p. 66) every juror was sworn not to divulge his own vote or that of any of his fellows.

[2] Cic., Fam., xv, 4, 12 ; Pliny, xxxiv, 14 (39), 139 ; Vell., ii, 47, 5 ; Ascon., ed. Clark, p. 37, ll. 18–21 ; p. 38, ll. 5–19 ; p. 39, ll. 1–10, 15–27 ; p. 40 ; p. 41, ll. 1–8, 14–8, 24–6 ; p. 42, ll. 1–4 ; p. 52, ll. 11–5 ; p. 53, ll. 11–25 ; p. 54, ll. 1–3, 9–20 (ed. Stangl, pp. 34–7, 44–5) ; Plut., Pomp., 55, 5 ; Cic., 35, 2–3 ; Dio (who wrongly says that Milo was not condemned for bribery), xl, 53, 2–3 ; 54, 2.

[3] Ascon., ed. Clark, p. 32, ll. 11–2 ; p. 54, l. 22 ; pp. 55, 56, ll. 1–5 (ed. Stangl, pp. 31, 45–6) ; App., ii, 24, 89 ; Dio, xl, 53, 1. 'That Pompey', says Mommsen (Röm. Gesch., iii⁸, 1889, p. 340 [Eng. tr., v. 1908, p. 149]), 'in order to appear impartial, did not prevent their condemnation was sheer folly' !

[4] Plut., Pomp., 55, 5 ; App., ii, 24, 90 ; Dio, xl, 53, 1–2.

52 B. C.   well, was tried for the same offence, Pompey insisted that the trial must take its course, which led to condemnation. But cool observers noted that when Pompey did not interfere, it was not from impartiality, perhaps also that he was less successful than his absent rival in protecting those whom he thought it expedient to assist. When his father-in-law, Scipio, was about to be tried for bribery, he summoned the jurors to his house and requested them to favour him, whereupon the prosecution was abandoned; but Plancus, who amongst others was charged with complicity in the burning of the Senate House, was less fortunate. Pompey, openly violating a clause in his own law, sent a letter to the jury, in which he eulogized the defendant and asked for an acquittal. Cato, who protested against the production of the document, stopped his ears while it was being read. It failed of its effect. Cicero was the prosecutor, and Plancus was convicted. ' I hated him ', wrote Cicero in his exultation, ' much more than even that scoundrel Clodius.' [1]

Caesar returns to Gaul.

Caesar had not awaited these events. He raised recruits throughout Cisalpine Gaul to repair the wastage in his legions, and when he learned that ' through the energy of Pompey the situation in the capital had improved ',[2] he returned with them to stem the Gallic insurrection.

[1] *Fam.*, vii, 2, 3 ; Plut., *Pomp.*, 55, 3-4 ; *Cato min.*, 48, 3 ; Dio, xl, 55, 1. 4.

[2] *B. G.*, vii, 6, 1. In 1, 1 Caesar connects his own levy with the senatorial decree which authorized Pompey to raise troops ; but the decree, so far as we know, had no relation to Caesar, who certainly acted on his own responsibility. C. E. C. Schneider may, however, be right in supposing that he raised recruits partly to help Pompey. See the note in my edition of the *Bellum Gallicum*, p. 271.

CHAPTER XII

THE REBELLION OF VERCINGETORIX.—
COMPLETION OF THE CONQUEST OF GAUL

THE story of the riots that followed the murder of Clodius was of course embellished by the imagination of the Gauls; and at the final meeting of the conspirators a definite plan was formed. The great object was to prevent Caesar from rejoining his army. They persuaded themselves that there would be no difficulty in doing this; for the generals who commanded the legions would not venture to leave their quarters in Caesar's absence, and Caesar could not make his way to the legions for want of a sufficient escort. The question was put :—who would take his life in his hand, and strike the first blow for fatherland and freedom ? He might count upon receiving a liberal reward. The chiefs of the Carnutes instantly responded to the appeal, only requiring a solemn assurance that their fellows would not leave them in the lurch. Making a sheaf of their military standards—a religious ceremony of the most awful import —the assembled leaders swore to be true to their countrymen ; and a date was fixed for the insurrection to begin.

Cenabum, the chief town of the Carnutes and the dépôt for the grain that came from the plain of La Beauce and down the Loire from the fertile Limagne d'Auvergne, stood upon the site now occupied by Orléans. Some Roman corn brokers were settled there, and one of Caesar's commissariat officers. When the appointed day came round, a band of the Carnutes, led by two desperadoes, Cotuatus and Conconnetodumnus, rushed into the town, massacred the Romans, and plundered their stores. The tidings spread swiftly through the length and breadth of Gaul ; for whenever an important event occurred, the

52 B. C
bystanders made it known by loud shouts, and those who heard them passed on the cry over the country-side. When Cenabum was attacked, it was just sunrise. By eight o'clock that night the news, flying from man to man, had reached the country of the Arverni, a hundred and forty miles to the south.

The news reaches the Arverni.

Gergovia.

Gergovia, the chief stronghold of this people, was situated on a mountain, two thousand four hundred feet above the sea and four miles south of the gently sloping eminence now covered by the streets of Clermont Ferrand. The vast plain of the Limagne, watered by the Allier and backed by the distant range of Le Forez, extended on the north-east : beyond wooded hills and valleys on the west, its summit crowned by the holiest sanctuary of Gallic worship, towered the huge blunt cupola of the Puy de Dôme ; and all around, as far as the eye could reach, rose the cones of the volcanic land where the Arvernian mountaineers had made their home.

Vercinge-torix, not-with-standing the oppo-sition of the Ar-vernian govern-ment, rouses popular enthusi-asm for rebellion.

At that time there was living in the town a young noble named Vercingetorix, who had shared in the counsels of the conspirators, and had perhaps been chosen as their head. Caesar had already discerned his ability and attempted to purchase his support.[1] His father, Celtillus, had been the most powerful chief in Gaul ; but he had tried to restore the detested monarchy, and had paid for his ambition with his life. The boy, we may believe, like other youths of gentle birth, had been schooled in Druidical lore ; and doubtless his imagination had been fired by the bards who at his father's table sang the brave deeds of Arvernian heroes.[2] For six years his fellow-tribesmen had watched the conquest of Gaul, doing nothing which the conqueror thought worthy of record, only sending their yearly contingent to swell his cavalry. But the Arvernians had been the first to withstand Roman invasion ; and he would lead them in a last effort to shake off the Roman yoke. We may be sure that, like Hannibal, he prayed his gods to bless his mission ; for

---

[1] Dio, xl, 41, 1.
[2] See *Anc. Britain*, p. 266 and n. 4.

religion had its part in every act of Gallic life. When the 52 b. c.
news from Cenabum arrived he summoned his retainers,
and communicated to them his plans. Their passions
were easily inflamed, and they answered with alacrity
the call to arms. The leading men, however, among
whom was a brother of Celtillus, regarded the movement
as quixotic, and ordered the young chief to leave the
town. But Vercingetorix persevered. He took into his
pay all the outcasts and desperadoes in the district. He
went from village to village and harangued the people ;
and all who listened caught the fire of his enthusiasm.
At the head of his levies he returned to Gergovia, and
banished the chiefs who had lately banished him. His   Most of
adherents saluted him as king. He sent out his envoys   the tribes
                                                          between
in all directions : soon nearly every tribe in Western Gaul   the Seine
from the Seine to the Garonne joined the movement ;   and the
                                                          Garonne
and the impressionable Celts, recognizing Vercingetorix   join him,
as the man of destiny who was to save their country,   and elect
                                                          him Com-
unanimously bestowed upon him the chief command.[1]   mander-
                                                          in-Chief.
He levied from each state a definite quota of troops and
of hostages, and ordered each to manufacture a definite   How he
quantity of weapons by a fixed day. He knew that the   raised an
                                                          army.
tribal militiamen would be of little use except for guerrilla
warfare, and therefore devoted all his efforts to strengthening his cavalry. Waverers and laggards he soon brought
to their senses by ruthless severity. Torture or the stake
punished grave breaches of discipline ; while minor
offenders were sent home with their ears lopped off or
an eye gouged out, to serve as a warning to their neighbours. These methods were effective. An army was
speedily raised ; and the bulk of the Celtican patriots
were united, for the first time, under one great leader.

It must not, however, be supposed that even now the   The dis-
movement was general. Even in the insurgent tribes—   sentient
                                                          tribes.
even among the Senones and Carnutes—the Nationalists

---

[1] Caesar does not say that the conspirators chose Vercingetorix as their
head, though his narrative suggests that they did. Perhaps mutual jealousy
prevented them from choosing any one : if they chose Vercingetorix, their
choice was evidently confirmed by a general council.

52 B. C.   must have had to reckon with adherents of Rome. The Aedui, jealous of their old rivals, the Arverni, and not prepared to break with Caesar, still kept aloof : the tribes who looked up to them remained passive. The Remi and the Lingones had long since made their choice ; and from them and their dependants no help was to be expected. The Treveri, enfeebled by the chastisement which Labienus had inflicted, were distracted by German raids ; and the other eastern tribes, if their hearts were with the insurgents, were severed from them by the Roman army. The Aquitanians took no heed of what was going on among the aliens beyond the Garonne. The Belgae had been terribly punished for their late rebellion ; and either for this reason or because they were jealous of their Celtican kindred, they left them alone. It remained to be seen whether Vercingetorix would be able, by the spell of his personality or by the victories which he might gain, to rouse the whole people into united action.

The mission of Lucterius.   His first step was to send a chief named Lucterius, the most daring of his lieutenants, to deal with the Ruteni, who dwelt in the district, bordering on the Roman Province, which is now called Aveyron. If they and their neighbours, the Nitiobroges, could be induced to join, the Province would be exposed to invasion ; Caesar would be obliged to succour it, and his separation from his army would be indefinitely prolonged. Vercingetorix himself moved northward with the remainder of the force into the great plain of the Berri, which belonged to the Bituriges, hoping to detach them from the Aedui, whose supremacy they recognized, and to link them with the Carnutes, the Senones, and his other allies in the north. The Bituriges at once sent envoys to the Aedui to ask for help ; and the Aedui, on the advice of Caesar's generals, dispatched infantry and cavalry to their assistance. The troops marched to the banks of the Loire, which separated the two peoples, halted there for a few days, and then returned. They excused themselves to the Roman generals on the plea that they had had reason

to fear that, if they crossed the river, the Bituriges would
combine with the Arverni to surround them.   Caesar
could never find out whether their plea was true or false.   The Bitu-
Directly after they had turned their backs the Bituriges   riges join
threw in their lot with Vercingetorix.   torix.

But what was Labienus doing ?   Did he make no   Why did
attempt to crush the rebellion before his chief could   Labienus
return ?   He had already paralysed the activity of Com-   the
mius ; and if he did not stir, it was not from lack of   field ?
initiative.   Perhaps, as he expected that Caesar would
soon arrive, he judged it best to do nothing that might
derange his plans.   But there is a sentence in the narrative
of Hirtius, Caesar's friend and secretary, which may
supply the clue.[1]   At the very outset of the revolt,
Drappes, a chieftain of the Senones, called his slaves
to arms, reinforced them with a band of outlaws and
brigands, and succeeded in cutting off some Roman convoys.   Caesar never mentions him ; and it is clear that
he struck before Caesar returned.   May we infer that in
the short space in which Labienus was free to act he
could not take the field because the supplies on which
he counted did not come ?

When Caesar reached the Province, his first difficulty,   How shall
as the conspirators had foreseen, was to rejoin his army.   Caesar
The legions were quartered at Agedincum, on the plateau   his le-
of Langres, and in the neighbourhood of Trèves, two   gions ?
hundred miles and more to the north.   If he were to
send for them, they would be compelled to fight a battle
as they marched southwards, and he was unwilling to
trust the issue to his lieutenants`: on the other hand, it
would be foolhardy for him, with only a slender escort,
to attempt to make his way to them.   Even the Aedui
were believed to be untrustworthy ; while Lucterius had
just won over the Ruteni and the Nitiobroges, and, having
raised fresh levies, was threatening to cross the Tarn and
descend upon the opulent city of Narbo.   Hastening   [Nar-
thither, Caesar assured the anxious provincials that there   bonne.]
was no cause for alarm, and posted detachments, drawn

[1] B. G., viii, 30, 1.

52 B. C.

He
rescues
the Pro-
vince :
from the native troops who garrisoned the Province, in
the surrounding country and also in the districts round
Toulouse, Albi, and Nîmes. Having thus checkmated
Lucterius, he went to join his new levies, which had been
ordered to concentrate in the country of the Helvii,
a Provincial tribe who dwelt in the Vivarais, on the
eastern side of the Cevennes. He now saw his way to
reach the army. Beyond the Cevennes lay the country
of Vercingetorix—undefended, for Vercingetorix was in
the Berri, a hundred miles away. But the mountain
tracks were buried beneath snow, and no one had ever
before attempted the journey under such conditions.
Nevertheless Caesar advanced. Moving up the valley of
the Ardèche, he made for the watershed between the

crosses
the Ce-
vennes,
invades
Auvergne,
and forces
Vercinge-
torix to
come to
its relief :
sources of the Allier and the Loire.[1] By prodigious efforts
the men shovelled aside the snow ;[2] and the Arverni,
who had never dreamed that any one would venture to
cross their mountain barrier, were astounded to see the
Romans descending into the plains. Caesar's horsemen
swept over the country in small parties, burning villages
and ravaging the farms. The news soon spread ; and
Vercingetorix, reluctantly yielding to the entreaties of his
tribesmen, hurried to the rescue. This was just what
Caesar had anticipated. Now that the rebel army was
withdrawn, he might with comparative safety travel
northward to join his legions ; and so confident was he
in the soundness of his forecast that, before he learned
that Vercingetorix had commenced his march, he acted
as if he had done so. He left Decimus Brutus with the
troops to occupy the enemy's attention ;[3] and for fear
his design might become known, he announced that he
was only going to procure reinforcements, and would
return within three days. Then, passing between the
Cevennes and the mountains of the Forez, he hastened

[1] *Caesar's Conquest of Gaul²*, 1911, p. 134, n. 1.
[2] A photograph in the *Rev. des études anciennes* (xii, 1910, p. 85) of a snow-drift, taken in the Col du Pal, shows that we need not suspect Caesar of exaggeration when he says (*B. G.*, vii, 8, 2) that the snow was six feet deep.
[3] Probably Brutus, after he had fulfilled his mission, retreated to the Province.

to Vienna on the Rhône; picked up there a body of Provincial cavalry,[1] which he had sent on in advance to wait for him; pushed on up the valley of the Saône as swiftly as horses could carry him,[2] hoping to elude the Aedui, in case they were hostile; rejoined the legions which he had left near Langres; and, before Vercingetorix knew where he was, concentrated the whole army in the neighbourhood of Agedincum.

Vercingetorix, however, quickly recovered from this surprise. Not far from the confluence of the Allier and the Loire, there was a town called Gorgobina, belonging to the Boi, whom, it will be remembered, Caesar had placed in dependence upon the Aedui. To strike at Caesar's allies would be equivalent to striking at Caesar himself. Vercingetorix accordingly prepared to besiege this stronghold. Caesar was again in a dilemma. If he left Gorgobina to its fate, the tribes that still remained loyal would conclude that he could not be relied upon to protect his friends, and would therefore probably join the rebels. If, on the other hand, he undertook a campaign so early in the year, the army would be in danger of starvation; for, owing to the severity of the weather, it was very difficult to transport supplies. But anything was better than to lose the confidence of his allies. He must trust to the Aedui to provide grain, and take what he could get from the enemy's magazines. Leaving two legions at Agedincum to guard his heavy baggage, and sending messengers to tell the Boi that he was coming and encourage them to hold out, he marched for Gorgobina. Instead, however, of taking the direct route southward, he intended to go round by way of Cenabum; for, although time was precious, it was of paramount importance to punish, first of all, the people who had been the first to rebel, and who, by the massacre of Roman citizens, had outraged the majesty of Rome.[3] Moreover,

52 B. C. then seizes the opportunity to rejoin his army.

About March 7 (Feb. 15)? Vercingetorix besieges Gorgobina.

Caesar marches from Agedincum (Sens) to relieve it:

---

[1] *Caesar's Conquest of Gaul[2]*, p. 581.   [2] *Ib.*, p. 136, n. 2.

[3] This seems a sufficient explanation of Caesar's having made a détour; but it is possible that if there were any bridges over the Loire above Cenabum, Vercingetorix had destroyed them. See also Meusel's second note on *B. G.*, vii, 11, 1.

by ravaging the lands of the Carnutes and Bituriges, he might count on forcing Vercingetorix to relax his hold on Gorgobina. His cavalry were comparatively weak, for some of the tribes which in former years had furnished contingents were now in revolt ; but he had reinforced his Gallic and Spanish horsemen by four hundred Germans, whose value he had first recognized in the campaign against Ariovistus. At the close of the second day's march he laid siege to Vellaunodunum, a stronghold of the Senones, probably on the site of the modern Montargis, in order to avoid leaving an enemy in his rear, who captures might obstruct the movement of his convoys. In three Vellauno- dunum days the garrison surrendered, and Caesar pushed on across the forest of Orléans for Cenabum, which he reached in two long marches. The Loire was spanned by a bridge, the northern end of which could only be reached from within the town. The Carnutes, who had expected that Vellaunodunum would hold out longer, were not prepared to resist, and tried to escape in the night over the bridge : but Caesar, foreseeing their attempt, had kept two legions captures under arms ; the gates were instantly fired, and the town and punishes seized ; and as the thronging masses were struggling Cenabum : forward through the narrow streets, the legions fell upon them, and almost all were taken prisoners.[1] The booty was given up to the soldiers ; the town was set ablaze ; and the army passed over the bridge and moved on to crosses relieve Gorgobina. Noviodunum, which lay on their line the Loire, and of march, promptly surrendered. Hostages had been captures delivered up, and centurions were collecting arms and Novio- dunum ; horses when the cavalry of Vercingetorix, who had hurriedly raised the siege of Gorgobina, were descried in the distance. Seizing the weapons which they had begun to pile, the townsmen manned the walls and tried to shut the gates ; but the centurions were too quick for them, and with swords drawn withdrew their men unharmed. The rebel cavalry, who were beginning to overpower Caesar's Gallic levies, scattered before the charge of the

---

[1] *Caesar's Conquest of Gaul*[2], p. 138, n. 1.   Cf. Meusel's note on *B. G.*, vii, 11, 8.

German squadron ; the baffled townsmen again surrendered ; and Caesar marched southward for Avaricum,
the capital of the Bituriges, now occupied by the famous
cathedral city of Bourges.

So far Vercingetorix had met with a succession of
disasters. But his spirit was indomitable, and he knew
how to learn from experience. He saw that the war
must be conducted on a totally different principle.
Nothing was to be gained by defending towns which
could offer no resistance ; and it was hopeless to encounter
the Romans in the open field. But he had thousands of
light horse who could scour the country and cut off their
supplies. The grass was not yet grown ; months must
elapse before the corn could ripen ; and although Caesar
had probably found grain in the towns which he had
captured,[1] he could only replenish his stores by sending
out detached parties to rifle the granaries. Vercingetorix
called his officers together, and told them his plans. They
must hunt down the Roman foragers wherever they could
find them, and attack the baggage-train. They must
make up their minds to sacrifice their own interests for
the national weal. Every hamlet, every barn where the
enemy could find provender, must be burned to the
ground. Even the towns must be destroyed, save those
which were impregnable, lest they should tempt men who
ought to be in the field to go to them for shelter, and
lest the Romans should plunder their stores. This might
sound very hard ; but it would be far harder for them
to be slain while their wives and children were sold into
slavery ; and if they were beaten, this would inevitably
be their doom. This uncompromising speech was greeted
with unanimous applause. Within a single day more
than twenty villages in the Berri were burned down ;
and all round the great plain, wherever the Romans
looked, the sky was aglow. But Vercingetorix could only
govern by character and tact ; and, though he might
venture to be severe, he could not afford to lose his
popularity. The question was raised, whether Avaricum

[1] *B. G.*, vii, 14, 9. Cf. C. Jullian, *Hist. de la Gaule*, iii, 1909, p. 441.

52 B. C. should be defended, or destroyed like the lesser towns.
But, con- The Bituriges were not restrained by the sense of dis-
trary to
his advice, cipline ; and their spokesmen eloquently pleaded their
they re- cause. Their capital was wellnigh the finest town in the
solve to
defend whole of Gaul ; and, moreover, its position was so strong
Avaricum. that they could easily defend it. Vercingetorix strongly
opposed their appeal ; but they pleaded so pathetically,
and their brother chiefs showed such sympathy with
them, that he was obliged to give way. Following Caesar
by easy stages, he finally halted about fourteen miles
north-east of Avaricum,[1] on a strong position, from which
he could communicate with the garrison and harass the
besiegers.

Siege of Avaricum was surrounded, on every side except the
Avaricum. south, by marshes intersected by sluggish streams. On
the south-east it was approached by a natural causeway,
which, about a hundred yards from the wall, suddenly
shelved down so as to form a kind of huge moat. Behind
this neck of land Caesar pitched his camp. As the marshes
rendered it impossible to invest the position, he proceeded
to construct a terrace, by which picked troops were
ultimately to advance to the assault. The flanking parts
were to serve as viaducts, to carry the towers in which
artillery was placed ; and it is probable that the platform
intended for the columns of assault occupied only the
front portion of the intervening space. The artillerymen
who manned the towers kept their catapults playing upon
the defenders of the wall. When the viaducts were completed, the towers could be moved backwards or forwards
along the surface ; while the sheds which had protected
the workmen were ranged on either side, and served as
a means of safe communication. The central mound was
probably raised higher than the other two, in order to
facilitate the assault ; and sheds were placed upon it
also, to screen the assailants from observation and attack.

Meanwhile the new policy of Vercingetorix was beginning to make itself felt. Organized patrols kept him
informed of Caesar's movements, and conveyed his

[1] *Caesar's Conquest of Gaul*[2], pp. 742-3.

instructions to the garrison. Whenever the Romans went 52 B. C.
out to forage or procure corn, his horsemen kept them
in sight, and attacked them if they ventured to disperse.
Caesar did all that ingenuity could suggest to baffle him,
sending the men out at odd times and in varying directions ; but the enemy seemed ubiquitous. Supplies were
running short, and Caesar called upon the Aedui and the
Boi for corn ; but the Aedui were half-hearted, and the
Boi, though they did their best, had little to give. For
several days the soldiers had no bread, and were obliged
to kill the cattle, driven in from distant villages, in order
to subsist at all. Caesar went among them as they worked
upon the terrace, and did all that he could to keep up
their spirits. He would abandon the siege, he told them
(for he knew their temper), if they found the want of
their accustomed food too hard to bear. But they would
not hear of such a thing. They reminded him that they
had fought under his command for six years with un-
tarnished honour, never abandoning any operation which
they had undertaken ; and they would cheerfully endure
every hardship if only they could avenge the massacre
at Cenabum.

Vercingetorix, when his provender was consumed,
moved several miles nearer the town. Some prisoners
reported that he had left his infantry in their new encampment, and gone with his cavalry to lie in wait for the
Roman foragers in the place where he expected that they
would be found on the following day. Caesar imagined
an opportunity, and marched at midnight to attack the
encampment. But the enemy, well served by their
patrols, removed their wagons and baggage into the
recesses of a wood ; and in the early morning Caesar
found them securely posted on a hill surrounded by a belt
of morass, not more than fifty feet wide. They had
broken down the causeways which spanned the morass,
and posted piquets opposite the places where it was
fordable. The legionaries clamoured for the signal to
advance ; but Caesar told them that victory could only
be purchased by the slaughter of many gallant men, and

that their lives were more precious to him than his own reputation. For the first, but not for the last time they had been forced to abandon an operation which they had begun ; and perhaps when Caesar led them back to resume the labour of the siege, he suspected that he had himself been duped.[1]

Vercingetorix, on returning to the encampment, was accused of treachery. His officers told him to his face that he would never have left them without a leader, exposed to that well-timed attack, if he had not intended to betray them. He ought never to have moved from his original position. It was plain enough that he wanted to reign as Caesar's creature, not by the choice of his countrymen. Vercingetorix was at no loss for an answer. He had moved, he reminded them, at their own request, simply in order to get forage ; and they had not been in the slightest danger, for the position in which he had left them was impregnable. He had purposely refrained from delegating his command to any one, for fear they should worry his substitute into risking a battle ; for he knew that they had not resolution enough to adhere to a system of warfare which required patient toil. They ought to be thankful that the Romans had tried to attack them, because they could now see for themselves what cowards the Romans were. He had no need to beg Caesar for a kingdom which he could win for himself by the sword ; and they might take back their gift if they imagined that they were doing him a favour, and not indebted to him for their safety. ' And now ', he said, ' to satisfy yourselves that what I say is true, listen to Roman soldiers.' Some camp-followers, whom he had captured a few days before, and had kept on starvation diet, were then told to step forward. They had been carefully drilled in the part which they were to play. Questioned by Vercingetorix, they stated that they were legionaries, and had secretly left the camp in the hope of finding something to eat ; that their comrades, one and all, were half-starved and too weak to get through

[1] *Caesar's Conquest of Gaul*[2], pp. 744-5.

their work ; and that Caesar had made up his mind, 52 B. C. unless within three days he had achieved some tangible results, to abandon the siege. ' You see ', said Vercinge-torix, ' I—I whom you call a traitor—have brought this mighty army, without the loss of a drop of your blood, to the verge of starvation. No course is open to them but an ignominious retreat, and I have arranged that not a single tribe shall give them refuge.' Clashing their weapons, as their custom was, the tribesmen swore that Vercingetorix was the greatest of generals, and that they would trust him through thick and thin. They realized how much was staked upon the safety of Avaricum ; and ten thousand picked men were sent into the town.

In devising expedients to baffle the operations of the besiegers the Gauls showed a resourcefulness which astonished Caesar. ' They are a most ingenious people ', he remarked, ' and always show the greatest aptitude in borrowing and giving effect to ideas which they get from any one.' [1] The wall, compacted with transverse balks and longitudinal beams of timber, was too tough to be breached by the battering ram ; and, being also largely composed of stone and rubble, it was proof against fire. The Roman engineers used powerful hooks, riveted to stout poles, to loosen and drag down the stones. These hooks the garrison seized with nooses ; and then, by means of windlasses, pulled them up over the wall. They made daily sorties, fired the woodwork of the terrace, and harassed the workers by frequent attacks. They erected towers along the wall, in imitation of those of the besiegers, and filled them with archers and slingers. They drove galleries under the terrace, and dragged away the timber of which it was composed ; and, assailing the Roman sappers with sharp stakes, heavy stones, and boiling pitch, they stopped the galleries by which they were approaching to undermine the wall.[2]

The siege had lasted twenty-five days ; and, in spite of numbing cold and drenching rains and harassing opposi-

---

[1] *B. G.*, vii, 22, 1.
[2] *Caesar's Conquest of Gaul*[2], pp. 600–2.

tion, the legionaries had built up the terrace, three hundred and thirty feet wide and eighty feet high, till it almost reached the wall. About midnight, when they were putting the finishing touches to the work, a cloud of smoke was seen rising above it. Some miners had burrowed underneath, and set the woodwork on fire. A yell of exultation rang from the town. Flaming brands shot down from the wall ; pitch and logs were flung on to the blaze ; and the enemy's masses came streaming through the gates. But Caesar, who had been personally superintending the workmen, was on the spot. Two legions regularly bivouacked in front of the camp, ready for emergencies ; and while some cohorts threw themselves upon the enemy, others drew back the towers out of reach or dragged asunder the timbers of the terrace to save the hinder part of it from being ignited ; others again endeavoured to quench the flames. More than once, however, it seemed that the Gauls were winning ; and Caesar himself was moved to admiration by their stubborn valour. He saw a man taking lumps of fat and pitch from his comrades, and flinging them into the flames. A bolt from a catapult pierced him, and he fell dead. Another man stepped across his prostrate body, and took his place. He, too, was struck : but in a moment a third was doing his work, and presently a fourth ; nor was the post abandoned until the Romans finally extinguished the fire, and the Gauls, beaten at every point, were forced back into the town.

Vercingetorix, seeing that it was useless now to prolong the defence, sent word to the garrison to slip out in the dark and come to his camp. They were confident that the marshes would prevent the Romans from getting at them. Night came on ; and the men, gathered in the streets and open places, were just starting when suddenly, rushing out of their houses, women flung themselves weeping at their husbands' feet, and besought them not to abandon them and the children who belonged to father and mother alike to the vengeance of the Romans. Deaf to their entreaties, the men pressed on. Frantic with

terror, the women screamed and gesticulated, to put the 52 B. C.
besiegers on their guard ; and the men, fearing that the
Roman cavalry would block the roads, abandoned their
attempt.

Next day Caesar completed the repair of the terrace, Storming
and moved forward one of the towers. Rain fell in of Avari-
torrents ; and noticing that the guards on the wall were cum.
posted carelessly, he determined to deliver the assault.
The workmen were told to loiter, in order to put the
garrison off their guard. The troops were concealed within
and in the rear of the sheds which stood upon the terrace.[1]
Caesar harangued them, and promised rewards to those
who should be the first to mount the wall. The artillerymen in the tower made play with their engines, to give
their comrades every chance. The signal was given.
Instantly the columns, darting forth from their cover,
streamed over the front of the terrace and swarmed up
the ladders ; and, panic-stricken and confounded, the
defenders were overborne and driven down on to the
space below. Quickly rallying, they formed up in compact wedge-shaped masses, resolute to fight it out if they
should be attacked. But the Romans were too wary to
attack them. They lined the wall all round ; and not
a man of them would come down. Throwing away their
weapons, the Gauls ran for their lives through the town
to its furthest extremity ; and there many, jostling one
another in the narrow gateways, were slaughtered, while
others, who shouldered their way out, were cut down by
the cavalry. Plunder was forgotten. Exasperated by the Indis-
long weariness of the siege, burning to avenge the massacre criminate
at Cenabum, the Romans slew the aged, they slew women massacre.
and infants, and spared none. Some forty thousand
human beings—all but eight hundred who made their way
to the camp of Vercingetorix—perished on that day.

It was late at night when the survivors approached the
camp. Vercingetorix, fearing that their pitiable plight
might arouse the sympathies of his turbulent host and
lead to disturbance and subversion of discipline, sent out

[1] *Caesar's Conquest of Gaul*[2], pp. 749-51.

the leading men of the several tribes to which they belonged, who waited for them on the road, and conducted them in separate groups to their several quarters

Vercinge-torix consoles his troops.

in the camp. Next day he called the united host together, and addressed them. They must not, he said, be disheartened ; for no experienced warrior would expect invariable success. The Romans had not beaten them in fair fight : they had merely stolen an advantage over them by superior science. As they all knew, he had never approved of defending Avaricum ; but he would soon repair the loss. He would gain over all the dissentient tribes to the cause ; and against a united Gaul the whole world could not stand in arms. Meanwhile he had a right to expect that in future they should adopt the Roman custom of regularly fortifying their camps. The multitude could not but admire his cheery courage : they could not but admit that the event had proved his foresight ; and they respected him because he had had the courage to confront them in the hour of defeat, when another leader might not have dared to show his face. So far then from lessening, the disaster only increased the estimation in which he was held.

He raises fresh levies.

He immediately set to work to fulfil his promise. Agents, chosen for their eloquence and tact, bore lavish bribes and still more lavish promises to the dissentient chiefs. New weapons and new clothing were provided for the survivors of the siege. New levies, including large numbers of bowmen, were speedily raised ; and Teutomatus, King of the Nitiobroges, though his father had been honoured by the Senate, hastened to join Vercingetorix with his own cavalry and with others whom he had hired from the Aquitanians. Thus the losses which had been incurred at Avaricum were made good ; while those who had already fought under Vercingetorix had learned a salutary lesson, and, in spite of their natural laziness and impatience of discipline, were in the humour to do or to suffer whatever he might command.

Winter was nearly over. The hungry Romans found an abundance of corn in Avaricum ; and Caesar remained there a few days to recruit their strength. The Gauls, in their new-born zeal, had entrenched their camp ; but, if he could not lure them into the open, he would blockade and force them to surrender. Suddenly his attention was distracted by serious news from the Aedui. Two chiefs, Cotus and Convictolitavis, were contending for the first magistracy, each insisting that he had been legally elected : their retainers were up in arms ; and a civil war was imminent. A deputation of leading men begged Caesar to arbitrate. He saw that it was of vital importance to prevent the weaker side from appealing for aid to Vercingetorix, and accordingly, though he was most reluctant to delay his operations, summoned the rivals and the council to meet him at Decetia, or Décize, on the Loire. Finding that Cotus had been nominated by his brother, the late Vergobret, in defiance of an Aeduan law which prescribed that no man should hold office while any member of his family who had done so survived, he settled the dispute in favour of Convictolitavis, who had been appointed with the sanction of the Druids. Before dismissing the council, he urged them to forget their differences, and told them that, if they wanted to share in the spoils of victory, they must help to suppress the insurrection. He should require ten thousand foot to guard his convoys, and all their cavalry. Then, sending Labienus with four legions, including the two that had been left at Agedincum, to reduce the Senones and Parisii, he marched southward with the remaining six up the eastern bank of the Allier, to strike a blow at Gergovia,— the heart of the rebellion.

On the hill now crowned by the cathedral of Nevers, which rises above the Loire, in the peninsula formed by its confluence with the Nièvre, was an Aeduan town called Noviodunum. Caesar had marked the strength of the position, and here he established his chief magazine ; but he could not spare a force sufficient to make it secure.

Vercingetorix was still on the western bank of the Allier. As soon as he heard of Caesar's advance he broke down all the bridges, but left the lower parts of the

Caesar, at the request of the Aedui, decides between rival claimants for the office of Vergobret.

He sends Labienus to suppress rebellion in the basin of the Seine, and marches to attack Gergovia.

He establishes a magazine at Noviodunum (Nevers) :

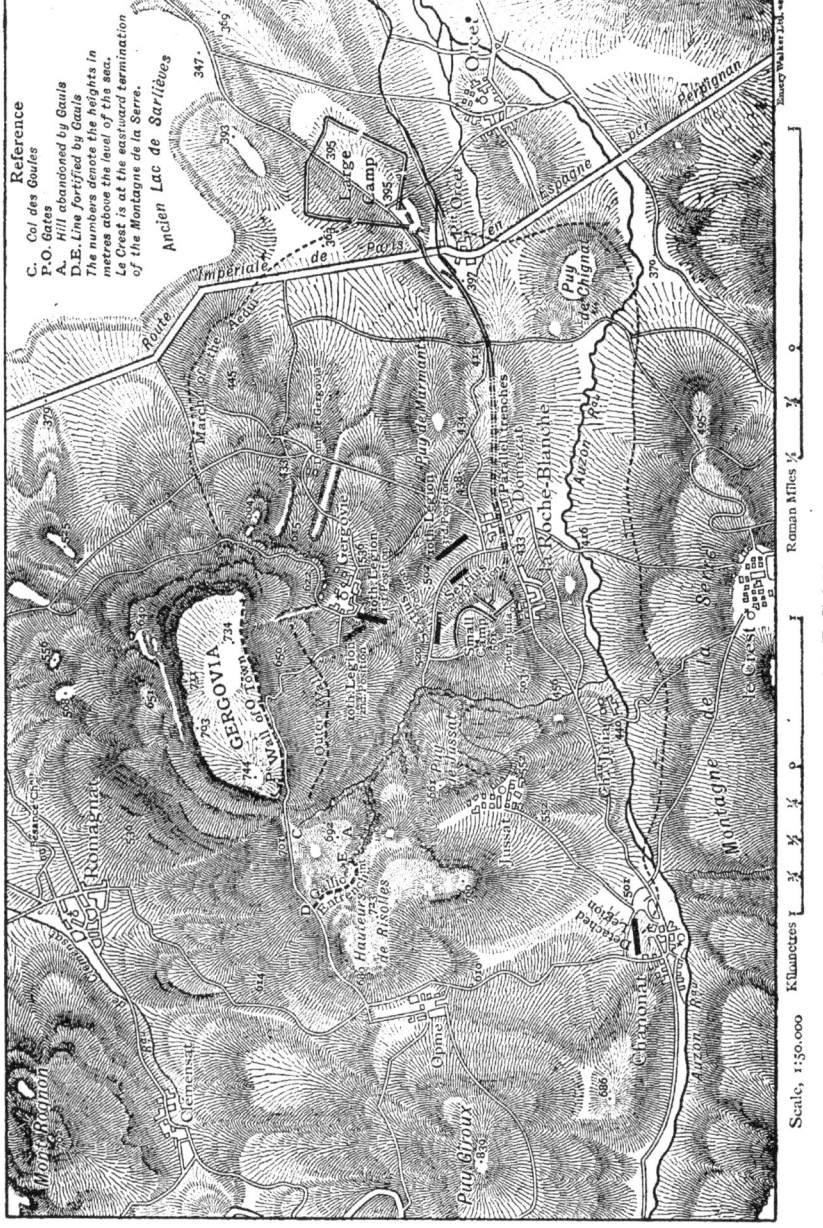

Reference

C. Col des Goules
P.O Gates
A. Hill abandoned by Gauls
D.E. Line fortified by Gauls
The numbers denote the heights in
metres above the level of the sea.
Le Crest is at the eastward termination
of the Montagne de la Serre.

Ancien Lac de Sarlièves

GERGOVIA

Scale, 1:30.000 Kilometres 1 ¾ ½ ¼ 0 1 Roman Miles ½ ¼ 0 1

piles intact. The two armies moved in full view of one
another, with the river between them. The Gallic patrols
were so vigilant that Caesar found it impossible to repair
any of the bridges ; and he began to fear that he might
be barred by the river during the entire summer. But
Vercingetorix had not yet learned the necessity of watching his rear. One evening, Caesar encamped on a wooded crosses
spot, opposite one of the bridges. Next morning he the Allier by a
took forty out of the sixty cohorts composing his force ; strata-
arrayed them in six divisions, so that, seen from a dis- gem ;
tance, they would look like the six legions ; and ordered
them to make a long march on with the entire baggage-
train. Vercingetorix suspected nothing. Caesar remained
behind with the rest of the force, waiting for the hour
when, as he calculated, the four legions and the enemy
should have encamped for the night. Then he set the
men whom he had kept behind to work at the repair
of the bridge. When it was finished, he made them cross
over, and sent for the other cohorts. Vercingetorix,
finding that he had been outwitted, and unwilling to risk
a battle, hurried on southward by prodigious marches.

Caesar followed more leisurely, and moving across the
level expanse of the Limagne, found himself, early on
the fifth day, approaching the mountain of Gergovia.
He had committed himself to a task the magnitude of
which he had neglected or had failed to estimate. Rising
on his right front, fully twelve hundred feet above the
plain, the northern face, with its upper terraces broken
here and there by precipices, manifestly defied attack ;
and, as he moved on past the long spurs, he saw that the
eastern side, steep, rugged, and scored by deep ravines,
was equally unassailable. His cavalry were soon engaged
in a skirmish ; and in the afternoon he reconnoitred the
stronghold from the south. The town stood on an oblong
plateau, which formed the summit, extending about seven
furlongs from east to west, and six hundred yards wide.
The higher terraces, and also the outlying heights of
Risolles, linked by a col or depression to the south-
western angle of the plateau, were bristling with the tents

of the Gauls ; and the tribal camps were protected by a wall of loose stones, which, about half-way up the slope, ran along the whole southern side. From the very foot of the mountain, below the central point of the wall, a low but steep hill, now called La Roche Blanche, projected southward at right angles, and terminated in an almost sheer precipice. A small stream, the Auzon, flowed eastward through the meadows which extended past the base of the hill ; and two miles beyond the valley, on the left as one looked up the stream, the view was closed by a long ridge, the Montagne de la Serre. Beyond the heights of Risolles was the pass of Opme, which at one point gave access to them by a comparatively easy slope, and separated them from the distant Puy Giroux.

The result of the reconnaissance was not encouraging. The ascent appeared less difficult on the south than on the other sides ; but even on the south it was not easy. Even if the Romans could gain the col on the south-west, they would still be confronted by a steep though short incline. All round the plateau ran a natural glacis, to climb which, in the face of a determined enemy, would be hopeless ; and the usual expedient of approaching by a terrace was obviously impracticable. To besiege or to assault the town was therefore out of the question ; and Caesar resolved to make sure of his supplies before proceeding to blockade it. Meanwhile he pitched his camp on a low plateau north of the Auzon, about half a mile north-west of the modern village of Orcet and three thousand yards from the south-eastern corner of the town.

and encamps before Gergovia.

First operations at Gergovia. For some days no event occurred more important than a cavalry combat. Vercingetorix kept his troopers busy, interspersing archers among their ranks ; and frequent skirmishes took place in the plain between the south-eastern spurs and the Roman camp. He made the tribal chiefs repair daily to his quarters before sunrise, to furnish their reports and to receive his instructions. But one detail, which Caesar had noted, escaped his vigilance. The Roche Blanche, which commanded the descent from

the town to the rich meadows of the Auzon, was inade- 52 B.C.
quately garrisoned ;[1] and he had either neglected to
fortify it or had been prevented by want of time. If
Caesar could get possession of this hill, he would cut
off the Gauls from the chief source of their supplies.
The ascent on the eastern side was practicable. In the
dead of night Caesar stole out of camp with two legions,
drove out the startled garrison before reinforcements
could arrive, and occupied the hill. There he constructed
a small camp, and connected it with the larger one by
a pair of parallel trenches, so that men might pass securely
from camp to camp under cover of the ramparts formed
by the excavated earth. Even now, however, he had
cause for anxiety ; for his entire force was hardly more
than thirty thousand men—too few to invest a position
more than twelve miles in extent.

Meanwhile the Aedui had been considering what policy
would best promote their interests. Diviciacus, if he was
still alive, had lost his influence.[2] He had never been
able to silence the anti-Roman party ; and even the
Caesarians were no longer staunch. If they adhered to
Caesar, they would no doubt be rewarded—if Caesar
gained the day. But was it certain that he would ?
Vercingetorix might perhaps succeed after all ; and then
their old rivals, the Arverni, would supplant them. If,
on the other hand, they threw in their lot with him, their
strength would surely turn the scale. To them would
belong the glory of liberating Gaul ; and then they would
hold sway, not as Caesar's servile nominees, but as the
champions of a great and independent confederation.
The ringleader was no other than Convictolitavis, the
Vergobret, whose election Caesar had himself secured.
Vercingetorix had offered him a bribe ; and he promptly
responded to that most potent spur of Gallic patriotism.
He in turn talked over some of the younger chiefs, and
gave them part of the money. The council, which would

Defection of the Aeduan Vergobret.

---

[1] *Caesar's Conquest of Gaul*[2], p. 151, n. 1.
[2] There is no evidence that Diviciacus played any part in the Gallic
War after 57 B.C.

52 B. C.

An
Aeduan
contin-
gent,
marching
to join
Caesar,
persuaded
by its
leader to
declare
for Ver-
cinge-
torix.

certainly think twice before venturing to turn against their patron, were not consulted. The infantry contingent which Caesar had demanded was just starting for Gergovia. A chief named Litaviccus was placed in command of it ; and, to avert suspicion, his brothers were sent on ahead to join Caesar. About half-way to Gergovia, he halted the column, and delivered an inflammatory harángue. The troops were horrified to hear that all the Aeduan cavalry with Caesar, and among them two chiefs named Eporedorix and Viridomarus, had been massacred on a trumped-up charge of treachery. Putting themselves in the hands of their leader, they vowed that as soon as they reached Gergovia, they would join Vercingetorix and avenge the slaughter of their countrymen. Some Roman citizens were travelling under the Aeduan escort with grain and stores for Caesar. Litaviccus had them tortured and killed ; and, before resuming his march, he sent off messengers to spread the news of the pretended massacre among the Aedui, and urge them to arm.

Rumour flew fast. The intrigue was soon known at Gergovia. Eporedorix himself came to Caesar in the Caesar
makes a
forced
march,
overawes
the con-
tingent,
and
returns
just in
time to
rescue his
camp. middle of the night, and told the whole story. He entreated him not to allow a few wrong-headed men to drag a friendly people into revolt : if Litaviccus and the ten thousand succeeded in joining Vercingetorix, the Aeduan authorities would have no choice but to support them. Caesar was intensely anxious ; but he did not hesitate. He determined to go and intercept the deluded infantry at once, though he knew that the large camp would be exposed in his absence to a most serious risk. The camp on the Roche Blanche, in the hands of a few resolute men, would be virtually impregnable. Before starting, he ordered the arrest of Litaviccus's brothers ; but they had already fled. He took with him all the cavalry and four legions, leaving two only to hold the camps. The defence was entrusted to Fabius, who, two years before, had joined in the relief of Cicero. Caesar told his men that he must call upon them to make a most

trying effort ; but, he added, the occasion was urgent, and they would not grumble. They were in the best of spirits and ready for anything. They had marched twenty-three miles down the valley of the Allier when the Aeduan column was descried. Sending on the cavalry to stop them, but warning them to do violence to no man, Caesar made Eporedorix and Viridomarus show themselves and converse with their countrymen. The Aedui were overawed ; and they saw that they had been duped. They grounded their arms and begged for mercy ; but Litaviccus managed to escape with his retainers, and made his way to Gergovia. Caesar, foreseeing that his action would be misrepresented, took the precaution of sending messengers to give the Aeduan authorities a true account of what had passed, and to impress upon them that he had treated the mutinous contingent with for-bearance. Three hours were allowed for rest, and then the Aedui went back quietly with the legions. Darkness was now closing in. On the march a party of horsemen, dispatched by Fabius, met the column, and reported that Vercingetorix had been attacking the large camp with desperate fury. The artillery had enabled the little garri-son to hold out ; but many had been wounded by sling-stones and arrows, and Fabius was busily erecting breast-works upon the rampart, in view of a renewed assault. The news stimulated the tired men to do their utmost. Pressing on all through the small hours, Caesar reached the camp before sunrise, having accomplished the extra-ordinary march of forty-six miles in little more than twenty-four hours, just in time to avert the destruction of his exhausted legions.[1]

For the moment the danger was over ; but there were unmistakable signs that the Aedui would soon go over to

[1] It has been suggested that Caesar was imprudent in trying to reconcile the Aeduan factions, and that, if he had left them to fight out their quarrel, one or the other would have been forced to take his part. Who can tell, and what would the leading men who invited him to arbitrate have done if he had rejected their appeal ? I dare say that he still felt that on the infor-mation available at the time he had not done wrong in trying to keep the entire people on his side.

Outrages
of the
Aedui
against
Roman
citizens.
the rebels. The ignorant populace, taking for granted the truth of the news about the massacre of the cavalry, burst open the dwellings of Roman residents, robbed them, murdered them, sold them as slaves. Convicto-litavis worked upon their passions. Once they had committed themselves, he saw, they would feel that Caesar would never forgive them, and that they had everything to gain and nothing to lose by taking up arms. The Aedui took care of course to send apologies and explanations to Caesar, as soon as they heard that their contingent was in his power. The Government, they said, had not sanctioned the outrages which had been committed : the property of Litaviccus had been confiscated ; and full restitution should be made. Caesar received their envoys courteously ; but he was not for a moment deceived.

There was perhaps just a chance that, if he affected to believe that the authorities were not responsible for the excesses of the rabble, they might be wise enough to draw back. Meanwhile he would prepare for the worst. The defection of so powerful a state would inevitably give a fresh stimulus to the rebellion ; and it seemed probable that, if he delayed where he was any longer, he might find himself hemmed in. Yet, besides the humiliation of failure, to abandon the blockade would of itself encourage waverers to turn against him. How was he to get away and rejoin Labienus without leaving the impression that he was obliged to flee ?

While he was considering this problem, he ascended the Roche Blanche in order to inspect the works of the camp. Standing upon the plateau, he noticed with astonishment that a hill forming part of the mass of Risolles was abandoned. What could this portend ? Some deserters explained the mystery. Vercingetorix was greatly alarmed for the safety of the col which connected Risolles with Gergovia ; for if the Romans captured this place as well as the hill on the south which they already occupied, it would be hardly possible for foragers to get out, and the garrison would be starved into surrender. Every available man therefore had been called away to fortify

the western approach to Risolles, where alone the ascent
was practicable.

Caesar immediately devised a stratagem. About midnight he sent several squadrons of cavalry up the valley
of the Auzon, whence they struck off to the left along
the lower slopes of the Montagne de la Serre, as though
they intended to make for the pass of Opme. In obedience
to orders they moved with a show of excitement and
made a noise, in order to attract attention. At daybreak
a number of baggage-drivers, equipped to look like
troopers, rode after them, accompanied by a few regular
cavalry, who were to roam further afield, in order to
increase the effect. One of the legions followed, and,
after advancing a short distance, crossed the Auzon, and
concealed itself in a wood near the hamlet of Chanonat.
Vercingetorix, who from his commanding position could
discern these movements, became thoroughly alarmed,
and sent the rest of his forces to push on the work of
fortification. Now was Caesar's opportunity. He made
the soldiers move in small parties, so that they might
not be observed, from the larger camp to the foot of the
Roche Blanche. Some cohorts of the 13th legion were
detailed for the protection of the smaller camp ; while
the 10th was to remain as a reserve under Caesar's personal command, and the Aedui were dispatched from the
larger camp to ascend the mountain from the right.
When all was ready, Caesar explained his plans to his
generals. The ground, he said, being so unfavourable, he
did not want to fight a battle, but to effect a surprise :
their one chance of success was to ascend with all possible
speed ; and he particularly warned them not to allow
the men, in their eagerness for plunder, to get out of
hand. Once in possession of the tribal camps, he doubtless hoped that they would have time to cut off the
Gallic troops from the town.

The legions were formed up on the right of the Roche
Blanche. From where they stood the actual distance to
the town was rather more than two thousand yards, while
the place which the Gauls were fortifying was barely five

furlongs from the nearest gate. The legionaries advanced rapidly until they came to the outer wall : over it they clambered, and took possession of three of the camps, while the few men who had been left in them fled up the hill. Caesar was with the 10th legion on the hill-side, on the right of a valley by which the column had ascended. Perhaps he had reason to believe that it would be impossible to follow up his advantage : possibly he intended to re-form the scattered legionaries, retain possession of the camps, and force Vercingetorix to fight : anyhow, he made his trumpeter sound the recall. Separated from him by the valley, the troops did not hear the blast of the trumpet, and, heedless of the commands of their officers, pressed on still higher up the hill, close to the southern gate of the town. Lucius Fabius, a centurion of the 8th legion, who had reminded his comrades of the rewards that Caesar had offered before the assault of Avaricum, and had boasted that no one should get into Gergovia before him, was hoisted on to the wall by three of his men, and then hauled them up in turn. A cry of terror rose. Women threw down money and clothes to appease the soldiers and, craning over with bare breasts and outstretched hands, besought them not to treat them as they had treated the women and children at Avaricum ; others were let down from the wall and offered themselves a sacrifice to lust ; while many in the distant parts of the town, fancying that the Romans were inside, ran for their lives. Now, however, the men who had been engaged in fortifying Risolles, hearing the uproar and stimulated by a succession of messages, came hurrying back and formed up at the foot of the wall. The women held up their little ones in their arms and screamed to their menfolk to protect them. Standing high above, these dense and ever-growing masses were too much for the tired legionaries ; and they had to fight desperately to hold their ground. Anxiously watching the struggle, Caesar moved with the 10th a little nearer to the outer wall, at the same time sending an order to Sextius, the officer whom he had left in command of the smaller camp, to

lead out his cohorts and form them up at the foot of 52 B. C.
Gergovia, so that in case the legions were repulsed, he
might fall upon the right flank of their pursuers. Meanwhile the panic in the town had subsided. The centurion
and the soldiers who had got in first were killed, and their
bodies were pitched over the wall. Marcus Petronius,
another centurion of the 8th, while attempting to hew
down one of the gates, was surrounded and severely
wounded, but, rushing into the thick of the enemy, killed
two of them, forced back the rest a little way and enabled
his men, whom he would not suffer to attempt to rescue
him, to rejoin the legion. The battle was still raging The
when the Romans caught sight of a column moving over attack
repulsed
the shoulder of the hill on their right flank. It was the with
Aedui, whom Caesar had sent up the eastern slope to heavy
loss.
create a diversion ; but the Romans, deceived by their
armour, took them for enemies : the Gauls were closing
in on every side ; and now thoroughly unnerved, they
were driven back, and fled headlong down the valley.
Blindly pursuing them, the Gauls were roughly checked,
on right and left, by the cohorts of Sextius, and by the
10th, who had moved lower down the slope. As soon as
they reached level ground, the runaways halted and faced
the enemy, who then moved off ; but forty-six centurions
and nearly seven hundred privates lay dead upon the hill.[1]

Next day Caesar assembled the troops, and reprimanded Caesar
them severely for their disobedience. He admired their marches
to rejoin
spirit, he told them ; but discipline was as necessary to Labienus.
a soldier as courage, and it was the height of presumption
in them to imagine that they knew how to gain a victory
better than their general. Still they must not be disheartened ; for they had only been beaten because they
had been rash enough to fight on unfavourable ground.
To give effect to his words, he formed them up in line
of battle on the most advantageous position which he
could select ; but Vercingetorix of course refused to walk
into the trap. On that day, however, and the next, there

[1] Regarding the operations at Gergovia, see *Caesar's Conquest of Gaul*[2],
pp. 756-67.

52 B. C.   were slight cavalry skirmishes, in which the Romans had
the advantage. Then, feeling that he had done something
to abate the exultation of the enemy and to restore the
confidence of his men, Caesar quitted Gergovia, and
marched down the valley of the Allier—to begin the
campaign anew.

His   The situation was serious indeed. The Gauls had found
critical
position.   out that he was not invincible. He had under-estimated
their force and deliberately weakened his own. The division which he had assigned to Labienus could not now
crush rebellion in the north : the legions which he had
kept for himself were doomed from the first to waste
their strength against the strongest fortress in Gaul.
Vercingetorix, however, was too wary to pursue him ;
and probably his purpose was to let the Romans starve
between his own force and the insurgents of the north.
On the third day of the retreat Caesar repaired one of
the bridges over the Allier. He had only just recrossed
the river when Eporedorix and Viridomarus told him that
Litaviccus had left Gergovia with the Gallic cavalry, and
gone to recruit for Vercingetorix among the Aedui. Might
they go too ? It was of the last importance that they
should reach home first, so that they might persuade their
brother chiefs to return to their allegiance while there was
yet time. Caesar was convinced that the Aedui were lost
irretrievably, and he believed that the departure of the
chiefs would precipitate the rupture ; still he thought it
best to let them go, as it would be wiser not to betray
any anxiety or to give the slightest ground for saying
that he had treated his allies as enemies. When they
took their leave, he reminded them of all that he had
done for their people, and made a last earnest appeal
to their loyalty. It is just possible that they may have
meant what they said ; but when they reached Noviodunum and found that Litaviccus had been officially
welcomed at Bibracte and that the Vergobret and the
council had definitely declared for Vercingetorix, they
saw their opportunity. Two or three days after their
departure, Caesar learned that they had seized Novio-

dunum, where all his hostages, his stores, treasure, and 52 B. c.
cavalry remounts were collected, plundered and burned Epore-
it to the ground, sent off all the hostages to Bibracte, Virido-
and massacred the slender garrison and the Italian traders marus
who had settled in the town. Cavalry were scouring the Novio-
country to cut off his supplies, and infantry threatening dunum,
to prevent him from crossing the Loire. The water, prevent
swollen by the melting of the mountain snows, was from
rushing like a torrent. The Aeduan infantry had deserted crossing
him. The Arverni, elated by their victory, were on his
rear ; on his left the Bituriges, exasperated by the bitter
memory of Avaricum : the perfidious Aedui barred the
road in front. The Province itself was insufficiently protected. The object of the Aedui was to hem him in
between the Allier and the Loire, and there starve him
into surrender ; or if, in desperation, he should make
a dash for the Province, to cut him off from the easier
way over the Loire, and drive him back towards the
Cevennes into the clutches of Vercingetorix. Retreat,
however, was not to be thought of : with the mountains
barring the way, it would be very difficult as well as
disgraceful ; and above all, he could not leave Labienus
and his four legions to perish.[1] Probably it would be
necessary to build a bridge ; and at any cost he must
reach the Loire before the Aedui had had time to assemble
in strength. They had not burned their granaries in
accordance with Vercingetorix's plan ; and he might perhaps get supplies in their country. Night and day he He saves
marched till he reached the river a few miles south of himself by
Nevers.[2] Some troopers rode to look for a ford, and ordinary
found one which was just practicable, the water being marches.
breast-high. The cavalry rode into the river, and formed
a line from bank to bank, to break the force of the
current : then the infantry, holding their weapons above
their heads, waded across the stream. The Aedui were
so confounded by Caesar's unexpected arrival that they
fled without attempting to dispute the passage : the
soldiers took all the grain and all the cattle that they

[1] *Caesar's Conquest of Gaul*[2], pp. 769–74.　　　[2] *Ib.*, p. 774.

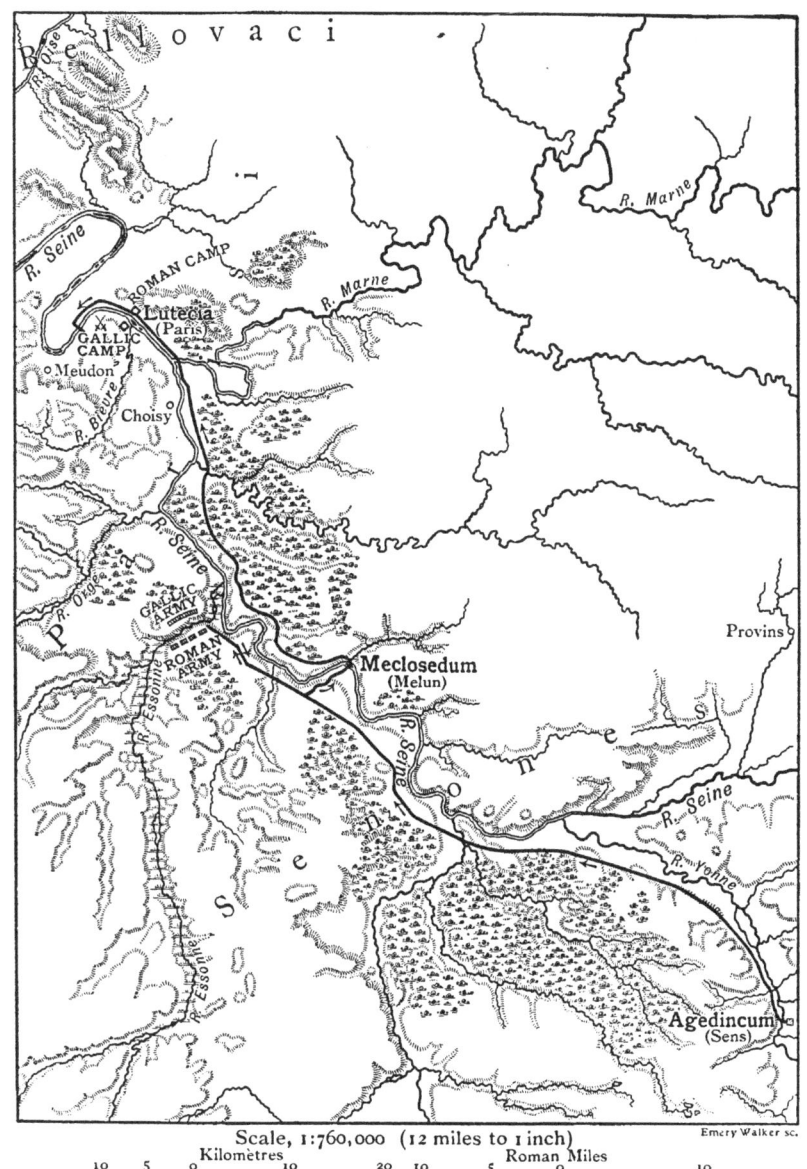

Scale, 1:760,000 (12 miles to 1 inch)

Emery Walker sc.

needed ; and the army marched on towards the valley
of the Yonne to succour Labienus.

That officer meanwhile was in great peril. Leaving the
heavy baggage at Agedincum in charge of the recruits
who had accompanied Caesar from Italy, he had marched
with his four legions down the left bank of the Yonne
and of the Seine, for Lutecia, the capital of the Parisii.
A large force, commanded by an aged chieftain named
Camulogenus, assembled to oppose him. On the approach
of the Romans, he encamped on the edge of a far-reaching
morass, about twenty miles south of Paris, through which
the Essonne crept sluggishly to join the Seine. Labienus
tried to construct a causeway across the slush ; but
finding this impossible in the face of an enemy, he silently
quitted his camp in the night ; marched back as far as
Meclosedum, or Melun, a town standing on an island in
the Seine ; seized some fifty barges and rapidly lashed
them together ; threw a detachment across ; chased away
the panic-stricken inhabitants ; repaired the bridge which
they had demolished ; transported his army to the opposite bank ; and then moved down the valley in the
direction whence he had come. The townsmen who had
fled from Meclosedum hurried with the news to Camulogenus. He at once sent messengers to order the destruction of Lutecia, and then moved northward from the
marsh. The barges accompanied the Roman column ;
and with their aid Labienus crossed the Marne. Lutecia
was situate upon the island in the Seine on which now
stands the cathedral of Notre-Dame. Labienus, finding
on his arrival that the bridges had been broken down
and the town burned to the ground, encamped just
opposite the island ; and the enemy established themselves over against his army on the southern bank.

Just at this time the news arrived that Caesar had
been forced to retreat from Gergovia, and that the Aedui
had joined the rebellion. Labienus was dependent on
Gallic peasants for his information ; and their statements
were positive. Caesar had tried to cross the Loire and
had failed : he could get no supplies ; he was in full

retreat for the Province. The Bellovaci immediately rose in arms. Labienus found himself threatened by this war-like people on the north-east : on the south the Parisii and their allies confronted him ; while the broad flood of the Seine separated him from his base at Agedincum. Back to that town he must somehow find his way ; for he saw that in his altered circumstances it would be folly to think of an offensive campaign. But how to return ? He might have gone, as he had come, by the right bank of the Seine : but he had never yet fled before the face of an enemy ; and to flee at such a crisis would shatter the enfeebled prestige of the Roman arms. Besides, to reach Agedincum, he must, sooner or later, recross the river ; and, hurry as he might, cross where he would, the enemy would be there to dispute his passage. There was nothing for it but to cross there and then by some skilful stratagem ; and, if he must fight, to clear the way by victory.[1]

The barges which he had brought from Meclosedum were lying under the bank, ready for use ; and a flotilla of small boats was also collected. Labienus placed each of the barges under the charge of an officer, and ordered them to drop down stream about ten o'clock for a distance of four miles, and there to await his arrival. He left half a legion to protect the camp ; sent the other half with the baggage-train up the bank, bidding them make as much noise as they could ; and ordered the boats to be rowed alongside of them with a loud splashing of oars. Soon after midnight he moved stealthily in the opposite direction with his remaining legions, till he came to the spot where the barges were waiting, near the southern end of the Bois de Boulogne. A storm was sweeping over the valley ; the troops were ferried across the river ; and in the rush and roar of wind and rain the enemy's outposts were surprised and cut down. The stratagem, however, only partially succeeded. About daybreak mes-

---

[1] I doubt whether the threatening attitude of the Bellovaci deterred Labienus from returning by the right bank of the Seine ; for he had a long start.

sengers hurried one after another into the Gallic encampment, and reported that there was a great uproar in the
Roman camp, soldiers tramping and oars splashing up
the stream, barges crossing below. Camulogenus, who
fancied that the Romans were crossing the river in three
places and would soon be in full retreat,[1] sent a small
detachment in the direction of Meclosedum, and, leaving
another to watch the Roman camp, marched in person
against Labienus.

Just before sunrise the armies met. The Gallic left
broke before the first charge ; but the right fought with
extraordinary resolution, and for a long time the issue
was doubtful. The aged Camulogenus was in the fore-
front of the battle, cheering on his men. At length the
victorious Roman right fell upon their rear. Even then
not a man would give way ; but all were surrounded
and slain. The troops which had been detached to watch
the Roman camp hurried to the rescue, and established
themselves on the hill of Mont Parnasse, but were speedily
dislodged, and, mingling with the runaways from the left
wing, were slaughtered—all who failed to find shelter in
the woods and on the hills—by the Roman cavalry. The
road to Agedincum was again open. Labienus returned
thither to take up the heavy baggage, and thence marched
southward to rejoin Caesar.[2]

He extricates himself from a perilous position by victory, and marches to rejoin Caesar.

Still the rebellion was rapidly gaining ground. The
defection of the Aedui was a turning-point in the war.
They won over other tribes by their influence and their
gold, and terrified waverers by threatening to put to
death the hostages who had been captured at Noviodunum. But discord and jealousy even now made themselves felt. The Aedui requested Vercingetorix to come
to them and concert operations ; and he readily consented. Forthwith they claimed the right of directing
the campaign : but their demand was disputed ; and
a general assembly was convened at Bibracte to settle
the question. The Remi and the Lingones, who steadily

The rebellion stimulated by the adhesion of the Aedui.

They claim the direction of the war.

---

[1] See the note in my edition of the *Commentaries* on vii, 61, 4.
[2] *Caesar's Conquest of Gaul*[2], pp. 775-85.

52 B.C.

adhered to the stronger side, and the Treveri, who were themselves hard pressed by the Germans, alone failed to appear.[1] It was the supreme moment in the life of Vercingetorix. A few weeks before, while they were still smarting under defeat, he had told his men that he would win over the rest of Gaul to the cause ; and now his promise seemed about to be fulfilled. With a fraction of the people he had vanquished the invincible conqueror ; and the whole people was rallying to his side. Chieftains and their retainers defiled through the streets of the mountain city, and thronged the open terrace where Vercinge-affairs of state were discussed.[2] The question was put torix re-elected to the vote ; and, without one dissentient, the repre-Com-sentatives of the Gallic nation chose Vercingetorix as mander-in-Chief. their general. Bitterly chagrined, the Aedui repented the rashness with which they had flung aside the friendship of the Romans : but it was too late now to draw back, and Eporedorix and Viridomarus reluctantly submitted to the Arvernian king.

His plan of cam-paign.

Vercingetorix determined to adhere to his original plan of campaign, and to limit his force to the number which could act without losing that mobility which was its strength. His infantry—eighty thousand chosen men— were sufficient for a guerrilla warfare ; and he contented himself with requiring levies from his new allies which raised his cavalry to fifteen thousand.[3] Relying on his superiority in this arm, he intended simply to cut off his enemy's supplies ; and once more he appealed to his countrymen to destroy their crops and to burn their

---

[1] It will of course be understood that the Aquitanian tribes were not represented. I am inclined to infer from certain significant omissions in the list (B. G., vii, 75) of the tribes which sent contingents for the relief of Alesia that the Remi, the Lingones, and the Treveri were not the only tribes unrepresented in the council, and that others, particularly the Suessiones and the Leuci, were influenced by the two former to hold aloof. It seems unlikely, moreover, that the Eburones and the other ' Cisrhenane Germans ' sent delegates.

[2] B. G., vii, 63, 6, and the note in my edition ; J. G. Bulliot, *Fouilles du Mont Beuvray*, i, 1899, p. x ; ii, 61.

[3] See my second note on B. G., vii, 64, 1, and cf. Meusel's, in his posthumous edition (1920), on the same passage.

granaries that they might achieve their liberty. That 52 B. C.
he might have a stronghold to retreat to in case of necessity, he fortified and provisioned Alesia, a town belonging
to the Mandubii, which covered the plateau of Mont
Auxois, in the highlands of the Côte-d'Or. But he
intended also to carry the war into the enemy's country.
If he could seize the Roman Province or could seduce
the Provincials to join him, the triumph of his cause
would be assured. He hounded on the neighbours of the *He*
Helvii and the Volcae Arecomici to attack them ; and, *hounds on*
the
believing that the Allobroges were still smarting under *neigh-*
the punishment which Rome had inflicted upon them *bours of*
the Pro-
a few years before, he sent envoys to bribe the chiefs *vincial*
and to hold out to the council the prospect of supremacy *tribes to*
attack
over the Province, and raised a levy of ten thousand *them.*
Aeduans, whom he reinforced with eight hundred cavalry,
to coerce them if persuasion should fail.

It was a master-stroke ; and Caesar knew that if it
succeeded, he would be in extreme peril. The Allobroges
had been badly treated by former Governors, and before
he entered Gaul they had been the most disaffected subjects of Rome. But he had rescued them from the Helvetii ; he had distinguished two of their leading men,
who had rendered him signal services, by special marks
of favour ; [1] and he had taught them to believe that his
cause was theirs. The Helvii, who risked a battle, were
defeated with heavy loss and driven into their strongholds : but the Allobroges, forming a chain of piquets
on the Rhône, presented an impenetrable front to the
enemy ; while ten thousand men, raised in the Province
itself and commanded by Lucius Caesar,[2] were posted at
various points on the threatened frontier. Meanwhile
Caesar contrived a plan for counteracting the enemy's
superiority in cavalry. No reinforcements could be expected from the Province, for the roads were blocked.
He therefore sent across the Rhine to the tribes which *Caesar*
he had subdued, and procured from them numbers of *enlists*
German
horsemen with their attendant light infantry, who eagerly *cavalry.*

[1] *B. C.*, iii, 59, 3. [2] See vol. i, p. 251.

52 B. C.

welcomed the chance of sharing in the plunder of Gaul. But the German horses, though hardy, were small and light ; and Caesar, seeing that his new allies would be at a disadvantage when they encountered the Gallic troopers, remounted them on the horses of his tribunes and body-guard and of the retired centurions and legionaries who, on his invitation, had volunteered for service, and were accordingly privileged to ride on the march.[1]

He marches to succour the Province.

Some weeks had passed since Caesar had rejoined Labienus. The meeting had taken place on the south of Agedincum, near the confluence of the Armançon and the Yonne ; and, as Agedincum itself had been abandoned, the united army took up its quarters not far from Troyes, among the friendly Lingones.[2] The Remi, steadily loyal to Caesar and steadily false to their countrymen, were close by on the north, to support him and to receive his support : the Aedui were on the south ; and while he was near enough to watch their movements, he could collect fresh stores and rest his troops in comparative security. But the Province was still threatened ; and he saw that he must march to its relief. Probably he meant also to reinforce his army with Provincial levies, and then to return and make an end of the rebellion. Accordingly he moved down the valley of the Tille, intending to cross the Saône near St. Jean-de-Losne, and to establish himself in the country of the Sequani. Vercingetorix with his infantry and his fresh hosts of horsemen moved off from Alesia to intercept him, and took up a position behind a stream, not far north of Dijon,[3] about ten miles from the spot where the Romans were encamped. His line of retreat was secure ; and he was protected in front by the slopes of the valley. He made up his mind to risk an action, although, only a few weeks before, he had declared that he would not tempt fortune ; so much harder is it to pursue than to adopt a wise plan of campaign. It would be rash, however, to affirm that

[1] I conjecture that the Germans used their own horses except in action.
[2] *Caesar's Conquest of Gaul²*, pp. 785–90.
[3] *Ib.*, pp. 791–801 ; p. 287, *infra*.

he consciously departed from his original resolution.[1] He
did not contemplate a pitched battle ;[1] and he was
perhaps ignorant that Caesar had been reinforced by
those doughty squadrons from beyond the Rhine. The
legions were of course too strong to be attacked : but
they were hampered by an immense baggage-train ; and
they must either lose precious time in defending it, or
abandon it at the cost of their honour, nay, of their means
of subsistence. He would draw up his infantry in front
of his encampment, to encourage his cavalry and to overawe the Romans. If he allowed Caesar to reach the
Province, he would soon come back stronger than ever ;
and then all hope of liberating Gaul would be at an end.
Such were the arguments by which he tried to animate
his cavalry officers ; and in an outburst of enthusiasm
the knights bound themselves by a solemn oath to break
the enemy's line. Next morning the Roman column was
discerned beyond the stream, each legion followed by its
own baggage-train.[2] Vercingetorix must have exulted at
this sign of carelessness. But between him and Caesar
was a hill, which a leader gifted with the intuition that
can divine an enemy's intentions would have seized.
Vercingetorix ranged his infantry in front of his encamp-   Vercinge-
ment, while the cavalry swept down upon the Roman   torix attacks
vanguard and on either flank. Caesar was surprised as   Caesar's
completely as in the battle on the Sambre. The lie of the   cavalry,
ground had prevented him from observing the approach
of the Gauls ; and, marching securely through a friendly
country, he had neglected to send out patrols. He made
his dispositions, however, with his usual calmness. He
sent his cavalry in three divisions to repel the triple
attack, while the legions gradually formed a hollow square
outside the baggage, ready to support them if they were
hard pressed.[3] For a time the Gauls had a slight advantage ; but the legions prevented them from following it

---

[1] R. Grosse (*Deutsche Literaturzeitung*, Sept. 6, 1913, col. 2285) insists
that I am wrong. Has he not forgotten the words *neque fortunam templa-
turum aut acie dimicaturum* (*B. G.*, vii, 64, 2) ?
[2] *Caesar's Conquest of Gaul*[2], p. 168, n. 1.   [3] *Ib.*, n. 2.

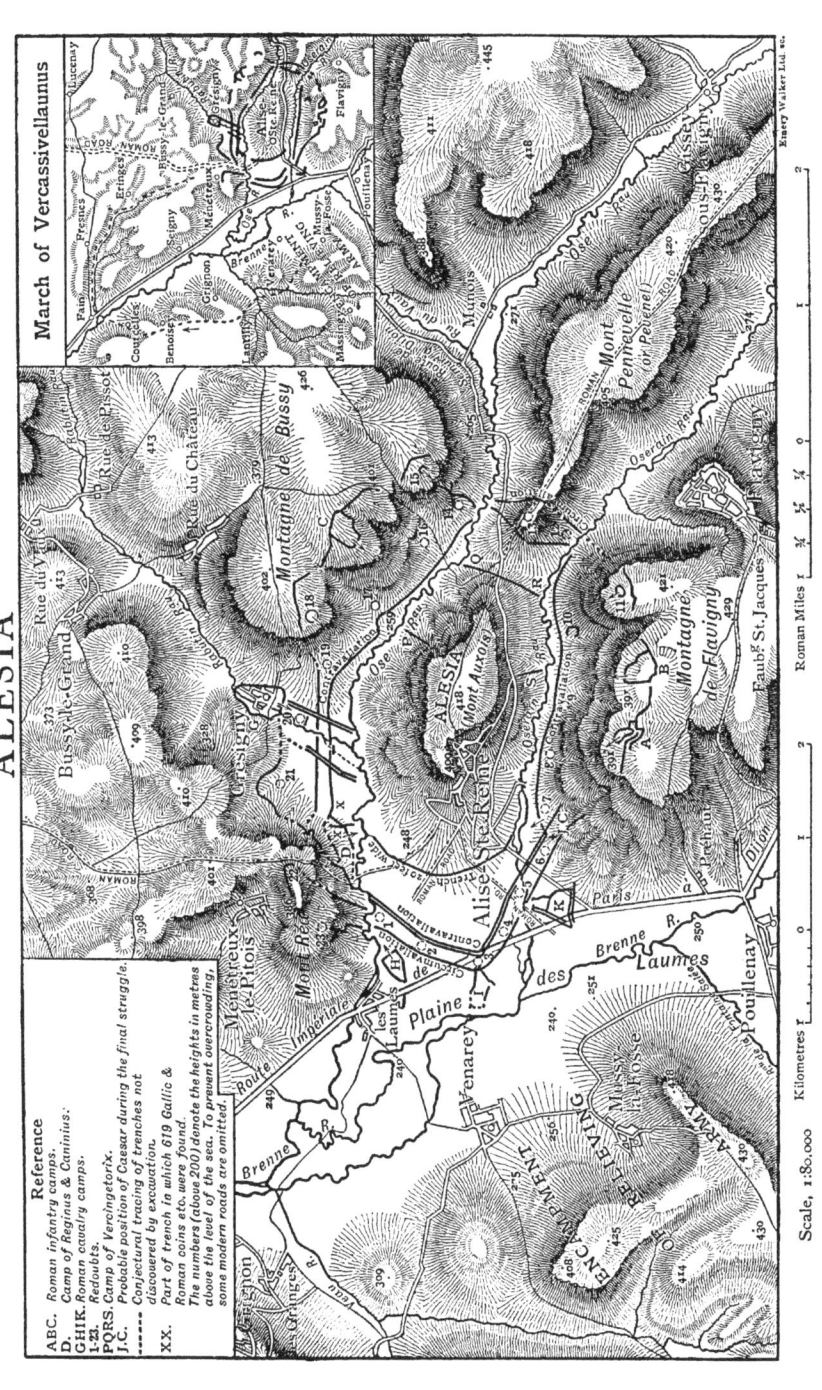

ALESIA

March of Vercassivellaunus

Reference

ABC. Roman infantry camps.
D. Camp of Reginus & Caninius.
G.HIK. Roman cavalry camps.
1-23. Redoubts.
PQRS. Camp of Vercingetorix.
J.C. Probable position of Caesar during the final struggle.
       Conjectural tracing of trenches not
       discovered by excavation.
XX. Part of trench in which 619 Gallic &
       Roman coins &c. were found.
The numbers (above 200) denote the heights in metres
above the level of the sea. To prevent overcrowding,
some modern roads are omitted.

Scale, 1:80,000

Emery Walker Ltd. sc.

up. And where were the Gallic infantry—those eighty 52 B.C.
thousand chosen men, with whom Vercingetorix had promised to support his cavalry ? Were they inferior to the
levies of the Seine, who had so borne themselves against
the veteran soldiers of Labienus as to merit Caesar's
praise ? Why did Vercingetorix, since he had risked
a battle, not throw them into the scale ? We cannot
tell. The knights, who had tried to redeem their pledge,
fought on without support. At length from the hill on
the Roman right the German horse came thundering
down on their flank,[1] and drove them with heavy loss
towards the stream. The rest of the Gauls, fearful of
being surrounded, galloped for their lives ; the infantry,
passive spectators of the slaughter, fell back upon their and re-
camps ; and Vercingetorix, ordering his baggage-drivers treats, beaten, to
to follow him, hastened westward towards Alesia. By Alesia.
nightfall, when his pursuers halted, three thousand of the
fugitives were slain ; and all that he had achieved in six
months by sustained effort was lost in a day.

Next morning the Romans were approaching the stronghold where Vercingetorix had prepared to make his final
stand. The column descended a valley closed on the
right and the left by the hills of Bussy and Pevenel. On
their left front, connected with Pevenel by a broad neck
of land, rose a hill, much lower than Gergovia, but still
too steep to be taken by assault. The Gauls were swarming on the eastern slope, beneath the scarped rocks of the
plateau, on which stood the town ; and Vercingetorix
had made them build a wall and dig a ditch to protect
their encampment. Just at their feet the legions saw
a stream, the Oze, winding like a steely thread through
the greenery that fringed the north of the hill ; and
beyond its southern side, parallel to the Oze, but invisible,
flowed the little river Ozerain. Moving down past the
hill of Réa, the soldiers came to a miniature plain, which
extended, three miles in length, beneath the western slope
of Alesia, and was bounded on its further side by a range

---

[1] 'The charge of 10 horsemen on the flank is more effective than that of
100 on the front.'—Lord Wolseley, *The Soldier's Pocket-book*[5], 1886, p. 376.

52 B. C.

of heights : the river Brenne, which received the waters of the Oze and the Ozerain, meandered through it from south to north ; and beyond the Ozerain the steep declivities of Flavigny completed the zone of hills.

Caesar invests Alesia.

Caesar harangued his troops and encouraged them to brace themselves for a toilsome effort. As it was evident that the place could not be taken except by a blockade, he drew a line of investment fully nine miles in length, along which a ring of camps was constructed. Those intended for the cavalry were on low ground—three in the plain and one in the valley of the Rabutin, which entered the Oze from the north : the rest were strongly placed upon the slopes of the outlying hills. Twenty-three redoubts were erected within the circuit of the camps ; and strong piquets were placed in them, to guard against any sudden sortie.

The Gallic cavalry make a sortie, but are beaten.

Soon after the commencement of the works, Vercingetorix sent all his cavalry down the hill ; and a desperate combat was fought in the western plain. Caesar's Gallic and Spanish horse were soon in trouble, and he sent his Germans to reinforce them. The legions were drawn up in front of their camps, to support the cavalry and to deter the enemy's foot from attempting a sortie. The Gauls were beaten, and galloped back along the valleys of the Oze and the Ozerain, hotly pursued by the Germans ; but the gates of the camp being too narrow, many of the thronging fugitives were cut down, while others threw themselves off their horses and tried to scramble over the wall. The legions, by Caesar's order, moved forward a little. The Gauls inside the wall were smitten with panic, many of them fleeing helter-skelter up the hill-side ; and Vercingetorix was obliged to shut the gates of the town, for fear the camp should be left unprotected.

Vercinge-torix sends them to fetch succour.

He had hoped perhaps that Caesar, who had failed so ignominiously at Gergovia, would not be strong enough to enforce a systematic blockade. But there were now ten legions instead of six ; and wherever he looked, over the plain or down in the valleys, there were soldiers at work with axe or spade. There was nothing for it but

to appeal to the whole Gallic people to extricate him 52 B. C.
from the trap in which he was caught. The ring of
redoubts was not yet complete ; the Romans were far
too few to guard the whole circuit of the mountain ; and
the cavalry might steal out in the dark without attracting
notice. He charged them to go, each to his own country,
and bring back with them every man who could wield
a sword. By reducing the rations, he reckoned that he
might make the supply last a little over a month. Every
thing depended on their using all speed : if they left
him to perish, the whole garrison would perish with
him.

Caesar learned the whole story from some deserters. Caesar
Its effect was to stimulate his inventive genius. If he constructs
lines of
could keep the army of Vercingetorix from breaking out, contraval-
he could also keep the relieving force from breaking in ; lation and
circum-
and unless they could break in quickly, they would be vallation.
forced to disperse for want of food. The most vulnerable
part of his position was the open meadow on the western
side of the mountain. Across this expanse, from the Oze
to the Ozerain, a trench was dug, twenty feet wide with
perpendicular sides, to prevent the enemy from attacking
the troops while they were constructing the proper works.
About four hundred yards behind the ends of this trench,
but bending outwards, was traced the line of contravallation, which was prolonged so as to surround Alesia, and
ran along the lower slopes of the encircling hills and
across the valley of the Rabutin. First of all, two parallel
trenches were sunk, each fifteen feet wide and eight feet
deep, the outer of which extended only across the plain,
while the inner, embracing the whole circuit of the hill,
was filled, where the level permitted, with water drawn
from the Ozerain and the Rabutin. Just behind the outer
trench, and also behind that portion of the other which
encompassed the rest of the position, a rampart was
formed, surmounted by a palisade, with an embattled
fence of wattle-work in front, from the bottom of which
projected stout forked branches. Wooden towers were
erected upon the western section of the rampart at

intervals of one hundred and thirty yards,[1] and also at certain points along the rest of the contravallation. To repel the reinforcements for which Vercingetorix had sent, a line of works somewhat similar to these, forming the circumvallation, was traced along the heights of Flavigny, Pevenel, and Bussy, and across the intervening valleys and the plain. The circuit of this line was about twelve miles.

But even these works were not deemed sufficient. The Gauls made frequent and furious sallies. Comparatively few of the Romans were available as combatants ; for many had to go in quest of corn and timber, while others were labouring on the works. Caesar therefore devised various subsidiary defences. Ditches, five feet deep, were dug just inside the large moat that was filled with water ; and five rows of strong boughs were fixed in each, with one end protruding above ground, sharpened and with the branches projecting so as to form a kind of abatis. In front of them and rising a few inches above the ground, but carefully concealed by brushwood, were sharp-pointed logs embedded in small pits. In front of these again, concealed, but barely concealed, beneath the turf, were barbed spikes fixed in pieces of wood. Fringed by these formidable defences, Caesar expected that contravallation and circumvallation would be alike impregnable.

Nevertheless, the struggle was likely to be prolonged ; and it would certainly tax to the utmost the endurance and the fighting power of the men. As soon as the relieving army should arrive, the Romans would be hemmed in between two desperate enemies. Every moment for preparation was precious. Flying parties scoured the country for corn and provender ; but they could not collect a sufficient supply, and the rations had to be reduced.[2] Every day—even by night, when the moon was up, or in the glow of the watch-fires—the besieged could see the indefatigable legionaries labouring

---

[1] *Caesar's Conquest of Gaul*[2], p. 810, n. 7.
[2] *B. C.*, iii, 47, 6. Cf. H. Delbrück, *Gesch. d. Kriegskunst*[2], 1908, p. 530, n. 2.

to finish their works before the time for the great hazard 52 b. c. should arrive.

Meanwhile Vercingetorix had abandoned his camp, and withdrawn the troops who occupied it into the town. He took every precaution to husband his resources. Meat was tolerably abundant, for the Mandubii had driven large numbers of cattle into the stronghold ; but he ordered the whole of the grain to be thrown into one common stock and brought to him for safe keeping, and he let it be known that the penalty of disobedience would be death. From time to time each man received his scanty dole.

A council of chieftains had already met to consider his Organiza- appeal. Probably the Aeduan delegates were minded to tion of an wreck the plan ; but there is no reason to doubt that army of relief. the majority were whole-hearted in supporting the leader who, a few weeks before, had been unanimously acclaimed. Vercingetorix, in his great need, had asked for a universal levy ; but the cooler judgement of the council rejected his demand. So vast a multitude would become unmanageable, and it would be impossible to find food for so many mouths. It was resolved therefore to call upon each tribe for a limited contingent. Several, however, were finally omitted, doubtless because it was known that they could not or would not help. The Treveri were still struggling with the Germans : the Eburones had been wellnigh exterminated ; the Atuatuci and the Menapii, who had suffered much, were naturally excused. The Remi and the Lingones were of course obdurate ; and certain tribes were influenced or obliged to follow their lead.[1] Forty-three in all were named. The summons was obeyed with alacrity ; and from north and south and east and west, from the Seine, the Loire, and the Garonne, from the marshes of the Scheldt and the Sambre and the mountains of the Vosges and the Cevennes, from the Channel and the Atlantic Ocean horse and foot came swarming to save the hero of Gaul. His fame had travelled to remote Helvetia ; and six thousand devoted men—a remnant of the host which had bled on

[1] The Suessiones, Viromandui, and Leuci.

52 B. C. the hill of Armecy—once more set their faces towards the west. But even in this supreme moment, in one instance, tribal jealousy prevailed over patriotism. The Bellovaci peremptorily refused to send a single man. They intended, they said, to attack Caesar on their own account, and had no intention of being dictated to by any one. They consented, however, as a personal favour to Commius, who had great influence with them, to dispatch a small contingent. Four generals were chosen ; for, except Vercingetorix himself, there was no one leader of sufficient eminence to command universal respect ; and, as if this weakening of authority was not enough, the generals were fettered by civil commissioners, whose instructions they were to follow in the conduct of the campaign. One of the four was Commius, who had good reason to abhor the Roman name ; his colleagues were Eporedorix and Viridomarus, representing the Aedui, and Vercassivellaunus, a cousin of Vercingetorix. The vast host mustered in the country of the Aedui, eight thousand horsemen and nearly two hundred and fifty thousand foot,[1] and marched for Alesia in the certain confidence of victory.

Famine in Alesia. By this time the garrison were in great straits. Their grain was all consumed. Day after day they strained their eyes, trying to catch a glimpse of the relieving army ; but there was never a sign. At length the chieftains called a council of war. Some advised surrender : others were clamorous for a grand sortie ; but an Arvernian called Critognatus denounced these proposals as half-hearted. Reminding his hearers that their fathers, when they were driven into their fastnesses by the Cimbri and Teutoni, had sustained life by feeding upon the flesh of those who were useless for warfare, he urged that, to give the garrison strength to hold out to the last against the tyrants who made war only to enslave, this glorious precedent should be followed. Finally it was decided

Critogna-
tus pro-
poses can-
nibalism.

---

[1] Readers versed in military history will perhaps doubt whether Caesar (*B. G.*, vii, 76, 3) was correctly informed. See *Caesar's Conquest of Gaul*[2], p 242, n. 10.

that all who were too old, too young, or too feeble to
fight should be expelled from the town ; that those who
remained should try every expedient before having
recourse to the desperate remedy of Critognatus ; but
that, if the relieving army failed to arrive in time, they
should even follow his counsel rather than surrender.
Accordingly the Mandubii, to whom the town belonged, The fate
were compelled to depart, with their wives and children. of the
Mandubii.
They presented themselves, many weeping, before the
Roman lines, and begged the soldiers to receive them as
slaves—only give them something to eat. To grant their
prayer was impossible ; and a line of guards, whom Caesar
posted on the rampart, forbade any attempt to escape.

But suspense was nearly at an end. It was just after Arrival of
the expulsion of the Mandubii when the anxious watchers the army
of relief.
on the hill saw, moving over the plain, a multitude of
cavalry. The infantry were on the heights of Mussy-la-
Fosse behind. In a fever of exultation men ran to and fro,
exchanging congratulations. Presently the garrison,
provided with fascines for filling up the trenches and
movable huts to protect their approach, descended the
hill and prepared for a sortie. Soon a fierce combat of
horse was raging over the plain. The legionaries were The final
posted, ready for emergencies, along the outer and the struggle.
inner lines. Archers were scattered among the Gallic
ranks ; and the arrows fell so thick and fast that scores
of wounded men were seen riding off the field. Every man
fought like a hero ; for they knew that on the heights
around friends and enemies alike were anxiously watching.
The numbers of the Gauls began to tell ; and their
countrymen, behind and before, encouraged them by
loud yells. All through the afternoon the battle raged
uncertain. But Caesar had kept his best troops in reserve.
Towards sunset the ever-victorious Germans charged in
a compact body, and threw the division opposed to them
into disorder : the archers were exposed and killed : the
rout was general ; and the besieged who had sallied forth
turned in despair, and reascended the hill.[1]

[1] 'In all Cavalry encounters with Cavalry', says Lord Wolseley (*The*

But Commius and Vercassivellaunus were still hopeful. Next day their men were hard at work, making fascines, scaling-ladders, and grappling-hooks for a grand assault on the Roman lines. About midnight they quitted their camp, and moved in silence across the plain. As they approached the works, they raised a simultaneous shout, to put the besieged on the alert ; and, as they flung their fascines into the ditch, the trumpet was heard, calling the garrison to arms. Stones flew from slings : arrows whizzed through the air ; and, though the Romans too plied their slings, and supports hurried from the neighbouring redoubts to the relief of any point that was too hardly pressed, the enemy were too many for them, and they suffered heavily : but when their assailants pressed on to storm the entrenchment, they trod upon the spikes, or, stumbling into the pits, impaled themselves on the pointed logs, while heavy pikes were hurled upon them from rampart and towers, and artillery made havoc in the seething multitude. Towards dawn they retreated, fearing an attack in flank ; and the besieged, who had lost much time in attempting to cross the outer trenches,[1] went back before they could strike a blow.

One chance remained. The leaders of the relieving army questioned the rustics about the lie of the ground on the north and the nature of the Roman defences. Mont Réa, which bounded the plain and rose above the further bank of the Oze, extended so far northward that Caesar had not been able to enclose it in his circumvallation.[2] On the southern slope, close to the stream, stood one of the Roman camps, held by two legions—perhaps about eight thousand men—under Reginus and Caninius. Soon after dark sixty thousand [3] picked men, under the

---

Soldier's Pocket-book[5], 1886, p. 376), ' the side that is able to bring up a fresh reserve when his opponent has exhausted all his, will, as a rule, win the day '.

[1] *Caesar's Conquest of Gaul*[2], pp. 813–5. Meusel disagrees, I think on insufficient grounds, with my interpretation of *priores fossas* (B. G., vii, 83, 3), but is unable to offer another.

[2] *Caesar's Conquest of Gaul*[2], pp. 361–2.

[3] Here again some readers may perhaps be sceptical (*ib.*, p. 242, n. 10).

command of Vercassivellaunus, left the Gallic camp, and, passing right round the northern hills, halted before daybreak for a rest in a hollow north-east of Mont Réa. About noon, just as they were moving down on the camp, the cavalry, by a pre-concerted arrangement, streamed over the plain towards the Roman lines : the rest of the infantry showed themselves in front of their encampment ; and Vercingetorix, observing these movements from the citadel, descended the hill and moved towards the plain.

This time there was no delay. The inner trench had been filled up at certain places with earth and fascines : stout sappers' huts, destined to protect the men when they should approach to storm the lines, poles fitted with hooks for tearing down the rampart, long pikes, and other implements which Vercingetorix had provided, were carried across ; and the besieged moved on to make their last effort.

A desperate struggle then began. Wherever there was a weak spot in the defences, the Gauls threw themselves upon it ; and the Romans, comparatively few in numbers, and scattered owing to the vast extent of their lines, found great difficulty in massing themselves upon the exposed points. Moreover, they were painfully distracted by the roar of battle in their rear ; for both on the inner and the outer line men felt, as they fought, that they must perish if their comrades behind suffered the enemy to break through. From the slope of Flavigny, south of the Ozerain, Caesar directed the battle, and sent supports to every point where he saw his men hard pressed. The attack on the circumvallation in the plain was comparatively feeble ; for the bulk of the relieving force was formidable only in numbers. Nor were those numbers wisely directed. The Aedui may have been treacherous : the generals may have disagreed, or they may have been fettered by the civil commissioners ; anyhow, the Gauls made no serious attempt except on Mont Réa and in the plain.[1] Behind Mont Réa they

---

[1] It is not certain that the relieving army did more than make a demonstration in the plain (*ib.*, p. 816).

were so densely massed that Vercassivellaunus could always send fresh men to relieve their comrades. Coming down on the camp from a higher level, the assailants hurled their missiles with fatal momentum : they shot earth in heaps over the pointed logs and the spikes, and, locking their shields over their heads, passed unscathed to the rampart ; and then their numbers began to tell. The Roman cavalry were unable to create a diversion ; for they were kept inactive by the Gallic troops in the plain.[1] Suddenly a galloper rode up and told Caesar that the garrison were worn out, and their stock of missiles failing. He immediately sent Labienus with six cohorts to the rescue, telling him to hold on as long as he could and when he could hold on no longer to sally forth and fight it out in the open. Then, riding down between the lines on to the plain, he harangued his weary soldiers and adjured them not to give in : just one short hour, and the prize was won. At last the besieged abandoned in despair the attempt to break through, and, wheeling to the left, crossed the Ozerain, and flung themselves against the works at the foot of Flavigny. They drove the artillerymen from the towers with volleys of missiles : they shot earth and fascines into the ditch, and made their way across ; they tore down palisade[2] and breastworks with their grappling-hooks ; six[3] cohorts, then seven[3] more were sent down to help, and still they pressed on—till Caesar himself hurried to the spot with fresh reinforcements, and drove them away. Everywhere, except at Mont Réa, the victory was sure. Caesar called out four cohorts from the nearest redoubt, told his cavalry to follow him, and dispatched a horseman to the northern cavalry camp to send another detachment down upon the enemy's rear.[4] By this time they were swarming over the rampart ; and, as a last resource, Labienus summoned every available man from the neighbouring redoubts to his aid. And now, conspicuous

[1] *Caesar's Conquest of Gaul*[2], p. 179, n. 1.
[2] *B. G.*, vii, 86, 5. Cf. p. 133, n. 1.
[3] *Caesar's Conquest of Gaul*[2], p. 179, n. 3.
[4] *Ib.*, pp. 818–9.

in his crimson cloak, Caesar was descried, hurrying
across the plain. The enemy made a supreme effort, but
they were left without support : Labienus gave the word,
and his cohorts charged into the thick of the stormers.
As Caesar approached, he heard the shouts of the combatants : he saw the camp abandoned and the short
swords flashing over the slopes beyond. Suddenly the
cavalry appeared on the heights above the enemy's rear :
Caesar's reserves came up to attack them in front ; and
they fled in bewilderment into the midst of the hostile
squadrons. Vercassivellaunus himself was captured, and
seventy-four standards ; and of the sixty thousand
chosen men who had marched out of camp the night
before only a remnant returned. The whole scene was
visible from the town ; and in despair the officers left
in command sent to recall their comrades from below.
The vast host without vanished in the gathering darkness.
The legions were too tired to follow, or all might have
been destroyed : but at midnight the cavalry were sent
in pursuit ; and when day broke they were still hunting
the fugitives and capturing or slaying them in scores.[1]

All was lost : so Vercingetorix clearly saw. In the
night he formed his resolve. Next morning he gathered
the tribal chiefs around him. He told them that he had
fought, not for himself but for national liberty ; and,
since they must needs all bow to fortune, he was ready
to place himself at their disposal—to die, if they wished
to appease the Romans by his death, or to yield himself
up as a prisoner of war. They accepted his offer, and
consented to purchase life by sacrificing the leader of their
choice. Ambassadors were sent to learn the pleasure of
the conqueror. He ordered the chiefs to be brought out,
and all the arms to be surrendered. The chiefs were led
forth ; and Caesar, seated on his tribunal, received their
submission. Vercingetorix, mounted on a gaily capari-
soned charger, rode round the tribunal, and then, leaping
to the ground, took off his armour, laid down his sword,

*The self-
sacrifice
of Vercin-
getorix.*

*Surrender
of the
garrison.*

---

[1] All questions relating to the operations at Alesia are discussed in *Caesar's
Conquest of Gaul*[2], pp. 804–20.

52 B. C.   and bowed himself at Caesar's feet. He was sent to Rome, and imprisoned in the dungeon where the Catilinarian conspirators had been executed, to await the day of Caesar's triumph and of his own doom.

·   ·   ·   ·   ·   ·   ·   ·   ·

Caesar distributes his legions for the winter.   Caesar determined, instead of going to Italy, to spend the winter in the Aeduan capital ; for he knew that though Gaul was sore smitten, it was not yet tranquillized. For the moment all was still. The Aedui were ready and eager to return to their allegiance ; the Arverni were quite cowed, and promised implicit obedience for the future. Caesar, too politic to bear hardly upon either, restored to them the prisoners whom he had taken, though he demanded a large number of hostages. But the soldiers had to be rewarded for their protracted labours ; and every man received, by way of booty, a captive, whom he might sell as a slave. The legions were then distributed for the winter, to safeguard the loyal, to overawe the disaffected, to cover the Province, and to be ready for mutual support. Though a thanksgiving service was decreed in Caesar's honour, he was aware that Pompey had begun to work against him.

Various tribes prepare to renew the struggle.   The winter had hardly set in when the legions were again called out ; for, though the victory at Alesia was decisive, some of the more resolute patriots were preparing to renew the struggle. They knew, indeed, that all the men whom they could muster had no chance of standing against Caesar in a battle ; but they allowed themselves to hope that, if they all rose simultaneously, his forces would not be strong enough to engage them all at once in detail. Such is the account, based probably upon the reports of Caesar's spies, which Aulus Hirtius [1] has given us. But it may perhaps be doubted by those who have analysed his narrative whether the rebellious tribes had any such definite and concerted plan. It is probable that they were actuated, not jointly but severally, by sheer abhorrence of a foreign yoke, by sullen despair, by desire

---

[1] The last book of the *Commentaries* was written by Aulus Hirtius. See *Caesar's Conquest of Gaul*[2], pp. 824-6, and *Philol.*, lxix, 1910, pp. 484-5.

for plunder, perhaps by the vague hope that when Caesar
was gone, his successor would leave such obstinate rebels
to themselves.

The Bituriges, who had not forgotten the massacre at
Avaricum, were the first to stir. The single legion which
had been quartered in their country was powerless to
restrain them. Caesar was anxious to give a long rest
to his soldiers, who were tired out by the extraordinary
duration and severity of the late campaign ; but before
the year was out he took the field, and while the chiefs
were still talking over their plans another legion was upon
them. Thousands of peasants were captured while they
were working in the fields : others had just time to flee :
but hurry where they might, Caesar was too quick for
them ; and his swiftness so impressed men's minds that
the friendly tribes saw that it was their interest to remain
loyal to a Governor who was strong enough both to protect
and to punish, while waverers hastened to sue for peace.
Caesar sent the legions back to quarters with the promise
of a substantial present for every officer and man, while
he himself returned to his civil work at Bibracte. But
in little more than a month his tranquillity was interrupted. When the humbled Bituriges begged for his aid
against the Carnutes, who had turned upon them, he
summoned two legions from the valley of the Saône ; and
on the mere rumour of his coming the Carnutes fled in
every direction. Chased from place to place by cavalry
and auxiliary infantry, numbed by the cold and drenched
by the rains, they finally dispersed among the neighbouring tribes; and their pursuers returned, laden with plunder. The lesson sufficed for the time ; but the legions
were left at Cenabum, to keep the tribesmen in awe.

Still, there was another tribe to be reckoned with, the
warlike Bellovaci, who had some grudge against the
Suessiones, and were mustering their forces and those of
the neighbouring tribes to attack them. The leaders
were a Bellovacan chief called Correus, who had incited
his fellow tribesmen to rebel in defiance of the tribal
council, and Commius, whose spirit was not subdued by

his defeat at Alesia. On Caesar's approach they established themselves in the forest of Compiègne, on Mont St. Marc, a hill protected by a marshy watercourse, which oozed northward into the river Aisne.[1] Caesar, who had assembled four legions, was anxious to bring on a battle, and advanced in a formation which partly concealed his strength ; but as the enemy were too wary to quit their vantage ground, he encamped on Mont St. Pierre, the height just opposite theirs. During the next few days frequent skirmishes took place, and the Gauls succeeded in surrounding some foraging parties, which were unavoidably isolated. Caesar's enemies at Rome were gladdened by a rumour that his cavalry had been annihilated, that the 7th legion had suffered a defeat, and that he himself was hemmed in by the Bellovaci.[2] In fact, he had under-estimated his task. It was impossible to storm the camp without excessive loss ; and, as a large force was needed to invest it, he sent for the three legions which he had left at Cenabum and in the country of the Bituriges.

When the rebel leaders heard of their approach, they remembered the fate of Alesia, and determined to send off their non-combatants and baggage in the night. The long train of wagons was barely in motion when day broke, and the Romans caught sight of them. The enemy formed up in front of their camp to cover the retreat, intending to follow as soon as possible. On their left and separated from their camp by a narrow depression, was a plateau with gently sloping sides. Caesar rapidly bridged the marsh, led his troops across, ascended the plateau, and just on its edge placed engines to throw missiles against the enemy's masses. Not daring to retreat, lest the tribal contingents might become confused as they broke into detachments, and fall victims to the Roman cavalry, they remained for some hours under arms. Caesar made a new camp on the plateau, formed up the legions in front of it, and kept the troop-horses bridled, ready to charge at a moment's notice. Towards nightfall, as the enemy could not remain where they were

---

[1] See pp. 287–91.　　　　　　[2] Cic., *Fam.*, viii, 1, 4.

any longer without food, they had recourse to a stratagem. 51 B.C.
Bundles of straw and sticks were laid in front of the line
and set ablaze. In a moment a wall of flame hid the
entire multitude, and they instantly fled. Suspecting,
though he could not see what they had done, Caesar made
the legions advance cautiously, and sent his cavalry up
the hill in pursuit. But the cavalry were afraid to ride
through the fiery barrier ; and a few bold troopers who
spurred in could hardly see their horses' heads for the
smoke. Meanwhile the enemy made good their retreat
and took refuge on a strong position, perhaps Mont
Ganelon on the further bank of the Oise.

Not far from the confluence of the Aisne and the Oise
there was a large meadow, the luxuriance of which,
Correus expected, would attract the Roman foragers.
In the woods which encompassed it he posted a strong
force of horse and foot. Having learned his design from
a prisoner, Caesar sent his foragers down the valley of
the Aisne, escorted by cavalry and light-armed auxiliaries,
and, following in support with the infantry, took post as
near the meadow as he could without being perceived.
Discerning the cavalry as they approached, the Gauls
rode out from the wood and charged ; but the disciplined
squadrons sustained the shock with admirable coolness :
supported by the auxiliaries, they baffled every attempt
to outflank them ; and they had already won the day
when the infantry appeared. The flying Gauls, caught
in their own trap, were hunted down and slaughtered in
the woods and by the banks of the Oise. Correus, standing
alone upon the field, refusing to accept quarter, struck
fiercely at his opponents and wounded many of them,
until, infuriated by his obstinacy, they hurled a volley
of javelins into his body, and he fell dead. Commius
escaped to wage a guerrilla warfare, but afterwards made
his peace with the conqueror, stipulating only that, as
a concession to his well-grounded fears, he might never
again look upon a Roman face.[1]

[1] An account of the successful close of his career will be found in *Anc.
Britain*, pp. 361, 365–6, 371.

51. B. C.   This was the expiring effort of the Bellovaci. Pleading that Correus was alone to blame, they appealed to Caesar's clemency, and obtained a contemptuous forgiveness. Their allies, who had been waiting to see what terms they would obtain, submitted likewise and gave hostages.

Caesar again harries the Eburones.

Caesar, accompanied by Labienus and reinforced by a legion under Mark Antony, marched against the remnant of the Eburones, and sent out flying columns to ravage, burn, and slay. Ambiorix evidently was not to be captured ; but Caesar resolved that he should never dare to show his face again among the people upon whom he had ·brought such a terrible doom.

Labienus punishes the Treveri.

The end was at hand. Labienus, who had been commissioned to deal the Treveri a final blow, captured their chieftains, and among them an Aeduan noble, Surus, who, scorning the tergiversations of his countrymen, remained a brave, unwavering, incorruptible patriot. The most warlike states were now subdued or overawed : only some tribes in the west were still restless. The Carnutes had been left free to strike by the withdrawal of the three legions from Cenabum. A rebel chief named Dumnacus, with a motley force from their country and from Brittany, was besieging Lemonum, on the site of the modern Poitiers, in which an adherent of Caesar had taken refuge.

Fabius compels Dumnacus to raise the siege of Lemonum.

Fabius compelled him to raise the siege, and while he was hurrying to escape across the Loire, pounced upon him and defeated him twice with heavy loss. Flying alone from the battlefield, he wandered to the uttermost parts of Gaul ; and history knows him no more. Two thousand of the fugitives, rallied by the Senonian adventurer, Drappes, and Lucterius, the chief who had so ably supported Vercingetorix, went off to plunder the Province ; but, finding themselves hotly pursued by Caninius, they took refuge in the fortress of Uxellodunum, the modern Puy d'Issolu,[1] of which, before the great rebellion, Lucterius had been the over-lord.

Drappes and Lucterius take refuge in Uxellodunum.

They had hardly shut the gates before their pursuers

[1] See pp. 291-2.

arrived. The hill overlooked the left bank of the river
Tourmente, which, about two miles to the south-west,
flowed into the Dordogne. It rose fully six hundred feet
above the valley ; steep rocks on every side forbade any
attempt to assault ; and to approach by an embankment
was utterly impracticable. Caninius therefore proceeded
to invest the town. On the west, rising beyond the
valley of the Tourmente, there were two hills of considerable height, and a third on the north-east, linked to
the stronghold by a broad neck of land. Caninius made
a camp on each of the three, and began to connect them
by a line of contravallation. Watching the progress of
the works, the garrison remembered the story of Alesia :
Lucterius had been there, and knew how Vercingetorix
and his people had suffered ; unless his own men bestirred
themselves, they too would be starved into surrender.
It was agreed that he and Drappes should make an
attempt to procure supplies. On the following night,
leaving two thousand men to hold the town, they stole
out with the rest of the force. For several days they
scoured the surrounding country, collecting corn. During
this time they occasionally attacked the Romans with
such vigour that Caninius was obliged to suspend the
construction of his lines ; but a detachment which
attempted to convey the stores into the fortress was
destroyed. Lucterius with a few followers escaped ; but
Drappes, who commanded another division, was surprised, and every man who escaped the sword was made
a prisoner. Resenting the indignity of bonds, or dreading
the penalty of obstinate rebellion, Drappes starved himself to death.

Meanwhile Caninius was reinforced by the legions of
Fabius, who, following up his victory over Dumnacus,
had fallen upon the Carnutes, already weakened by the
losses which they had suffered in that battle, and overwhelmed them. This warlike people, who had never been
thoroughly subdued, were now completely cowed and
forced to give hostages ; and the maritime states of
Brittany, which, like them, had supported Dumnacus,

51 B. C.   hastened to follow their example. Caesar, who had been making a political progress and trying to conciliate the humbled chiefs, was now at Cenabum; while Mark -Antony, whom he had left behind, was holding the Belgae in awe. The Carnutes were still uneasy at the remembrance of the provocation which they had given in the great revolt; and it seemed likely that despair might drive them to fresh excesses. Caesar saw that the only way to allay their fears and to restrain their turbulence was to make an example of the leader who had incited them, and frankly to forgive the rest. He therefore demanded that Cotuatus, who had been the author of the massacre at Cenabum in the preceding year, should be delivered up to him for punishment; and the people, eager to purchase the favour of the conqueror, hunted him down and brought him a prisoner

Execu-   to the Roman camp. Caesar, if Hirtius is to be believed,
tion of
Cotuatus.   was unwilling to order his execution, but could not afford to disregard the clamours of the soldiery. But Caesar knew how to silence any clamour; and if he had told the story, he would have told it without excuse. Cotuatus was flogged till he was insensible; and his head was then cut off.

Caesar   Caesar now received a series of dispatches informing
marches
for Uxel-   him of the resistance of Uxellodunum. Contemptible
lodunum.   as were the numbers of the rebels, their example might encourage other states to renew the struggle. Only one more summer had to pass, as the malcontents had doubtless reckoned, and his government would be at an end. But Caesar determined that before that time they should be for ever subdued. Taking his cavalry with him, he hurried southwards, followed by two legions, for Uxellodunum.

He de-   He instantly detected the weak point in the enemy's
prives the   position. His lieutenants had merely intended a blockade.
garrison
of water.   But the garrison, whose numbers had been greatly reduced, were amply provisioned; and the only way of reducing them in time was to cut off their supply of water. Archers, slingers, and artillery were posted on the western bank

of the Tourmente ; and thenceforward the Gauls could 51 B. C. get no water except from a spring on the western slope of the hill. Opposite this spring Caesar proceeded to construct a terrace. From the heights above the enemy hurled down missiles, and many of the workers were struck : but the rest toiled doggedly on ; and the terrace was built up nearer and nearer still. A tower was erected upon it, of the extraordinary height of ten stories, enough to overtop the spring ; and the garrison dared not approach under the shower of stones and arrows which its engines rained down. As a last resource, they set fire to a number of barrels, filled with pitch, grease, and shavings, and rolled them on to the terrace. The woodwork and the sheds were presently ablaze. The garrison flung down missiles to deter their assailants from advancing to put out the fire ; and although the Romans did all that brave men could do, lives were sacrificed in vain. In this extremity Caesar sent several cohorts to climb the hill and feign an assault upon the town. Panic-stricken, the garrison recalled their comrades from below ; and the moment they turned their backs the Romans ran forward and extinguished the flames. Still the Gauls held out ; for the spring was still untouched. At length, however, a party of sappers crept through a gallery which had been secretly driven into the hill-side to the source of the spring, and diverted its flow. Then at last, feeling that Surrender of the Heaven was fighting against them, the garrison surrendered. garrison.

Caesar saw that if rebellions were allowed to recur Their punishment. indefinitely, his work would never be at an end. He determined, therefore, to inflict upon the garrison a punishment so appalling that all malcontents should in future remain quiet. He would not put his prisoners to death, because, if he did, their fate, though it might be talked of for a time, would soon be forgotten. They were to remain a living warning to intending rebels. He ordered their hands to be cut off, and sent them forth to exist as they best might.

One notable survivor of the great rebellion was still

51 B.C. at large. Lucterius, the man who, as Caesar said, was
The ready to dare anything, had wandered far from Uxello-
fate of
Lucterius. dunum. He knew that for him there was no forgiveness ;
and he went from place to place in fear of betrayal. At
length he fell into the hands of a renegade Arvernian,
who brought him in chains to Caesar ; and what was his
fate we can only guess.

Caesar's Caesar was now at leisure ; and he used it in writing
Commen- the memoirs whose directness and unadorned elegance
taries.
Cicero[1] praised, which Turenne, Napoleon,[2] and Wolseley,[3]
commended to students of the art of war, and of which
the greatest scholar of all time wrote, 'The noble work
deserves all the labour that can be spent upon it : the
enormous difference between these Commentaries and
everything else that is called Roman history cannot be
adequately realized '.[4] The purity of the Latin, the
lucidity, the terseness, and the vigour of the narrative,
the skill that excites emotion by virtue of restraint and
appeals to admiration by statement of fact without the
impertinence of praise, have been generally acclaimed :
the critic [5] who reproached Caesar with having failed
to recognize the nobleness of Vercingetorix, forgot that
he had himself learned to recognize it from Caesar alone.
Apart from exaggerations due to defective information,
the general trustworthiness of the record has been
vindicated by analysis of the arguments by which it was
impugned. It has been assumed, however, that the work
was essentially a manifesto, in which Caesar strove to
justify his conquest and the successive levies which he
had made in order to achieve it.[6] Whom was the manifesto
designed to influence ? Caesar was not so simple as to
imagine that any colouring which he could give to his

---

[1] *Brut.*, 75, 262.
[2] *Mém., notes et mélanges*, ii, 155 ; G. F. R. Henderson, *Stonewall Jackson*,
i, 1898, p. 504.
[3] *The Soldier's Pocket-book*[5], 1886, p. 286.
[4] Th. Mommsen, quoted by H. Meusel, *C. I. Caesaris comm. de b. c.*, 1906,
p. 10.
[5] R. Y. Tyrrell, *The Correspondence of Cicero*, v, 1897, p. xlvii.
[6] Th. Mommsen, *Röm. Gesch.*, iii[2], 1889, p. 615 (Eng. tr., v, 1908, p. 499).

story would induce the Catonian party to refrain from 51 B. C. the prosecution which he knew that he must expect unless he could evade it by retaining his command until he should enter upon his second consulship ; and when he wrote he knew that, despite the agreement which had been made at the conference of Luca, his enemies were scheming to recall him as a private citizen before that time. Cato was hardly to be conciliated by the frankness with which Caesar narrated the massacre of the Usipetes and Tencteri ; and though the speech which he ascribed to Diviciacus has suggested to a cynic that, with the aim of moulding Roman opinion, he had told him what to say, he attributed to Ariovistus the most telling arguments which an advocate of Ariovistus could have devised. To keep his supporters loyal no manifesto was required. If, then, the *Commentaries* were designed as a political document, they must have been intended to influence waverers or to win over those who were indifferent. The question remains whether Caesar's purpose, whatever it may have been, led him to misstate facts or to warp their true significance ; and on this I have said in former volumes what I had to say.[1]

But Caesar left his tale unfinished, for he had other work to do. He knew that conquest can never be complete until coercion has been followed by conciliation. When he deemed it necessary to have recourse to terrorism, he did not fail to terrorize ; but the clemency for which he took credit in his memoirs was attested by his enemies,[2] as well as by his friends. In little more than a year he would be leaving Gaul ; and he must contrive to leave it at peace. The time had not come, nor had he the authority to organize a government : it would be enough if his successors could accomplish that task without encountering resistance. He had no wish to oppress the Gauls or to hurt their national pride ; and towards the end of the war he had raised a native legion, called Alaudae, upon which he afterwards bestowed

He follows up coercion by conciliation

---

[1] See pp. 271–81. [2] e. g. Gaius Cassius (Cic., *Fam.*, xv, 19, 4).

Roman citizenship.[1] He fixed the tribute of the Gauls at a moderate amount,—forty millions of sesterces,[2] or about four hundred thousand pounds ; and, mindful of the evils entailed in other provinces by the farming of the taxes, he arranged that, like the Spanish tribes, they should be free to raise the sum themselves. He did not interfere with their institutions, though he doubtless used his influence to promote his own adherents to power. He loaded the chiefs with presents : he won their hearts by the charm of his address ; and if, when he quitted Gaul, he were confronted by another foe, they would send their bravest warriors to fight under his flag.[3]

Reasons of his success.

It may not be superfluous to consider by what means, apart from self-evident military skill, the conquest, fraught with illimitable issues, had been achieved. With all their dash and nervous enthusiasm, the Gauls lacked the tenacity of the Roman : rushing vehemently to the attack, they fell away at the first reverse. This weakness, which Caesar often notices, may have been inherent in the race : it may have been wholly or in part the result of a want of mutual confidence. Their naïve credulity was observed by Posidonius ; [4] and, unwarned by experience, they precipitated themselves, again and again, into the simplest traps. Nor, for the most part, were the heterogeneous levies who opposed Caesar the equals of the Gauls who had routed a Roman army on the banks of the Allia. The Helvetii, the Parisii, the Senones, and a few of the Belgic tribes alone maintained the ancient renown of the Celtic infantry. The Gauls had no regular troops, no science, no discipline, and, until Vercingetorix arose, they had no great leader : their conqueror, master of a compact, disciplined, and well-equipped army, was free in opposition to their sporadic efforts to pursue a definite aim. He knew that a well-organized commissariat is the foundation of success in

[1] Suet., 24, 2. Cf. Cic., *Phil.*, i, 8, 20.
[2] Suet., 25, 1 ; Eutrop., vi, 17.
[3] See Cic., *Att.*, ix, 13, 4, and Caes., *B. C.*, i, 39, 2.
[4] Strabo, iv, 4, 2. 5.

war ; and the truth of this maxim is borne in at every
turn upon the reader of his memoirs. While his enemies
were obliged to strike prematurely or to disperse because
they had not secured their means of subsistence, he was
able to keep his forces together and to choose his own
time. With cool calculation he took advantage of the
fears, the necessities, the intestine broils, the spasmodic
revolutions, the petty ambitions of those incoherent
multitudes. For it must never be forgotten that, as the
British conquered India with the aid of Indians, Caesar
conquered Gaul with the aid of Gauls. Fortune, which,
as he so often said, ' is a great power in war, as in all other
affairs ', was no fickle friend to him. The aristocracies
broke the triumvirate which threatened to anticipate him,
and deprived the Helvetii, who, unaided, were almost his
match, of allies who would have been irresistible. The
Romanized Provincials supported him throughout ; and
in the great rebellion their assistance was indispensable.
Gallic patriotism was choked by jealousy ; and when
Vercingetorix was fighting for the fatherland, there were
many who had as much to fear from his success as from
his failure. Those who courted Caesar's favour and
espoused his cause were distinguished by every mark of
favour, and might reckon with certainty upon his support.
The Aedui adhered to him for six years, and when they
changed their minds they found that they had served
his turn : the Remi saw from the first that he was going
to win, and, having made their choice, abided by it to
the end. The Aquitanians cared nothing for the Gauls,
and their isolated resistance was paralysed in one campaign. The Arvernian oligarchy executed the chief who
had restored the traditional glory of their kings, and
while his son was still too young to play his part, reduced
the state which had been the rival of Rome's strongest
ally to such insignificance that for five years it remained
unnoticed in the record of the war. Indutiomarus and
Ambiorix and Acco struck too soon ; and when their
help was needed, one had vanished and two were slain.
The Celticans, with the exception of the Senones, the

Carnutes, and the maritime tribes, submitting, for the most part, without an effort, looked on with folded hands until, at the eleventh hour, Vercingetorix aroused them ; and then the Belgae, who had hitherto borne the brunt, held aloof until it was too late. And there was one other factor which we must not forget. Against Vercingetorix even Caesar's fortune and his genius might have failed if the hereditary enemies of Gaul had not crossed the Rhine to his aid.

And after he had gone, what motive had the Gauls to rebel ? Many of the weaker tribes had been subject to a stronger ; and it was less humiliating to obey an alien than one of their own race. Rome was distant ; and her grandeur wrought upon the imagination. Rome was the resistless power which, for centuries, had been bringing, one after another, the peoples of the earth within her empire ; and for the Western in that partnership there was a germ of pride. If adventurers in Gaul, as in India, regretted the good old days when they could win thrones by their wits and by their swords, the many gained more than they had lost ; and so it happened that the few sporadic outbreaks which followed Caesar's departure were foredoomed to fail, and that his conquest, of which the French nation remains the monument, was effected once for all.

CHAPTER XIII

THE GATHERING OF THE STORM

WHILE Caesar was fighting at Alesia his enemies in 52 B.C. Rome were scheming to effect his ruin.

It will be remembered that by the law which Pompey and Crassus had carried in pursuance of the agreement which Caesar had made with them at Luca the proconsulship of Caesar was prolonged for a second period of five years, and was therefore legally secured until the end of February, 49. Virtually indeed it was secured until the end of that year ;[1] for under the Sempronian law of Gaius Gracchus his successor would be one of the consuls elected in July, 50, and could not in the ordinary course arrive in Gaul until after the expiry of his consulship.[2] It will also be remembered that a clause of the law carried by Pompey and Crassus provided that the question of appointing a successor should not be raised before the 1st of March, 50. But it was vitally important that when Caesar returned to Rome he should return as consul ; for he knew that if he were not then protected by the sanctity of office, Cato or another enemy would prosecute him on some charge connected with his government of Gaul.[3] He could not legally become consul before the 1st of January, 48,[4] and the difficulty was that, unless he could obtain a dispensation, he would be obliged to present himself for election as a private individual in the summer of 49. It would seem that the tribunes who favoured him desired nevertheless to associate him as joint-consul with Pompey for the latter part of 52, but that he preferred to remain in

---

[1] Strictly speaking, to the end of 705 (Nov. 2, 49 B.C.).
[2] Cf. Cic., De prov. cons., 7, 17.
[3] Suet., Div. Iul., 30, 3 ; App., B. C., ii. 25, 97.
[4] Or rather Jan. 1, 706 (Nov. 3, 49 B.C.).

52 B. C.   Gaul and finish his work.[1] Probably, as I have remarked .
in a previous chapter, he had arranged at Luca with
Pompey and Crassus that he should be enabled to pass
direct from his province to a second consulship. At all
events he asked Cicero, whom he met at Ravenna after
the campaign of 53, to induce Caelius, who was then a
tribune, to support a bill which should authorize him to
stand for the consulship without presenting himself at
Rome.[2] Cicero consented, and, if we may believe his own
words, fulfilled his promise. Pompey used his influence
for the same end,[3] although Cicero, as he himself afterwards said, endeavoured to dissuade him.[4] We are told
by Dio that Pompey persisted because he wished to
prevent Caesar from becoming his colleague and also
because he was unwilling to offend him ; but it is more
reasonable to suppose that Pompey was fulfilling a secret
pledge than to accept the statement of a writer who was
Caesar au- always ready to invent a motive. Notwithstanding the
thorized   determined opposition of Cato,[5] the bill, which is known
to stand
for the   as the Law of the Ten Tribunes,[6] was passed. But
consul-   Pompey, influenced doubtless by the Catonian party,
ship in
absence.   soon afterwards stultified his own action. He was no
longer sole consul, for in July or August he had nominated
his father-in-law, Metellus Scipio, as his colleague ;[7]
but the nomination itself shows that he was still supreme,
and Scipio, though he repealed the law by which Clodius
had weakened the power of the censors,[8] virtually

---

[1] Suet., 26, 1 ; Dio, xl, 50, 4 ; 51, 1.

[2] Cic., *Att.*, vii, 1, 4. See pp. 316–7.

[3] *Ib.*, viii, 3, 3 ; *Fam.*, vi, 6, 5 ; Suet., 26, 1 ; App., ii, 25, 96 ; Dio,
xl, 51, 2.

[4] *Phil.*, ii, 10, 24.   [5] *B. C.*, i, 32, 3 ; Livy, *Epit.*, 107.

Cic., *Att.*, vii, 3, 4 ; viii, 3, 3 ; Flor., ii, 13, 16. See p. 316.

[7] App., ii, 25, 95 ; Dio, xl, 51, 3 ; Plut., *Pomp.*, 55, 5, who says that
Pompey made his father-in-law his colleague for the remaining five months
of the year. Drumann (*Gesch. Roms*, iv², 1910, p. 535), who failed to see
that πέντε μῆνες was a round number, inferred that Scipio became consul
on the 1st of August. Apart from Plutarch's statement we only know that
he entered office between June 13, when Pompey was still sole consul
(*C. I. L.*, i², p. 734), and September 13, when, as an inscription shows
(*Eph. epigr.*, iii, 1877, p. 204), Scipio was his colleague.

[8] Dio, xl, 57, 1. See vol. i, p. 330.

remained a mere figure-head.   Pompey now re-enacted · 52 B. C.
the law which ordained that all candidates for office must
attend in person, and confirmed a resolution which the
Senate had passed in the preceding year, that no consul
and no praetor should be eligible for a provincial governorship until five years had elapsed from the expiration of
his office.[1]   Caesar's supporters of course protested, for This privi-
either of these laws was enough to ruin his career : the lege en-
former nullified the Law of the Ten Tribunes ; under by later
the latter, which practically abrogated the Sempronian tion.
law, the Senate might send a new Governor to succeed
Caesar on the day after the legal termination of his
command.[2]   Pompey, either yielding to pressure or
wishing to correct an error which he had made through
oversight, on his own responsibility added a clause to
the former law, to the effect that only those persons
might stand for office in their absence to whom permission to do so had been expressly granted.[3]   But this
clause, even if it was not legally invalid, could not exempt
Caesar from the operation of Pompey's other law ; for
he would gain nothing by it if before his election and
during the interval between his election and his consulship he were a private person and therefore liable to
prosecution.   The only security that remained to him
rested upon a technical point.   Under the Sempronian
law the tribunician veto could not be exercised against
any settlement of consular provinces ; but now that the
Sempronian law was defunct this disability was removed,
though the Senate, if it were prepared to take the risk
of civil war, could still in the last resort treat a refractory
tribune as a public enemy.   Pompey, moreover, in viola-
tion of his own enactment, soon afterwards accepted
from the Senate the prolongation of his government of
Spain for another period of five years.[4]   Thus, if Caesar
became consul in 48, he would be without an army,

---

[1] Suet., 28, 3 ; Dio, xl, 30, 1 ; 56, 1.   Cf. P. Willems, Le sénat, &c.,
ii, 1883, p. 588, and see p. 302.
[2] See p. 302.   [3] Cf. Suet., 28, 3, with Dio, xl, 56, 2-3.
[4] Plut., Caes., 28, 3 ; Pomp., 55, 5 ; App., ii, 24, 92 ; Dio, xl, 56, 2.

52 B. C.   while Pompey would still retain command of the legions
in Spain. Cato, regarding Pompey and Caesar as equally
dangerous and hoping to thwart them before they could
either attack one another or renew their coalition, offered
himself as a candidate for the ensuing consulship. His
rivals were Marcus Claudius Marcellus and Sulpicius
Rufus, the distinguished jurist, whose candidature had
failed in the time of Catiline. Cato induced the Senate
to decree that the candidates should conduct their
canvass without employing agents. The shopkeepers,
artisans, and idlers of Rome, who throve on bribery and
enjoyed the importance of being solicited for their votes,
resented the innovation ; for evidently the candidates

Futile
candida-
ture of
Cato.

would not have time to canvass every one. Moreover,
Cato, maintaining that citizens ought to vote in obedience
to principle, scorned the electioneering methods which
Quintus Cicero had recommended to his brother, and
would not even condescend to shake hands with the
electors. They of course revenged themselves by leaving
his virtue to reward itself.[1]

Of the new consuls Marcellus was notoriously opposed
to Caesar ; Sulpicius was lukewarm, but anxious to maintain peace.[2] Pompey threw out a hint that he intended
to go at last to Spain. Cicero was so alarmed at the
prospect of his leaving Rome, which he alone could
preserve from anarchy, that he urged Theophanes,
Pompey's Greek secretary, to exert his influence and
persuade his master to remain.[3] In the early spring
Marcellus showed his hand. Caesar had settled new
colonists in the Latin colony of Comum, to whom, in
virtue of a law passed in his consulship by his satellite
Vatinius, he granted Roman citizenship. In doing so,

A sena-
torial
resolution
against
Caesar
vetoed.

however, he had in some way exceeded his authority.[4]
Marcellus, who, like all the members of his party, regarded
many of the acts of Caesar's consulship as null, moved
that the colonists should be disfranchised.[5] The motion

[1] Plut., Cato min., 49, 2 ; Dio, xl, 58.
[2] Cic., Fam., iv, 1, 1 ; 2, 3 ; 3, 1.   [3] Att., v, 11, 3.   [4] See pp. 317–20.
[5] Suet., 28, 3. Cf. C. C. L. Lange, Röm. Alt., iii, 1871, p. 372.

was apparently carried, but vetoed by Caesarian tribunes, for on the 10th of May Cicero wrote to Atticus from his villa near Pompeii, 'No trustworthy report has yet reached us here as to how Caesar took the news that the senatorial resolution was put on record.'[1] It was rumoured that Caesar had actually on his own responsibility carried out the intention which he had long since formed of enfranchising the population of Transpadane Gaul : 'If that is so,' Cicero added, 'I fear there will be a great disturbance.'[2] A few days later, however, he learned that the rumour had died out ; that Marcellus had not yet brought before the Senate the question of appointing a successor to Caesar ; and that he had postponed his intended motion till the 1st of June.[3] Premature though the motion was, his supporters complained of his inaction ; and Caelius, who had a gift of terse characterization, remarked in writing to Cicero, 'You know Marcellus, how slow and inefficient he is, and Servius, what a dawdler.'[4] Servius, however, to whom Cicero listened with approval, did not shrink from warning the House of the danger of civil war.[5] But Cicero, sorely against his will, was now obliged to tear himself away from Italy, and he saw that for a year or more he would be prevented from taking part in a political controversy more sensational than any which he had yet known. In accordance with Pompey's recent law, he was obliged to accept the governorship of the province of Cilicia.[6] 'Do not imagine', he wrote to Atticus, 'that anything can console me for this awful bore, except the hope that it won't last more than a year.'[7] Before he started he published his treatise *On the State* as a counsel of perfection to politicians,[8] and made Caelius promise to keep him regularly informed of every important event that might occur at home.[9] 'See',

Apr. 8, 51 B. C.

Apr. 30.

Cicero reluctantly leaves Rome to govern Cilicia.

---

[1] *Att.*, v, 2, 3. See p. 308, n. 12.   [2] *Ib.*   [3] *Fam.*, viii, 1, 2.
[4] *Ib.*, 10, 3.   [5] *Ib.*, iv, 3, 1.   [6] *Ib.*, iii, 2, 1.
[7] *Att.*, v, 2, 3.
[8] *Fam.*, viii, 1, 5. Cf. O. E. Schmidt, *D. Briefwechsel d. M. T. Cicero,* 1893, p. 75.
[9] *Fam.*, viii, 1. 1.

51 B. C.   he afterwards said, 'what a compliment I am paying
you ; and not undeservedly, for I have never in all my
life known any one more *au fait* in political questions
than you.' [1] Atticus, who of course undertook to attend
to his private affairs during his absence, exhorted him to
govern righteously ; and Cicero repeatedly begged his
[£8,200.]   friend to see that a loan of eight hundred and twenty
thousand sesterces, which he had received from Caesar,
should be at once repaid.[2] As he was travelling towards
Brundisium, where he was to embark, he observed that
in the country towns there was much vague anxiety
Pompey   about the political situation ; [3] but Pompey, at whose
relieves   villa near Tarentum he stayed for a few days, completely
his
anxiety   reassured him. ' It is a great patriot ', he told Atticus,
about the   ' that I am leaving and one thoroughly prepared to ward
political
situation.   off the dangers which we dread.' [4] Caelius was sceptical.
' If ', he wrote, ' you have come across Pompey, as you
wished, write to me fully what you thought of him,
what he said to you, and what he professed to want ;
for he generally thinks one thing and says another, and
yet isn't clever enough to hide his real aims.' [5] But
Cicero was still under the spell. After he had read this
letter he assured Caelius that Pompey was ' a great
patriot, prepared in heart and head for all emergencies '.[6]

Antece-   It was a happy thought of Cicero to choose Caelius as
dents of   his special correspondent, for without his letters we
Caelius,
who un-   should have scant original information about one of the
dertakes   most momentous years in the life of the Republic. Caelius
to supply
Cicero   knew intimately the world of politics and the world of
with news.   fashion ; if his judgement was unsound, he had keen
discernment ; and he wielded a pungent pen. He had
served his political apprenticeship under Cicero himself,
and had been initiated by him into the life of the Forum.
As a youth of twenty-five,[7] he, like so many of his con-

---

[1] *Fam.*, ii, 8, 1.
[2] *Att.*, v, 1, 2 ; 4, 3 ; 5, 2 ; 6, 2 ; 9, 2 ; 13, 3 ; &c. The debt still remained
unpaid after Cicero returned to Italy (*ib.*, vii, 8, 5).
[3] *Ib.*, v, 3, 1.   [4] *Ib.*, 7.   [5] *Fam.*, viii, 1, 3.   [6] *Ib.*, ii, 8, 2.
[7] Caelius, as P. Groebe has shown (*Hermes*, xxxvi, 1901, pp. 612-4),
was born in 88 or possibly 89 B.C., not, as Pliny (*Nat. Hist.*, vii, 49 (50),

temporaries, fell under the influence of Catiline. He 51 B.C.
prosecuted Gaius Antonius,[1] who had been the colleague
of Cicero in the consulship, and won fame not only as
a formidable forensic antagonist, but also as an eloquent
speaker. Quintilian[2] named him among the foremost
orators of the time. His handsome face,[3] his caustic
wit, his graceful dancing,[4] perhaps also his impulsive
generosity, attracted Clodia ; when she tired of his
friend Catullus he became her lover ; and when he had
broken from her or she from him he paid his tribute to
her personality. Quintilian[5] has recorded the nickname
which he flung at her—' the twopenny-halfpenny Clytemnestra '—which suggested to those who knew the
low life of Rome that, after murdering her husband, she
had sunk to the level of the lowest prostitute. ' Woman ',
said Juvenal,[6] ' is most savage when wounded pride spurs
her hate.' Instigated by Clodia, one Atratinus, whose
father Caelius had prosecuted, charged him with having
attempted, amongst other crimes, to poison his former
mistress. Caelius defended himself with characteristic
violence,[7] and Cicero, who rejoiced in the opportunity
of castigating the woman whom he hated, successfully
pleaded his cause. Thenceforward he and Cicero, notwithstanding their difference in age, became close friends.[8]

165) says, in 82 ; for Cicero (*Pro Cael.*, 7, 18) remarks that he became eligible
for the quaestorship, the minimum age for which was 30, in 59, and he
held the praetorship, the minimum age for which was 40, in 48 B.C.
[E. Meyer (*Caesars Monarchie*[2], 1919, pp. 451 note, 577 note) insists that
there was no minimum age for the quaestorship, and that it was only necessary for candidates to have completed 10 years of military service. But
this rule was obsolete (Th. Mommsen, *Röm. Staatsr.*, i[3], 1887, p. 567). After
the reforms of Sulla the quaestorship gave admission to the Senate ; and
since Pompey, when he was sent at the age of 24 to Sicily, was far below
the senatorial age (Cic., *De imp. Cn. Pomp.*, 21, 61), I see no reason for dissent-
ing from the orthodox view (Daremberg and Saglio, *Dict. des ant. grecques
et rom.*, i, 271 ; iii, 1533). Anyhow, what I have said about Caelius's praetorship holds good.]

   [1] See vol. i, p. 317.
   [2] *Inst.*, vi, 3, 69 ; x, 1, 115 ; 2, 25 ; xii, 10, 11. Cf. Cic., *Brut.*, 79, 283.
   [3] Gell., xvii, 1, 11.   [4] Cf. Cic., *Pro Sest.*, 54, 116.
   [5] *Inst.*, viii, 6, 53. Cf. Plut., *Cic.*, 29, 2.
   [6] x, 328-9.   [7] Quint., xi, 1, 51.
   [8] The evidence—*Att.*, ii, 12, 2 (*de lituis βοώπιδος*) which Tyrrell (*The Corre-

51 B. C.   Even before Cicero arrived in his province sensational
The consul reports began to reach him. Marcellus, before the day
Marcellus
from   to which he had postponed his motion, on some pretext
animus   ordered one of the citizens of Comum, who happened to
against
Caesar   be in the capital, to be flogged ; and, explaining that the
flogs a of punishment had been inflicted in order to show that his
citizen of
Comum.   Roman citizenship was a sham, bade him go and exhibit
his scars to Caesar.[1] Cicero, notwithstanding his political
sympathies, was scandalized ; for not only was Comum
connected with the family of Pompey, but all the Transpadanes already possessed Latin rights, and it was a
question whether the injured man was not an ex-magistrate and therefore entitled to the franchise. ' Marcellus ',
he wrote, ' behaved outrageously in the case of the
citizen of Comum. Even if he did not hold a magistracy,
still he was a Transpadane. So Marcellus seems to me
to have given no less cause of offence to our friend Pompey
than to Caesar.'[2] When, however, the Senate assembled
Apr. 30. on the 1st of June Marcellus did not bring forward his
promised motion,—' not ', said Caelius, ' as it seems to
me, from lack of energy, but from policy '.[3] The sequel
may perhaps suggest that he was restrained by Pompey.
June 19. On the 22nd of July the Senate met in the temple of
Apollo, outside the boundary of the city ; and Pompey
was therefore able to attend. He was about to start for
Ariminum to inspect his troops. One of the members
questioned him about the legion which he had lent to
Caesar. He replied that it was in Gaul. So much everybody knew, and the coterie who were most bitterly
opposed to Caesar taunted Pompey for irresolution and
insincerity. At last under pressure he promised to recall
the legion. The question of appointing a successor to
Caesar was then mooted ; and a resolution was passed
that Pompey should return to the capital as soon as
possible, in order that he might be present when the

spondence of Cicero, iii[2], 1914, p. xlvii) cites for his assertion that Cicero
knew that Clodia ' had sounded the clarion in the attack [of Clodius] on
himself ' is nullified by his own note on the words which he quotes.
[1] See pp. 317–20.   [2] *Att.*, v, 11, 2.   [3] *Fam.*, viii, 2, 2.

question was discussed. ' I think ', Caelius added, ' the 51 B. C
matter will be debated on the 13th of August. There will July 11.
certainly be a settlement of some sort, unless it is
obstructed by a scandalous use of the veto.' [1]   But
Caelius was disappointed. On the 13th of August a
cousin of Marcellus, Gaius, one of the consuls-desig-
nate, who had been elected under the influence of
Pompey, was undergoing trial for bribery ; and the
question of the provinces was postponed till the 1st of July 28.
September. On that day the attendance of senators Pompey
was very small. Marcellus, however, moved that Caesar negatives
should be required to resign his command on the 1st of a proposal
March, 49 ; but Pompey resisted this proposal, which, quiring
being premature, was plainly illegal, and Sulpicius also resign on
spoke against it.[2] Pompey himself moved that at present March 1,
no decree should be passed about the Gallic provinces ; 49 B. C.
Scipio that the question should be brought before the
House on the 1st of March, 50, and discussed without
reference to any other provinces. ' This motion ', wrote
Caelius, ' made Cornelius Balbus look very blue, and
I know that he remonstrated with Scipio.' [3]   On the
29th of September, after repeated postponements,[4] the Aug. 25.
matter came to a head. Staunch Conservatives were
afraid that Caesar, if ever he obtained a second consulship, would wreck the constitution ; and everybody
knew that Pompey, notwithstanding the clause which
he had added, in favour of Caesar, to his own law,
strongly objected to his being allowed to retain his
province after the legal term. Having regard, however, to the law which he had passed four years before
in conjunction with Crassus, he stated emphatically that
he could not without injustice settle anything about
the Gallic provinces before the 1st of March, but that

---

[1] *Fam.*, viii, 4, 4.

[2] Dio, xl, 59, 1. See p. 308, and Dr. Hardy's article in *Journ. of Philol.*,
xxxiv, 1918, pp. 164, 173, 177, 204. If the motion was pressed, we may
assume that it was vetoed.

[3] *Fam.*, viii, 9, 5.

[4] *Ib.*, 5, 3 ; 8, 4. The postponements were necessary because Marcellus
could not get a quorum.

after that day he would not hesitate. ' What ', asked
a senator, ' if Caesar resolves to be consul and also to
keep his army ? ' ' What ', Pompey angrily retorted,
' if my son chooses to whack me with his stick ? '

The
Senate
resolves
that the
question
of ap-
pointing
Caesar's
successor
shall be
settled on
March 1,
50.

Finally, the Senate adopted a series of resolutions, the
first two of which Scipio and Curio, amongst others,
had drafted :—that on the 1st of March the consuls
should bring forward the question of the consular
provinces, and that this question should take prece-
dence of all others ; that if any magistrate then hindered the settlement of the question, he should be
deemed guilty of high treason ; that an inquiry should
be held concerning all the soldiers in Caesar's army
who had served their full time or who claimed their
discharge ; and that not only the eight provinces then
governed by ex-praetors, but also Cilicia should, when
they became vacant, be assigned to magistrates of
praetorian rank. The object of the last resolution was
plain : it meant that on the 1st of March, when the
consular provinces were to be fixed, Syria and Caesar's
two provinces would alone be available ;[1] as was to be
expected, therefore, this resolution as well as the second
and the third were vetoed by tribunes who supported
Caesar. To Caelius it seemed evident that the object
of the decree which was to be moved on the 1st of March
would be to compel Caesar, if he should determine to
stand for the consulship, first to resign his province and
to disband his troops. ' As far as I can see ', he concluded, ' Caesar means to adopt one of two alternatives,—
either to remain in his province and not be a candidate
in the ordinary course, or, if he succeeds in getting elected,
to leave his province. Curio is prepared to oppose him
at every point ; but what he can do I don't know.'[2]
Caelius, as he himself afterwards saw, and as the sagacious
reader has already seen, was mistaken in his forecast :
it was safe to prophesy that Caesar, if he were elected
consul, would in self-defence remain in Gaul until the
beginning of his consulship.

[1] Hardy, op. cit., pp. 181–2.   [2] Fam., viii, 8, 4–10; 9, 5.

Caesar was of course informed of these proceedings.
His immediate aim was to purchase the support of every
one who could serve him in the Senate, by intrigue, or in
the field. He had acquired enormous wealth in Gaul. He
had already enriched his officers and bestowed much prize-
money upon the rank and file.[1] He now virtually doubled
the pay of the private soldiers.[2] He lent money to those
who could repay, paid the debts of impoverished spend-
thrifts, and even made presents to slaves whom he knew
to have influence with their masters. Lucius Aemilius
Paullus, one of the consuls-elect, who had inveighed
against him in the Senate after the recent resolutions
had been passed, accepted a bribe soon after he entered
upon his office.[3] But the man whose support he was
most anxious to gain was the younger Curio, though the
elder had publicly denounced him in an epigram worthy
of Tacitus as *omnium mulierum virum et omnium virorum
mulierem.*[4] An excellent speaker, popular with the lower
orders, master of all the arts of parliamentary intrigue,
and, notwithstanding the effeminacy with which even
his friends reproached him, proof against intimidation
and clamour, Curio, stung perhaps by Caesar's marked
neglect, perhaps also infected by his father's rancour,
had attacked him systematically throughout the past
year.[5] Cicero, on hearing that he had been elected a
tribune, wrote him an affectionate letter of congratula-
tion, tempered by advice :—' I exhort you to regulate
your whole conduct by your own good sense and not
allow yourself to be carried away by the suggestions of

---

[1] *B. G.*, vii, 89, 5 ; viii, 4, 1 ; *Caesar's Conquest of Gaul²*, 1911, p. 183.

[2] Suet., 26, 3. Cf. vol. i, p. 116 and n. 5. The word ' now ' is tentative.
Willems (*Le sénat*, &c., ii, 407), remarking that Caesar had no power to
increase the pay of Roman soldiers ' comme une mesure générale ', the
right of doing so belonging to the Senate or the people, conjectures that
he utilized booty, as he was entitled to do, to increase the pay of his own
army.

[3] Cic., *Att.*, vi, 3 ; *Fam.*, viii, 1, 5 ; 10, 3 ; Plut., *Caes.*, 29, 2 ; *Pomp.*,
58, 1 ; Suet., 26, 2–3 ; 27 ; 29 ; App., ii, 26, 101 ; Dio, xl, 60, 1. 3.

[4] Suet., 52, 3.

[5] Cic., *Att.*, i, 14, 5 ; *Fam.*, viii, 4, 2 ; *Brut.*, 81, 280 ; Livy, *Epit.*, 109 ;
Dio, xl, 61, 2.

others. No one can give you sounder advice than you can give yourself : you will never stumble if you will listen to your true self . . . commune with yourself, take yourself into council, hearken to yourself, obey yourself.' [1]

He bribes Curio to rat to his side.

Caesar did not offer advice, but he offered what was more acceptable. Curio by reckless extravagance, against which Cicero warned him,[2] had incurred enormous debts ; and Caesar paid them.[3] Curio kept his own counsel. With simulated indignation he continued to harangue the populace in the Forum against Caesar. Meanwhile, in order that he might find a pretext for deserting his party and at the same time obstruct the expected debate on the Gallic provinces, he introduced various bills, which, as he knew, would inevitably be thrown out.[4] When he proposed to insert an intercalary month, his object became clear. The proposal was of course rejected, whereupon Curio threw off the mask and began to speak openly on behalf of Caesar. His desertion provoked an outburst of invective which did not ruffle him. ' He is being cut up ', said Caelius, who sometimes mixed his metaphors, ' like blazes.' [5] ' The last page of your letter ', Cicero replied, ' took my breath away. What ! Curio standing up for Caesar ! Who had expected it ? Except me ! For, as I live, I thought it would come. Ye gods ! How I wish we could laugh over it together ! ' [6] Curio meanwhile was resolutely carrying out his policy of obstruction ; and the settlement fixed for the 1st of March did not then take place. ' I have the city gazette ', wrote Cicero to Atticus, ' up to the 7th of March, from which I gather that, thanks to the persistence of my friend Curio, they will debate everything rather than the provinces.' [7] What Curio intended was that if Caesar were required to disband his army, Pompey should do likewise : he knew that Pompey would never consent to

---

[1] *Fam.*, ii, 7, 1-2.   [2] *Ib.*, 3, 1.
[3] Vell., ii, 48, 3-4 ; Plut., *Caes.*, 29, 2 ; Suet., 29, 1 ; App., ii, 26, 101 ;
Dio, xl, 60, 2-3. See p. 321.
[4] *Att.*, vi, 1, 25 ; *Fam.*, viii, 6, 5 ; App., ii, 27, 102 ; Dio, xl, 61.
[5] *Ib.*, 62, 2 ; *Fam.*, viii, 6, 5.
[6] *Ib.*, ii, 13, 3.   [7] *Att.*, vi, 2, 6.

make this sacrifice ; and he therefore determined by 50 B. C.
unflinching exercise of the tribunician veto to secure
the same privilege for his paymaster.[1] The masses,
irritated by the vindictive legislation of Pompey,[2] were
on his side ; and he knew that the bulk of the Pompeians
shrank from precipitating a rupture with Caesar. He
knew also that if his exercise of the veto were threatened,
Caesar would not hesitate to support him ; and the
unconstitutional conduct of Pompey in remaining at
Rome instead of going to his province put a weapon into
his hands.

Pompey meanwhile was preparing to take a step the
significance of which Caelius apparently did not appreciate. A Parthian army had crossed the Euphrates ;
and at Rome, where the recollection of Carrhae was still
fresh, there was serious alarm. In January Pompey Dec.,
wrote to tell Cicero that he would probably be called upon 51 B. C.
to undertake a campaign against the invaders.[3] This
intention was abandoned, but in May Pompey repre- Apr.
sented to the Senate that the Roman army in Syria
needed to be reinforced, and in obedience to his suggestion
they decreed that he and Caesar should each contribute
one legion. Pompey had no intention of giving up any He is
of the troops which he himself commanded, and accord- obliged
ingly requested Caesar to send back the legion which he the legion
had lent to him two years before.[4] Caesar readily com- lent to
plied ; but in bidding the men farewell he presented Pompey
each with the equivalent of a year's pay. On his own and to
give up
account he dispatched the 15th legion, one of the newest another.
and perhaps the least efficient in his force.[5] Whether the
Parthian alarm was a pretext or not,[6] when the legions
reached Italy all danger had passed, and they were
accordingly encamped at Capua. The officer who had

[1] Vell., ii, 48, 1 ; App., ii, 27, 104–5 ; Dio, xl, 62, 3–4.
[2] App., ii, 27, 105. See p. 168.
[3] Fam., viii, 10, 2 ; Att., v, 21, 2–3 ; vi, 1, 14.
[4] B. G., viii, 54, 3 ; Plut., Pomp., 56, 3 ; Caes., 29, 2 ; App., ii, 29, 114 ;
Dio, xl, 65, 1–3. See p. 323.
[5] Plut., l.c. ; App., ii, 29, 115 ; Dio, xl, 65, 4.
[6] See pp. 321–2.

50 B. C.   conducted them from Gaul assured Pompey that Caesar's
army was war-weary and disaffected.[1]

Before this time the question of the Gallic provinces
had reached a further stage.   Gaius Marcellus, it
Feb. ?   would seem, had in April moved that Caesar should
Curio   resign on the 1st of March, 49 ; and the motion had been
vetoes
C. Mar-   blocked by Curio.[2]   Towards the end of the month the
cellus's   Senate proposed a compromise, which was in reality a
motion
that   trap.   About the beginning of May Caelius wrote a letter
Caesar   to Cicero which illuminates the situation :—' All contro-
shall re-
sign on   versy centres on one point,—the provinces.   So far
March 1,   Pompey seems to have thrown his weight on the side of
49.
the Senate's wish that Caesar should leave his province
Sept. 28.   on the 13th of November.[3]   Curio is resolved to go all
lengths rather than allow this : he has thrown overboard his other proposals.   Our party, whom you know
so well, dare not push matters to extremes.   The scene on
our stage is this : Pompey, professing not to be attacking
Caesar, but to be making a settlement which he considers
fair to him, says that Curio is seeking pretexts for a
quarrel.   However, he is strongly against and evidently
afraid of Caesar's becoming consul-designate before
handing over his army and province.   Curio is handling
him pretty roughly and severely criticizing his whole
second consulship.   Mark my words,—if they push
Curio too hard, Caesar will defend him in exercising the

[1] Plut., *Pomp.*, 57, 3 ; *Caes.*, 29, 3 ; App., ii, 29, 115 ; 30, 116.

[2] See p. 309.

[3] See pp. 302–7.   An attempt has recently been made to explain why the
13th of November was chosen as the date.   Prof. Tenney Frank (*Class. Rev.*,
xxxiv, 1919, p. 69) argues that ' Since Pompey's proposal . . . pretended to
be fair to Caesar, Pompey apparently undertook to prove that it gave
Caesar his legal term. . . . His offer therefore probably contained a clause
which was to restore in February of 49 the forty-five days that the calendar
had lost by two previous failures to insert intercalary months, for if these
were restored *there would be exactly 365* [*sic.* Read 354] *days in the year 49
before the Ides of November* '.   M. Cary (*ib.*, p. 109) supports the professor,
pointing out that two months before Pompey made his offer Curio had
made a futile proposal to intercalate (*Fam.*, viii, 6, 5).   Pompey, he adds,
' had a double interest in reviving the question of intercalation.   Not only
. . . would a manipulation of the calendar enable him to make a specious
offer . . . but it would place Curio in a dilemma '.   Would it ?   Curio was not
so easily nonplussed.

veto : if they shrink—and it looks like it—Caesar will
stay where he is as long as he chooses.' [1] One sees that
Pompey had approved the compromise in the hope of
disarming Curio ; but what he really wanted was that
Caesar should resign on the 1st of March. Curio, who was
not gullible, vetoed or threatened to veto the proposal
that Caesar should be recalled in November.[2] Marcus
Marcellus, however, mustered courage to propose that
Curio and the tribunes who had supported him in
blocking the motion of Gaius should be censured.[3]
But the great majority of the Senate shrank from provoking Caesar to resort to force. Caelius, who apparently
thought that Cicero would approve their action, immediately wrote an account of the incident :—' You will
be anxious, Cicero, to learn that our friend Curio had
a brilliant finale to his veto about the provinces. A motion
about the veto (ordered by decree of the Senate) was
brought before the House, and Marcus Marcellus proposed
that the tribunes should be admonished, whereupon a
full Senate voted dead against him. "The Great" is
at present so out of sorts that he can hardly find anything
to suit him. The Senate has come round to this,—that
Caesar is to be allowed to stand for the consulship without
giving up army or provinces. How Pompey is likely to
stand this I will write and tell you as soon as I know.' [4]

Pompey, indeed, who had gone to Naples, was seriously
ill. The Neapolitans, whose example was followed by
other municipalities, offered prayers and sacrifices for his
recovery ; and when he became convalescent and was
travelling back to Rome, the people of every town
through which he passed flocked to welcome him and
strewed his path with flowers, so that his journey

---

[1] *Fam.*, viii, 11, 3.

[2] See pp. 309–10. Tyrrell and Purser (*op. cit.*, vol. iii, p. lxxxi = lxxxii-
lxxxiii of the 2nd ed.), after remarking that Curio resisted Pompey's pro-
posal, say, ' The majority of the Senate were in favour of a compromise. . . .
They said, let him [Caesar] retire on July 1st [49 B.C.]. The letter of
Cicero (*Fam.*, xvi, 12, 3) to which they refer was written on Jan 27, 705
(=Dec. 9, 50 B.C.), and described a proposal which had been received from
Caesar only four days before. The chronology of the co-editors (pp lxxxi-
lxxxiii) is confused.   [3] See p. 310.   [4] *Fam.*, viii, 13, 2.

50 b. c. resembled a triumphal progress.[1] Their homage was offered not, perhaps, to the cause which he represented, but to the popular hero, whose victories had extended the empire and whose authority had rescued the State from anarchy.[2]

The settlement upon which the Senate had decided in the absence of Pompey did not last long. ' As to political June. prospects ', wrote Caelius in August,[3] ' I have often told you that I see no chance of peace lasting a year, and the nearer the struggle comes—for come it must—the clearer does the danger appear. The point on which the men in power are sure to fight is this : Gnaeus Pompeius has made up his mind not to allow Gaius Caesar to become consul, unless he first hands over his army and pro- vinces ; Caesar is convinced that there is no safety for him if he quits his army. He proposes, however, as a compromise, that both should give up their armies. So their mighty love for each other and their detested alliance has not drifted into secret bickering, but is breaking out into open war. What line I personally should take I cannot conceive—and I have no doubt that making up your mind on this point will worry you too—for between myself and the Pompeians there are ties of good feeling and close connexion, while on the Caelius other side it is the cause, not the men that I dislike.' Then throws in Caelius considered how he should break to Cicero the his lot with news that he intended to follow the example of his friend Caesar. Curio. He too, it would seem, like Curio, had been bought, though Caesar did not value his support at so high a price ; [4] and he expected that when Caesar won, debts would be abolished and the property of rich Pom- peians distributed among Caesar's friends.[5] ' You cannot, I am sure,' he continued, ' fail to see that when dissen-

---

[1] Vell., ii, 48, 2 ; Plut., *Pomp.*, 57, 1 ; App., ii, 28, 107.

[2] According to Appian (ii, 28, 107–111), whose statement is unsupported, Pompey, while he was ill, wrote insincerely to the Senate with the view of putting Caesar in the wrong, offering to give up his army and provinces, and renewed the offer when he returned to Rome ; but Curio denounced it as a sham.   [3] *Fam.*, viii, 14, 2.   See pp. 323–4, 326.

[4] *Att.*, vii, 3, 6.   [5] See vol. iii, p. 223.

sions arise in home affairs, so long as the contest is carried
on constitutionally without violence, one ought to support
the party which is in the right, but when it comes to
blows and open war, the stronger. In this quarrel I can
see that Gnaeus Pompeius will have on his side the
Senate and the judicial body ; that Caesar will be joined
by all who have everything to dread and little to hope
for ; and that between the armies there is no comparison.
On the whole, there is time enough to appraise the
resources of both and to choose sides. . . . You want
my opinion of the future. Unless one of the two goes
to the Parthian war, I see that a tremendous quarrel is
impending, which will be decided by the sword and by
force.   Both are ready, determined, and thoroughly
equipped. If only it could be acted without deadly
peril, fortune is rehearsing for you a great and enthralling
drama.' [1]

Caesar meanwhile was preparing for eventualities.
About the time when he received the order to send back
the two legions Mark Antony, who had served as one of
his brigadiers in the last two campaigns, set out for
Rome to stand for a vacant place in the college of augurs
and also for a tribuneship. Caesar was of course aware
that his enemies would do their utmost to oppose Antony,
and that to secure his election would enhance his own
prestige. Moreover, Antony was one of his most loyal
supporters, and he was anxious to do his best for him.
He therefore wrote to the municipal authorities in *Caesar*
Cisalpine Gaul, urging them to canvass in the interest of *backs An-*
Antony.[2] Curio worked hard in the same cause, and *tony's candida-*
Caesar kept him plentifully supplied with money.[3] But *ture for office.*
Antony had to contend against a very strong candidate,
Domitius Ahenobarbus, who had the advantage of being
a consular, and was still an irreconcilable enemy of
Caesar. A courier was sent to inform Caesar that the
opposition was formidable. Towards the end of July
Caesar started for Cisalpine Gaul, intending to exert his

---

[1] *Fam.*, viii, 14, 3-4.   [2] *B. G.*, viii, 50, 1-2.
[3] Plut., *Ant.*, 5, 1. Cf. Cic., *Phil.*, ii, 2, 4.

personal influence with the electors. On the road he met a second courier, from whom he learned that Antony had been elected both as tribune and as augur, but that Servius Galba, who conducted the campaign in the Valais,[1] had failed in his candidature for the consulship; that two of his own opponents, Lucius Lentulus and Gaius Marcellus, a brother of Marcus, had been returned; and that the Pompeians were exulting at his discomfiture. He resolved therefore to continue his journey and to devote himself to strengthening his hold upon Cisalpine Gaul.

Enthusi-
astic wel-
come of
Caesar in
Cisalpine
Gaul. During the next month Caesar was making a progress through the province. The inhabitants of the chief towns received him with demonstrations of affectionate respect. His victorious campaigns awakened enthusiasm, and the Transpadanes were grateful for his championship of their cause. Roads and gateways were gaily decorated; men, women, and children streamed out of the towns to welcome their Governor; thanksgiving services were celebrated and sacrifices were offered in the shrines.[2]

July. Early in September Caesar, leaving Labienus with the 13th legion in charge of Cisalpine Gaul,[3] returned to his [Arras.] camp at Nemetocenna, and ordered all the legions in the other camps to assemble in the country of the Treveri, near the site of the modern Trèves. There, perhaps in order to impress the neighbouring German tribes, he reviewed the whole army and performed the time-honoured religious ceremony of lustration. It was rumoured that an attempt would be made to deprive him of a part of his army and that his enemies were endeavouring to seduce Labienus; but he refused to believe that his second-in-command would forsake him, and when his friends urged him to strike he declined, being convinced that Curio would look after his interests and that a majority of the Senate were disposed to let him keep his province until he should have become consul.[4] He wrote frequently in cordial terms to Cicero,[5] whose

---

[1] See pp. 49-50.   [2] B. G., viii, 50, 3-4; 51.
[3] See pp. 326-7.   [4] B. G., viii, 52, 1-4.   [5] Att, vii, 1, 3; 3, 11.

support he always desired ; but the mode in which he disposed his army for the winter proves that he did not intend to adopt an attitude of menace and that he hoped for peace. Though he was about to return to Cisalpine Gaul, he did not take any of his legions with him.[1] Four of them were quartered near Matisco (now Mâcon) under Gaius Fabius ; four under Trebonius in the country of the Belgae, seven hundred miles or more from the Italian frontier. The legion called Alaudae, which, as the Gauls who composed it had not yet received the franchise, was ignored by the writer who recorded the distribution, was perhaps stationed in the Transalpine Province. Some time in November Caesar moved south-ward[2] and before the middle of December arrived at Ravenna.

On the 1st of December two motions were brought forward in the Senate by the consul Gaius Marcellus : —should a successor be sent to replace Caesar [on the 1st of March] ? Should Pompey be required to resign his command ? The first motion was carried : the second was rejected by a large majority.[3] Curio then proposed that both Caesar and Pompey should be required to resign. Only twenty-two senators voted against this motion : three hundred and seventy voted for it.[4] Like that which Marcellus had carried, it was of course futile ; for the earlier motion of Marcellus, which required Caesar to resign on the 1st of March, was still blocked by the veto of Curio,[5] and the Senate had no power to

Margin notes: 50 B. C. His arrangements in Transalpine Gaul prove his desire for a peaceable settlement.

Oct. 15.

The Senate accept Curio's proposal that both Caesar and Pompey shall resign.

---

[1] G. Veith (*Gesch. d. Feldzüge C. J. Caesars*, 1906, p. 233) thinks that Caesar left the bulk of his army in Transalpine Gaul not only to avoid provoking his enemies, but also to maintain his hold on Gaul and to guard against invasion from Spain. But Caesar had no more reason to fear a Gallic insurrection then than a few months later, when he withdrew all his veteran legions from the province, and he guarded later against invasion from Spain by sending three legions to the neighbourhood of Narbo, to watch the passes of the Pyrenees. See p. 255.

[2] *B. G.*, viii, 54, 4–5 ; 55, 1.

[3] If Appian is right in saying that C. Marcellus introduced these motions, he of course intended that the second should be rejected.

[4] Plut., *Pomp.*, 58, 4 ; App., ii, 30, 118–19. See pp. 324–6, and cf. Hardy, *op. cit.*, p. 217, n. 1 with F. W. Sanford (*Univ. Studies*, Lincoln, Nebraska, xi, 1911, p. 317, n. 97).   [5] See p. 310.

50 B. C. compel Pompey to resign before his legal term. Curio, however, perhaps hoped to divert attention from the question of Caesar's successor and to sow dissension between Pompey and the Senate.[1] Evidently the Senate as a whole desired nothing so much as to avert civil war. 'Have your own way', exclaimed the consul, 'since you want Caesar for your master.'[2] Curio in exultation hurried out of the House to the Forum and harangued the populace, who welcomed him with shouts of applause and threw bouquets on to the Rostra.[3] A rumour was current that Caesar was about to march upon the capital. Next day therefore Marcellus assembled the Senate, and proposed that the two legions should be summoned from Capua to oppose the public enemy. Curio, insisting that the rumour was false, vetoed the motion,[4] whereupon Marcellus moved that such obstruction should be marked by a vote of censure. The motion was rejected,[5] and the consul announced that he would act in the interest of the State on his own responsibility.[6]

C. Marcellus calls upon Pompey to act against Caesar. Going to Pompey's house outside the city, he handed him a sword and, calling upon him to lead the two legions against Caesar, authorized him to raise additional levies. Pompey accepted the commission, remarking, 'unless I can find a better way'.[7]

The friends of Caesar immediately dispatched a courier to inform him of what the consul had done. Although the intentions of his adversaries were now clear, he determined to leave nothing undone in order to keep the peace ;[8] but, to prepare for emergencies, he ordered the

Caesar prepares for emergencies.

[1] Cf. Hardy, op. cit., p. 216.   [2] App., ii, 30, 119.
[3] Plut., Pomp., 58, 4. Cf. Caes., 30, 1-2, where Plutarch relates the same or a similar incident in connexion with the proceedings of the following Jan. 1.
[4] App., ii, 31, 120.   [5] Dio, xl, 64.
[6] G. Plaumann (Klio, xiii, 1913, p. 369) maintains, with the approval of E. Meyer (Caesars Monarchie², 1919, pp. 274-5) that the action of Marcellus was constitutionally correct. That a consul was constitutionally justified in making what was virtually an ultimate decree not only on his own responsibility, but in opposition to the Senate, seems to me questionable.
[7] Plut., Pomp., 59, 1 ; App., ii, 31, 120-2 ; Dio, xl, 64, 4. Orosius (vi, 15, 1) wrongly says that the two legions were at Luceria when Pompey received his commission.   [8] B. G., viii, 55, 2.

scattered detachments of the 13th legion to assemble at 50 b. c.
Ravenna and summoned the 8th and 12th from the
camp at Matisco.[1] Fabius, who was thus left with only
two legions, was to take over another from Trebonius
and to move from Matisco to Narbo, evidently in order
to prevent any attempt which Pompey's lieutenants
might make to invade Gaul from Spain : Trebonius was
to move southward and occupy the camp abandoned by
Fabius.[2] Late on the 6th of December Caesar's secretary, Oct. 20.
Aulus Hirtius, arriving in Rome on a mission the nature
of which is unknown, learned that Pompey was to start
for Capua on the following day and that Balbus intended
to confer with Scipio at daybreak, probably in the hope
of inducing him to dissuade Pompey from proceeding
to extremities. Without waiting to learn the result of
the conference he returned forthwith to report. Four Dec. 10
days later Curio, whose tribuneship had just expired, and (Oct. 24).
who had demanded in vain that the consuls should forbid joins
any one to respond to Pompey's levy, quitted Rome and Caesar at
joined Caesar at Ravenna.[3] Ravenna.

If this narrative has achieved its aim, the reader The ques-
should now be able to form a judgement about the tion at
question that was at issue between Caesar and his rival. between
When Pompey virtually abrogated the Sempronian law Caesar
and made it possible, unless the Caesarian tribunes could Pompey
maintain their veto, to recall Caesar before he could
stand for the consulship and thus to expose him to the
attacks of his enemies, he violated the compact of Luca,
to which he owed his own power. Moreover the Law of
the Ten Tribunes had been passed at the instance of
Pompey himself ; and to deprive Caesar of the advantage
which it conferred, while nominally permitting him to
use it, was the merest trickery. One may imagine how
Caesar who, as a hostile critic [4] has observed, never
failed to discharge a debt of honour or to stand by a
friend, smarted when his former coadjutor played him

---

[1] See pp. 324–5.   [2] See p. 322.
[3] Cic., Att., vii, 4, 2 ; App., ii, 31, 123 ; Dio, xl, 66, 5. See pp. 325–6.
[4] Strachan-Davidson, Cicero, 1894, p. 265. Cf. Cic., Fam., vii, 17, 2.

50 B. C.

false. Nevertheless he was still determined, if by any
means it were possible without political suicide, to avoid
civil war. If, as Cicero said,[1] he often quoted the couplet
of Euripides,

' If sin one must, for power 'tis best to sin,
    In all things else to keep the moral law,'[2]

the wise will not pervert his meaning. Every statesman
who deserves the name obeys some principle : none
allows scruple to enfeeble action.

Cicero's
govern-
ment of
Cilicia.

Cicero had by this time returned to Italy after a
proconsulship which deserves notice in the history of
Roman provincial administration. No one who can appreciate a self-revealed character would need to be told
that the prosecutor of Verres was, from self-respect as
well as from sympathy, a humane and, so far as certain
weaknesses permitted, conscientious governor ; every one
would expect to find that his letters and even his official
dispatches were enlivened by naïve self-glorification.[3]
On his outward journey he abstained from accepting even
the contributions that were allowed by the stringent law
which Caesar had passed in his consulship ;[4] and his
staff, almost without exception, followed his example.[5]
' Nothing ', he told Atticus, ' could be more equitable,
mild, and dignified than my administration of justice . . .
never in all my life have I felt such pleasure as I do at
my own integrity ' ;[6] ' my administration of justice is
enlightened and withal mild and courteous to a marvel.'[7]
He had the good taste to refuse to allow the provincials
to erect temples in his honour,[8] and he did his best to
encourage municipal self-government.[9] It is true that
he had not the least enthusiasm for his work or the least
comprehension of its importance : it was to him merely

[1] De off., iii, 21, 82. Cf. Suet., 30, 5.

[2] εἴπερ γὰρ ἀδικεῖν χρή, τυραννίδος πέρι
κάλλιστον ἀδικεῖν, τἆλλα δ' εὐσεβεῖν χρεών (Phoenis., 524–5).

[3] Att., v, 11, 5 ; 13, 1 ; 14, 2 ; 15, 1 ; 16, 2 ; 17, 2. 6 ; 18, 2 ; vii, 1,
5–6 ; 3, 8 ; Fam., ii, 17, 4 ; xv, 1, 3 ; 4, 1.

[4] Att., v, 10, 2.   [5] Ib., 17, 1 ; 21, 5.   [6] Ib., 20, 1. 6.

[7] Ib., vi, 2, 5.   [8] Ib., v, 21, 7. Cf. Q. fr., i, 1, 26.

[9] Att., vi, 1, 15 ; 2, 4. Cicero's administration is praised by Plutarch
(Cic., 36, 2) and Quintilian (Inst., xii, 1, 16).

a disagreeable duty, to be performed conscientiously, 51 B. C.
but to be escaped at the earliest possible moment :
' I will endure it ', he said, ' as well as I can, provided
that it does not last more than a year '.[1] The persistence
with which he importuned his friends to exert all their
influence to prevent its being prolonged beyond that
period, and not to allow a month to be intercalated in
his absence,[2] is not so much wearisome as comical. ' The
whole business ', he complained, ' is unworthy of my
powers.' [3] He was longing to return to the scene where
the fate of the Republic, which he so much loved, was
soon to be decided :—' Rome, Rome, my dear Rufus,
stay in it and live in its sunshine ! All foreign service,
as I made up my mind in early life, is mere eclipse and
obscurity to those whose energy is capable of shining at
Rome.' [4]

When Cicero reached his province he found that under
his predecessor, Appius Claudius, the inhabitants had
suffered the normal evils of cruelty and extortion. ' It
was the same tale everywhere ', he wrote ; ' they could
not pay the poll-tax : everybody obliged to sell his
securities : groans and lamentations from the towns :
atrocities worthy of a wild beast rather than of a man.' [5]
He tried to relieve their misery,[6] and although he had
always thought that the great difficulty which beset a
conscientious governor was to keep on good terms with
the tax-gatherers without allowing them to oppress the
tax-payers,[7] he assured Atticus that he had succeeded
in solving this problem :—' I make pets of them, indulge,
compliment, and honour them, at the same time taking
care that they oppress no one.' [8] But he was not always
strong enough to withstand the pressure put upon him
by interested friends. Caelius was not ashamed to ask
him for a grant to defray the cost of the entertainments
which, as curule aedile, he was expected to give. Few

[1] *Att.*, v, 15, 1.

[2] *Ib.*, 2, 1 ; 9, 2 ; 11, 1 ; 13, 3 ; 14, 1 ; 17, 5 ; 18, 1 ; 21, 3 ; vi, 1, 14 ;
Fam., ii, 7, 4 ; 8, 3 ; 10, 4 ; iii, 8, 9 ; 10, 3 ; xv, 9, 2 ; 12, 2 ; 14, 5.

[3] *Fam.*, ii, 11, 1.   [4] *Ib.*, 12, 2.   [5] *Att.*, v, 16, 2. Cf. vi, 1, 2.

[6] *Fam.*, xv, 4, 2.   [7] *Q. fr.*, i, 1, 32–4.   [8] *Att.*, vi, 1, 16. Cf. 2, 5.

governors scrupled to tax provincials for such a purpose ;[1] but Cicero did, and in dealing with his former pupil he felt that he must be firm. ' I have advised him ', he told Atticus, ' (for I am really fond of him) that, after prosecuting others, he should be extra-careful as to his own conduct.'[2] But there was a more important matter in which excessive complaisance led Cicero to sacrifice his principles : ' the noblest Roman of them all ', the hero of Plutarch and Dio, of Lucan and Velleius, the man of whom Atticus said that ' if Cicero brought back from his province nothing but the gratitude of Brutus, he would have good reason to be satisfied ',[3] of whom Cicero himself said, ' he is already the first among the rising generation and will soon, I hope, be the first man in the state '[4]—Marcus Brutus played the leading part in this scandal. The province of Cilicia still included Cyprus. Six years before the people of Salamis, the chief town of the island, had endeavoured to raise a loan in Rome. It will be remembered that a law, passed in the interest of the Roman money-lenders who transacted business in the provinces, forbade provincials to borrow in the capital ;[5] but Brutus, unwilling to neglect a profitable investment, secretly offered to advance the money, arranging that a Cilician banker, named Scaptius, should pose as the lender, and charging interest at the rate of forty-eight per cent. Scaptius of course stipulated for immunity from arrest ; and accordingly Brutus used his influence to get two senatorial decrees passed,—the first indemnifying both Scaptius and the Salaminians against any penalty for breach of the law, the second declaring the bond which registered the transaction to be legally valid. Scaptius, armed with a letter of introduction from Brutus, requested Cicero to appoint him commander of a troop of horse in Cyprus, in order that he might be able to recover the money. Cicero, who knew that Scaptius had held a similar command under Appius Claudius, and had taken advantage of it to recover

---

[1] *Q. fr.*, i, 1, 26. [2] *Att.*, vi, 1, 21. [3] *Ib.*, § 7.
[4] *Fam.*, iii, 11, 3. [5] See Vol. i, p. 131.

debts from the Salaminian Senate by starving five of 51 B. C
them to death, peremptorily refused the request ; but,
afraid of offending Brutus, he sent for the Salaminian
debtors and ordered them to pay, threatening that
unless they obeyed he would use force. They professed
themselves willing to pay interest at twelve per cent,—
the rate allowed by Cicero's edict. Scaptius, appealing
to the senatorial decrees, insisted that they must pay
what they had promised,—forty-eight per cent. ; but
Cicero pointed out that the decrees could not legalize
what was illegal. The Senate indeed, realizing at last
that the extortions of Roman money-lenders were
injurious to the reputation of the State, had recently
decreed that even in the provinces the rate of interest
must not exceed twelve per cent. Scaptius, who expected
(with good reason) that the next governor would be less
scrupulous, then asked Cicero to leave the matter open,
explaining that the real creditor was Brutus. Cicero
consented. ' I gave in ', he confessed, ' to the fellow's
shameless importunity.' [1] Nor was this all. Cicero
condescended to act as the agent of Brutus and of
Pompey in recovering moneys owed by Ariobarzanes,
a grandson of the king whom Pompey had restored.
In order to pay Pompey the King was obliged to
wring thirty-three talents, or about eight thousand
pounds, a month from his wretched subjects, which did
not cover even the interest of his debt, while Brutus
received in one year the equivalent of twenty-five
thousand pounds.[2] The truth was, though Cicero could
not or would not see it, that under the Republican
constitution, to which he clung, it was hardly possible
for the best-intentioned governor to govern with perfect
justice : if he refused to wink at some extortion, he could
not but offend the equestrian order, to which the tax-
gatherers belonged, and whose support was essential
to the stability of the State. To effect any real improve-
ment, it was necessary not only to reform the system of

[1] *Att.*, v, 21, 12–3 ; vi, 2, 8. See pp. 327–8.
[2] *Att.*, vi, 1, 3 ; 3, 5. Cf. *Fam.*, xiii, 56 , 3.

51 B. C.

taxation, but also to make the governors responsible to a central authority which could without fear or favour exercise control.

Every Roman governor was also a commander-in-chief ; and Cicero found himself obliged to conduct a campaign, which requires notice because it had some bearing upon subsequent events. On arriving at Iconium from Italy, he learned that the Parthians were invading Syria ; and it seemed probable that they would push on into Cappadocia, which was open to incursion on the Syrian side.[1] His army consisted of only two legions, which, owing to the negligence or the parsimony of the Senate, had fallen far below their normal strength ; [2] but he was supported by his brother, who had come fresh from his experience in Gaul to serve under him ; [3] and before he left Iconium he collected a considerable force of auxiliaries from the self-governing communities and the kings who were clients of Rome. Fortunately Gaius Cassius, who after the disaster at Carrhae had rallied the remnant of the beaten army, remained as governor in Syria, where he suppressed a Jewish revolt.[4] Towards

July.

the end of August Cicero marched to Cybistra in the south-western corner of Cappadocia, intending to cover Cilicia and to hold Cappadocia itself. There he heard that the Parthians had threatened Antioch, the capital of Syria, but that an advanced party, which had actually penetrated into Cilicia, had been defeated by one of his auxiliary corps. In order to safeguard Cilicia, he moved on and, crossing Mount Taurus by the pass of Pylae, marched to the range called Mount Amanus, the boundary between Cilicia and Syria, where he learned that Cassius had compelled the Parthians to fall back. In the neighbourhood of Mount Amanus he defeated a band of refractory natives, seized some of their fastnesses, and was saluted, not ironically, by his army as Imperator. Having thus prepared the way for a further advance, he

---

[1] *Fam.*, xv, 2, 1 ; 3, 1 ; 4, 2–3 ; *Att.*, v, 20, 2.   [2] *Ib.*, 15, 1.
[3] Quintus arrived in Cilicia in the summer of 51 B.C. (*ib.*, 20, 5, compared with 10, 5). These texts correct a mistake which I made in *Caesar's Conquest of Gaul*[2], 1911, p. 565.   [4] Jos., *Ant.*, xiv, 7, 3 ; *Bell. Iud.*, i, 8, 9.

invested Pindenissus, the principal stronghold of the 51 B. C.
Cilician mountaineers, captured it on the 17th of December Nov. 10.
after a siege of fifty-seven days, and sold the garrison for
twelve millions of sesterces, or about one hundred and
twenty thousand pounds.[1] Writing to a friend, Papirius
Paetus, he jestingly alluded to his campaign :—' You
don't know what a great general you're dealing with !
My well-thumbed *Cyropaedeia* has been thoroughly
exemplified throughout my command.'[2] Caelius, who
mixed scandal with political reports, could not resist
the temptation to banter his old mentor. ' Servius
Ocella ', he wrote, ' would never have convinced any
one that he was a rake if he had not been nabbed twice
in three days. You will ask " Where ? " . . . I leave
you something to find out from others ; for I rather like
the idea of an Imperator asking one person after another
with what woman So-and-so has been caught.'[3] But
while Cicero did not overrate his own exploits, he was
jealous of his colleagues. He told Atticus that Cassius
had contributed nothing to the overthrow of the Parthians,[4] although, as his own letters [5] prove, he knew
that Cassius had compelled them to retreat. Writing to
influential friends, he begged them to procure for him the
honour of a thanksgiving service ; [6] but although his
efforts were successful, his pleasure was alloyed by one
of the replies which he received. ' I am glad ', wrote
Cato, ' that the thanksgiving was decreed, if you prefer
our thanking the gods rather than giving the credit to
you. . . . But if you consider a thanksgiving an earnest
of a triumph, and therefore prefer fortune having the
credit rather than yourself, let me remind you that a
triumph does not always follow a thanksgiving.'[7]

On the 24th of November, 50, Cicero landed at Brun- Oct. 9.
disium,[8] and thence travelled leisurely across the peninsula

[1] *Fam.*, xv, 4, 3–10 ; *Att.*, v, 20, 1–5. .   [2] *Fam.*, ix, 25, 1.
[3] *Ib.*, viii, 7, 2.   [4] *Att.*, v, 21, 2 ; vi, 1, 14.
[5] *Fam.*, xv, 4, 7 ; ii, 10, 2. Cf. *Phil.*, xi, 13, 45.
[6] *Fam.*, iii, 9, 4 ; xv, 4, 11 ; 10, 2 ; 13, 3. Cf *Att.*, vi, 4, 2.
[7] *Fam.*, xv, 5, 2. Cf. viii, 11, 1–2.
[8] *Att.*, vii, 2, 1.

into Campania.   His mind was troubled by the impending

He re-
turns to
Italy:
his inter-
views
with
Pompey
and re-
marks on
the politi-
cal situa-
tion.
crisis. ' You ask ', he wrote to Atticus, ' what is to happen
when the consul says, " Your vote, Marcus Tullius ? "
I shall answer *tout court*, " I agree with Gnaeus Pompeius ".   Nevertheless in private I shall exhort him to
keep the peace.[1] . . . On our side every one is doing his
utmost to avert an appeal to arms.' Next day he met
Pompey at Capua,[2] conversed with him for about two
hours, and immediately reported the conversation to his

friend.   Pompey, he wrote, ' did not encourage me to
hope for peace : " he had felt before that Caesar was
alienated from him, and had recently become convinced
of it.   Hirtius, Caesar's most intimate friend, had come
on a mission from his chief, but had not called on him.[3]

He had arrived on the evening of the 6th, and, finding
that Balbus had arranged to visit Scipio on the 7th
before daybreak, and talk over the whole question, he
had started late at night to rejoin Caesar."   This seemed
to Pompey " proof positive " of alienation.'[4]   Did it
never occur to Pompey or to Cicero that when Balbus,
who was also an intimate friend of Caesar, arranged ' to
talk over the whole question ' with the father-in-law of
Pompey, he could have had no other aim than to effect
a compromise ?   Cicero was much disturbed by the
expressions of his leader ; and many who thought that
the recruiting mission on which Pompey was engaged
portended war, shared his alarm. From Capua he went
to his villa at Cumae, where Caelius visited him. Cicero
remarked that he would endure anything rather than
leave Italy to take part in a civil war.[5]   A day or two
later he moved northward to Formiae.   ' I am more
anxious ', he wrote to Atticus, ' about the political
situation every day. The Conservatives are not, as
people think, united. Have I not seen many knights
and many senators ready to inveigh against the whole
policy, and especially this progress on the part of

---

[1] *Att.*, vii, 3, 5.
[2] L. Holzapfel (*Klio*, iv, 1904, p. 334, n. 7).
[3] See p. 255.   [4] *Att.*, vii, 4, 2.   [5] *Fam.*, ii, 16, 3.

Pompey ? [1] . . . I am one of those who think it more   50 B.C
expedient to yield to Caesar's demands than to fight.' [2]
This, he assured Atticus, was also the feeling of almost
every one with whom he had discussed the state of
affairs.[3]   Appius Claudius indeed, who, as one of the
censors, had expelled many senators, including Sallust,
from the House, and branded sundry knights with
ignominy, had unwittingly driven those of them who
were half-hearted to embrace the cause of Caesar.[4]   Still,
Cicero asked his friend whether the Senate did not
deserve blame for having suffered Curio (whose force of
character he did not appreciate) to maintain his veto :—
' Curio would never have held out if he had been tackled ;
but the Senate would not adopt this course, with the
result that no successor was named to Caesar.'   From
the information which he could gather he concluded that
the farmers of the taxes were disposed to support Caesar,
while the financiers and the yeomen had no intention of
backing Pompey, but only desired peace.[5]   Caesar had
been so long away from Italy that his character was
not generally known :   ' Every one ', said Cicero, ' is
convinced that if the Conservatives are beaten, Caesar
will massacre the aristocracy as ruthlessly as Cinna and
plunder the rich with the rapacity of Sulla.' [6]   On the
25th of December he had another long interview with   Nov. 8
Pompey.   If we may trust his account, it would seem
that Pompey, like Napoleon when he spoke of Wellesley
as ' a sepoy general ', did not yet appreciate Caesar's
military genius.—' As far as I could gather from Pompey's
conversation—he spoke at great length and weighed his
words—he hasn't even the wish for peace.   His view is
that if Caesar becomes consul, even if he first disbands

---

[1] These words, written about the 16th of December, suggest that Pompey
was already raising troops. Cf. *Att.*, vii, 8, 4. Stoffel, who maintains (*Hist.
de J. César*, i, 1887, p. 208) that he did not begin to do so till the end of the
month, cites Plut., *Pomp.*, 59, 2, which only shows that he had begun in
or before the first week of January, and *B. C.*, i, 6, 3, from which we learn
that after January 7 the Senate ordained a levy.

[2] *Att.*, vii, 5, 4–5.   [3] *Ib.*, 6, 2.   [4] Dio, xl, 63, 3–4.
[5] *Att.*, vii, 7, 5.   [6] *Ib.*, § 7.

50 B. C.

his army, there will be a *bouleversement* of the constitution. Besides, he thinks that when Caesar hears that preparations are being made energetically to resist him, he will abandon the consulship for this year and prefer retaining his army and his province. But, supposing that he were to act like a madman, he expressed a hearty contempt for his capacity [1] and felt confident in his own and the national resources. . . . I felt my anxiety removed while I listened to a man of such courage, military skill, and supreme influence discoursing like a statesman on the dangers of a sham peace. We had in our hands a report

Nov. 4.

of Antony's speech, delivered on the 21st of December, which contained an invective against Pompey from his boyhood . . . and a threat of open war. Pompey exclaimed apropos, " What do you suppose Caesar himself will do, if he obtains supreme power, when his penniless quaestor, a man of straw, dares to talk like this ? " In short he appeared not merely not to desire the peace you talk of, but even to dread it. What most makes him hesitate, I fancy, is that it would be undignified to abandon the city. What galls *me* is that I *must* pay that money to Caesar and devote what I had provided for the expense of my triumph to that. For " it looks ugly to be in debt to a political opponent ".' [2] The anxiety which Pompey had dispelled soon returned. Cicero saw that his preparations were not complete, and Pompey had told him that if Caesar were elected consul he would

Dec. 27 (Nov. 10).

himself go to Spain. On the very next day he wrote again to his friend, enumerating all the contingencies by which the Pompeians were menaced, and begging him to say which of them he thought the most tolerable. ' Do ', he concluded, ' suggest anything that occurs to you. Night and day I am on the rack.' [3]

At the moment when Cicero wrote these words Curio, who had spent the last fortnight with Caesar at Ravenna, was leaving with an official letter for the Senate. If we may believe Appian,[4] as soon as he had joined his

---

[1] Vehementer hominem contemnebat.   [2] *Att.*, vii, 8, 4-5.
[3] *Ib.*, 9, 2-4.   [4] ii, 32, 125-7.

chief, he urged him to send instantly for all his legions and march on Rome ; but Caesar, rejecting this advice, directed his supporters to propose that he should be allowed to retain two legions only, with Cisalpine Gaul and Illyricum, until he entered upon his consulship. That he made this offer, evidently in the hope of escaping prosecution, is certain ; but there is some reason to suspect that he had made it before Curio arrived.[1] Pompey, it would seem, was willing to accept it ; but the consuls would not agree. Thereupon Caesar wrote another letter, which was virtually an ultimatum. He was ready, he said, to resign his command if Pompey would do the same ; but to require him to resign while Pompey retained his army would be unfair : it would simply leave him at the mercy of his enemies. If his offer were rejected, he would have no alternative but to vindicate his rights, with which those of the public were involved.[2] The Senate was to meet on the 1st of January, when the consuls-elect would enter upon office ; and if Curio hastened he would be in time. Travelling eighty miles a day, he reached Rome on the eve of the meeting, and, presenting himself in the Senate on the following morning, delivered the dispatch.[3] The consuls perused it. Evidently they were determined to reject the offer, for they declined to communicate the letter to the House, and it was only after Antony and his brother tribune, Quintus Cassius, vehemently insisted, that they reluctantly allowed it to be read. But the Senate could come to no decision about the offer unless some magistrate would submit it for discussion ; and this the consuls absolutely declined to do,[4] for they were afraid that those senators who wished to avoid war would vote in its favour. It was useless for Cassius and Antony to authorize the discussion ;[5] for they knew that the

Marginal notes:
50 B. C.

Caesar's final proposals for a compromise rejected.

He sends Curio with an ultimatum to the Senate.

Jan. 1, 705 (Nov. 13, 50 B. C.)

---

[1] See pp. 331–3.

[2] *B. C.*, i, 9, 3 ; Cic., *Fam.*, xvi, 11, 2 ; Livy, *Epit.*, 109 ; Plut., *Caes.*, 30, 1 ; App., ii, 32, 128 ; Dio, xli, 1, 4.

[3] *B. C.*, i, 1, 1 ; App., ii, 32, 127 ; Dio, xli, 1, 1.

[4] *B. C.*, i, 1, 1. In regard to the credibility of Caesar's report of the proceedings in the Senate see pp. 329–31. [5] See Cic., *Fam.*, x, 16, 1.

Pompeian tribunes would interpose their veto. Accordingly the consuls merely proposed the political situation in general terms as the subject for debate.[1] Pompey was debarred by his military position from attending the House. Lentulus himself spoke first. He declared that if members would pluck up courage to avow their convictions, he would take a strong line ; but if they tried to curry favour with Caesar, as they had done on former occasions, he would consult his own interests, for he too had the means of securing Caesar's favour if he chose. Scipio said that Pompey was prepared to support the Government if the Senate were compliant ; but if they hesitated or procrastinated, it would be useless for them, when they found out their mistake, to solicit his aid. Everybody knew that Scipio was the mouthpiece of his son-in-law.[2] On the following day the debate was resumed. Notwithstanding the menaces of Scipio and Lentulus, several senators counselled moderation. Marcus Marcellus urged that it would be better to postpone all discussion until the levies were completed and the new army enrolled, when the Senate would be able to enforce their decision. Marcus Calidius, an ardent Caesarian, bluntly suggested that Pompey should go to Spain and govern his own provinces : then there would be no occasion for a quarrel ; as it was, Caesar naturally feared that the two legions which he had surrendered would be used against him. Caelius said substantially the same. Lentulus, turning upon them fiercely, refused to put the motion of Calidius to the vote ; and Marcellus, cowed by the invective of the consul, withdrew his proposal.[3] Scipio then moved that Caesar should resign his command on or before the 1st of March,[4] and that if he refused he should be declared a public enemy. Overawed by the violence of Lentulus and the threats of other prominent Pompeians, the moderates for the most part voted with Scipio,[5] and the

[1] B. C., i, 1, 2.
[2] B. C., i, 1, 2–4 ; 2, 1.
[3] Ib., §§ 2–5.
[4] See p. 306, n. 1.
[5] B. C., i, 2, 6–7 ; Dio, xli, 2, 1 ; 3, 4 (chronologically inexact). According

resolution was passed. Antony and Cassius of course 50 B. C.
vetoed it. The House was called upon to decide what Caesar declared a public enemy: Antony and Q. Cassius veto the resolution.
notice should be taken of the veto, and it was evident
from the vehemence with which the Pompeians spoke
that they intended to arm the magistrates with extraordinary powers to enable them to act in spite of it.[1]

In the evening the session was adjourned, and Pompey
invited all the senators to come to his house on the
following day and confer with him. Commending those
who had supported him, he inveighed against the waverers,
and, by way of stimulating their resolution or coercing
them, he summoned all his own friends and all the
enemies of Caesar who had not been present at the
sessions of the previous days to attend. At the same time
he sent for drafts from the legions which Caesar had
restored, moved troops into the city, and offered rewards
to retired legionaries who had served under his command
to rally round him.[2]

On the 4th of January, while Pompey was still con- Nov. 16.
ferring with the senators, Cicero, escorted by the lictors
who attended him as Imperator, arrived in the outskirts
of Rome. Notwithstanding the political tension, his
mind was preoccupied with thoughts of a triumph and
of the recognition which he expected of his achievements.
Lentulus assured him that as soon as the public safety
was secured he would bring forward a motion for a Cicero's desire for a peaceable settlement ignored.
triumph. ' Nothing ', Cicero wrote, ' could have been
more imposing than the procession that came out to
meet me.'[3] He had recently received a letter from
Caesar, urging him to work for a peaceable settlement ; [4]

---

to Plutarch (*Ant.*, 5, 2) many senators considered that the terms offered
by Caesar were reasonable ; but Dio implies that only two voted against
Scipio's proposal. If, however, many of the rest were, as Caesar says,
overawed, Dio's statement is compatible with that of Plutarch.

   [1] *B. C.*, i, 2, 8 ; Plut., *Caes.*, 30, 3 ; Dio, xli, 2, 2.

   [2] *B. C.*, i, 3, 1-4.   [3] *Fam.*, xvi, 11, 2-3.

   [3] *Att.*, vii, 21, 3. Cicero says that this letter was dated ' before Caesar
began his violent proceedings ', that is, as I understand, before he wrote
the letter which Curio handed to the consuls. O. E. Schmidt (*D. Briefwechsel d. M. T. Cicero*, 1893, p. 104), citing *Fam.*, vi, 6, 5 (which does not
necessarily refer to the time when Cicero returned), affirms that on reaching

50 B.C. but the leaders of his party would not listen to him. ' I was unable ', he explained, ' to do any good ; for I came too late, I was isolated, and I was regarded as imperfectly acquainted with the facts.'[1] Nevertheless, he was clearsighted enough to discern the aims of the chief actors. At a later time, recalling what had happened before the crisis came, he said, ' I saw . . . that our friends desired war, whereas Caesar did not desire it, but did not fear it '.[2]

Nov. 17. The 3rd and the 4th of January were days on which the Senate could not legally meet ; but on the 5th the debate was renewed. All the Pompeians and the enemies of Caesar who had not yet appeared were summoned ; and numbers trooped into the House. Caesar's father-in-law, Lucius Calpurnius Piso, and one of the praetors, Lucius Roscius, who had served in Gaul, pleading that it would be only just to let Caesar know how his proposal

the outskirts of Rome he renewed the proposal of Calidius that Pompey should go to Spain and that Caesar should be allowed to stand for the consulship. Tyrrell and Purser in their note on the passage which Schmidt quotes remark that if Cicero ever ' publicly urged that Pompey should go, it must have been at the council in Capua at the end of January, 705 (49) [see vol. iii, p. 8]. . . . But ', they add, ' he may have suggested it in the private meetings he had with Pompey in December, 704 '. Purser in his new edition (1918) of *The Correspondence of Cicero* (vol. iv) adds, ' it is more likely that Cicero . . . had often said unofficially to his friends . . . that it would be better for Pompey to go to Spain, and that he never urged it forcibly on Pompey himself '. I agree : in December, 704 (50 B.C.) Pompey himself told Cicero that he intended, if Caesar were elected consul, to go to Spain (see p. 264).

[1] *Fam.*, iv, 1, 1. Cf. Plut., *Cic.*, 37, 1.

[2] *Fam.*, ix, 6, 2. Schmidt (*op. cit.*, p. 106) says that the whole tone of the letter of January 12 (*Fam.*, xvi, 11) in which Cicero describes the situation, as it appeared to him, when he returned to Rome, shows that war was not expected to break out yet : the senators hoped to keep the peace till July 1 [or rather March 1]—the date by which Caesar must resign his province and his army (see p. 266)—and meanwhile to make their preparations undisturbed. The tone of the letter seems to me very different : Cicero says (§ 2), ' I found myself in a blaze of civil discord *or rather civil war* ' (*incidi in ipsam flammam civilis discordiae v e l p o t i u s c i v i l i s b e l l i*), and (§ 3) 'now, *when it is too late*, [Pompey] begins to fear Caesar ' (*Caesarem s e r o coepit timere*). Again in *Fam.*, xvi, 12, 2, written on January 27, he says, ' when I reached the capital a mad passion for fighting had seized . . . even those who are regarded as constitutionalists, though I loudly insisted that nothing could be more lamentable than civil war ' (*Equidem ut veni ad urbem . . . mirus invaserat furor . . . etiam iis qui boni habentur, ut pugnare cuperent, me clamante nihil esse bello civili miserius*).

had been received, volunteered to go to Ravenna and
report to him, undertaking to return in six days. Several
other senators urged that an official deputation should
be sent. But the opposition of the Pompeians was too
strong. Cato was not only a conscientious Conservative,
but also an old enemy of Caesar. Lentulus was deeply
in debt ; and while he had no prospect of satisfying his
creditors if peace were to be maintained, he looked
forward to a war in which he might repair his fortunes
by the plunder of a province and by selling the title of
King to Asiatic chiefs who would support Pompey.
Scipio, whose creditors, as Cicero said, were ' actually
preparing to sell him up ',[1] knew that unless there were
a war, his enemies would bring him to trial ; and he
too hoped to retrieve his position by the profits of a
provincial governorship, while, as the father-in-law of
Pompey, he might count upon getting an important
command. Pompey himself, as even his own supporters
allowed, could not brook a rival.[2] The proposal of Piso
and of Roscius was rejected ; and on the 7th of January Nov. 19.
Antony and Cassius were warned by the consuls, if Antony
they wished to escape violence, to quit the House. and
Cassius
Antony vehemently protested ; but the soldiers of warned to
Pompey were outside, and it was time for him and his quit the
House.
colleague to be gone. Immediately after their departure
the Senate passed a decree identical with that which The
had armed Cicero against Catiline : consuls, proconsuls, Senate
passes the
praetors, tribunes were empowered to dispense with ' ultimate
all constitutional checks and to act against the common decree '.
enemy. Antony and Cassius determined of course to
join their chief, and Curio and Caelius were ready to
accompany them. A carriage was hired for the party.
After sunset Caelius visited Cicero, who charged him to
implore Caesar, in his name, to strive for peace.[3] The
fugitives quitted Rome in the night, and on the 10th Nov. 22.

[1] *Att.*, ix, 11, 4.
[2] *B. C.*, i, 3, 5–7 ; 4 ; Vell., ii, 49, 3 ; Lucan, i, 125–6 ; Flor., ii, 13, 14 ;
Dio, xli, 54, 1.
[3] See p. 333.

50 B.C.

Caesar
harangues
the 13th
legion, se-
cures Ari-
minum,
and
crosses
the
Rubicon.

reached Ariminum.[1] A few hours later the news reached Ravenna. Caesar immediately paraded his solitary legion and delivered an harangue, the accuracy of which, in one particular, has been impugned by scholars who perhaps forgot that oratory and history are not the same.[2] He began by recounting the wrongs which his personal enemies had done to him : they had alienated from him the friendship of Pompey, who from envy and the desire of depreciating his renown had attacked the friend who had always supported him. The violence offered to Antony and Cassius was an unprecedented outrage : even Sulla, though he reduced the power of the tribunes to insignificance, had left them their veto unrestricted : Pompey, who was supposed to have restored their power, had actually deprived them of what they enjoyed before. The extreme senatorial decree, against which they had not been allowed to protest, had never before been passed save when it was necessary to suspend the law in order to stem revolutionary violence, which at the moment no one dreamed of. Finally he adjured them to defend the good name and the honour of their general, who had so often led them to victory, under whose command they had subdued the whole of Gaul, and also Germany. With one universal shout officers and men declared themselves ready to avenge their general and the outraged tribunes.[3]

Caesar immediately sent a detachment under Hortensius, a son of the famous orator, to secure Ariminum.[4] Between that town and Ravenna flowed the little stream which separated his province from the rest of Italy.[5] To overpass it in arms was to declare war against the Government of Rome. On the 11th of January Caesar crossed the Rubicon and next day joined the tribunes.[6] The Civil War had begun.

Nov. 23.

---

[1] B. C., i, 5 ; Cic., Fam., viii, 17, 1 ; xvi, 11, 2 ; Livy, Epit., 109 ; Plut., Caes., 31 ; Ant., 5, 3 ; App., ii, 33, 131-3 ; Dio, xli, 3, 2-3 ; Oros., vi, 15, 2.
[2] See pp. 330-1.   [3] B. C., i, 7. See pp. 334-7.
[4] Plut., Caes., 32, 1 ; App., ii, 35, 137.
[5] Pliny, iii, 15 (20), 115.   [6] See pp 334-7 and vol. iii, p. 1.

PART II

CAESAR'S CONQUEST OF GAUL AND INVASIONS OF BRITAIN

In *Caesar's Conquest of Gaul* (second edition, 1911), *Ancient Britain* (1907), and my edition of the *Bellum Gallicum* (1914) I discussed all the questions that related, directly or indirectly, to Caesar's operations in the years 58–51 B. C. Here I need only take account of the publications relevant to this history that have since appeared. The pages referred to at the beginning of various notes belong to the present volume.

PAGE 3. ' It was about the seventh century before the Christian era that the tall fair Celts began to cross the Rhine ', with which compare *Ancient Britain*, pp. 432–3. M. David Viollier,[1] who claims to have attained greater precision, has proved that a Celtic group appeared in the valley of the Rhine in the sixth century, but not that they were the first comers.[2] J. Déchelette,[3] followed by J. Loth,[4] argued on archaeological grounds that Celts were already settled in Franche-Comté and Burgundy in the Bronze Age.[5]

PAGE 14. In *Ancient Britain*, pages 289–90 and Caesar's *Conquest of Gaul²*, pp. 32–3, 523–4 I argued that Druidism was pre-Celtic. Camille Jullian, who formerly [6] held that it was purely Celtic and originated in the third century B. C., has recently [7] given reasons for accepting the view which I maintain.

Salomon Reinach on Caesar's narrative of his first two campaigns in Gaul.—In *Caesar's Conquest of Gaul* [8] and *Ancient Britain* [9] I discussed all the criticisms that had been directed against the credibility of Caesar's *Gallic War*. Recently, however, M. Salomon Reinach has made a fresh attack.[10] Its object is the *First Commentary*, which has provoked more hostile comment than all the rest. Remarking at the outset [11] that the narrative consists of two parts—chapters 2–29 and 30–54—he affirms that between them there are contradictions so glaring that this Commentary cannot have been either written or published at one time.—

[1] *Festgabe Hugo Blümner*, 1914, pp. 261–6.
[2] His readers should check his argument by *Caesar's Conquest of Gaul²*, p. 305, and J. Déchelette's *Manuel d'archéol.*, ii, 3, 1914, pp. 1014–5.
[3] *Op. cit.*, ii, 1910, pp. 136, 150–3.
[4] *Rev. celt.*, xxxviii, 1921, p. 286.
[5] Cf. *Caesar's Conquest of Gaul²*, pp. 274, 852.
[6] *Hist. de la Gaule*, ii, 1908, pp. 88–9.
[7] *Rev. des études anc.*, xxi, 1919, p. 32.
[8] 1899, pp. 173–244 ; 2nd ed., 1911, pp. 211–56.   [9] Pp. 666–72.
[10] *Rev de philol.*, xxxix, 1915, pp. 29–49.   [11] *Ib.*, p. 29.

1. The motives which Caesar alleges for the Helvetian emigration [1] are inadmissible : if the Helvetii were too numerous for their territory, their sensible course would have been to send out a colony ; and a universal emigration is even less credible if their purpose was to conquer Gaul, for countries are not to be conquered by invaders who are accompanied by women, children, and old men.[2] I reply, first, that universal migrations occurred more than once in ancient times, witness the migrations of the Cimbri and Teutoni [3] and of the Usipetes and Tencteri ; [4] secondly, that German, if not Celtic, conquerors were accompanied by women and children.[5]

2. The reasons, says Reinach,[6] which Caesar gives for having attacked the Helvetii are just as bad : ' he was afraid that the Helvetii, if they settled near the Atlantic, would be close to Tolosa (Toulouse) and the Province,[7] as if they were not nearer still while they continued to inhabit Helvetia ! ' Again, Caesar would have us believe that the danger with which Rome had been threatened by the Cimbri and Teutoni was renewed by the Helvetian emigration ; this is manifestly false, for the Helvetii were Gauls, not Germans, and Caesar never calls the Gauls ' barbarians '. When he recounts the abortive projects of Orgetorix, he does so in order to strengthen the impression that the Helvetii were dangerous to Rome ; but whereas in another quarter there was a real danger, from Ariovistus, he took care not to say one word about it, or even to make a passing mention of that chieftain's name. Why ? Because, in order to justify himself for having attacked the Helvetii, it was necessary to ascribe the Helvetian migration to the unscrupulous designs of the Helvetii themselves.[8]

I have argued elsewhere [9] that the Helvetii were really dangerous, and I need only point out here that the Senate as well as Caesar appreciated the danger.[10] Reinach is mistaken when he says that Caesar never called the Gauls ' barbarians ' ; for he did so six, or if we count the Eburones as Gauls, seven times.[11] Unquestionably there was a danger resulting from the victories of Ariovistus, about which Caesar, while he is describing the Helvetian campaign, says nothing. But unless Reinach can prove that the sole motive of the Helvetian emigration was to escape from an invasion threatened

---

[1] *B. G.*, i, 2, 30, 4.   [2] *Op. cit.*, p. 30.
[3] Plut., *Marius*, 11, 2-3.   [4] *B. G.*, iv, 14, 5.
[5] *Ib.*, i, 51, 3 ; iv, 14, 5 ; Flor., i, 38 ; Plut., *Marius*, 11, 3 ; 19, 8 ; 27, 2-3. Cf. Strabo, iv, 4, 2. A. Klotz (*Neue Jahrb. f. d. klass. Altertum*, xxxv, 1915, pp. 617, 623) reasonably infers from *B. G.*, i, 29, from the extreme slowness of the march of the Helvetii, and from their having taken 20 days to cross the Saône with only three-fourths of their number that their movement was a national emigration.
[6] *Op. cit.*, p. 31.   [7] *B. G.*, i, 10, 1.
[8] Caesar frankly says (*ib.*, iv, 4) that the Usipetes and Tencteri were pushed into Gaul by the Suebi ; but that was no reason why he should not drive them out.
[9] *Caesar's Conquest of Gaul*², pp. 225-6. Cf. Klotz, *op. cit.*, pp. 613-4.
[10] Cic., *Att.*, i, 19. 2.
[11] *B. G.*, i, 40, 9 ; iii, 14, 4 ; 15, 2 ; 16, 4 ; 23, 2 ; v, 34, 1 ; 54, 4.

by Ariovistus, his remark loses its point. To this question I will return later.

3. Caesar, says Reinach,[1] resorted in chapter 30 to an artifice in order to give a semblance of truth to his narrative. If Diviciacus really uttered the words which Caesar puts into his mouth in §§ 2–3, they were dictated to him by Caesar ; for the motives there alleged for the war which the Romans waged against the Helvetii are precisely those which Caesar himself insisted upon, and they will not bear examination. Is it credible that the Gauls would have considered Caesar's personal grievance connected with the campaign of 107 B. C. as a justification of the war which he had waged against the Helvetii ? Or that they even remembered the episode ?

Now the words to which Reinach refers were not spoken by Diviciacus, nor is there any allusion in the chapter to Caesar's personal grievance ; but these are minor inaccuracies. Here (immediately following the statement [2] that ' On the conclusion of the campaign against the Helvetii, envoys from almost every part of Gaul . . . came to congratulate Caesar ') are the words which Caesar is supposed to have dictated : ' They were aware, they said, that if he had exacted atonement from the Helvetii by the sword for the wrongs they had done in the past to the Roman People, yet his action was just as much to the advantage of Gaul as of the Romans ; for, though the Helvetii were perfectly well off, they had quitted their own abode with the intention of attacking the whole of Gaul, usurping dominion, selecting for occupation out of numerous tracts the one which they deemed the most suitable and the most fertile in the whole country, and making the other tribes their tributaries ' (*intellegere sese, tametsi pro veteribus Helvetiorum iniuriis populi Romani ab his poenas bello repetisset, tamen eam rem non minus ex usu terrae Galliae quam populi Romani accidisse, propterea quod eo consilio florentissimis rebus domos suas Helvetii reliquissent uti toti Galliae bellum inferrent imperioque potirentur, locumque domicilio ex magna copia deligerent quem ex omni Gallia oportunissimum ac fructuosissimum iudicassent, reliquasque civitates stipendiarias haberent*). I suspect that the Gallic envoys were quite shrewd enough to speak in this sense without dictation. Whether the war against the Helvetii was just or unjust is a question of casuistry, which I need not discuss. As for the motive which Caesar alleges for having attacked them, I have examined it elsewhere.[3]

4. Reinach insists [4] that the speech which Caesar ascribes to Divico [5] and his own reply[6] were inventions addressed to the Senate and to public opinion in Rome. By way of substantiating this assertion he affirms that the alleged devastation by the Helvetii of the lands of the Aedui would have been a gross blunder ; for it was the interest of the Helvetii not to make enemies, and, in view of the supplies with which they had provided themselves,[7] it is

[1] *Op. cit.*, pp. 31–2.   [2] *B. G.*, i, 30, 1.
[3] *Caesar's Conquest of Gaul*, 1899, pp. 181–6 ; 2nd ed., 1911, pp. 225–6.
[4] *Op. cit.*, pp. 32–3.   [5] *B. G.*, i, 13, 3–7.   [6] *Ib.*, 14.   [7] *B. G.*, i, 5, 3.

hardly conceivable that they should have been so soon reduced to plunder their neighbours. No, the ravages were invented, in order to make the Romans believe that the allies of Rome had been wronged. What Divico would naturally have said was, 'We are hard pressed by Ariovistus'; but it would not have suited Caesar's purpose to record such words : he would not let it appear that the Helvetii saddled Ariovistus with the responsibility of their migration. This charge also is not new. I need only ask Reinach the same question that I asked Ferrero : [1] does he believe that a host numbering over 300,000 souls (or any figure which he may prefer to substitute for Caesar's estimate) [2] could have been prevented by their leader, however well they may have been supplied, from attempting to plunder ? I think that such discipline would have been too much to expect ; and probably Reinach has not forgotten the events of 1914. The responsibility of Ariovistus shall be considered anon.

5. Caesar then proceeds, says Reinach,[3] to justify his campaign against Ariovistus. In 30, 5 he anticipates the objection, ' You, Caesar, must have known all that [the oppression of the Aedui and the Sequani by Ariovistus] since March, 58 '. ' No,' Caesar could reply, ' it was a secret kept by the Gauls.' Then Reinach incidentally pays Caesar a compliment. It is difficult, he says, to believe that Gallic deputies came, as Caesar says,[4] to congratulate him after he had defeated the Helvetii, as if he were already master of Gaul ; ' but it was not from vanity—unlike Pompey, he was above that sentiment—that he tried to gain credence for his story. His object was infinitely more important : he wished to justify in the eyes of the Romans, Friends and Allies of King Ariovistus, the bold initiative which he was about to take against him '.

Another old charge in a new form.[5] No doubt Caesar knew all about the tyranny of Ariovistus by March, 58. But I cannot see why, even if he had written as a scientific historian, he should have mentioned it before he came to describe his campaign against Ariovistus,[6] unless Reinach is right in contending that the pressure exerted by Ariovistus was the real motive of the Helvetian migration, and that Caesar knew it. Let us hear the proof which he adduces of this contention.

---

[1] *Caesar's Conquest of Gaul*[2], p. 223.   [2] *B. G.*, i, 29.
[3] *Op. cit.*, p. 34.   [4] *B. G.*, i, 30, 1.
[5] See *Caesar's Conquest of Gaul*, 1899, pp. 187-9.
[6] Very likely, as A. Klotz argues (*Zeitschr. f. d. österr. Gymn.*, lxiv, 1913, pp. 883-4), Caesar, in order to justify his campaign against Ariovistus in the eyes of political opponents, used the speech of Diviciacus to make it appear that he had acted in compliance with the wish of the Aedui ; but he expressly adds (*B. G.*, i, 33, 2-5) that he had his own reasons for action. In a later paper (*Berl. philol. Woch.*, 1915, col. 1245) Klotz, while vindicating the credibility of Caesar's narrative, nevertheless holds that, in order to defend himself against the charge of having picked a quarrel with the Helvetii, he emphasized petty acts of aggression which, in the absence of iron discipline, were unavoidable when such large masses were migrating. Perhaps ; but it was no affair of his whether iron discipline was maintained or not : the Helvetii were a nuisance and a danger ; that was all that concerned him.

In chapter 31, he says,[1] we find the first real indication of the cause of the Helvetian migration,—to escape from the tyranny of the Germans; and it is needless to insist upon the contradiction between this passage and the preceding texts relative to the aims of the Helvetii.

Yes, 'to escape from the tyranny of the Germans', but not to escape from the tyranny of Ariovistus. Read the passage in question, which occurs in the speech of Diviciacus :—'Unless Caesar could help them, the Gauls must all do as the Helvetii had done,—leave house and home, seek another abode, other settlements, out of reach of the Germans', &c. (*Nisi quid in Caesare . . . sit auxilii, omnibus Gallis idem esse faciendum quod Helvetii fecerint, ut domo emigrent, aliud domicilium, alias sedes, remotas a Germanis, petant*).[2] Do these words support the contention that Ariovistus, by the menace of invasion, had expelled the Helvetii from Helvetia? I grant that fear of the ultimate designs of Ariovistus may have been one of the motives that impelled the Helvetii to emigrate. I have myself suggested that they 'had reason to fear that . . . Ariovistus would sever them from their Celtic kinsmen';[3] in other words, that if he succeeded in conquering Gaul, he would be free to turn his arms against them. But this is not the same as Reinach's view. At the time when the Helvetii were preparing to set out Ariovistus was fully occupied in Gaul; and it was not his pressure, but that of other Germans, which was thrusting the Helvetii towards the west. But suppose that, directly or indirectly, his pressure was the determining motive: how can Reinach tell that Caesar knew it? Even if he did, the 'absolute contradiction' on which Reinach insists is imaginary; for the Helvetii had their own designs, which conflicted with Caesar's policy, and that was all that interested him. The notion that he would have been ashamed to avow that the Helvetii desired to escape the tyranny of Ariovistus is really comical: he expressly stated that the Usipetes and Tencteri were forced to migrate by the pressure of the Suebi;[4] but that did not prevent him from destroying them.

6. The relentless critic then proceeds to develop the theory that Caesar wrote the *Commentaries* in instalments. Why, he asks,[5] did Caesar never mention Ariovistus until he had finished his narrative of the Helvetian campaign? This problem would be insoluble if Caesar had written his seven books continuously; he wrote the first in two instalments, and he avoided mentioning Ariovistus in the first because in his own consulship Ariovistus had been named Friend and Ally of the Roman People.[6] Reinach admits[7] that when Caesar published the seven books as a whole, he might have been expected to remove the contradictions which were due to the previous fragmentary publication. The reason, he explains, of his having omitted to do this must have been, partly

<hr>

[1] *Op. cit.*, pp. 35–6.
[3] *Caesar's Conquest of Gaul*[2], p. 38.
[5] *Op. cit.*, p. 38.   [6] *Ib.*, p. 41.

[2] *B. G.*, i, 31, 14.
[4] *B.G.*, iv, 1, 1–2; 4, 1–2.
[7] *Ib.*, p. 39.

that he had little time to spare, but principally that the various reports which form the *Commentaries* had had too great a circulation to admit of his introducing important corrections without writing an entirely new book. Then, citing the opinions as to the time when Caesar wrote his memoirs that have been expressed by 'the best modern authorities', including myself, and referring to the argument which I based upon the words of Hirtius—'others know the flawless excellence of his work ; I know more, how easily and rapidly it was done '[1]—he says,[2] 'I could vouch in the same terms for the facility of Gaston Boissier, for example, without having ever sat near him at his desk'. So, he concludes, 'the argument which Rice Holmes . . . thinks so strong is worth, to speak plainly, absolutely nothing'.

I like a hard hitter ; but I can parry this blow and counter it. Reinach can vouch that Boissier wrote easily and rapidly ; but, if I am not mistaken, he was not Boissier's secretary, as Hirtius was Caesar's. Also it may be doubted whether Boissier ever wrote a short book 'easily and rapidly' and yet published it in eight instalments, as Reinach will have it that Caesar did. Perhaps too Reinach will admit that since these eight instalments had such an extensive circulation, one of their readers must have been Cicero, who undoubtedly read what Reinach would call the complete edition, but instead of noticing the alleged glaring contradictions merely praised the style.[3] But if he had read the alleged instalments, he must have read carelessly ; for although the Nervii were mentioned ten times in the *Second Commentary*, played by far the most important part of all the Belgic tribes in 57 B. C., and were within an ace of beating Caesar on the Sambre, Cicero, whose brother was one of Caesar's generals, had apparently never heard of them before 54 : 'where those Nervii of yours are', he writes to Quintus, 'and how far off, I have no idea' (*ubi enim isti sint Nervii et quam longe absint nescio*).[4]

7. But Reinach has other arguments in reserve. Caesar, he reminds

---

[1] *B. G.*, viii, Praef., § 6. My argument ran as follows : ' if the statement that the *Commentaries* were written "easily and rapidly " is not absolutely inconsistent with the view that each book was written during the comparative leisure of the winter following the campaign which it describes, the natural meaning is that the whole work was the result of a continuous effort ' (*Caesar's Conquest of Gaul*[2], pp. 203–4) ; and again (p. 209), ' Hirtius's words show that he had himself witnessed the rapidity with which Caesar wrote his *Commentaries* : therefore it is morally certain that they were written at one time ; for the other theory, besides involving a forced interpretation of the Latin, would oblige us to assume that Hirtius regularly spent his winters with Caesar in Cisalpine Gaul '.

[2] *Op. cit.*, p. 40.   [3] *Brutus*, 75, 262.

[4] *Q. fr.*, iii, 8, 2. Cicero never mentions the *Commentaries* in his letters. This omission is intelligible enough if they were published as a whole in 50 B.C. ; for he was then in Cilicia and was distracted by anticipations of the imminent Civil War : but that he should never have noticed any one of the eight successive publications which Reinach postulates—not even in 54 B.C., when in his correspondence with his brother Quintus he was constantly referring to Caesar— is inconceivable.

us,[1] declared at the end of his second book [2] that the whole of Gaul was subdued : who will believe that he would not have modified this statement if, at the moment of writing, he had known that what his legions had achieved in the first two years of the war was nothing in comparison with the efforts which he was obliged to demand from them in later years ?

I will not say that this argument is ' worth absolutely nothing '. I merely ask Reinach to re-read the first sentence of the *Seventh Commentary*,—' Gaul was now tranquillized ; and Caesar, in accordance with his determination, started for Italy to hold the assizes ' (*Quieta Gallia Caesar, ut constituerat, in Italiam ad conventus agendos proficiscitur*). Immediately afterwards follows the narrative of the rebellion of Vercingetorix. Unless Caesar wrote the first sentence in the winter of 53/52, and then stopped short, he must have known at the moment of writing that what his legions had achieved in the first six years of the war was little in comparison with the efforts which he was obliged to demand from them later. Really of course, in this case as in the other, he was simply describing the condition of Gaul as it had appeared to him at a given time. In other words, he either implied in both cases that his foresight had failed or he only meant by *pacata* (ii, 35, 1) and *quieta* (vii, 1, 1) that Gaul was temporarily subdued.

8. Again, Reinach insists,[3] if Caesar wrote the second part of the *First Commentary* immediately after the campaigns of 58 B. C., he had good reasons for emphasizing the service which Publius Crassus had rendered in the battle with Ariovistus ; [4] but it would have been strange if he had written in this sense in 51 B. C., three years after the death of Publius and of his father, when there was no occasion either to compliment the one or to flatter the other. Besides, who will deny that, writing in 51, Caesar would have found something to say about the sad and heroic end of his lieutenant ?

I will deny it, for it was not Caesar's way to recall incidents, however sad or heroic they might have been, which were irrelevant to his narrative. But what baffles my understanding is how Reinach can assert that Caesar would have gratuitously recorded the heroism of Publius in Mesopotamia, and in the same breath deny that he would have recorded the bold initiative that turned the scale in a desperate battle in Gaul, unless he had had something to gain. Does Reinach mean that Caesar never chronicled meritorious deeds except from motives of self-interest ? I will not cite the case of Sextius Baculus,[5] because, as we shall see later, Reinach might object that in praising a centurion, as contrasted with an aristocratic officer, Caesar was paying court to the Roman populace. But what had he to gain by praising his Gallic friend Gaius Valerius Procillus ? [6] Does Reinach, who compliments Caesar on his freedom from vanity, suppose that he was incapable of generosity ?

---

[1] *Op. cit.*, p. 41.
[2] *B. G.*, ii, 35, 1.
[3] *Op. cit.*, p. 42.
[4] *B. G.*, i, 52, 7.
[5] *Ib.*, ii. 25, 1 ; iii, 5, 2 ; vi, 38, 1–4.
[6] *Ib.*, i, 47, 4 ; 53, 5–6.

9. If the reader is not yet sure whether he will accept Reinach's view, this final argument may help him to decide. Unless Caesar had known that Ariovistus had an understanding with his enemies at Rome, he would not have dared to attribute to him the words, ' Indeed if he put him [Caesar] to death, he should be doing an acceptable service to many of the nobles and leading men of Rome. This he knew as a fact, for he had it through their agents from their own lips ' (*Quod si eum interfecerit, multis sese nobilibus principibusque populi Romani gratum esse facturum—id se ab ipsis per eorum nuntios compertum habere*).[1] But this accusation dates itself—in 58 B. C.; for who, seven years later, could remember the Suebian emissaries in whom the Roman aristocrats who hated Caesar had put their trust ?

If this question requires an answer, let me answer it by another. Is *l'affaire Dreyfus*, which happened in the nineteenth century, forgotten by Reinach and his countrymen ? [2]

[1] *B. G.*, i, 44, 12.
[2] H. Meusel (Jahresb. d. philol. Vereins [*Sokrates*, i, 1913], pp. 30–1) has shown that the arguments for the annual composition of the *Commentaries* which had been adduced before the appearance of Reinach's article lose most of their value unless successive *publication* is assumed as well. O. Schulz, however (*Klio*, xi, 1911, pp. 48–82), has endeavoured by comparing what Caesar said about the manners and customs of the Germans in the *Fourth* and the *Sixth Commentary* respectively to prove that the seven books must have been published successively. In the *Sixth* (22, 2), he says (pp. 62–3), Caesar contradicts a statement which he made in the *Fourth* (1, 7). I reply that any clear-headed reader who compares the two passages will see that in the second Caesar repeats his earlier statement in other words. But Schulz tries again. It was not, he says (p. 75), until Caesar was about to write the *Sixth Commentary* that he had read the Greek books to which he there refers, and in which the Gauls were confounded with the Germans : if he had read them before, he would naturally have inserted in the *Fourth* the ethnographic chapters (vi, 11–24) in which he corrected this error and emphasized the contrast between the two nations. I think that Caesar understood the business of authorship better than his critic. In the whole of the *Bellum Gallicum* it would be difficult to find a place where the ethnographical digression would have been more glaringly incongruous than the beginning of the *Fourth Commentary*.
      Two more attempts have recently been made to prove that the *Commentaries* were written in instalments. F. Hartmann (*Glotta*, ix, 1917, pp. 10 ff.) argues that Caesar only gradually learned the difference between Gauls and Germans. After giving reasons, which do not require notice, for believing that at first he regarded the Germans as ' genuine Gauls ', he finds himself obliged to explain a passage of which the accepted version stultifies this view. In i, 47, 4 the *a* MSS. have (Commodissimum visum est C. Valerium Procillum C. Valerii Caburi filium . . .) *et propter fidem et propter linguae Gallicae scientiam, qua multa iam Ariovistus longinqua consuetudine utebatur* . . . (ad eum mittere). That is to say, Caesar knew that Ariovistus, whose native speech was German, had learned during the years which he had spent in Gaul to speak the language of the Gauls. The *β* MSS. have *quorum amicitia Ariovistus iam longinqua consuetudine utebatur et propter fidem et propter linguae Gallicae scientiam.* Needless to say that the editors have unanimously followed *a* ; but, according to Hartmann, they are wrong. When he insists that *quorum* can well refer to Procillus and his father, I am not concerned to contradict him ; but he fails to see that *propter fidem* is meaningless and that *propter linguae Gallicae scientiam* can only imply that Ariovistus had *learned* to speak the language. When he urges (p. 26) that Caesar, in describing his negotiations with Ariovistus,

10. One more instance of alleged bad faith remains. Commenting on Caesar's description of the panic at Vesontio [1] (Besançon), Reinach [2] admits that he will not go so far as to say that there is no truth in it ; but the truth is coloured by Caesar's demagogic policy : he shamed his officers by contrasting their conduct with that of the centurions and privates, thus at once reading a lesson to the aristocracy and paying court to the populace. Had Reinach forgotten this sentence—' Gradually even *legionaries, centurions,* and cavalry officers, who had had long experience of campaigning, were unnerved ' (*etiam ii qui magnum in castris usum habebant, milites centurionesque quique equitatui praeerant, perturbabantur*) ? [3] Had he forgotten that Caesar 'rated the centurions severely ' (*vehementer eos incusavit*),[4] and that when he told them that ' if no one else would follow him, he would go on with the 10th legion alone ' (*si praeterea nemo sequatur, tamen se cum sola decima legione iturum*),[5] he implied that in the other legions panic had taken possession not only of officers but also of the rank and file ?

Salomon Reinach is one of the most eminent of living savants ; but I do not think that he has made out a much better case than Guglielmo Ferrero. Read Caesar's *First Commentary* and then contrast the reconstructive essays of the two critics : you will be first edified and afterwards amused.

[Since I wrote the foregoing pages I have read the passage in which Professor Hans Delbrück [6] attempts to explain Caesar's narrative.

says nothing about linguistic difficulties, he forgets that Caesar had a staff of interpreters (i, 19, 3) ; when he reminds us that Cicero in 56 B.C. did not yet know the difference between Celts and Germans (*De prov. cons.*, 13, 32), we may remind him that two years later Cicero professed complete ignorance of the Nervii (*Q. fr.*, iii, 8, 2).

Max Radin (*Class. Philol.*, xiii, 1918, pp. 283–300) conjectures that the *Commentaries* were written in three instalments—i and ii in the winter of 57–56 B.C. ; iii–vi in the winter of 53–52 ; vii in the winter of 52–51. He cannot believe that after the war was over Caesar would have said that the campaign of 57 had resulted in ' the pacification of the whole of Gaul ' (*omni Gallia pacata* [ii, 35, 1]), for later events had shown that it was not subdued. I have confuted this argument (p. 277) in dealing with Reinach. Observing that when Caesar wrote (iv, 21, 7) that in 55 B.C. he ' believed Commius to be loyal ', he might seem to have had in mind the man's subsequent defection (vii, 76, 1–2), Radin admits that ' That would militate against ' his theory ; but he disposes of this difficulty by assuming that in the winter of 53–52 Caesar already knew that Commius was disloyal, for otherwise Labienus would not have attempted to kill him in the early part of 52. It is true that Labienus, when he made this attempt, had just found out that Commius was plotting (viii, 23, 3) ; but his messenger must have travelled to Italy on the wings of the wind if Caesar became aware of the plot while he was engaged on the second of the four books which *ex hypothesi* he wrote in the winter of 53–52. No one will gainsay Radin when he confesses that his arguments (one or two of which I have mercifully ignored) are not ' wholly conclusive ' ; but he does not realize that he has himself disproved them While he assures us that Caesar was too distracted by the disturbances in Italy to write his booklet *De analogia* in the winter of 53–52, he finds time for him in the same winter to write four commentaries.

[1] *B. G.*, i, 39.   [2] *Op. cit.*, p. 48.   [3] *B. G.*, i, 39, 5.
[4] *Ib.*, 40, 1.   [5] *Ib.*, § 15.
[6] *Gesch. d. Kriegskunst*, i², 1908, pp. 491, 494–6, 505–6.

In *Caesar's Conquest of Gaul* [1] I argued that the Helvetii, after they crossed the Saône, moved northward up its right bank because they found it more convenient to make this détour than to attempt to cross the mountains that intersected the direct route. Delbrück insists that the *ostensible* purpose of the Helvetii must have been to take the direct route, or they would not have crossed the Saône in the southern part of its course, and that the obstacles presented by the mountains were not to be compared with the danger of marching, pursued by Caesar, up the valley of the Saône. Caesar, he says, evidently expected that the Helvetii would follow the course of the Saône, for he had arranged that his supplies should be conveyed in barges up that river. Delbrück concludes that the proposed settlement in the country of the Santoni was merely a pretext, by which the Helvetian leader had persuaded his people to emigrate : if that country was his objective, why did he attack Caesar when the latter, ceasing to pursue him, marched for Bibracte ? Caesar's account of his motive [2] is incredible. The Helvetii could not have believed that Caesar was afraid of them : if they wished to prevent him from reaching Bibracte, they had no need to fight ; for if they won the battle, no Roman would need supplies again ; if the Romans won, they would not be prevented.

Delbrück then proceeds to develop his theory of the objects of the Helvetian emigration and of Caesar's campaign. The Helvetii intended, in conjunction with the Aeduan patriotic party, to resist Ariovistus. Caesar, who was informed of their purpose before he left Rome, resolved to anticipate them : he would himself rid Gaul of the German invaders. Divico requested him to allow the Helvetii to march through the Roman Province because he wished to keep up the fiction that they purposed to settle in the country of the Santoni. By the time when Caesar destroyed the Helvetian rearguard on the Saône the pro-Roman party among the Aedui had got the upper hand and, instead of welcoming the Helvetii, begged him to expel them. The Helvetii, seeing that their enterprise had failed, sent envoys to Caesar, asking permission to settle in any land which he might assign to them—in other words, to return to their own country. The mission failed because Caesar required the Helvetii to give hostages. They marched northward with the intention of returning to Helvetia, but diverged westward from the Saône into the uplands, where they would be better able to resist attack. When Caesar relinquished the pursuit in order to obtain supplies, they could have marched back to Helvetia unhindered ; but had they done so, they would have left their Aeduan allies and the whole of Central Gaul at Caesar's mercy. As Caesar had not hitherto attacked them, they may have hoped that he would finally abandon the pursuit, and, as they knew, his supplies must soon be exhausted.

I have summarized Delbrück's argument because he is a writer of recognized ability. Let us see how far his theory will bear examination. To begin with, one asks oneself whether the Helvetii would

<hr />

[1] 2nd ed., pp. 50, 232. [2] *B. G.*, i, 23, 3.

have gained anything, supposing that they intended to reach the country of the Santoni by a détour, by crossing the Saône further north : to those who can read a map the answer will be evident. If the proposed settlement in the country of the Santoni was a mere pretext, it matters nothing whether the obstacles presented by the direct route were more or less formidable than the danger of marching up the valley of the Saône ; but, Delbrück notwithstanding, the mountain tracks were not practicable for wagons, and, moreover, the Helvetii must have wished to avoid encountering the Arverni, who were enemies of their Aeduan allies. Again, if Divico marched towards the lower valley of the Saône in order to delude his followers into the belief that their goal was the country of the Santoni, they must have been extraordinarily docile if he could count upon their acquiescing in being compelled to diverge northward and abandon the settlement upon which *ex hypothesi* their hearts were set. Besides, if his purpose was to join the Aeduan patriots against Ariovistus, what did he mean to do when Ariovistus was disposed of ? He must have intended to settle somewhere. Why not in the country of the Santoni ?

Now as to Caesar's statement of the motive of the Helvetii for fighting. It does not seem to me incredible that they thought that Caesar was afraid of them ; but he states this merely as an alternative conjectural explanation of their action, and the other alternative was equally conjectural. If they wished to prevent Caesar from getting supplies—and assuredly they did, for they must have known that if he got them he would be able without difficulty to resume his pursuit and overtake their crawling column—how were they to gain that object without fighting ? The altruistic motive which Delbrück assigns for their action is fantastic. If, as he says, they wanted to return to Helvetia, is it credible that they would have risked a battle unless they had known that Caesar, after he had replenished his stores, could overtake them ? When Delbrück says that they may have hoped that Caesar would finally abandon the pursuit, I cannot conceive what he is driving at : surely that hope, if they entertained it, would have led them, not to attack him, but to go away.]

PAGE 20. In *Caesar's Conquest of Gaul*[2], pages 231-3, I gave reasons for believing that Plutarch and Appian were wrong in saying that Labienus, not Caesar, defeated the Tigurini. A. Klotz,[1] however, holds that their statements, being derived, as he believes, from Asinius Pollio, must be accepted, but that Caesar's version may be defended by comparison with the monument of Ancyra,[2] where Augustus said that he had compelled the Parthians to submit, although the actual commander was Tiberius.[3] But the cases are not parallel, and it seems more probable that the statements of Plutarch and Appian were ultimately derived from Labienus, who may be supposed to have commanded under Caesar's supervision.

[1] *Neue Jahrb. f. d. klass. Altertum*, xxxv, 1915, p. 610.
[2] *Res gestae divi Aug.*[2], 1883, 5, 40-2.   [3] Suet., *Tib.*, 9, 1.

282   CAESAR'S CONQUEST OF GAUL AND

PAGE 32. In *Caesar's Conquest of Gaul*[2], page 648, I gave reasons for rejecting the theory of C. Winkler that the battle between Caesar and Ariovistus was fought near Epfig, about 7 miles north of Schlettstadt. E. Fabricius [1] gives another. Glöckelsberg, 13 kilometres (about 8 miles) south-west of Strassburg, which Winkler identifies with the knoll or earthen mound (*tumulus terrenus*) where the interview between Ariovistus and Caesar took place, does not in the least correspond with Caesar's description : [2] it is not an isolated eminence, but the termination of a range extending from the Vosges into the plain of the Rhine.

PAGE 39. The late Lieutenant G. L. Cheesman [3] argued that as the *velites*—the auxiliary troops of pre-Marian times—were probably abolished by Marius, ' it necessarily follows that when, during the last fifty years of the Republic, a standing army came into existence . . . auxiliary regiments formed part of it ', and accordingly he concluded that the ' Cretan archers, Balearic slingers, and Numidian cavalry ' (*sic*) which he supposes that Caesar employed in 57 B.C.[4] ' had formed part of the regular troops which he found in the province '. But on the same reasoning it would follow that when the Italian cavalry, which had been attached to the legions, ceased to serve, foreign cavalry ' formed part of the regular troops ' : yet this Cheesman rightly denies.[5]

PAGE 91. Mr. A. H. Davis in an excellent school-book [6] offers a novel explanation of the statement in the *Commentaries* that the Usipetes and Tencteri fled *ad confluentem Mosae et Rheni*.[7] Assuming that the Rhine bifurcated at Wesel, about 8 miles east of Xanten, he tells us that the southern branch flowed past Xanten, Cleves, and Nimeguen ; that it was ' the branch known to Tacitus as the Waal ' ; and that in Caesar's time ' it may well have been known here as *Mosa*, because it joins up with the Meuse later on, and bears that name after the junction. What I would suggest therefore ', he continues, ' is that *confluentem Mosae et Rheni* may mean the place where the Meuse (*i.e.* the Waal) and the Rhine meet *as on a map* '—in other words, where the so-called Meuse does not flow into, but diverges from, the Rhine. ' The question is ', he candidly adds, ' whether *confluens* can possibly be used in this sense ' ; and Latin scholars will have no hesitation in answering. When Mr. Davis suggests that ' in comparison with the northern branch ' the so-called Meuse ' may have given the appearance of flowing in the

[1] *Zeitschr. f. d. Gesch. d. Oberrheins*, N.F., xxiv, 1909, p. 10.
[2] *B. G.*, i, 43, 1.
[3] *The Auxilia of the Roman Imperial Army*, 1914, p. 10.
[4] Meusel in his critical note on *B. G.*, ii, 7, 1 (p. 388 of his edition) argues that *Cretas* and *Baleares* were not written by Caesar. Anyhow, the Numidians in Caesar's army were not cavalry (cf. ii, 7. 1, 10. 1 with *Bell. Afr.*, 13. 1, 15. 1, &c.) ; nor were they archers, from whom in *B. G.*, ii, 10, 1 they are distinguished.
[5] *Op. cit.*, pp. 9–10.
[6] *Caesar and the Germans*, 1915, pp. 99–102.
[7] *B. G.*, iv, 15, 2. My view, that *Mosae* (or *Mosellae* ?) means the Moselle (*Caesar's Conquest of Gaul*[2], pp. 99, 691–706), is supported by Prof. E. Sadée (*Bonn. Jahrb.*, cxxiii, 1915, pp. 99–100).

opposite direction '—in other words, may have appeared to flow eastward when it was flowing westward—he forgets that Caesar emphasizes ' the force of the current ' (*vi fluminis*). [In regard to the question whether the description of the Meuse and the Rhine in *B. G.*, iv, 10 was an interpolation I refer to my edition (1914, page 136) and to my article in the *Classical Quarterly*, viii, 1914, pages 158–60.]

'**The solution of the Portus-Itius-Gesoriacus question.'**—The heading of this article is translated from the sub-title of a recent dissertation [1] by Dr. F. Ludwig Ganter. The ' solution ' is revolutionary. Ever since the question began to be discussed it has been an article of faith that Gesoriacum was on the site of Boulogne ; for many years the question of the identity of Portus Itius has been narrowed to a choice between Boulogne and Wissant.[2] Ganter tells us that Gesoriacum and Portus Itius must both be identified with the village, between Cape Blanc-Nez and Calais, where there is not and never was a harbour, Sangatte, and that when Caesar says that he ' ordered all the ships to assemble *at* the Itian harbour ' (*ad*—not *in*—*portum Itium convenir eiubet* [3]) he meant ' the neighbouring harbour of Calais with its river-mouth '—the mouth of the brook called Hames—' and the great gulf-like mass of water in its rear, which now forms a morass west of Calais '. [4]

Ganter [5] of course admits that the *Itinerary* of Antonine and the *Table* of Peutinger identify Gesoriacum with Boulogne, but he insists that there were two towns of the same name, while, among other eccentricities, he argues [6] that ' the further harbour ' (*ulteriorem portum* [7]), to which Caesar, just before he started on his first expedition, ordered his cavalry to march, was distinct from ' the upper port ' (*superiore portu* [8]), from which the cavalry transports started on the occasion of their second attempt, although to all other commentators it has always been obvious that the two adjectives are synonymous. The *ulterior portus*, he maintains, was Wissant, the *superior portus* was Sangatte ; and thence Caesar, on his first expedition, himself sailed !

Two facts alone dispose of Ganter's ' solution ', which, so far as Portus Itius is concerned, merely restates a view more than three centuries old : the alleged gulf west of Calais did not exist,[9] and, as I proved in *Ancient Britain*,[10] fortifying my own conclusion by the testimony of nautical experts, it would have been impossible for the gale that carried one division of Caesar's cavalry transports back to the port from which they had started to carry them to Sangatte. Furthermore, it might be interesting to hear Ganter explain why, if Sangatte was the *portus Morinorum Britannicus* and the most

---

[1] *Cäsars Fahrt nach Britannien*, 1914.
[2] I may refer to *Anc. Britain*, pp. 552–95 ; *Caesar's Conquest of Gaul*[2], pp. 432–8 ; and *Class. Rev.*, xxiii, 1909, pp. 77–81 ; xxvii, 1913, pp. 258–60 ; xxviii, 1914, pp. 45–7, 82–4, 193–6.
[3] *B. G.*, v, 2, 3.   [4] *Op. cit.*, p. 19. Cf. p. 30.   [5] *Ib.*, p. 12.
[6] *Ib.*, pp. 18–9.   [7] *B. G.*, iv, 23, 1.   [8] *Ib.*, 28, 1.
[9] *Anc. Britain*, pp. 517–8, 565.   [10] pp. 581–3.

famous port in Northern Gaul,[1] Boulogne was selected in the first half of the first century as the station of the Channel Fleet—the famous *classis Britannica*.[2] Some amusement might be derived from a minute examination of his arguments, but I reserve what I have written : the ' solution ' does not merit a sumptuous funeral.[3]

PAGE 111. ' Caesar determined . . . night.' It is evident from Caesar's narrative [4] that the object of the march which he made in the night after his second landing was simply to attack the Britons. But Mr. Henry Sharpe [5] knows better. ' The only reason possible ', he says, ' for the night march was want of water. . . . Caesar must have found out the year before that although the stream north of Deal supplied water enough for two legions, it did not supply enough for five,' &c., Mr. Sharpe forgets that the five legions spent ten days in the neighbourhood of Deal, constructing a naval camp.[6] If the stream did not supply enough water and there were no springs, they doubtless sunk wells.[7]

---

[1] Mela, iii, 2, 23.

[2] *C. I. L.*, xiii, p. 561. Cf. A. E. E. Desjardins, *Géogr. de la Gaule rom.*, i, 1876, pp. 364, 368.

[3] Ganter begins by attacking the universally accepted view that the great road which Agrippa constructed between Lugudunum (Lyons) and ' the Ocean ' (Strabo, iv, 6, 11) terminated at Boulogne, and offers a novel explanation of a passage in Florus (ii, 30, 26) which has puzzled commentators,—(Drusus) *Bormam* [v.l. *Bonam*] *et Caesoriacum* [*Gesoriacum*?] *pontibus iunxit classibusque firmavit* (' Drusus connected Borma [or Bonna ?] and Caesoriacum with bridges and strengthened them with fleets '). For *pontibus* read *Pontibus*, and all becomes clear : *Pontes* was a town mentioned in the *Itinerary* of Antonine (p. 363) between Ambiani (Amiens) and Gesoriacum, 36 Roman miles from the former and 39 from the latter ; and Ganter identifies it with Ponthoile, which, he says, incorrectly, is at the required distance from Amiens. What Drusus did was to prolong Agrippa's road, which terminated at Pontes [!] and connect it with the ' important naval stations, Bonna [Boulogne !] and Gesoriacum ' [Sangatte !]. Unhappily for Ganter Ponthoile is much too far from Sangatte ; and I need hardly add that he has no warrant for assuming that Boulogne was ever called Bonna. The statement of Florus occurs in the chapter in which he describes the campaigns of Drusus in Germany, and when I first read it it seemed to me unlikely that he would have interpolated a sentence about a Gallic road far away to the west (cf. *Sitzungsber. d. Königl. preuss. Akad. d. Wiss.*, 1899, p. 550, n. 1 and *C. I. L.*, xiii, p. 560, n. 3, where Hirschfeld says the same). C. Jullian (*Hist. de la Gaule*, iv, 1913, p. 104, n. 3) is inclined to think that Drusus connected Bonn (*Bonnam*) with a fort called Caesoriacum on the right bank of the Rhine. If, as Mommsen thought (*Röm. Gesch.*, v⁴, 1894, p. 28, n. 2 [Eng. tr., p. 31, n. 2]), Florus meant that Drusus linked the naval stations at Bonn and Boulogne by a military road, *pontibus* must mean a ' corduroy ' road ; but I agree with Hirschfeld and Jullian that this is most improbable.

Ganter frequently refers to the German translation, which, in respect of certain notes, is an adaptation (*Bearbeitung*), of Part I of my *Caesar's Conquest of Gaul* and Chapters VI–VIII of my *Ancient Britain*. If he had consulted the originals, he might have resisted the temptation to write note 2 on page 28 of his tract. The German translation—*unregelmässige*—of the word ' irregular ', which I used to represent Caesar's *instabilem* (*B. G.*, iv, 23, 5), is incorrect. The connotation of ' irregular ', which may mean ' unsettled ' or ' changeable ', is wider than that of *unregelmässig*.

[4] *B. G.*, v, 9, 1.   [5] *Britain B. C.*, 1910, p. 225.   [6] *B. G.*, v, 11, 5–7.

[7] Cf. *B. C.*, iii, 50, 5 ; *Bell. Alex.*, 6, 1 ; *Bell. Afr.*, 51, 6.

PAGE 117. 'What route . . . Bromley.'—Mr. Sharpe[1] argues that Caesar did not march from the neighbourhood of Canterbury to the Thames by either of the two routes which I have indicated, but took a circuitous course in order to have access to running water on every stage. But Caesar[2] estimates the distance from his landing-place to the Thames as about 80 Roman, or 73 English, miles, which is accurate if he took either of the direct routes, but on Mr. Sharpe's theory far short of the truth. Between the Medway and the Thames my itinerary presents no difficulty : from Canterbury to Aylesford on the Medway is very little more than 30 miles ; and if water was not to be obtained from springs or other sources, enough could surely have been carried to last for a couple of marches. Towards the end of the famous march from Corfinium to Brundisium Caesar covered 60 Roman miles without crossing a stream.

PAGES 111, 119-20. Th. Schiche[3] has endeavoured to correct the received chronology of several important letters which I have quoted or noticed in my narrative and of certain events recorded therein. In a long letter which Cicero wrote in instalments to Quintus in reply to four letters which he had received from him he said, ' As to events in Britain, I gather from your letter that we have no occasion either for fear or exultation' (*De Britannicis rebus cognovi ex tuis litteris nihil esse nec quod metuamus nec quod gaudeamus*).[4] The letter to which he here alludes was the first of the four, and the commentators have of course generally assumed that it was written in Britain. Schiche[5] says that they are wrong and insists that it was written while Caesar's army was weatherbound at Portus Itius ; [6] but who will believe that Quintus would then have prophesied that the expedition for which Caesar had made such elaborate preparations was going to be uneventful ? However, Schiche has something in reserve. Cicero, he remarks,[7] says later, ' Your fourth letter, dated August 10 in Britain, was delivered to me on the 13th of September ' (*Quarta epistola mihi reddita est Id. Sept. quam a. d. IIII. Id. Sext. ex Britannia dederas*).[8] Since Cicero implies that this letter was dispatched later than the other three, which, he thinks, were posted simultaneously,[9] and since he expressly says that it was written in Britain, we must conclude that the other three were not. This seems to me a flimsy argument ; but I need not anticipate my readers' decision. Having proved to his own satisfaction that those three letters were written not from Britain, but from Portus Itius, Schiche infers that a familiar passage in one which Cicero wrote to Quintus about the end of August[10] has been generally misunderstood : ' How I rejoiced at your letter from (?) Britain ! I was nervous about the sea and the coast of that island. I don't underrate what you have still to do ; but there is more ground for hope than for fear. . . . You, I can see, have a splendid subject for description,—topography,

[1] *Op. cit.*, pp. 248-9. [2] *B. G.*, v, 11, 8.
[3] Jahresb. d. philol. Vereins (*Zeitschr. f. d. Gymnasialwesen*, 1908), pp. 13-4.
[4] *Q. fr.*, iii, 1, 10. [5] *Op. cit.*, p. 15. [6] *B. G.*, v, 7, 3. [7] *Op. cit.*, p. 15.
[8] *Q. fr.*, iii, 1, 13. [9] *Ib.*, § 8 [10] See *Anc. Britain*, p. 728.

natural features of things and places, customs, peoples, battles, your general himself '. (*O iucundas mihi tuas de Britannia litteras! Timebam Oceanum, timebam litus insulae. Reliqua non equidem contemno, sed plus habent tamen spei quam timoris. . . . Te vero ὑπόθεσιν scribendi egregiam habere video. Quos tu situs, quas naturas rerum et locorum, quos mores, quas gentes, quas pugnas, quem vero ipsum imperatorem habes!* [1]) No wonder that the commentators assume that the letter which gladdened Cicero's heart came from Britain. Not at all, says Schiche : [2] *de Britannia* does not mean ' from Britain', but ' about Britain'. Let it mean ' about Britain' : what difference does that make ? Would Cicero have dwelt upon the dread, now removed, which he had felt about the voyage, if the voyage had not begun ? Would he have waxed enthusiastic about the British scenes which Quintus now had the chance of describing if Quintus had written while he was still whistling for a wind at Portus Itius ? But we must hear Schiche patiently to the end. Cicero, referring to Quintus's letter of August 10, writes, ' There was nothing new in it, except about your *Erigona* ' (*In ea nihil sane erat novi praeter Erigonam*),[3] one of four tragedies which Quintus had composed. That being the case, says Schiche,[4] fighting with the Britons had not yet begun : this letter was written immediately after Quintus landed, for it is incredible that he would not have instantly announced his arrival. Therefore the date of the voyage was probably August 10, which corresponded to July 17 [or rather July 16 [5]] of the Julian calendar. By this pronouncement Schiche seals the fate of his whole theory : he has forgotten to inform himself about the tides. As I showed in *Ancient Britain* (page 729), Caesar's statement that the tide turned westward soon after daybreak on the morning when he arrived in Britain [6] proves that he landed either about the time of full moon or about the time of new moon. The former is out of the question, for full moon occurred on July 21 (Julian): the previous new moon was on July 6.

'**Neglected British History.**'—Professor Flinders Petrie, in a paper [7] which bears this title, complains that I and other writers have ignored ' the so-called Tysilio's Chronicle ',[8] which, he argues, was based upon ' a British account of the first century A.D.' I ignored it because it adds nothing that is both important and trustworthy to Caesar's narrative, with which, as the professor says, it ' is in its main lines substantially in accord ' ; and when I found, among other blunders, that, according to the writer, the second expedition was two years later than the first, and that Caesar passed the winter after the second in London (the existence of which at that time was denied by Haverfield), I thought it best to discard a chronicle the details peculiar to which, if they were not manifestly false, could not be checked.

[1] *Q. fr.*, ii, 15, 4.   [2] *Op. cit.*, p. 16.   [3] *Q. fr.*, iii, 1, 13.
[4] *Op. cit.*, pp. 19–20   [5] See vol. i, pp. 339–41.   [6] *B. G.*, v, 8, 2.
[7] Reprinted from *Proc. Brit. Acad.*, vol. vii.
[8] See P. Roberts, *Chron. of the Kings of Britain*, 1811, pp. 73–82.

PAGE 208. ' Vercingetorix... took up a position behind a stream, not far north of Dijon,' &c. R. de Launay [1] has recently argued that the cavalry combat, immediately preceding the blockade of Alesia, in which Caesar defeated Vercingetorix,[2] took place near Perrigny on the left bank of the Armançon, 25 kilometres (about $15\frac{1}{2}$ miles) from Alesia His reasons are, first, that Caesar, marching to succour the Province, must have moved, probably from the country of the Senones, down the road which leads from Sens to Dijon; secondly, that the high ground from which his German cavalry charged the Gauls must, as the words *summum iugum* [3] prove, have been on a ridge, not on an isolated hill; thirdly, that he reached Alesia early on the morning after the battle, and therefore that Alesia must have been not more than 25 or, at the most, 30 kilometres from the battle-field; and lastly that the description of Alesia and the situation of the Gallic camp prove that he approached Alesia from the west. In *Caesar's Conquest of Gaul* [4] I gave reasons for believing that Caesar during the period of inaction that preceded his march remained, not in the country of the Senones, who were hostile, but in that of the Lingones, who were friendly; I agree that he was marching in the direction of Dijon, but when he encamped on the night before the battle he was marching ' through the most distant part of the country of the Lingones ' (*per extremos Lingonum fines*),[5] and, as I have shown in *Caesar's Conquest of Gaul*,[6] those words can only mean ' through that part of the country of the Lingones which was furthest from his starting-point in the direction in which he was going '; on my theory the words *summum iugum* have the meaning which de Launay gives them; there is no evidence that Caesar reached Alesia early in the morning after the battle, and, as he pursued the beaten army on the day of the battle as long as daylight lasted,[7] he could easily have covered the rest of the way— the entire distance from the battle-field which I indicated to Alesia being less than 30 miles [8]—on the following day; there is not one word in his description of Alesia which shows that he approached it from the west, while the Gallic camp faced the east.[9] The precise site to which I pointed [10] was avowedly provisional; but I adhere to the view, which Camille Jullian [11] shares, that it was not far from Dijon.

Caesar's campaign against the Bellovaci (51 B.C.).—The view which I advocated in *Caesar's Conquest of Gaul*,[12] that the Bellovaci encamped on Mont St. Marc, about 5 miles east of Compiègne, and Caesar on Mont St. Pierre, just south of their position, has lately

[1] *Rev. des quest. hist.*, xlix, 1914, pp. 5–23.   [2] *B. G.*, vii, 66–8.
[3] *Ib.*, 67, 5.   [4] Pp. 788–90.   [5] *B. G.*, vii, 66, 2.
[6] Pp. 792–3.   [7] *B. G.*, vii, 68, 2.
[8] De Launay himself (p. 17) insists that Caesar could march ' une quarantaine de kilomètres [about 25 miles] par jour '.
[9] *B. G.*, vii, 69, 5.   [10] *Caesar's Conquest of Gaul*², p. 800.
[11] *Rev. des études anc.*, x, 1908, pp. 347–50 ; *Hist. de la Gaule*, iii, 1909, p. 495, n. 1.
[12] 2nd ed., pp. 826–30.

been controverted by Dr. H. O. Forbes.[1] I omit to notice those of
his arguments which, if they have any force, tell equally against
any sites that have been or could be proposed, and are therefore
self-destructive.

Dr. Forbes objects that the sites which I, in agreement with
de Saulcy, Stoffel, General Creuly, and Camille Jullian, have indicated
are in the territory of the Suessiones, whereas he in common with
those authorities infers from the narrative of Hirtius that the
Bellovaci encamped in their own country ; that St. Marc ' is not,
nor could be, *surrounded* by a marsh ', whereas Hirtius describes the
Bellovacan stronghold as *locum . . . circumdata palude*,[2] and that
' To-day, whatever may have been the case in 52 B.C. ' [or rather 51],
it is not ' protected by any wet land of consequence ' ; that St. Marc
' cannot be considered " hard to ascend " ' *(tanto collis ascensu)*,[3]
for he has himself ' walked up leisurely ' from Rethondes ' across the
supposed site of the Belgic camp to its south-easterly edge and back
to the village in 45 minutes ' ; that the valley between St. Pierre and
St. Marc is not ' deeper than wide ' *(magis in altitudinem depressa
quam late patente)*;[4] that ' Hirtius's text . . . nowhere authorizes the
assumption that Caesar's camp was placed on a hill at all ' ; that
Caesar's ' ramparts . . . would be superfluous . . . on St. Pierre, whose
slopes rendered it protected as sufficiently as, or better than,
St. Marc ' ; that the plateau of St. Pierre, ' only some 700 yards
by 500 in extent seems . . . inadequate to accommodate the Roman
army, numbering . . . probably some 30,000 men ' ; that ' the
expression *procurrentibus* '[5] ' suggests a very different situation
from that of camps perched on steep eminences 2 miles apart ' ;
that no ' spot in full view of the two presumed camps ' can ' be
recognized answering to ' the *vada transitusque paludis*[6] (fords and
crossing-places of the marsh) which Hirtius mentions ; that the
depression between St. Marc and Mont Collet—the ridge *(iugum)*[7]
on which Caesar must have formed his second camp if the first was
on St. Pierre—is ' only 10 metres below their level ' and cannot be
described as a valley *(mediocri valle)* ;[8] finally, that ' the extreme
edge ' of the ridge, on which Caesar planted artillery, is ' more than
2 miles from the centre of St. Marc's plateau . . . while the range of
the Roman *tormenta* rarely exceeded 1,200 feet '. Dr. Forbes argues,
further, that Mont Ganelon, on the right bank of the Oise, could
not have been the stronghold to which the Bellovaci retreated,
because Caesar could have prevented them from reaching the Oise,
which, moreover, was unfordable ; that the meadow on the left
bank of the Aisne in which *ex hypothesi* they attacked Caesar's
cavalry[9] was so close to St. Marc and St. Pierre that it would have
been rifled by the foragers long before ; that Hirtius's account[10] of
the messages which Caesar sent to his troops during the action and
before he arrived on the scene shows that the meadow was much

---

[1] *Geogr. Journ.*, lix, 1922, pp. 195–206.   [2] *B. G.*, viii, 7, 4.
[3] *Ib.*, 14, 3.   [4] *Ib.*, 9, 2.   [5] *Ib.*, 10, 2.   [6] *Ib.*, 13, 1.
[7] *Ib.*, 14, 4.   [8] *Ib.*   [9] *Ib.*, 18, 1 ; 20, 1.   [10] *Ib.*, 19, 4.

more than 3,000 yards from his camp ; and that, if it had been so near, Hirtius could not have said that Caesar ' discovered (*videbat* [1]) ' ' the river flowing between the field and the " very strong place " ', for ' it must have been hourly in evidence during his occupation of Mt. St. Pierre '.

Now the extreme limits within which the operations must have taken place are known ; and if Dr. Forbes will examine sheets 32 and 33 of the *Carte de l'État-Major* or, like de Saulcy, explore the terrain, he will admit that, if St. Marc and St. Pierre do not satisfactorily answer to Hirtius's narrative, no other sites answer as well.

It is not certain that St. Marc and St. Pierre were in the territory of the Suessiones : Camille Jullian [2] argues that they were in that of the Bellovaci. But if, as Dr. Forbes evidently believes, the eastern frontier of the Bellovaci was the Oise, and if, as he insists, their camp and that of Caesar were within their territory, the strong place to which they afterwards retreated must have been east of the Oise ; for it was separated from Caesar's camp, and therefore also from the camp which they had abandoned, by a deep river,[3] and there was no other. Thus Dr. Forbes must admit that on his theory they fled from their own country into that of their enemies ! *Circumdata*, as every Latin scholar knows, does not necessarily mean ' surrounded ' [4] : Hirtius may only have meant that the hill on which the Bellovaci encamped was fringed by a marsh on the sides on which it was exposed to attack. The Ru de Berne, which flows between St. Marc and St. Pierre, may well have overflowed its banks in consequence of the recent heavy rains ; [5] the ground which Hirtius, perhaps loosely, calls a marsh, was constantly crossed by both the Belgae and the Romans ; and the Ru de Berne in that part of its course over which Caesar was obliged *ex hypothesi* to make causeways widens out into *étangs*. The short time which Dr. Forbes took to ascend St. Marc is irrelevant : if he had been one of Caesar's legionaries, he would have known that to ascend even a gentle slope in the face of an enemy was a perilous enterprise.[6] No valley that I know, except in one place the gorge of the Cheddar Cliffs, is ' deeper than wide ' : the words by which Hirtius, if my view is right, describes the valley between St. Marc and St. Pierre evidently mean that its depth—some 60 metres, or about 200 feet—was more impressive than its breadth—less than half a mile across the floor ; and, as Camille Jullian [7] wrote after he had seen it, ' L'expression *valle intermissa, magis in altitudinem depressa quam late patente* . . . me paraît désigner la vallée entre Saint-Marc et Saint-Pierre, vue surtout du nord de cette dernière colline.' Caesar generally encamped on rising ground ; and since a deep valley intervened between his position and the hill occupied by the Bellovaci, it is

[1] *Ib.*, 20, 1.
[3] *B. G.*, viii, 18, 1 ; 20, 1.
[5] *Ib.*, viii, 5, 4.
[7] *Op. cit.*, p. 547, n. 2.

[2] *Hist. de la Gaule*, iii, 1909, p. 547, n. 8.
[4] Cf. *B. G.*, i, 51, 2.
[6] Cf. *Anc. Britain*, p. 629 and n. 7.

U

self-evident that he too occupied a hill. Ramparts on St. Pierre would not have been ' superfluous ', because Caesar wished both to impress the enemy with the belief that he was afraid of them and to render his position, when he could only spare a few men to hold it, impregnable.[1] Does Dr. Forbes fancy that the wall of Gergovia,[2] on the summit of a mountain, was superfluous ? The area of the plateau of St. Pierre was about 62 acres ; Caesar's camp at Gergovia, which was occupied by 6 legions, whereas in the Bellovacan campaign he had only 4, covered only 87 acres ; and a camp described by Hyginus, considerably less than 100 in extent, accommodated 40,000 men.[3] The ' steep eminences ' were one, not two miles apart ; the valley that separated their bases was, I repeat, less than half a mile wide ; and if Dr. Forbes will consult Meusel's *Lexicon Caesarianum*, he will not find the slightest difficulty in ' the expression *procurrentibus* '. The *vada transitusque paludis* may have been paths, like those that now cross the Ru de Berne. Scrutinize the *Carte* or Napoleon's plan (Planche 29), which is on a much larger scale and exactly agrees with it, and you will see that what Camille Jullian [4] calls ' le ravin nord entre le mont Collet et le mont Saint-Marc ' might be called a *mediocris vallis* as reasonably as the depression on the southern side of the mountain of Gergovia which Caesar [5] calls ' a considerable valley ' (*satis magna valles*) : you will also see, within range not of ' the centre of St. Marc's plateau ' (which is irrelevant), but of the probable position of the Belgic front, the place where Caesar would have posted his artillery. The assertion that the Aisne and the Oise were ' unfordable ' is pointless : for the retreating Bellovaci crossed a river, which must have been one or the other ; and unless the Oise was fordable or, like other Gallic rivers,[6] spanned by bridges, how did the Bellovaci intend to invade the country of the Suessiones ? The Bellovacan baggage-train got away by night,[7] and the fact that Caesar did not attempt to cut off the retreat of the combatants need present no difficulty when one reflects that, encamped on St. Marc, they would have been much nearer than he both to the Aisne and the Oise, that they could have interposed in strength either in the narrow passage between the forest and the Aisne or in that between the Aisne and St. Marc, and that, being obliged to leave part of his army to defend his camp, he may not have been strong enough to risk the attempt. No soldier would see anything improbable in Hirtius's statement that Caesar sent gallopers to let the commander of his cavalry know that he was coming to the rescue even if the scene of the combat was only 7,000—not 3,000 [8]—yards away ; and Dr. Forbes, for

[1] *B. G.*, viii, 10, 1.   [2] *Ib.*, vii, 47, 3. 7.
[3] *Caesar's Conquest of Gaul*[2], p. 664.   [4] *Op. cit.*, p. 550, n. 2.
[5] *B. G.*, vii, 47, 2.
[6] *Ib.*, i, 6, 3 ; ii, 5, 6 ; vii, 11, 6 ; 34, 3 ; 58, 5–6 ; viii, 27, 2. The Oise near Compiègne may be unfordable *now* ; but it has been canalized. Cf. *Caesar's Conquest of Gaul*[2], p. 675.   [7] *B. G.*, viii, 14, 1.
[8] Measured on the *Carte de l'État-Major*, the distance in a straight line to the meadow opposite Choisy-au-Bac, where Napoleon placed the combat, is nearly 9,000 yards ; to the spot midway between Choisy and Rethondes,

whose translation of *videbat*, ' discovered ' (which Hirtius would have expressed by *compererat* or *cognoverat*) I would substitute ' saw ', forgets that Caesar saw (*videret*[1]) that his camp was separated from that of the Bellovaci by a marsh, which must also have been ' hourly in evidence ', after he had been many days on the scene. The combat may not have taken place in a meadow by the confluence of the Aisne with the Oise, and the strong place may not have been Mont Ganelon ; but I adhere to the view that Mont St. Marc and Mont St. Pierre are the most probable sites of any that have been or, in default of archaeological evidence, can be named.

PAGE 226. In *Caesar's Conquest of Gaul*[2] I concluded that Uxellodunum must be identified with the Puy d'Issolu, for these reasons :—of the other sites the claims of which have been advocated Uzerche is inadmissible, for it is not in the country of the Cadurci, but in the Limousin, and, moreover, the isthmus which the Vézère there forms was not, as the text of the *Bellum Gallicum*[3] requires, 300 feet, but about 500 metres wide : Capdenac and Ussel in no respect correspond with the description given by Hirtius : Luzech, though its isthmus is not much more than 300 feet wide, is in all other respects out of the question. On the other hand, at the Puy d'Issolu traces of the works by which Caesar deprived the garrison of water are said to have been found, and in every respect but one the site corresponds with the original narrative ; the isthmus alone is wanting. I therefore argued that Hirtius had been misinformed about the isthmus ; but although reason appeared to point to my conclusion, I could never satisfy myself that it was unassailable. Camille Jullian, the distinguished author of the *Histoire de la Gaule*,[4] agreed with me in choosing the Puy d'Issolu. Within the last few years, however, several new papers in favour of Uzerche have appeared in France.[5] Referring to the latest,[6] of which I tried in vain to procure a copy, M. Jullian[7] says that the author, M. J. Lejeune, accuses J. B. Cessac, on whose circumstantial account of the way in which the spring on the western slope of the Puy d'Issolu is said to have been diverted I relied in *Caesar's Conquest of Gaul*, ' d'avoir trompé Napoléon III dans ses constatations et fouilles sur le terrain '! Before I read M. Jullian's note I had asked myself this

where General Creuly placed it, more than 6,500. Dr. Forbes may reasonably insist that, as I freely admitted in *Caesar's Conquest of Gaul*, both these sites are less than 8 Roman miles from Mont Ganelon ; but when he says that the meadow in question ' was 8 miles from the strong place ', he does not accurately report the statement of Hirtius (20, 1), according to whom the camp on the ' strong place ' ' was said to be not further than 8 miles, more or less, from the battle-field' (*quae non longius ab ea caede abesse plus minus VIII milibus dicebantur*). [1] *B. G.*, viii, 14, 4.
[2] pp. 483–93.   [3] viii, 41, 1.   [4] iii, 1909, p. 557, note.
[5] Only one has been accessible to me—*Le dernier oppidum gaulois assiégé par César*, 1917—in which the writer, Monsieur B. Marque, argues, unconvincingly as it seems to me, that the name of the fortress was not Uxellodunum, but *Usercodunum*.
[6] *L'erreur hist., Puy d'Issolu = Uxellodunum ; Uzerche = Uxellodunum* ; Tulle, Serre, 1920.
[7] *Rev. des études anc.*, xxiii, 1921, p. 56.

question : Which is more likely—that Hirtius should have been misled into the belief that Uxellodunum was in the country of the Cadurci, or that he should have repeatedly affirmed that at Uxellodunum there was an isthmus, the breadth of which he stated with precision, but which did not exist ? The isthmus at Uzerche is, indeed, five times as wide as that which Hirtius (if the MSS. are right) described : but *passuum* (' paces ' equivalent to 5 Roman feet) and *pedum* were liable to be confused by copyists,[1] and it is conceivable that what Hirtius wrote was *passuum CCC intervallo*, or that his informant carelessly wrote *pedum* instead of *passuum*. Nevertheless I adhere to my former opinion. I do not insist upon the fact that the earliest known name of Uzerche was Userca,[2] for, as Noviodunum (Haeduorum) was in Gallo-Roman times called Nivernum,[3] the name Userca might have succeeded Uxellodunum. But, except perhaps its doubtful isthmus, Uzerche does not correspond to the description of the mountain stronghold ; [4] the Puy d'Issolu does so in every respect, except that it has no isthmus ; and Hirtius, a bad topographer, if he was not present at the siege, may have so far misunderstood his informant that he represented the Tourmente and the Sourdoire, which, after flowing beneath the western and the eastern side of the hill, converge below its southern end, as one stream nearly encircling it. ' On vient ', M. Jullian writes to me, ' de retrouver au Puy d'Issolu la source dérivée par César. Pour moi, Uxellodunum = Issolu me paraît maintenant aussi certain qu'Alèsia = Alise. . . . Dès que j'y serai autorisé je publierai le résultat des fouilles d'Issolu.'

CICERO'S ' PALINODE ' AND QUESTIONS THEREWITH CONNECTED

The object of this article is to ascertain as nearly as possible the dates of the conference at Luca and of Cicero's speech on the consular provinces ; to identify the composition which he called his ' palinode ' ; and to fix the chronological order of certain letters which relate to these points.

Writing on April 8, 698 (56 B. C.), Cicero tells his brother that on the 5th there was a debate in the Senate on the Campanian land ; that on the 7th he visited Pompey, who intended to start on the 11th for Sardinia and to embark at Labro (Leghorn ?) or Pisa ; and that he himself is on the point of leaving Rome, but intends to return on the 6th of May.[5] Two years later he wrote to Lentulus Spinther that in the debate of April 5, 56 it had been resolved ' that the question of the Campanian land should be referred to . . . the Senate

---

[1] Cf. A. Klotz, *Cäsarstudien*, 1910, pp. 212–23.
[2] A. Holder, *Alt-celt. Sprachschatz*, iii. 50.
[3] *Caesar's Conquest of Gaul²*, p. 464.
[4] So I am assured by M. Jullian : I have not seen Uzerche.
[5] *Q. fr.*, ii, 5, 1. 3. 4.

on the 15th of May '. 'After this decree ', he continued, ' had
passed in accordance with my motion, Pompey, without showing
the least sign of being offended with me, started for Sardinia and
Africa, and on the way visited Caesar at Luca. Caesar complained
a great deal about my motion, for he had already seen Crassus at
Ravenna, and had been irritated by him against me. Every one
knew that Pompey was much annoyed about it—so I . . . learned
definitely from my brother. When Pompey met him in Sardinia
a few days after he left Luca, he said, " You are the very man I want
to see . . . you went bail for your brother Marcus ; unless you speak
strongly to him, you'll have to pay up " . . . He spoke of his own
services to me ; recalled what he had often said to my brother about
Caesar's measures [in his consulship] and the pledge which my
brother had given for my conduct ; called my brother to witness
that what he had done to secure my recall [from exile] he had done
with the consent of Caesar ; and asked him to commend to me
Caesar's policy and aims and persuade me not to attack, even if
I would not or could not support them. My brother reported these
remarks to me, but Pompey nevertheless sent Vibullius to me with
a message, not to commit myself on the Campanian question till
his return ; so I reconsidered my position and, so to speak, asked
permission of the State itself . . . to fulfil the duty which gratitude
to my benefactors and the pledge which my brother had given
demanded.' [1]

In 56 B.C., considerably later than April 8, Cicero wrote from
Antium to Atticus, ' What ! Do you really think that I would
rather have what I write read and approved [legi probarique] by any
one than by you ? Why, then, did I send it first to anyone else ?
Because I was pressed by the man to whom I sent it, and had no
copy. And—well ! I am nibbling at the pill, but I must after all
swallow it—my recantation [παλινῳδία] did seem to me rather
ignominious ! . . . The treachery of the leading Conservatives is
incredible . . . and yet I did intend to stick by them in politics . . .
At last I have hearkened to you, and my eyes have been opened.
You will say that your advice only extended to action, not to writing.
The truth is that I wanted to bind myself to this new coalition
[Pompey, Caesar, and Crassus] that I might have no excuse for
slipping back to those who, even now when I deserve their sympathy,
are still jealous of me. However, when I did write I kept within
bounds : I shall be more expansive if he shows that he is pleased
with it.' [2]

Soon afterwards Cicero wrote again from Antium to Atticus, ' In
my present retirement I am thinking how to express my rejection
of the old policy, and when we are together you will keep me up to
the mark.' [3]

On or soon after May 15 he wrote to his brother, who was returning
from Sardinia, ' The debate about the Campanian land, arranged for
the 15th and 16th, did not come off. In this matter I am in a fix.' [4]

[1] Fam., i, 9, 8-10. [2] Att., iv, 5. [3] Ib., 6, 2. [4] Q. fr., ii, 6, 2.

Writing in the same year from Rome to Lentulus Spinther, he says, ' I have been all but driven from my old political standpoint ; ' [1] and towards the end of the same letter he gives this important information, ' with very slight opposition they [the triumvirs] have achieved all their aims through the Senate : money to pay his troops has been granted to Caesar as well as ten lieutenant-generals ; [2] and *no difficulty has been made in deferring the appointment, required by the Sempronian law, of his successor.*' [3] The italicized words prove that this letter was written after Cicero's speech on the consular provinces.[4]

Turning to Caesar's *Third Commentary*, we learn that, after the conference of Luca, ' as soon as the season permitted, he hastened to join the army ' in Gaul (*cum primum per anni tempus potuit, ad exercitum contendit*).[5]

From the foregoing evidence it is clear that the conference at Luca was held between the 11th of April, when Pompey left Rome, and the 15th of May, the day fixed for the adjourned debate on the Campanian land. Evidently it occurred some considerable time before the latter date ; for ' a few days ' elapsed after the conference before Pompey reached Sardinia, and afterwards he had time to dispatch Vibullius to request Cicero not to commit himself on the Campanian question until he should himself return to Rome. Moreover, it is clear from Caesar's words that he left Luca for Transalpine Gaul before May, the first day of which was equivalent to April 5 of the Julian calendar.[6] What probably happened was this. Cicero's speech of the 5th of April was reported to Caesar at

---

[1] *Fam.*, i, 7, 7.
[2] Cf. *De prov. cons.*, 11, 28 and *Pro Balbo*, 27, 61. Camille Jullian (*Hist. de la Gaule*, iii, 1909, p. 282, nn. 1, 3) holds that the ten *legati* were not lieutenant-generals, but a senatorial commission appointed to settle the administration of the conquered territory of Gaul. Apart from other reasons, my view seems to me proved by Cicero's words in the passage which I have quoted from his speech *Pro Balbo*,—*C. Caesarem senatus et genere supplicationum amplissimo ornavit et numero dierum novo. Idem in angustiis aerarii victorem exercitum stipendio adfecit, imperatori decem legatos decrevit*, &c. Test the effect of translating the passage in the sense which M. Jullian attributes to it. Again in the passage which I cite from *De prov. cons.* Cicero says that some senators were opposed to granting the ten *legati*, while others asked for precedents (*actum est de decem legatis, quos alii omnino non dabant, alii exempla quaerebant*). If it had been a question of sending commissioners, precedents were easy to find. Besides, is it likely, is it conceivable that Caesar, in the full tide of success and anxious to complete his work of conquest, while he was still fighting against the Veneti, would have asked that commissioners should be prematurely sent to interfere with him (see Cic., *Fam.*, i, 7, 10) ? M. Jullian actually argues that the grant of pay for Caesar's troops which Cicero mentions implied that the war was over ! Then why did Cicero, while he spoke and voted in favour of the grant, do his utmost to secure the prolongation of Caesar's command ? M. Jullian does not seem to see that Cicero's speech on the consular provinces was directed against the machinations of Domitius and his coterie. Both Suetonius (*Div. Iul.*, 24, 3) and Dio (xxxix, 25, 1), who never mentions the conference at Luca, entirely misunderstood the sense in which Cicero used the word *legati*.
[3] *Fam.*, i, 7, 10.
[4] See *De prov. cons.*, 2, 3 ; 7, 17.
[5] *B. G.*, iii, 9, 2.
[6] See vol. i, pp. 339-44.

Ravenna on the 8th or a day or two later ; for it was possible to travel from Rome to Ravenna in three days,[1] and in ordinary circumstances the journey would have taken not more than five. The distance from Rome to Luca by the coastal road was 218 Roman, or 200 English miles,[2] which Pompey would have accomplished without hurrying in five days. Probably, then, he reached Luca about April 16, and the conference was held immediately afterwards.

The speech on the consular provinces, in which Cicero eulogized Caesar and shortly before which he had spoken in the Senate on his behalf,[3] was evidently delivered after Pompey met Quintus Cicero in Sardinia and after Vibullius had conveyed his message to Marcus. The date was certainly later than the 15th of May, the debate fixed for which day did not come off. Mommsen[4] puts it at the end of May. I shall give reasons later for believing that it was in June.

Now we come to the ' palinode '. Tyrrell in his first edition,[5] after disposing of an absurd guess which identified it with Cicero's poem *De temporibus suis*, decided that ' far the most likely hypothesis is that which sees the παλινῳδία in the *Or. de prov. cons.*'. This speech, he remarked, was written before the *pro Balbo*, for ' it is plainly alluded to in *or. pro Balbo*, § 61, and in a recantation, if anywhere, *c'est le premier pas qui coûte* '. It is true, moreover, that, as Tyrrell said, the greater part of the oration on the consular provinces ' could hardly be better described than by the word παλινῳδία ; it is an *amende honorable* to Caesar '. Nevertheless it was not the παλινῳδία for which Cicero apologized to Atticus.

To begin with, Tyrrell assigned the letter in which Cicero mentioned the παλινῳδία to the ' end of April ' or the ' beginning of May ' ; but, as I have shown, on May 15 he had not yet delivered his speech on the consular provinces. Secondly, Cicero says in explanation of his not having sent his recantation to Atticus, ' I was pressed by the man to whom I sent it, and had no copy '. Tyrrell originally believed that ' the man ' was Pompey. If Pompey heard the speech, it is improbable that he would immediately afterwards have pressed Cicero to send him the only copy which he possessed ; anyhow it is improbable that Cicero, if he had already committed his speech to paper, had only one copy of a work which he was going to publish. Did it not occur to Tyrrell that, if he had parted with his solitary copy, he would have been obliged before the publisher could set his copyists to work, to beg ' the man ' to send it back to him ? Thirdly, Cicero anticipates that Atticus will say that his advice only extended ' to action, not to writing '. Would Cicero have expressed himself in this way—would he have said, ' When I did *write*, I kept within bounds '—if he had made a *speech* of the first importance, of which the palinode was only a record ?

---

[1] App., *B. C.*, ii, 32, 127.   Cf. Caesar., *B. C.*, i, 3, 6.
[2] *Itin. Ant.*, ed. Wesseling, pp. 289–93.
[3] *De prov. cons.*, 11, 28.
[4] *Röm. Gesch.*, iii⁸, 1889, p. 323, n. ** (Eng. tr., v, 1908, p. 130, n. 1).
[5] *The Correspondence of Cicero*, ii, 1886, pp. 47–8.

If he had already made the speech, Atticus, who was in Rome, must have heard of it. Fourthly, after explaining that in the palinode he 'kept within bounds', he promises to 'be more expansive if *he* shows that he is pleased with it ' : but surely he glorified the achievements of Caesar copiously enough in the speech ; nor was he ever ' more expansive ' until, eleven years later, he pleaded for Marcellus. Finally, when he told Atticus that he was ' thinking how to express his rejection of the old policy ', Atticus knew that he had written the palinode ; but if the palinode was the speech on the consular provinces, he had definitively expressed his rejection.[1]

Opening Tyrrell's new edition [2] (for which Dr. Purser is jointly responsible), I find that he has considerably modified his opinion. He still, indeed, holds that, ' if it was not a letter, far the most likely hypothesis is that which sees the παλινῳδία in the *or. de prov. cons.*' ' But ', he continues, ' it is not . . . certain that the " palinode " may not have been, as Dr. Reid has pointed out, a direct communication to Caesar.' The next two sentences are substantially identical with my own third argument. Then, after remarking that ' the dates too are troublesome if we regard the " palinode " as an oration ', but that ' it is just possible, but most unlikely, that a preliminary sketch of the *oratio de provinciis consularibus* is meant ', Tyrrell decides for ' the view that sees in the " palinode " a direct communication to Caesar written at the end of April or early in May, when the messages of the triumvirs [read ' the message of Pompey '] sent through Quintus reached Marcus Cicero '.[3]

Now ' the dates ' are not merely ' troublesome ', but damning ; and it is more than ' most unlikely '—it is impossible—that the palinode was ' a preliminary sketch of the *oratio de provinciis consularibus* '. The last of the reasons which I have given for rejecting the view that it was the extant version of the speech tells equally against the suggestion that it may possibly have been a ' preliminary sketch ' :—if it had been, how could Cicero have afterwards told Atticus that he was ' thinking how to express his rejection

---

[1] Tyrrell evidently thought that the speech was delivered before the palinode, which in his view recorded it, was written. To my mind the words *legi probarique* would imply that if the palinode was the *oratio de provinciis consularibus,* the written version preceded the delivery of the speech. But in that case the reasons which I have given for not identifying the palinode with the speech would still hold good : if Cicero had written what he was about to speak, he had already expressed his rejection of the old policy, and had no need to think how he should do so.

[2] 1906, pp. 57–9.

[3] Cicero, it will be remembered, told Lentulus Spinther that Quintus had ' reported ' Pompey's message to him (*Haec cum ad me frater pertulisset*, &c. [*Fam.*, i, 9, 10]) ; and on May 15 Quintus had not yet returned to Italy from Sardinia. If *pertulisset* is to be understood in the sense which Tyrrell ascribes to it, the use of the word can only be justified by the maxim, *Qui facit per alium facit per se.* Cicero had doubtless received Pompey's message from Vibullius before May 15 ; but I am inclined to believe that Quintus delivered the message that had been entrusted to him orally, and therefore after that date.

of the old policy ' ?   Tyrrell tacitly recants an unsound reason
which he gave in his first edition for refusing to identify the palinode
with a letter to Caesar.   But a sound reason there is, which has
escaped both him and Professor Reid.   It is evident—and Tyrrell
admits—that the palinode was not written until Cicero had received
Pompey's message from Vibullius, or his message from Quintus, or
both.   But if ' the man ' by whom he ' was pressed ' to send it was
Caesar, Caesar must surely have pressed him through the medium
of Pompey ; for Caesar, as we have seen, left Luca for Transalpine
Gaul immediately after the conference, and a direct message from
him would therefore have reached Cicero several days before
Pompey's admonition came from Sardinia.   Would Cicero, when
he told Lentulus how Pompey had put pressure upon him, have
omitted to mention that Caesar had already done the same ?   Anyhow, before Caesar could receive the palinode, he must have reached
the country of the Veneti, north of the estuary of the Loire !   What,
then, are we to make of Cicero's words, ' I shall be more expansive
if *he* shows that he is pleased with it ' ?   Cicero fulfilled this promise
in the speech on the consular provinces ; and he could not have heard
that Caesar was pleased with the letter until long after he had made
that speech.   Furthermore, if he had sent the palinode to Caesar, it
is unlikely that Atticus would have heard of it as early as he did.

What, then, was the palinode ?   Since it was not the speech on
the consular provinces, nor a letter addressed to Caesar, it must
have been a letter which Cicero wrote to Pompey after he received
from Vibullius the message in which Pompey requested him not to
commit himself on the question of the Campanian land and from
Quintus the message in which Pompey commended to him the policy
of Caesar.   When Cicero wrote to Atticus again, and told him that he
was thinking how to express his rejection of the old policy, he was preparing, or was about to prepare, his speech on the consular provinces.

It only remains to deal with the chronological order of the relevant
letters.   *Fam.*, i, 7, which Tyrrell in his first edition misplaced, was
evidently later than *Q. fr.*, ii, 6, and, as I have shown, was written
after the speech on the consular provinces.   Although, however, in
his second edition Tyrrell was induced by Purser to correct his
mistake, he adhered with the consent of his colleague to the opinion
that *Att.*, iv, 5 and 6 were earlier thàn *Q. fr.*, ii, 6.   The following
table shows the various arrangements of the five letters of 56 B. C.
to which I have referred in this article and of others (enclosed in
brackets) which belonged to the same year :—

	TYRRELL (1st ed.)	TYRRELL (2nd ed.)	G. RAUSCHEN
Q. fr., ii, 5	1	1	1
[*Att.*, iv, 4 B]	2	3	5
Att., iv, 5	3	4	6
[*Fam.*, v, 12]	4	5	4
Att., iv, 6	5	6	7
[*Att.*, iv, 7]	6	2	2
[*Att.*, iv, 8 A]	7	7	8
Fam., i, 7	8	9	9
Q. fr., ii, 6	9	8	3

Rauschen [1] has shown that *Fam.*, v, 12, *Att.*, iv, 4 B, *Att.*, iv, 5, and *Att.*, iv, 6 were written in rapid succession from Antium ; and the Irish editors agree with him. The question is whether these letters were earlier or later than *Q. fr.*, ii, 6, which was written at Rome. Rauschen thinks that they were later. This view compels him to suppose that after Cicero returned to Rome from the tour which he began on April 8 he went to stay at Antium. I agree with Rauschen, for these reasons. First, Cicero, announcing his projected tour to Quintus on April 8, says, ' Tomorrow I intend to be at Laterium [near Arpinum], thence, after five days at Arpinum, to go to my Pompeian property, and on the way back to look in at my villa at Cumae, with the view . . . of being at Rome on the 6th of May and, I hope, of seeing you on that day ', &c. He certainly did go first to Laterium, as is proved by the letters—*Att.*, iv, 7 and *Fam.*, v, 12—which he wrote from Arpinum. He says nothing about Antium in his letter of April 8, and, as the map will show, if he went there ' on the way back ',[2] he must have struck off from the Appian Way at Tres Tabernae, and spent several days at Antium, —why ? Secondly, when I read in the letter which he wrote to Quintus from Rome, ' The debate about the Campanian land, arranged for the 15th and 16th [of May] did not come off. In this matter I am in a fix ', the conviction forces itself upon me that he had not yet written the palinode. When he wrote it, and when he wrote about it to Atticus, he was certainly not ' in a fix ' : he had made up his mind to abandon all opposition to Caesar and Pompey and to give them his support. It seems probable therefore that soon after he wrote this letter to Quintus he composed the palinode, retired to Antium, and there thought out the speech which he was about to deliver on the consular provinces. Thirdly, I find it difficult to conceive how he could have written to Atticus about the palinode as early as the end of April or even the beginning of May,—the alternative dates which Tyrrell and Purser assign to the letter. Antium was more than 50 Roman miles—a day's journey —from Rome, where Atticus was. When Cicero wrote to Atticus, the latter had already heard of the palinode, either from Pompey to whom it was addressed, or from some one to whom Pompey had mentioned it, or from some one at Antium, to whom Cicero may have spoken of it ; and Atticus had written to complain to Cicero of its not having been first shown to him. At that time Pompey was apparently either in Sardinia or travelling to Africa ; Cicero must have written the palinode several days before he mentioned it to Atticus : yet he certainly did not write it before he received the message which Pompey sent him by Vibullius, nor before Quintus delivered the message with which he had been charged. Vibullius could hardly have reached Cicero before the end of April ; Quintus did not return to Rome until after May 15. It seems probable therefore that the palinode was written soon after May 15, and that

---

[1] *Eph. Tull.*, 1886, pp. 42–5 (§§ 53–4).
[2] Evidently he did not go to Antium on the way to Pompeii.

the speech on the consular provinces was delivered after Cicero returned to Rome from his sojourn, which lasted several days, at Antium, and therefore, as he had made another speech in the Senate a few days before, most probably in June.

DIO, xxxix, 25–30

The political events at Rome in 56 B. C. which followed the conference at Luca and Cicero's speech on the consular provinces are not illustrated by contemporary evidence. Dio apparently knew nothing of the conference, for he never mentions it. He says that Pompey was annoyed by the admiration which the Roman populace felt for Caesar's exploits, especially because certain senators were sent to Gaul as if it were already subdued, and because a large sum of money was voted by the people to Caesar. He is here evidently referring to the senatorial proceedings which followed the conference, and which Cicero described in one of his letters [1]; but he misunderstood them. His 'certain senators' were the ten *legati* who were sent to Caesar; [2] and the money was voted, not by the people but by the Senate, for the payment of Caesar's troops. When Dio asserted that Pompey was jealous of Caesar he was doubtless thinking of the differences that existed between them before the conference,[3] and did not know that their alliance had been re-cemented at Luca before the end of April. He goes on to say that Pompey drew closer to Crassus, and that the two concluded that if they could obtain the consulship they would soon be able to get the better of Caesar, but that, as they expected to encounter opposition, they contrived through Gaius Cato to prevent the election from being held in the current year in the hope that an *interrex* would be appointed and they might be elected afterwards.

Now we know that there was an interregnum,[4] and that Pompey and Crassus were not elected until 55 B. C., some time before the 11th of February,[5] but, being ignorant that the consulships of Pompey and Crassus had been prearranged nine months before at Luca, Dio ascribed to them imaginary motives.

THE *LEX POMPEIA LICINIA*

For nearly half a century after 1857, when Mommsen published his celebrated treatise *Die Rechtsfrage zwischen Caesar und dem Senat*, it was an article of faith that the date legally fixed for the expiry of Caesar's Gallic command was the 1st of March (more correctly the 28th of February), 49 B. C. In 1904, however, Otto Hirschfeld gave reasons for believing that Caesar's tenure was not expressly secured beyond March 1, 50 [6]; and although Ludwig

---

[1] *Fam.*, i, 7, 10.   [2] See p. 294.   [3] See p. 72.
[4] Dio, xxxix, 31, 1.
[5] Cic., *Q. fr.*, ii, 7 (9), 2–3. Cf. Livy, *Epit.*, 105; Plut., *Cras.*, 15, 7; *Pomp.*, 52, 1–3.   [6] *Klio*, iv, 1904, pp. 76–87; 1905, pp. 236–40.

Holzapfel vigorously defended the orthodox view,[1] Hirschfeld remained for several years in possession of the field. In 1913 Walther Judeich [2] argued that the date was December 29, 50. A few years ago in the *Classical Quarterly* [3] I vindicated Mommsen's conclusion. Since then Dr. Hardy has written a dissertation,[4] in which he demolishes the arguments of Hirschfeld and Judeich. My own paper, which I here reproduce in an abbreviated and amended form, will serve the purpose which I have in mind.

Until last year (1920) all scholars agreed that a passage in Cicero's speech *De provinciis consularibus* [5] proves that the five years for

[1] *Klio*, 1905, pp. 107–16.   [2] *Rhein. Mus.*, lxviii, 1913, pp. 1–10.
[3] x, 1916, pp. 49–56.   [4] *Journ. of Philol.*, xxxiv, 1918, pp. 161–221.
[5] 15, 37.—*mihi nihil videtur minus a dignitate disciplinaque maiorum quam ut qui consul Kalendis Ian. habere provinciam debet, is ut eam desponsam, non decretam habere videatur. Fuerit toto in consulatu sine provincia, cui fverit antequam designatus est decreta provincia ? Sortietur an non ? Nam et non sortiri absurdum est, et quod sortitus sis non habere. Proficiscetur paludatus ? Quo ? Quo pervenire ante certam diem non licebit. Ianuario, Februario provinciam non habebit. Kalendjs ei denique Martiis nascetur repente provincia.*
Cicero, who argued that Caesar's career in Gaul should not be interrupted, was replying to a senator who proposed that on the expiration of Caesar's legal term one of his provinces should be assigned to one of the consuls who would be elected in 56, a few weeks after he was speaking. He observed that the tenure of a province by a consul regularly began on January 1, the first day of his consulship [although, as a rule, he did not begin to administer the province until after his consulship]. But since Caesar's tenure was guaranteed up to the end of February, the consul who under the senator's proposal was to succeed him would not be in possession of a province when he entered upon his consulship. Nay, Cicero implies (*Fuerit . . . decreta provincia*), he will be without a province throughout his consulship, for during all that time it will belong to Caesar ; the consuls of 55, who must constitutionally draw lots for the provinces assigned before their election, will not be able to decide by lot about Caesar's province, which will not be in their power ; and even after their consulship is over neither of them will be able to take over Caesar's province before March 1. Therefore the senator's proposal, being absurd, must be rejected. R. Laqueur, however (*Neue Jahrb. f. d. klass. Altertum*, xlv, 1920, p. 242), concludes that the speech 'related, not to the provinces which the consuls of the following year (55) were to administer as proconsuls in 54, but to the provinces which, as consuls, they would legally hold from the 1st of January 55 '. But then he has to explain (or to explain away) the words immediately following (*Fuerit . . . repente provincia*), on which the unanimous conclusion of scholars has hitherto been based. How, he asks (p. 244), would they explain why Cicero mentioned January, February, and March without adding that he meant the first three months, not of the next year, but of the next but one ? Because, I reply, the addition was superfluous ; his meaning has been transparently clear to every commentator except Laqueur. If Cicero, when he said that Caesar's hypothetical successor would take over the province on March 1, was referring to 55, why did he say just before that he would have no province throughout that year ? Readers would only be exasperated if I were to reproduce further the arguments by which Laqueur struggles to make good a hopeless case. How could Cicero with the faintest show of reason have complained that a consul who entered upon his consulship on the 1st of January, 55, was not to enter upon his proconsulship until the 1st of March in the same year ? If, as Laqueur insists (p. 247), though Caesar's provincial government dated—so Laqueur (p. 241) maintains—from the 1st of January, 59, the Vatinian law, under which he had received it, provided that ' no successor should obtain the province before March 1 of the fifth year ' (*vor d. 1. März d. fünften Jahres darf kein Nachfolger d. Provinz erhalten*), the province was granted, not for five

which Caesar was originally appointed terminated on February 28, 54 B. C.; and a footnote may suffice to show that the solitary dissentient has wasted his time. The extension of Caesar's command, provided for at the conference of Luca, and confirmed by Pompey and Crassus in the following year (55), was to last, according to Cicero,[1] Velleius,[2] Plutarch,[3] Appian,[4] and Suetonius,[5] for another five years; but Dio[6] affirmed that it had been limited to three. In another passage,[7] however, he attributes to Antony the statement that Caesar was forced to return to Italy before the lawful time, and so far confirms the tradition which assigned a legal duration of ten years to Caesar s proconsulship. If, then, the date fixed by Mommsen is to be rejected, the reasons must be strong. Before we examine them it may be well to recall certain facts related to the question.

As Hirschfeld[8] observed, a letter which Caelius wrote to Cicero in 51 B. C. proves that the *lex Pompeia Licinia* contained a clause providing that the question of appointing a successor to Caesar should not be discussed before March 1, 50 :—(illa praeterea Cn. Pompeii sunt animadversa . . . ut) *diceret se ante Kalend. Mart. non posse sine iniuria de provinciis Caesaris statuere*).[9] Now under the Sempronian law of 123 the Senate was obliged to decide before the consular elections what provinces should be administered by the consuls after their term of office had expired.[10] It follows that Caesar's successor would be one of the consuls elected in July, 50; and in the ordinary course he could not arrive in Gaul until after the close of his consulship. Therefore, whether Caesar's command was to terminate legally on February 28, 49, or not, he might

years, but for four years and two months ! Laqueur (p. 247) tries to remove this absurdity by pointing to another passage (7. 17) in *De prov. cons.* Cicero desired that the consuls who were to hold office in 55 should succeed Gabinius and Piso respectively as governors of Syria and Macedonia. Remarking that he might move that Syria and Macedonia should be made praetorian, not consular, provinces, in order that Gabinius and Piso might be recalled by the beginning of 55, he said that such a motion would be useless because it would be vetoed by a tribune, and therefore that they could only be superseded by the Sempronian law which empowered the Senate without being subject to the veto, to name two consular provinces. Thus he made it clear that their successors would not be able to enter their provinces before the beginning of 54, and Laqueur infers that Gaul could not in practice be made a consular province before the same time. Did it not occur to him that, on his theory, Gaul might. if Caesar's enemies had had their way, have been made consular in 57 for March 1, 55, and is it credible that Caesar would have allowed the law which gave him his province to be drafted so clumsily as to shorten a nominal period of five years by ten months ? When Laqueur insists that Caesar's Gallic command dated from January 1, he forgets that the province which he held from that day was the insignificant one which the Senate had assigned to him (Suet., *Div. Iul.*, 19, 2) under the Sempronian law, and with which he had nothing more to do when the Gallic provinces were assigned to him—obviously from March 1—*by a special law.*

[1] *Att.*, vii, 7, 6 ; 9, 4 ; *Phil.*, ii, 10, 24.   [2] ii, 46, 2.
[3] *Cras.*, 15, 7 ; *Pomp.*, 52, 4 ; *Caes.*, 21, 3.   [4] *B. C.*, ii, 17, 63 ; 18, 65.
[5] *Div. Iul.*, 24, 1.   [6] xxxix, 33, 3 ; xliv, 43, 2.
[7] xliv, 43, 1.   Cf. xl, 44. 1, 59. 1. 3.
[8] *Klio*, 1904, p. 83.   [9] *Fam.*, viii, 8, 9.   [10] See vol i, p 26.

expect to retain his province and his army until the arrival of his successor in January, 48. The Sempronian law, however, was abrogated by Pompey in 52, and a law which he then passed enacted that no consul should be appointed to a provincial governorship until five years or more after the end of his consulship.[1] On March 1, 50, several consuls would be available for provincial commands ; and, even if Caesar's was secured until February 28, 49, the Senate would be entitled to make his province consular for that year and to supersede him on the 1st of March. A *plébiscite*, passed in 52, had indeed authorized him to stand for the consulship without presenting himself in Rome [2] ; and as he could not legally be elected consul before July, 49, this *plébiscite* virtually permitted him to retain his command until that date [3], if not until January 1, 48, when his year of office would begin : but the authorization was rendered useless by Pompey's law and infringed by another [4] which Pompey carried in the same year, to the effect that candidates for any magistracy must tender their names in person,[5] although, yielding to pressure, he declared informally that the law did not apply to Caesar.[6]

Hirschfeld tries to prove that no date was fixed for the termination of Caesar's command [7] : before March 1, 50, he could not be recalled, but how long afterwards he should remain in Gaul was left uncertain. Only on this hypothesis, he says, can we explain the apparent inconsistency between the demand that Caesar should be recalled after March 1 and the claim which he urged to retain his province until his second consulship. The evidence for the ' demand ' is a passage in one of Caelius's letters, written in October, 51,— ' it was quite evident that Pompey desired a decree to be passed for Caesar's quitting his province after the 1st of March ' (*plane perspecta Cn. Pompeii voluntate in eam partem ut eum decedere post Kalendas Martias placeret*[8]). Despite the testimony of Cicero, Velleius, Plutarch, Appian, and Suetonius, Hirschfeld insists that Caelius meant the 1st of March, 50. But, as we shall presently see, Hirschfeld's hypothesis is stultified by an unequivocal passage in Cicero [9] ; and it has been demolished by Judeich.[10]

In order to confute Mommsen, Hirschfeld takes his stand upon a well-known passage in Cicero's correspondence. In May, 50, Caelius wrote : ' So far Pompey seems to have thrown his weight on the side of the Senate's wish that Caesar should leave his province on the 13th of November. Curio is resolved to go all lengths rather than allow this. . . . Pompey, professing not to be attacking Caesar,

[1] See p. 237   [2] Cic., *Att.*, viii, 3, 3.
[3] Dr. Hardy (*op. cit.*, pp. 190, l. 37–191, ll. 1–3), apparently misled by or misunderstanding an assistant, has unwittingly misrepresented my meaning : he himself (p. 191, ll. 17–20) confirms what I say.
[4] Or perhaps by a clause of the law about provincial governorships. Dio, however, distinguishes the two.
[5] Dio, xl, 56, 1.
[6] *Ib.* ; *Att.*, viii, 3, 3 ; Suet., 28, 2.   [7] *Klio*, 1904, p. 84.
[8] *Fam.*, viii, 8, 4.   [9] *Att.*, vii, 7, 6.   [10] *Rhein. Mus.*, 1913, pp. 4–5.

but to be making a settlement which he considers fair to him, says that Curio is seeking pretexts for a quarrel. However, he is strongly against and evidently afraid of Caesar's becoming consul-designate before handing over his army and province ' (*adhuc incubuisse cum senatu Pompeius videtur ut Caesar Id. Novembr. decedat. Curio omnia potius subire constituit quam id pati. . . . Pompeius, tamquam Caesarem non impugnet, sed quod illi aequum putet constituat, ait Curionem quaerere discordias. Valde autem non vult et plane timet Caesarem consulem designari prius quam exercitum et provinciam tradiderit*[1]). If, Hirschfeld argues,[2] the *lex Pompeia Licinia* had provided that Caesar's term of office should not expire before February 28, 49, Pompey could not have claimed that the desire expressed in the Senate to recall him on November 13, 50, was reasonable. But when Caelius wrote *Id. Novembr.* did he mean the year 50 ? He had no need to specify the year which he had in mind, because Cicero of course knew in what year Caesar's command was to expire. Caesar could not become consul before January, 48 ; and to insist on his vacating his province more than thirteen months before that time could not be called a concession. If, on the other hand, Caelius was thinking of 49, Pompey might plausibly claim that he was making a reasonable compromise. As Tyrrell and Purser[3] say, ' A great deal was granted to Caesar—permission to stand for the consulship in his absence, and only a bare six weeks of private life, and that as consul-designate before he entered on the consulship '. Hirschfeld contends that if Pompey was allowing Caesar to stand for the consulship in his absence, Caelius could not consistently say that he was ' afraid of Caesar's becoming consul-designate before handing over his army ' ; but, as Dr. Hardy says,[4] ' It was only in the vain hope of shaking off the iron grip of Curio's *intercessio* [veto] that he had agreed to the suggested extension, and his . . . fear of Caesar's election remained. The word *autem* marks a strong contrast between his professed protest against Curio and his real feeling.' But, apart from this consideration, a significant passage of Hirtius proves, although Hirschfeld endeavours to turn it to his own advantage, that Caesar's government did not legally expire before the end of 50, and therefore that Caelius must have meant 49. Hirtius, describing the siege of Uxellodunum, says that the Gauls, as Caesar was aware, knew that the summer of 50 B. C. would be the last in which he would be free to deal with them (*cum omnibus Gallis notum esse sciret reliquam esse unam aestatem suae provinciae, quam si sustinere potuissent, nullum ultra periculum vererentur*).[5] Hirschfeld, however, insists that the passage has hitherto been misunderstood. He tells us that C. Bardt (a well-known Ciceronian scholar) pointed out to him that *unam aestatem* must mean, not the summer of 50, but the summer of 51 B. C.,—the year in which the siege occurred. How,

[1] *Fam.*, viii, 11, 3.   [2] *Klio*, 1904, p. 82. Cf. *ib.*, 1905, p. 239.
[3] *The Correspondence of Cicero*, iii[2], 1914, p. lxxxi.
[4] *Op. cit.*, pp. 211–2.   [5] *B. G.*, viii, 39, 3.

he asks, could Caesar's personal intervention in the siege have been explained by Hirtius on the ground that his only remaining summer in command was that of 50 B. C.? If he could have looked forward to another entire summer, in which he would be free to dispose of his army, why should he have been so anxious to capture Uxellodunum at once?[1] But Hirschfeld's interpretation does violence to the meaning of a plain Latin sentence. It is certain that when Caesar started for Uxellodunum the summer of 51 was already far advanced; for immediately after the capture of the fort, when he went to Aquitania, only the fag-end of the summer remained.[2] Now consider the earliest chronological indication which Caesar gives in regard to his first invasion of Britain,—' only a small part of the summer remained' (*exigua parte aestatis reliqua*).[3] And only a small part of the summer of 51 remained when Caesar started for Uxellodunum. Therefore, if Hirschfeld is right, *reliquam esse unam aestatem* is equivalent to *reliquam esse exiguam partem aestatis* ! If Hirtius had meant this, would he not have said it ? If he had written *reliquos esse duos annos*, Hirschfeld will admit that he would have meant ' two whole years '. Why, then, should *unam aestatem* be distorted into meaning ' a small part of one summer ' ? I ask Hirschfeld to look through Meusel's *Lexicon Caesarianum*, ii. 1615 ff. He will not find there one solitary instance in which *reliquus*, coupled with a noun, denotes a part only of the thing signified by that noun. Nothing, then, can be more certain than that, if Hirtius had intended to convey the meaning which Hirschfeld attributes to him, he would have written, not (reliquam esse) *unam aestatem*, but *exiguam partem aestatis*.

The reason which Hirschfeld gives for accepting Bardt's misinterpretation can be easily disposed of. Caesar hastened in person to crush the resistance of Uxellodunum because he knew that if the garrison succeeded in defying his lieutenants, the malcontents throughout Gaul would be encouraged to prolong the guerrilla war into the summer of 50 B. C. ; and he resolved that that final summer should be free from all disturbance. He had been obliged to spend eight years in coercing the Gauls : he intended to spend the last in conciliating them.[4]

---

[1] *Klio*, 1904, p. 83.

[2] *In eam partem* (sc. *Aquitaniam*] *est profectus, ut ibi extremum tempus consumeret aestivorum* (*B. G*, viii, 46, 1). Holzapfel (*Klio*, 1905, pp. 113–4) has anticipated me in calling attention to this passage.

[3] *B. G.*, iv, 20, 1. See also iv, 4, 7 (*reliquam partem hiemis*) ; v, 31, 4 (*reliqua pars noctis*) ; vii, 10, 1 (*reliquam partem hiemis*) ; vii, 25, 1 (*reliqua parte noctis*) ; *B. C.*, iii, 28, 6 (*reliquam noctis partem*), &c.

[4] What I have written in the text disposes of the attempt which Hirschfeld made (*Klio*, 1905, p. 237) to answer Holzapfel (see n. 2 above). Hirschfeld, however, insists that even if by *unam aestatem* Hirtius meant the summer of 50, ' this can only be used as an argument to prove that Hirtius had in view the actual facts of the case, namely, that Caesar, considering the resolutions passed by the Senate in Rome, might only remain on in Gaul for the summer of 50 '. Hirschfeld seems to have forgotten that the Gauls could not in the summer of 51 have foretold senatorial resolutions the earliest of which were passed on the 29th of September of that year. The only way of evading the conclusion

Let us see whether Judeich has succeeded better than Hirschfeld. It is, he insists, certain that Caesar's command was to terminate at the end of 50 [1] : that is proved unmistakably by Cicero's words, written (between December 18 and 21 [2]) to Atticus,—' What then ? Ought we to allow a man who still retains his army after his legal term has expired to stand for the consulship ? . . . Do I approve of *the ten-year term of military authority*, carried too in the way that it was ? ' (*Quid ergo ? exercitum retinentis, cum legis dies transierit, rationem haberi placet? . . . a n n o r u m e n i m d e c e m i m p e r i u m et ita latum ⟨placet⟩?*[·3] ; and by a passage in another letter, written on December 26 or 27 [4],—' *You have held a province for ten years*. . . . That period—not one of law but of your own self-willed choice, but still let us say of law—has elapsed, and a vote is passed for your successor' (*t e n u i s t i p r o v i n c i a m p e r d e c e m a n n o s . . . praeteriit tempus non legis, sed libidinis tuae : fac tamen legis : ut succedatur de-cernitur*[5]). Judeich admits of course that the period for which Caesar was originally appointed did not end until February 28, 54, and that the extension was to last for another five years ; but he regards the difference between ten years and nine years and ten months as negligible ! His point is that, since Cicero said in December, 50, first, that Caesar's term of office was a ' ten-year term ', and, secondly, that he had already held office for ten years, the term legally expired at the end of that year. Judeich is very matter-of-fact, and his literalness recoils against himself. For if he insists upon pinning Cicero down to the statement that Caesar had already ' held a pro-vince for ten years ', he must perforce admit that, since Cicero wrote on the 26th or the 27th of December, Caesar's term expired not, as he maintains, on December 29, 50, but on or before Decem-ber 27 ; and since he understands *tenuisti* literally, why does he not take *decernitur* in the same sense, and argue that on the 26th or the 27th of December the Senate was actually appointing Caesar's successor ? To any one who has a spark of imagination Cicero's meaning is unmistakable. As Tyrrell and Purser put it, ' The Senate would not make their decree appointing a successor till the beginning of January, 705 (49). So when Cicero writes *praeteriit* and *decernitur* he is anticipating, and referring to what will take place in a few days, not to the actual present.' [6] The Irish editors

which I have drawn from the statement of Hirtius would be to adopt a theory which Albert Watson notices (*Cicero, Select Letters* [3], 1881, p. 287),—that Caesar's second term of five years was to run ' from the day of the enactment of the consular law [*lex Pompeia Licinia*]. . . supposed to have been November 13'. Now on November 15 Cicero, writing from Tusculum, says (*Att.*, iv, 13, 2) that Crassus has already left Rome for Syria ; and it is evident from the narra-tive of Dio (xxxix, 33–9) that the law had been passed long before.

[1] *Rhein. Mus.*, 1913, pp. 1–2.
[2] O. E. Schmidt, *D. Briefwechsel d. M. T. Cicero*, 1893, p. 101.
[3] *Att.*, vii, 7, 6.　　[4] Schmidt, *op. cit.*, p. 102.　　[5] *Att.*, vii, 9, 4.
[6] *Op. cit.*, p. 323. ' I cannot agree with Dr. Rice Holmes ', says Dr. Hardy (*Journ. of Philol.*, xxxiv, 218, n. 1), ' that *decernitur* is equivalent to *decretum est* '. I have nowhere said or implied anything so absurd. Dr. Hardy must have been misled by some one who devilled for him.

might have added that ' the [legally] fixed day ' (*certa dies*)[1] by which the Senate would then require Caesar to resign was March 1. The absurdity of supposing that the *lex Pompeia Licinia* was so loosely drafted as to make it possible to confound five years with four years and ten months or ten years with nine years and ten months is self-evident.

However, Judeich has other strings to his bow. By the Trebonian law, passed in 55 B. C., the province of Syria was assigned to Crassus and the provinces of Spain to Pompey, for five years. Judeich asserts that ' There is not the slightest ground to suppose that in this case there was any departure from the rule which prescribed the 1st of January of the year following the consulate as the beginning of the proconsular year ',[2] and accordingly he affirms that Pompey and Crassus were to hold their provinces from January 1, 54, till December 29, 50. Caesar's command, he argues, could not have outlasted that of Pompey.[3] Now there is the strongest possible ground for supposing that the proconsulship of Crassus began before 54, for he left Rome in his official dress (*paludatus*) for Syria before November 15, 55 [4]; he and Pompey were of course possessed of their provincial commands from the time when they were assigned to them by the Trebonian law. Pompey's actual tenure, however, was secure until the end of 50.[5] If it was not legally secured as long as Caesar's, the explanation may be that at the time of the conference of Luca Caesar was the predominant partner in the triumvirate.[6] But Pompey secured himself still more effectively by providing in 52 that his command should be prolonged for five years—in other words, till the end of 45.[7]

Judeich, like Hirschfeld, maintains that when Caelius said that the Senate wished Caesar to leave his province on the 13th of November, he meant of 50 B. C.; but here he is confronted by Hirschfeld's argument :—if (as Judeich argues) Caesar's term did not legally expire till December 29, 50, how could Pompey claim that the Senate's proposal was reasonable ? Judeich struggles

---

[1] See Caes., *B. C.*,·i, 2, 6. Cf. Plut., *Caes.*, 30, 3, and Hardy, *op. cit.*, p. 186. Prof. E. T. Merrill (*Class. Philol.*, vii, 1912, pp. 247–9) observes that ' all the commentators appear tacitly to assume that *ante certam diem* is Caesar's own expression, while the resolution itself embodied a specific date. . . . Not one . . . betrays any surprise that Caesar substituted the vague phrase *certam diem* for the definite date which they believe to have stood in the resolution '. Merrill fails to see that *ante certam diem* was not a vague, but a precise and well-understood phrase (cf. Cic., *De prov. cons.*, 15, 37) ; that it denoted the known date, March 1, before which Caesar, under the *lex Pompeia Licinia* and after Pompey's law of 52 B. C., was bound, if required, to resign ; and that Cicero (*l.c.*) had used the same phrase to denote the same day (March 1), which in 54 would terminate Caesar's original quinquennial period.

In *Class. Quart.*, 1916, p. 55, n. 1 I wrongly inferred from Caesar's complaint (*B. C.*, i, 9, 2) that his enemies, by disregarding the tribunician law which had authorized him to stand for the consulship in his absence, deprived him of six months' tenure of his command, that the *certa dies* was July 1.

[2] *Rhein. Mus.*, 1913, p. 3.   [3] *Ib.* p. 7.
[4] Cic., *Att.*, iv, 13, 2.   [5] Cf. Cic., *De prov. cons.*, 7, 17 ; 15, 37.
[6] Hardy, *op. cit.*, pp. 193–4.   [7] See p. 237.

desperately to wriggle out of this *impasse*. ' The question ', he replies, ' is here only of surmises on the part of Caelius, which relate to the fact that in the Senate the proposal was mooted that Caesar should hand over his province on November 13 : Pompey in his indecisive way took up no definite attitude on the matter and only let it be seen privately that the proposal was acceptable to him.' Besides, ' Caelius's description of Pompey's vacillation enables us to see clearly that even Pompey, when he concurred with the proposal of the Senate, had an uneasy conscience '.[1] Judeich sees what he wishes to see ; but that the settlement, sanctioned by the Senate, which Pompey considered ' fair ', was not only unfair but also illegal, is simply inconceivable.[2]

Such are my grounds for thinking that Hirschfeld and Judeich have failed to upset Mommsen's conclusion. Unless Cicero, when he said ' ten years ', meant nine years and ten months, or rather nine years nine months and twenty-seven days, Caesar's command was assured by the *lex Pompeia Licinia* until February 28, 49 B. C.[3]

---

[1] *Rhein. Mus.*, 1913, pp. 6–7.   [2] Cf. Hardy, *op. cit.*, p. 212.

[3] Since I finished this article Laqueur has published a second paper (*Neue Jahrb.*, 1921), in which, starting from his unique conclusion, that the first five years of Caesar's command were terminable on March 1, 55, not 54, he deals with the events of 51–50. He shares (pp. 234–5) the delusions of his compatriots about the meaning of *Fam.*, viii, 8, 4 and 11, 3, of *Att.*, vii, 7, 6 and vii, 9, 4. The kernel of his paper (pp. 238 n. 1, 243–4, 246) is that the *plébiscite* which authorized Caesar to stand for the consulship in absence applied to the year 704 (50 B. C.) ; that Caesar saw that if he stood then, his candidature, owing to the presence of Pompey's army, would fail ; and that he therefore [truly] insisted (*B. C.*, i, 32, 2) that he could not legally become consul until after the lapse of ten years from his former consulship, and that the *plébiscite* meant this. Dio (xl, 51, 2), he says, adopts Caesar's view ; Suetonius that of the Senate.

Laqueur's notion that Caesar, in accordance with the *plébiscite*, originally intended to stand in 50 B. C. is based upon a remark of Caelius in October, 51 (*Fam.*, viii, 8, 9) and upon a remark of Cicero in December, 50 (*Att.*, vii, 7, 6). ' I fancy ', wrote Caelius, ' that Caesar intends to adopt one of two alternatives —either to remain [in Gaul] and not stand *in the year in question*, or, ' &c. (*Itaque iam, ut video, alteram utram ad condicionem descendere vult Caesar, ut aut maneat neque hoc anno sua ratio habeatur*, &c.). Laqueur insists that *hoc anno* means ' in this [electoral] year ', that is in 50 : Dr. Hardy (p. 189), replying to Hirschfeld, who said the same, maintains that there could not be ' the smallest ambiguity as to the identity of *hoc anno* '—in other words, that Cicero, to whom Caelius wrote, must have seen that *hoc anno* could only mean the first year, 49, in which Caesar could legally stand. I would add that even if it meant 50, if Caelius did not make a slip, it would be folly to base an argument upon an idle guess that Caesar intended to break Sulla's law. Self-evidently, moreover, the *plébiscite* must have indicated the year to which it applied, and have left Caesar no room for quibbling. As to *Att.*, vii, 7, 6 (part of which I have already quoted)—*Quid ergo ? exercitum retinentis, cum legis dies transierit, rationem haberi placet ? Mihi vero ne absentis quidem. Sed, cum id datum est, illud una datum est*—which Laqueur (p. 246) takes to mean that the *plébiscite* authorized Caesar's candidature in absence only during the *de facto* period of his command, supposed by Laqueur to have ended on December 29, 50, I must repeat what I have already shown ; Cicero did not mean that on the day when he wrote (between December 18 and 21, 50) Caesar's legal term had expired. What he meant by the words *Sed cum . . . una datum*

[I may discuss here certain questions which arise in connexion with the subject of the foregoing article.

1. When did Marcus Marcellus bring forward his premature motion, mentioned by Hirtius,[1] Suetonius,[2] Appian,[3] and Dio,[4] and alluded to by Cicero,[5] for terminating Caesar's command on March 1, 49 ? Certainly not before the last week of May, 51, for Caelius then reported that Marcellus had not yet brought before the Senate the question of appointing Caesar's successor.[6] If the motion was that, relating to the Gallic provinces, of which Caelius recorded the repeated postponement,[7] it was not made before the 1st of September ; and if it had been made between the 1st and the 29th, when the famous senatorial resolution was passed by which discussion of the question of the consular provinces was fixed for the 1st of March, 50,[8] one might suppose that Caelius would have said so. I was therefore originally inclined to think that Marcellus introduced his motion on the 29th, but withdrew it when Pompey said that the question could not without injustice be discussed before the 1st of March.[9] But on the 2nd of September Caelius told Cicero that Pompey had moved that no decree about appointing a successor to Caesar ought yet to be passed.[10] After this Marcellus would hardly have persisted. I can only conjecture that he made his proposal on the 1st,[11] and that it was frustrated on the same day by Pompey's opposition.[12]

est was, as Tyrrell and Purser explain (cf. Hardy, p. 191), that the *plébiscite* involved ' the further concession of allowing ' Caesar ' to be a candidate without laying down his command ' on March 1, 49. There is no contradiction between Suetonius and Dio. Suetonius, as Dr. Hardy shows (pp. 163–4), believed that Caesar's ' command was to last till the end of 49 ', for he speaks (25, 1) of the nine years (58–50) during which Caesar exercised it in Gaul (*gessit autem novem annis, quibus in imperio fuit, haec fere*), ' so that he must have regarded 49 as the tenth '. Dr. Hardy's argument, to which I have not space to do justice, should be studied.

Let me conclude by noticing an imbroglio in which Laqueur has landed himself. Quoting Caesar's remark (*B. C.*, i, 9, 2) that he had been deprived of six months of the period during which he might have expected to hold his command, and assuming, as his theory forces him to do, that ' the fixed day ' (*certa dies*) before which the Senate decreed that Caesar must resign (*B. C.*, i, 2, 6) was January 1, 705 (50 B.C.), he concludes that the six months were the first six of the year. He forgets that the senatorial decree was passed on January 2, and therefore that on his theory Caesar was required to resign on the day before that on which the decree was passed ! The *certa dies*, as I have shown, was March 1 ; the six months were the last six of the year. Laqueur (p. 242, note) actually infers from Caesar's remark (*B. C.*, i, 9, 3) that he had endured the loss of the six months with equanimity, that when he made the remark they had begun ! Can he not see that the loss was involved in the fact that Caesar had been ordered to leave his province before ' the fixed day ' ? As Dr. Hardy observes (p. 186), the fact that towards the end of January, 705, Caesar was called upon to return from Italy to his province (*B. C.*, i, 11, 1) proves that ' his term had not yet expired '.

[1] *B. G.*, viii, 53, 1.   [2] *Div. Iul.*, 28, 2.   [3] *B. C.*, ii, 26, 99.
[4] xl, 59, 1.   [5] *Att.*, viii, 3, 3. Cf. Livy, *Epit.*, 107.
[6] Cic., *Fam.*, viii, 1, 2.   [7] *Ib.*, 2, 2 ; 4, 4 ; 5, 3 ; 9, 2 ; 8, 4.
[8] *Fam.*, viii, 8, 5.   [9] *Ib.*, § 9.   [10] *Ib.*, 9, 5.   [11] *Ib.*, § 2.
[12] Dr. Hardy (*op. cit.*, pp. 179, 204) apparently thinks that Marcellus made and withdrew his proposal in June or earlier. According to Suetonius, he stated as a reason for his motion that the Gallic war was over : could he have said

2. Was the question of the consular provinces raised in the Senate on March 1, 50, in accordance with the resolution that had been passed on September 29 in the previous year ? Dr. Hardy [1] assumes that on the appointed day a decree was passed ' declaring the Gallic provinces . . . consular from March 1, 49 ' ; and Drumann,[2] though he admits that direct evidence is wanting, infers from the letter [3] in which Cicero tells Atticus that he has copies of the Gazette (*acta diurna*) up to March 15, and gathers therefrom that ' thanks to the persistence of . . . Curio, they will debate everything rather than the provinces ' (*Curionis nostri constantia omnia potius actum iri quam de provinciis*), that the decree was passed and vetoed on March 1. It seems to me on the contrary that if this had happened Cicero would have said so, and that we should rather infer that, owing to the obstruction of Curio, the question was postponed. Moreover, Paullus, who had been bought by Caesar,[4] may, as the senior consul,[5] have presided in March,[6] and may have found some way of delaying the discussion. Appian [7] appears to refer the motion of Gaius Marcellus for recalling Caesar to the time (April or May) when Pompey was unwell ; but, as Dr. Hardy remarks,[8] if his account is accurate, Curio could not have exercised his veto, for Appian says that Curio supported the motion of Marcellus, but at the same time moved that Pompey should resign as well. Appian's chronology is here, as often, open to suspicion, for he relates that the populace presented Curio with bouquets, an incident which, if we may trust Plutarch,[9] happened near the end of the year. On the whole it seems to me probable, for reasons which I shall give in the next paragraph, that that motion was made in April.

3. Did the attempt that was made in May, 50, to censure Curio for having exercised his veto relate, as Dr. Hardy says,[10] to a veto by which he had blocked the motion of Gaius Marcellus or to one by which he had frustrated the proposal that Caesar should resign on November 13, 49 ? Dr. Hardy [11] thinks that this proposal was dropped in consequence of ' Curio's threatened opposition '. Nothing, so far as I can see, in the letter [12] that records the attempted

this in or before the last week of May, when it was rumoured in Rome (Cic., *Fam.*, viii, 1, 4) that Caesar had suffered a disaster ? Suetonius, indeed, implies that Marcellus made his motion early in the year, before he attempted to disfranchise the colonists whom Caesar had settled at Novum Comum (see p. 238) ; but this is disproved by what Caelius wrote in May, unless Caelius meant that Marcellus then contemplated a motion such as that which was carried on September 29. There is no evidence that Cicero's remark on May 10 (*Att.*, v, 2, 3) as to ' how Caesar took the news that a senatorial resolution [which had been vetoed] had been put on record ' referred to Marcellus's premature motion—if it did, why did not Pompey oppose the motion then ?— and not to his motion for disfranchising the colonists. If Hirtius was right in saying that the former was rejected by the Senate, Cicero evidently did not refer to it. The chronology of Suetonius is often loose.

[1] *Op. cit.*, p. 185. [2] *Gesch. Roms*, iii², 1906, p. 347, n. 6.
[3] *Att.*, vi, 2, 6. [4] Suet., 29 ; App., ii, 26, 101. Cf. *Att.*, vi, 3, 4.
[5] Cic., *Fam.*, viii, 4, 4. [6] See p. 325, n. 9.
[7] ii, 27–8, §§ 103–7. [8] *Op. cit.*, p. 217, n. 1. [9] *Pomp.*, 58, 4.
[10] *Op. cit.*, p. 213. [11] *Ib.*, p. 209. [12] *Fam.*, viii, 11, 3.

compromise supports this view. Immediately after saying that Curio ' is resolved to go all lengths rather than allow ' the proposal to take effect (*Curio omnia potius subire constituit quam id pati*), Caelius observes that the Pompeians ' dare not push matters to extremes ' (*Nostri porro . . . ad extremum certamen rem deducere non audent*), a remark which he qualifies later by saying that ' if they push Curio too hard, Caesar will defend him in exercising the veto ; if they shrink—and it looks like it—Caesar will stay where he is as long as he chooses ' (*si omnibus rebus prement Curionem, Caesar defendet intercessorem : si—quod videntur—reformidarint, Caesar quoad volet manebit*). No doubt these words are consistent with the supposition that Curio had only threatened to use his veto ; but they may also imply that he had actually done so, and that it was still doubtful whether his action would be marked by a vote of censure. What makes me believe that the proposal was not dropped is that Caelius immediately after the words which I have just quoted adds, ' The vote given by each [senator] is in the memorandum of city events ' (*Quam quisque sententiam dixerit in commentario est rerum urbanarum*). Surely these votes related to the proposal. Still, even if Curio did then use his veto, it does not follow that the attempt to censure him related to that occasion. Caelius, after telling Cicero that Curio ' had a brilliant finale to his veto about the provinces ' says that ' The Senate has come round to this,—that Caesar is to be allowed to stand for the consulship without giving up army or provinces '.[1] Evidently this means that as the proposal that Caesar should leave his province on November 13 had been defeated, and as the motion for passing a vote of censure on Curio had been rejected, the Senate had decided—for the moment—to acquiesce in Caesar's demands. Now the proposal would never have been made if Gaius Marcellus had not already moved that Caesar should resign on the 1st of March, 49, and if that motion had not been blocked. It seems to me therefore practically certain that, as Dr. Hardy says, the proposed vote of censure related to the veto by which Curio and other Caesarian tribunes had blocked the motion of Marcellus.]

CAESAR'S TREATISE *DE ANALOGIA*

What is known about the *De analogia*, fragments only of which survive, amounts to this :—it was written when Caesar was crossing the Alps to rejoin his army in Gaul[2] ; it was dedicated to Cicero,[3] whom Caesar complimented as the great master of oratory[4] and

---

[1] *Fam.*, viii, 13, 2.   [2] Suet., *Div. Iul.*, 56.   [3] Cic., *Brut.*, 72. 253.
[4] Prof. Hendrickson (*Class. Philol.*, 1906, pp. 118–19) thinks that the famous eulogy of Cicero in Pliny's *Nat. Hist.*, vii, 30 (3), 117—*Salve primus omnium parens patriae appellate, primus in toga triumphum linguaeque lauream merite, et facundiae Latiarumque litterarum parens atque, ut dictator Caesar hostis quondam tuus de te scripsit, omnium triumphorum laurea maior*—was taken from the *De analogia*.

who quotes from it; numerous extracts, made by later writers [1] show that it dealt largely with the true forms of words; and we learn from Gellius and Macrobius that Caesar was conservative in matters of style, deprecating the use of new-fangled words.

Professor Hendrickson [2] conjectures that the idea of writing the book was suggested by certain passages in Cicero's *De oratore*, which was finished in November, 699 [3] (55 B. C.) and probably published early in the following year. H. Köchly and W. Rüstow [4] argue that the book was finished in the winter of 53–52; for Caesar spent the winter of 54–53 and of 52–51 in Gaul. But if we accept the statement of Suetonius, the only part of the winter of 53–52 in which Caesar could have written the treatise was that in which he was returning from Cisalpine Gaul to oppose Vercingetorix; and in the anxiety which he must then have felt, to say nothing of the impression which the recent murder of Clodius and the disturbances that followed it left upon his mind, is it likely that he would have been in the mood to compose a grammatical treatise? By far the most probable supposition seems to me to be that the journey to which Suetonius referred was that which Caesar made in the spring of 54, just after Quintus Cicero had joined his staff and when his relations with Marcus were most cordial.[5]

[Since I wrote the foregoing paragraph Max Radin [6] has argued that the only winter in which Caesar had leisure to compose the treatise was that of 57–56: for in 56–55 he was preparing to repel the invasion of the Usipetes and Tencteri; in 55–54 he was making arrangements for the second invasion of Britain; in 54–53 he knew that 'grave troubles were brewing'; and in 53–52 he was distracted by the news of the disturbances that followed the murder of Clodius. Any one who has read the *Commentaries* carefully will see that the first two statements are misleading; the third may be ruled out because in the winter of 54–53 Caesar did not cross the Alps at all. But what puzzles me is that while Radin denies that Caesar could have written *De analogia* in the winter of 53–52, he argues that he wrote four of the *Commentaries* then! [7]]

GABINIUS'S SETTLEMENT OF THE GOVERNMENT OF JUDAEA

What Josephus [8] meant when he said that Gabinius divided Judaea into five σύνοδοι has occasioned controversy. E. Schürer [9] regarded them as districts formed for judicial and fiscal purposes, thereby implying that Gabinius made Judaea a Roman province,

---

[1] B. Kübler gives the quotations in his ed. of *Bell. Hisp.*, 1897, pp. 140–5.
[2] *Op. cit.*, pp. 97–8, 103.   [3] Cic., *Att.*, iv, 13, 2.
[4] *Einleitung zu C. J. Cäsars Comm.*, &c., 1857, p. 91, n. 59.
[5] E. Meyer (*Caesars Monarchie²*, 1919, p. 202, n. 1), who argues that the book must have been written in the spring of 53, because otherwise it would have been mentioned in Cicero's correspondence of 54, forgets that in 53 Caesar did not cross the Alps into Gaul.
[6] *Class. Philol.*, xiii, 1918, p. 296.   [7] See p. 279, note.
[8] *Bell. Iud.*, i, 8, 5.   [9] *Gesch. d. jüd. Volks*, &c., i, 1890, p. 275.

for which there is no evidence and which, moreover, as G. F. Unger argued,[1] is disproved by the statement of Josephus that Gabinius committed the government to an aristocracy. What he really did, says Unger, was merely to substitute aristocracy for monarchy without disturbing the arrangement of Pompey, by which the country had been placed under the superintendence of the Governor of Syria.[2] Schürer,[3] admitting that the words of Josephus— ἐν ἀριστοκρατίᾳ διῆγον, ἐπὶ προστασίᾳ τῶν ἀρίστων, ἀριστοκρατίᾳ διῳκοῦντο [4]—tell in Unger's favour, denies that σύνοδοι can bear the meaning which Unger puts upon it. Since σύνοδος primarily means an assembly or a meeting, and the words which Schürer quotes are unmistakable, his denial is nugatory.

THE PARTHIAN CAMPAIGNS OF CRASSUS

The date of the meeting between Crassus and the envoys of Orodes. —Dio [5] clearly implies that the envoys of Orodes met Crassus during his first campaign, that is in 54 B. C. Plutarch [6] refers the event to the spring of the following year, when Crassus was leaving his winter-quarters. Florus [7] says that the meeting took place at Nicephorium, which is in Mesopotamia, on the northern bank of the Euphrates ; and since Plutarch's statement, viewed in the light thrown upon it by Florus, is inconsistent with his description of the campaign of 53, we must conclude that he mistook the date. As Kurt Regling remarks,[8] if Crassus had marched southward in 53 from the latitude of Zeugma to Nicephorium, and had met the envoys there, he would not have turned northward to encounter the Parthians between Ichnae and the fort of Carrhae ; moreover, the road that leads from Nicephorium to the battle-field runs through the valley of the Belik, and accordingly Holzapfel, who assigned the meeting to that year, was obliged to regard Plutarch's description of the march through the desert as romance.[9] Dio, who says that Orodes sent the envoys ἐς τὴν Συρίαν, may appear at first sight to give the lie to Florus ; but, as Regling observes, Orodes could not tell where his envoys would meet Crassus, and Dio's words may well mean ' *towards* Syria '.

The battle-field.—Just before the battle, Crassus, coming from the eastern bank of the Euphrates, reached the river Bilechas [10] (Belik). During the battle his son Publius charged a Parthian division, which, by a feigned retreat, lured him away from the rest of the Roman army and then overwhelmed his troops. He himself was urged by friends to escape to Ichnae, which was not far off.[11] Three hundred Roman horsemen, fleeing from the battle-field,

[1] *Sitzungsber. d. phil.-philol. u. d. hist. Cl. d. K. b. Akad. d. Wiss. zu München*, 1897, pp. 194-5.   [2] See vol. i, p. 218.
[3] *Gesch.*, &c., i[3], 1901, p. 340, n. 8.   [4] *Ant.*, xiv, 5, 4.   [5] xl, 16, 1.
[6] *Cras.*, 18, 1-2.   [7] i, 46, 4.   [8] *Klio*, vii, 1907, p. 366, n. 10.
[9] *Berl. philol. Woch.*, 1901, col. 851-2.   [10] Plut., *Cras.*, 23, 5.
[11] *Ib.*, 25, 2-13 ; Dio, xl, 21, 3.

reached Carrhae about midnight.[1] Evidently, then, the battle-field was between Carrhae and Ichnae, the shortest distance between which is 47 miles. Regling[2] locates it near a hill,[3] Tell Wazz Gol, 20 miles south of Carrhae.

The formation of the Roman army in the battle.—Plutarch[4] says that when patrols reported the approach of the enemy, the legions were following the cavalry; that, in deference to the advice of Cassius, Crassus extended 'the phalanx of legionaries as far as possible over the plain to avoid being surrounded, and distributed the cavalry on the wings'; but that he presently changed his mind, forming a square, each side of which comprised 12 cohorts (ἀμφίστομον ἐποίησε καὶ βαθὺ πλινθίον ἐν δώδεκα σπείραις προερχομένης τῶν πλευρῶν ἑκάστης), and assigning a troop of cavalry to each cohort; that he placed Cassius in command of one wing and his son Publius of the other, while he took up his own position in the centre; and that in this formation (the baggage presumably being inside the square) he advanced to the Belik. Plutarch here accounts for 48 cohorts only, though he says that Crassus marched from Zeugma, where he crossed the Euphrates, with 7 legions[5] (70 cohorts) : a square cannot be properly said to have any wings; only three divisional commanders are mentioned, not, as one would have expected, four; and when we read that Publius Crassus charged a Parthian division which was threatening to attack him in the rear (κατὰ νώτου[6]), we ask ourselves how such an attack could have been made against one 'wing' of a closed square. According to Groebe,[7] the square was not a square, but a parallelogram : 25 cohorts marched in front, 25 in the rear; the flanks were each composed of 10. Plutarch, says Groebe, included the 'corner-cohorts' (*Eckkohorten*), and so counted 12 cohorts instead of 10. This seems to me a gratuitous distortion of Plutarch's statement; and, moreover, it leaves out of account the 7,000 infantry, whom Crassus had left to garrison the Mesopotamian towns which he occupied in his first campaign.[8] May we not conclude that the 7 legions were incomplete (Caesar often used the term *legiones* in an elastic sense); that the 8 cohorts with which Publius charged were not included in the 48 which formed, or were ordered to form, the square; that the 7 legions therefore comprised 56 cohorts; and that the 14 which had been detached were identical with the 7,000 infantry which garrisoned the captured towns?[9] So far I am disposed to agree with Mr. Francis Smith, who has written an interesting study of the campaign.[10] Let us see how he corrects Plutarch's description. Anticipating the objections which

---

[1] Plut., *Cras.*, 27, 7.   [2] *Klio*, 1907, p. 382, n. 8.
[3] Cf. Plut., *Cras.*, 25, 11.   [4] *Cras.*, 23, 2–5.
[5] E. Meyer (*Caesars Monarchie²*, 1919, p. 171, note) conjectures that Crassus had left one legion to hold Syria, for the number assigned to a proconsul was almost invariably even.   [6] Plut., *Cras.*, 25, 1.
[7] W. Drumann's *Gesch. Roms*, iv², 1908, p. 115, n. 4.
[8] Plut., *Cras.*, 17, 4.
[9] Florus (i, 46, 2) says that Crassus had 11 legions, Appian (*B. C.*, ii, 18, 66) that he had 100,000 men. Both statements are incredible.
[10] *Hist. Zeitschr.*, cxv, 1915, pp. 241–2.

I have made, he adds that if the square had been complete, the charge which Publius made in obedience to his father would have destroyed the whole formation, and that as Publius with all his force perished, the 8 cohorts that formed part of it were evidently not included in the square.[1] Again, after the army reached the Belik, the direction of the march changed : the troops did not cross the river, but moved southward.[2] A square, as Smith remarks,[3] would have merely diverged to the right, and thus the right flank would have become the front : obviously then, if Publius commanded a ' wing ' of the alleged square before, he could not have done so after the direction changed. Smith concludes that at the moment of the first encounter the square was not yet formed, and that the army was divided into three groups.

Smith then proceeds to expound his own conception of the movements. When Crassus learned that the enemy was approaching, he threw out ' wing columns ' (Flügelkolonnen) right and left, which he placed respectively under Publius and Cassius. Two-thirds of the cavalry, which formed the advanced guard—in all 2,600 men [4]— were ranged alongside the wings : the rest reconnoitred in front. Behind came the baggage and the rearguard. Possibly the manœuvre, which required a considerable time, was incomplete when Crassus changed his mind and resolved to form a square, of which the centre, marching in front of the baggage, the two wings, and the rearguard were to form the sides. Meanwhile the army neared the Belik and had to diverge to the right. The right wing [under Publius], extending southward, remained where it was to guard against attack ; the other troops advanced in order to change front and to form on the left of Publius. Before this evolution was completed Crassus ordered the right wing to advance, thereby giving the Parthians a chance of surrounding the exposed division.[5]

The theory seems plausible, and it is supported to some extent by Dio,[6] according to whom the charge of Publius was the first incident of the battle : but Plutarch refers the charge to a much later period ; and Smith, who says that the right wing was to form one side of the square, and yet denies that the eight cohorts which charged under Crassus were included in the square, does not explain why they were excluded, or what purpose they were originally meant to serve. It seems to me, then, that we must be content with the knowledge that at some period of the battle Publius charged, and

---

[1] Hist. Zeitschr., cxv, 1915, p. 249.
[2] Plut., Cras., 23, 6. Cf. Klio, 1907, pp. 381–2.   [3] Op. cit., pp. 250–1.
[4] When Plutarch (20, 1) says that Crassus had nearly 4,000 cavalry after he crossed the Euphrates, he apparently includes the thousand whom he had left the year before in the surrendered towns ; for Crassus needed every trooper whom he could get. The argument by which Regling (Klio, 1907, p. 373) tries to prove that he had raised 1,900 in Syria does not convince me (we do not know how many Crassus had brought from Italy) ; but the point is unimportant.   [5] Op. cit., p. 252.
[6] xl, 21, 2. Dio (23, 1) also says that in the course of the battle Abgarus of Osrhoene attacked the exposed Roman rear, which implies that the square was not then complete.

that the Parthians won because their mounted archers could keep on shooting without coming to close quarters and because the Roman cavalry were inadequate. Accuracy in tactical details is not to be expected from Plutarch or from Dio.

The date of the battle.—The date of the battle of Carrhae is fixed by Ovid [1] in lines that relate to the festival of Vesta, which was celebrated on the 9th of June [2] :—' Crassus near the Euphrates lost his eagles, his son, his troops ; last of all he was himself put to death ' (*Crassus ad Euphraten aquilas natumque suosque | Perdidit, et leto est ultimus ipse datus*). Yes, says Groebe, but Crassus was killed at least three days after the battle, in which his son fell : then did Ovid refer to the earlier event or to the later ? ' Von Gutschmid,' he remarks, ' so far as I know, is the first and only writer who took June 9, 701 [53 B. C.] to be the day of the battle of Carrhae.' [3] Von Gutschmid was a sensible man ; and one marvels that the other eminent scholars, of whom Groebe conscientiously gives a list, did not see that the memorable date was the date of the disaster, and that the death of Crassus, which resulted therefrom, was quite a secondary matter. Having propounded his question, Groebe endeavours to demonstrate that the battle was fought on June 9,[4] and therefore that (if we may trust Plutarch [5]) Crassus was killed on June 12. I am not satisfied with his arguments [6] ; but I forbear to inflict upon my readers, who will not require their support, a paragraph in which I have examined them.

THE THIRD CONSULSHIP OF POMPEY

The date of the 'ultimate decree'.—Professor A. C. Clark [7] observes that the ' ultimate decree ' ' is antedated by Dio,[8] who assigns it to the evening of Jan. 19 [that is to the day following the murder of Clodius]. This ', he says, ' is inconsistent with ' the narrative of Asconius. G. Plaumann,[9] on the contrary, insists that Asconius supports the chronology of Dio. It is certain that the decree was not passed until successive *interreges* had failed to hold the elections [10] ; and Clark is therefore right.

The date of the trial of Milo.—I have stated (pages 169–70) that the trial of Milo began on the 4th of April and ended on the 7th. The former date is attested by Asconius,[11] who, however, also says,[12] if the manuscripts are right, that Cicero's speech was delivered on the 8th (*a. d. VI Id. April.*), the last day of the trial, which would

---

[1] *Fasti*, vi, 465–6.   [2] *C. I. L.*, i², p. 319.
[3] *Hermes*, xlii, 1907, p. 315, n. 2.
[4] *Ib.*, pp. 315–20. Cf. Drumann's *Gesch. Roms*, iv², 114, n. 7.
[5] *Cras.*, 28. 1, 29, 1. 3, 29. 6, 31. 9.
[6] They are astronomical, based upon Plut., *Cras.*, 29, 4, and Dio, xl, 25, 3.
[7] Cic., *Pro Milone*, 1895, p. xxiv, n. 2.
[8] xl, 49, 5.   [9] *Klio*, xiii, 1913, p. 348, n. 1
[10] Ascon. ed. Clark, p. 33, l. 25—34, ll. 1–6 (ed. Stangl, p. 32).
[11] Ed. Clark, p. 39, ll. 7–8 (ed. Stangl, p. 35).
[12] Ed. Clark, p. 30, ll. 1–2 (ed. Stangl, p. 30).

thus have continued for five days. But it appears from Asconius's minute description [1] that it lasted only four. Some critics have tried to remove the inconsistency by assuming that although, as Asconius says, Milo appeared before the court on April 4, that day was spent in preliminaries, and the trial did not begin until the 5th. Professor Clark, remarking that while in the former of the two passages in which Asconius mentions the date of Cicero's speech the manuscripts have *a. d. VI Id. April.*, in the latter [2] they have *a. d. II* or *a. d. III*. Thus in at least one passage there is plainly a corruption, and the professor reads *a. d. VII* in both.[3] He confesses, however, that a difficulty remains. Cicero's speech was delivered, as he himself tells us,[4] on the *centesima lux et, ut opinor, altera* since the death of Clodius, and the professor says that, ' according to the natural meaning of the words,' Cicero meant the 102nd day. If so, the speech was delivered on April 8, for Clodius was killed on the 18th of January.[5] ' It is of course possible ', says the professor, ' that Cicero is calculating roughly, and perhaps not impossible that *centesima et altera* may mean 101st.' [6] Now Cicero was certainly not calculating roughly, as the words *ut opinor* show ; and it is not merely not impossible, but certain, that *centesima et altera* means 101st : for as *altera* in relation to *prima* means 2nd, so *centesima et altera* means the ordinal number immediately following 100th, that is 101st.[7] I therefore have no doubt that the speech was delivered on April 7.

Caelius and the Law of the Ten Tribunes.—According to Tyrrell and Purser,[8] who follow Ludwig Lange,[9] Caelius originally intended to veto the Law of the Ten Tribunes, ' for . . . he saw . . . that it was . . . fraught with the greatest danger to the Senatorial party ', but Pompey

---

[1] Ed. Clark, pp. 39–41. It was formerly supposed that Asconius's statement (p. 39, ll. 18–19) that *quarta die adesse omnes iuberentur . . . dein rursus postera die sortitio iudicum fieret* implied that the trial was to last five days, and was therefore inconsistent with his account of the proceedings ; but, as Prof. Clark says in his edition of Cicero's speech (p. 128), ' It is now generally accepted that the supposed discrepancy rests upon a mistranslation. When he [Asconius] says *quarta die . . . iuberentur*, he means that ' they were ordered to be present on the fourth day ', not ' on the fourth day they were ordered to be present ', i. e. next day. Is it not astonishing that the mistranslation was ever made ?

[2] Ed. Clark, p. 40, l. 25.

[3] Cic., *Pro Milone*, 1895, p. 128.

[4] *Pro Mil.*, 35, 98.

[5] Jan. 18–29 . . . . . . =12 days.
    Feb. . . . . . . =28 ,,
    Intercalary month . . . . =23 ,,
    March . . . . . . =31 ,,
    April 1–8 . . . . . = 8 ,,
    _____
    102 ,,

[6] ' I should, however, prefer ', the professor adds, ' to say that our knowledge of the Roman system of intercalation is not sufficiently certain ', &c. But it is quite certain that the intercalary month was either 22 or 23, never 24 days.

[7] See *B. C.*, iii, 54, 2 and my note on the meaning of *altero die* in *Caesar's Conquest of Gaul²*, 1911, pp. 738–40.

[8] *The Correspondence of Cicero*, iii², 1914, p. lxiv.

[9] *Röm. Alt.*, iii, 1871, p. 360.

'commissioned Cicero to dissuade Caelius,' &c. I doubt whether the letter (*Att.*, vii, 1, 4) to which the two editors refer proves their point. What Cicero there said was, ' I helped to secure him [Caesar] this privilege, for I was asked by Caesar himself at Ravenna to induce Caelius, as a tribune, to support the bill. By Caesar ? Aye, and by our friend Gnaeus also ' (*Nam ut illi hoc liceret adiuvi, rogatus ab ipso Ravennae de Caelio tribuno pl. Ab ipso autem ? Etiam a Gnaeo nostro*).[1] This may only mean that both Caesar and Pompey urged Cicero to use his influence with Caelius, whose support would be valuable ; it does not prove that Caelius had manifested any intention to oppose the bill, though Caesar may have feared that he might.

THE FLOGGING OF A CITIZEN OF NOVUM COMUM

We learn from Strabo [2] that Pompey's father established a colony at Comum, and from Asconius [3] that he gave the Transpadane colonies (of which Comum was one) Latin rights : Strabo adds that Caesar settled at Comum 5,000 additional colonists, 500 of whom were non-resident Greeks of distinction, upon whom he conferred citizenship (τούτοις δὲ καὶ πολιτείαν ἔδωκε). Appian,[4] remarking that Caesar established a colony at Novum Comum and bestowed upon it Latin rights, which implied that any one who had held a magistracy in the town became a Roman citizen, says that Marcellus flogged one of the ex-magistrates—' a punishment never inflicted upon Romans '—and explained that the punishment meant that he was not a Roman citizen. Plutarch,[5] after observing that Marcellus and Lentulus [6] disfranchised the colonists whom Caesar had settled in the town, states that the man whom Marcellus flogged was one of the local senators (which is not inconsistent with his having formerly been a magistrate) and goes on to make the same remark as Appian about the significance of the punishment. Suetonius,[7] who does not mention the flogging, says that Marcellus moved that the colonists whom Caesar had settled in Comum under the Vatinian Law should be disfranchised, because the citizenship had been granted to them irregularly (*ultra praescriptum*). ' Marcellus ', wrote Cicero,[8] ' behaved outrageously in the case of the citizen of Comum. Even if the man did not hold a magistracy (*etsi ille magistratum non gesserit*), still he was a Transpadane. So Mar-

---

[1] Tyrrell and Purser in their note on the passage which I have quoted say, ' viz. when asked by Caesar to induce Caelius to propose a bill allowing him to stand in his absence ', &c. The word ' propose ' is not authorized by the evidence.

[2] v, 1, 6. [3] Ed. Clark, p. 3, ll. 8–12 (ed. Stangl, p. 12).
[4] *B. C.*, ii, 26, 98. [5] *Caes.*, 29, 1.
[6] Plutarch was wrong in speaking of [C. Claudius] Marcellus and Lentulus, the consuls of 49 B. C. The Marcellus in question was M. Claudius Marcellus, one of the consuls of 51.
[7] *Div. Iul.*, 28, 3. [8] *Att.*, v, 11, 2.

cellus seems to me to have given no less cause of offence to our friend
[Pompey] than to Caesar.' Most of the commentators, however,
read *gesserat* (an emendation), according to which Cicero meant
' even though he had not held a magistracy '.

The reader will have noticed that Appian implicitly contradicts
Plutarch and Suetonius, if not also Strabo. Moreover, his testimony
is inconsistent with that of Cicero, if Cicero wrote *gesserat*; and he
ascribes to Marcellus a senseless outrage, for if Caesar had only established a new Latin colony at Novum Comum, he had not violated
the law, and Marcellus (unless he was misled by reports which
Appian does not mention) had no conceivable motive for his action.
Besides, as Dr. Hardy observes,[1] the evidence of Appian ' is fatally
vitiated by his ignorance of the fact that Comum had been a Latin
colony long before the time of Caesar. He clearly regards Caesar's
colonization as equivalent to the conferment of Latin rights upon
the town '. The only point which his evidence seems to Dr. Hardy
to establish ' is that the person scourged claimed by virtue of some
act of Caesar to be a Roman citizen '. I rather doubt whether
Cicero would have written *gesserat* unless his correspondent had
urged that the injured man was not an ex-magistrate and had
pleaded that as an excuse for the flogging. Supposing that Caesar
had established a Roman colony at Novum Comum and that Marcellus by disfranchising the colonists had reduced the town to the
status of a Latin colony, it seems to me not unreasonable to suppose
that the man may have been an ex-magistrate and therefore a Roman
citizen. Professor Reid,[2] however, and Dr. Hardy,[3] who differ on
other points, agree in denying that he could have been
a Roman : ' if ', says the latter, ' the man had been a magistrate
in a Latin colony, neither Marcellus nor any one else would have
dared openly . . . to violate the lex Porcia.' Is this quite certain ?
Marcellus in his hatred of Caesar may not have stopped to inquire
into the man's position ; and Cicero, if he wrote *gesserit*, implied
that he might have violated the Porcian law. Did not Piso in 63 B. C.
illegally *execute* a Transpadane ?[4] Professor Reid[5] asserts that
Cicero's words are ' unintelligible unless Novum Comum was a Latin
colony. The reference to the magistracy would be meaningless ;
also the words *erat tamen Transpadanus* ;[6] for the *Transpadani* in
general were notoriously Latin.' Commenting on this, Dr. Hardy[7]
insists that ' the passage is unintelligible on the supposition that
Novum Comum was established as a Latin colony by Caesar. For in
that case there would have been no motive for the outrageous action
of Marcellus.' Dr. Hardy himself holds,[8] following Suetonius (who,

---

[1] *Journ. of Philol.*, xxxiii, 1914, p. 113.
[2] *Journ. Rom. Studies*, i, 1911, p. 74.
[3] *Op. cit.*   [4] Sall., *Cat.*, 49, 2.   [5] *Op. cit.*, p. 74.
[6] Mr. Caspari (*Class. Quart.*, v, 1911, p. 117) offers an original explanation.
' " Transpadanus " ', he says, meaning that the law, passed by the elder
Drusus, which exempted Latins from the punishment of flogging, was still
in force, ' is synonymous with " Latinus " '. See vol. i, pp. 350–1.
[7] *Op. cit.*, p. 123   [8] *Ib.*, pp. 120–2.

however, does not say that the motion of Marcellus for disfranchisement was carried), that Novum Comum was, at the time of the outrage, again a Latin colony ; but, against Professor Reid, his argument is unanswerable.

Professor Reid, however, appeals [1] to Strabo, arguing that he draws ' a distinction between the 500 distinguished Greeks . . . and the remainder of the colonists ', while he contends that Suetonius's words *ultra praescriptum* distinctly imply that ' Caesar had been commissioned to create so many citizens and no more, and that he had exceeded the fixed number '.[2] Perhaps he had, though the words of Suetonius are not sufficiently precise to prove it ; [3] but does Professor Reid believe that Caesar, who, as every one knows, encouraged the Transpadanes to hope for the franchise, would, if he had been empowered to create 500 Roman citizens and no more, have selected Greeks to the exclusion of Transpadanes ? Dr. Hardy [4] denies that Strabo's words imply any difference of status between the Greeks and the other colonists, ' or that he even directly states them to have been Roman citizens at all ; ' for if he had meant this, he would have written, not (ἔδωκε) πολιτείαν but τὴν πολιτείαν.

One crux still confronts us. In the original draft of this article I wrote, ' It is difficult, notwithstanding the statements of Strabo, Suetonius, and Plutarch, to believe that Caesar would have drawn an invidious distinction by granting the citizenship to Novum Comum alone while the other Transpadane communities were without it ; ' and long afterwards I found that Professor Reid [5] had said much the same. But the difficulty is not insuperable : the other communities would have known that Caesar's power was limited, and might well have regarded the enfranchisement of Novum Comum as an earnest of favours to come. In fine it seems to me probable, if not morally certain, that Caesar had been empowered

---

[1] *Op. cit.*, p. 70.

[2] ' It would be quite unnatural ', says Prof. Reid, ' to interpret Suetonius as meaning that Caesar had added to the number of colonists, all Roman, whom he had been enjoined by the law to place at Novum Comum ; or that all these colonists were to lose their Roman franchise because Caesar had exceeded his rights in creating Roman burgesses '. I reply that it would be unnatural to interpret the words of Suetonius—*rettulit etiam* [Marcellus] *ut colonis quos rogatione Vatinia Novum Comum* [Caesar] *deduxerit civitas adimeretur, quod per ambitionem et ultra praescriptum data esset*—as meaning that the citizenship was to be taken away from those colonists to whom Caesar had arbitrarily given it, while many other colonists had only received Latin rights. If Suetonius meant what he said, he meant that all the colonists whom Caesar had settled at Novum Comum were to be deprived of the citizenship, because he had in some way exceeded his authority in granting it. Dr. Hardy, who thinks it probable that Marcellus acted on the principle that ' many of the laws . . . passed in 59 B. C. [the year of Caesar's first consulship] were strictly null and void, as having been carried by force, or against the auspices, or in defiance of the *intercessio* ' (tribunician veto), holds that the reasons given by Suetonius for his action in proposing to annul the grant of citizenship were invented by Caesar's enemies.

[3] Is it not conceivable, for instance, that Caesar may have been authorized to enfranchise those colonists only who had served in his army ?

[4] *Op. cit.*, pp. 115–17.　　　　　　　　　　　　　　[5] *Op. cit.*, pp. 76–7.

by the Vatinian law to found a colony of Roman citizens,[1] and that Marcellus, either because he regarded the Vatinian law and other laws of Caesar's consulship as null and void [2] or because Caesar had in some way exceeded his authority, proposed to disfranchise the colonists,[3] one of whom he subsequently flogged.[4]

[1] If a colony was ever founded in which some colonists were to be Roman citizens while the rest had only Latin rights, I never heard of it. Professor Reid, however (op. cit., pp. 72-3), remarking that 'It may be asked, Was it possible to create a new colony in which the colonists had not all the same legal status', concludes that 'there seems to be no difficulty in the supposition that Caesar created a mixed community at Novum Comum'. Dr. Hardy. on the other hand, says (op. cit., p. 117), 'the fact that permission to create Roman citizens was contained in what is admitted to have been a colonial law is . . . a conclusive proof that the citizenship was the result of incorporation in a colony, and that the colony must therefore have been a Roman colony'.

[2] See p. 319, n. 2.   [3] See p. 238.

[4] Mommsen (Hist. of Rome, v, 1908, p. 131 [Röm. Gesch., iii⁸, 1889, p. 324]. with which cp. Hermes, xvi, 1881, p. 30, n. 1) remarks that ' the Transpadanes. who, according to the existing constitution, possessed only Latin rights, were practically treated by Caesar . . . as Roman citizens', and he supports his opinion in the following note :—' This is not stated by our authorities. But the view that Caesar levied no troops at all from the Latin communities, that is, from by far the greater part of his province, is in itself absolutely incredible, and is directly refuted by the fact that the opposition slightingly designates the force levied by Caesar as " for the most part natives of the Transpadane colonies " (Caes., B. C., iii, 87, 5); for here the Latin colonies . . are evidently meant. There is, however, no trace of Latin cohorts in Caesar's Gallic army ; on the contrary, according to his express statements, all the recruits levied by him in Cisalpine Gaul were added to the legions or distributed into legions. It is possible that Caesar combined with the levy the bestowal of the franchise ; but more probably he adhered in this matter to the standpoint of his party, which instead of seeking to procure for the Transpadanes the Roman franchise rather regarded it as already legally belonging to them. . . . Only on this hypothesis could the report have spread that Caesar had introduced on his own authority the Roman municipal constitution among the Transpadane communities (Cic., Att., v, 3, 2 ; Fam., viii, 1, 2). This hypothesis too explains why Hirtius designates the Transpadane towns as " colonies of Roman citizens " (B. G., viii, 24, 3), and why Caesar treated the colony which he founded at Comum as a burgess-colony (Suet., Caes., 28 ; Strabo, v, 1, p. 213 ; Plut., Caes., 29), while the moderate party of the aristocracy conceded to it only the same rights as to the other Transpadane colonies, namely Latin rights, and the extremists even declared the civil rights conferred on the settlers altogether null, and consequently did not concede to the people of Comum the privileges attached to the tenure of a Latin municipal magistracy.' Mommsen, then, evidently holds that Cicero (Att., v, 11, 2) wrote gesserit, and, unlike Professor Reid and Dr. Hardy, believes that Marcellus did venture to scourge an ex-magistrate.

Now the rumour to which Mommsen alludes speedily died out (Cic., Fam., viii, 1, 2), and that Caesar regarded the franchise as ' already legally belonging to ' the Transpadane soldiers whom he had levied is simply incredible. Morally no doubt, but not legally. Dr. Hardy (op. cit., p. 109), remarking that ' the practice of admitting peregrini [aliens] to the legions with the simultaneous conferment of the franchise was carried to excess in the civil wars ' [after Caesar's death], thinks it probable that ' Caesar was the first to set an example of doing what was shamelessly abused by the triumvirs ' (cf. Reid, op. cit., pp. 71-2) ; but if he had enfranchised thousands of legionaries, surely Cicero, if not the historians, would have mentioned so momentous a step. Hirtius does not, at all events expressly, designate the Transpadane towns as colonies of Roman citizens : he may have referred only to Comum and the Cispadane

THE BRIBE PAID TO CURIO

The estimates of the bribe which Curio accepted from Caesar range from 1,000,000 sesterces [1] (£10,000) to 60,000,000 [2] (£600,000). Appian [3] says that it was more than 1,500 talents (£360,000); Servius [4] 2,700,000 sesterces (£27,000); Velleius [5] leaves it an open question whether Curio ratted without reward or for a bribe of 10,000,000 sesterces (£100,000). Dio [6] and Plutarch [7] wisely content themselves with saying that Caesar paid Curio's debts, which were heavy; Suetonius [8] merely observes that the bribe was large. Mommsen [9] accepts the highest figure, remarking that 'the price was high, but the commodity was worth the money'. Remembering the African campaign, I doubt whether it was; but anyhow the wealth which Caesar had acquired by plundering Gaul was not inexhaustible, and he had to disburse many other bribes besides finding money for the war. I have therefore followed the cautious vagueness of Plutarch, Suetonius, and Dio.

CAESAR'S COMPLAINT IN *B. C.*, i, 9, 4

Caesar complained that the two legions which he was obliged to send back to Italy in 50 B.C. 'had been withdrawn from him on the pretext of war with the Parthians'; but perhaps he only meant that after they had been withdrawn for the expected war they were retained when the danger had passed. Before February 20 Cicero received at Laodicea a letter from Pompey, who told him that he expected to be entrusted with the command against the Parthians; [10] and a letter written on July 18, in which Cicero said that if news of the restoration of peace in Syria were received in time the legions would doubtless not be sent thither,[11] implies that it had been originally intended to send them. As late as June 5 he thought that the danger was not over; [12] and although on January 23 in the following year he remarked that the legions were

Roman colonies, Eporedia, Mutina, and Parma. If he was really thinking of Transpadane towns, he may have meant that Caesar regarded them as entitled to the citizenship: anyhow he knew that they had not actually received it until it was granted to them, at the instigation of Caesar, by the *lex Roscia* in 49 B.C. (Dio, xli, 36, 3). [In a later article (*Journ. Rom. Studies*, vi, 1916, pp. 70-3) Dr. Hardy points out that many of the recruits mentioned in the passage (*B. C.*, iii, 87, 5) which Mommsen cites had been raised since the Transpadanes had been enfranchised by the *lex Roscia* of March, 49. and also that for more than thirty years before Caesar founded the colony of Novum Comum 'the number of Roman citizens in the Transpadane colonies had been yearly increasing by the continuous enfranchisement of magistrates and their families', &c.]

[1] A scholiast on Lucan, iv, 820. [2] Val. Max., ix, 1, 6.
[3] *B. C.*, ii, 26, 101. [4] Ad *Aen.*, vi, 621. [5] ii, 48, 4.
[6] xl, 60, 3. [7] *Caes.*, 29, 2. [8] *Div. Iul.*, 31.
[9] *Röm. Gesch.*, iii⁸, 1889, p. 366 (Eng. tr., v, 1908, p. 183).
[10] *Att.*, vi, 1, 14. [11] *Fam.*, ii, 17, 5. [12] *Att.*, vi, 4, 1.

'somewhat treacherously retained ',[1] he never said that they had
been unfairly recalled.   I therefore doubt whether Plutarch [2] was
justified in saying that they were originally sent for on the pretext
of war.

HOW CAESAR MODIFIED THE DISTRIBUTION OF
HIS LEGIONS IN THE WINTER OF 50–49 B. C.

Caesar says that while he was delayed at Massilia [in April or May,
705 (49 B. C.)] he ordered Gaius Fabius to march for Spain with three
legions, ' which he had quartered for the winter at Narbo and in the
adjacent districts.' [3]   Reading these words, one remembers that,
according to Hirtius,[4] Caesar, immediately before he returned to
Cisalpine Gaul in the autumn of the previous year, quartered four
legions under Trebonius in Belgium and four under Fabius in the
country of the Aedui.   It is therefore evident that in the course of
the winter he made a change.   I have no doubt that he decided upon
it in December, 704, when, inferring from the commission which
Gaius Marcellus had given to Pompey to arm that the efforts which
he had made to avert war would probably fail, he summoned the
8th and the 12th legion to join him.[5]   Evidently both these legions
belonged to Fabius's division, which was much nearer than that of
Trebonius to Italy.[6]   Fabius was thus left with only two legions.
Caesar doubtless ordered Trebonius to march southward, occupy the
camp of Fabius, and transfer one of his four legions to him, while
Fabius was to march to Narbo.[7]   The fact of his having been sent
thither proves that Caesar already contemplated fighting in Spain.
Probably Fabius's legions had been quartered in and around Matisco
(Mâcon) ; for that town was situated at the junction of several roads,
and Caesar had chosen it as the winter-quarters of a legion after the
fall of Alesia.[8]

---

[1] *Att.*, vii, 13 A, 2.
[2] *Pomp.*, 56, 3.   Cf. App., ú, 29, 114–5 and Dio, xl, 65, 2.
[3] *B. C.*, i, 37, 1.   [4] *B. G.*, viii, 54, 4.   [5] See p. 255.
[6] For this reason I cannot agree with Camille Jullian, who thinks (*Hist.
de la Gaule*, iii, 1909, p. 578, n. 1) that Caesar must have taken the 12th from
Fabius and the 8th from Trebonius.   It is true that the 8th joined Caesar
a fortnight later than the 12th (*B. C.*, i, 15, 2 ; 18, 5) : but it had more than
110 miles further to march ; and if it had come from Durocortorum (Reims),
near the southern frontier of the Belgae, where Trebonius's division was
probably quartered, the courier would have required four days longer to reach
it, and it would have taken at least a fortnight longer than the 12th to reach
Auximum.   Evidently it started later than the 12th,—because its quarters
were somewhat farther north, because its mobilization was more protracted,
or for some other unexplained reason.
[7] After writing so far I find that my view coincides with that of Stoffel
(*Hist. de J. César*, i, 1887, p. 207).
[8] *B. G.*, vii, 90, 7 ; viii, 4, 3.

THE CHRONOLOGY OF EVENTS FROM THE RECALL OF TWO OF CAESAR'S LEGIONS TO THE DEPARTURE OF CURIO FROM ROME

In pages 247–55 of my narrative I have derived great assistance from an able dissertation,[1] written by Professor Sanford, of the University of Nebraska. The time when the Senate decreed that Caesar should give up one of his legions for the Parthian war can be approximately fixed. On July 18, 50 B. C., Cicero wrote from Tarsus to Gnaeus Sallustius, ' You ask my opinion about the legions which have been ordered for Syria. I had my doubts before about their coming ; now I have no doubt, if news is received in time that tranquillity prevails in Syria, that they will not come ' (*Quod quaeris quid existimem de legionibus quae decretae sunt in Syriam, antea dubitabam venturaene essent : nunc mihi non est dubium quin, si antea auditum erit otium esse in Syria, venturae non sint).*[2] On June 26 Cicero had written from Tarsus, ' Syria is ablaze ' (*arderet Syria*)[3] ; in other words, he did not then know that the Parthians had gone. ' The date of their retreat,' says Professor Sanford,[4] ' may be fixed at about July 1 ; *antea* therefore refers to a period prior to that date.' Surely prior to the date when Cicero heard of the retreat ? It seems to me that all we can safely say is that Cicero heard of the retreat, the news of which would have taken, say, four or five days to reach him, at some time between July 1 and 17 ; and evidently he had been informed of the senatorial decree some days before the latter date. The news would have taken a month or more to travel from Rome to Tarsus ; so we may be sure that the decree was passed not later than the beginning of June, probably in May.

Professor Sanford begins by examining the theory, elaborated by H. Nissen[5] and W. Sternkopf,[6] that Antony was elected an augur in the latter half of September, 704 (50 B. C.). These scholars maintain, first, that Hirtius, when he said that Caesar started for Italy to support the candidature of Antony, *hibernis peractis,*[7] meant ' after inspecting the winter quarters,' not ' at the end of winter ' ; secondly, that, according to the current emendation—(Scio Domitio) *comitiorum* (diem) *timori ·esse*—of a corrupt passage in one of Caelius's letters (Cic., *Fam.*, viii, 12, 4), which was certainly written in September, Caelius was then looking forward to the augural election ; thirdly, that, as Caelius announced the result in *Fam.*, viii, 14, 1, that letter was evidently written later than the other ; finally, that *Fam.*, viii, 14, being one of the letters which the courier Acastus delivered to Cicero at the Piraeus on October 14, the twenty-first day after he left Rome, was probably written on September 23 [8] (August 9 of the Julian

[1] *University Studies*, Lincoln, Nebraska, xi, 1911, pp. 293–342.
[2] *Fam.*, ii, 17, 5.   [3] *Att.*, vi, 5, 3.   [4] *Op. cit.*, p. 329.
[5] *Hist. Zeitschr.*, xlvi, 1881, pp. 48–105. See especially 67 n. 4, 68, 69 n. 2.
[6] *Quaest. Chronol.*, 1884. See especially 28, 24, 26–7.
[7] *B. G.*, viii, 50, 1.
[8] Cf. O. E. Schmidt, *D. Briefwechsel d. M. T. Cicero*, 1893, pp. 88, 400.

calendar), and therefore that the election occurred in September, shortly before. Sanford[1] shows that *hibernis peractis* can only mean at the end of winter, and therefore that Caesar must have started for Italy long before September; he observes that the current emendation of *Fam.*, viii, 12, 4, though ' satisfactory from a paleographical point of view ', is ' nowise decisive '; [2] he points out [3] that Cicero [4] was informed at Ephesus on September 29 that the elections of consuls, praetors, and tribunes had taken place ; that the transmission of news from Rome to Ephesus would hardly have taken less than 35 days, and therefore that those elections were probably over before August 24 ; [5] and he argues [6] that as Antony, who successfully stood for a tribuneship as well as for the vacant place in the college of augurs, ' could not have known what date would be set for the election of tribunes,' and would have assumed that it might be ' the earliest possible ', July 14, and as it was necessary for him to announce his candidature at least 17 days before the election, he must have arrived in Rome not later than June 27, and must have left Nemetocenna (Arras) early in the month if not before.

At what time in the autumn of 50 B. C. did Caesar arrive finally in Cisalpine Gaul ? Hirtius says that he learned on his arrival that the two legions which he had been obliged to surrender for the [expected] Parthian war had been assigned by the consul Gaius Marcellus to Pompey.[7] Appian [8] and Dio [9] relate that Pompey was commissioned to arm against Caesar just before the end of Curio's tribuneship, that is, before December 10. Sanford [10] rightly holds that it was the news of this commission which impelled Caesar to summon the 8th and the 12th legion from Transalpine Gaul —evidently from the nearer camp, at Matisco (Mâcon), in the country of the Aedui.[11] The 12th, he remarks, overtook Caesar ' at Auximum, or very soon after he left that place, certainly before he reached Firmum [12] (February 2 [50 B. C.]) '.[13] Between the date of Pompey's commission and February 2 (or 4 ?) a courier or couriers travelled from Rome to

---

[1] *Op. cit.*, pp. 298–9.

[2] *Op. cit.*, p. 301. Sanford recognized of course that it was incumbent upon him to propose a new emendation. The MS. reading is *Scis Domitio diem tumorae est. Te exspecto*, &c. Sanford (pp. 45–6) offers a choice of three:—(1) *Scis Domiti odium timori esse. Te* (exspecto) ; (2) *Scis Domiti odium in tumore esse. Te* (exspecto) ; (3) *Scis Domiti odium. Tu moraris. Te* (exspecto). The second seems to him the most plausible. I doubt whether any of the three is more than plausible ; but the question is unimportant, for, as the reader will see, Sanford has proved that when the letter was written the augural election was over.

[3] *Ib.*, pp. 300–1.   [4] *Att.*, vi, 8, 2.

[5] The argument is reasonable, but not conclusive. Sanford observes (p. 301, n. 40) that, ' to judge from the evidence furnished by Cicero's letters from Cilicia, thirty-five days under ordinary conditions were quick time from Rome to Ephesus ' : a freedman of Trebonius, however, travelled from Seleucia Pieria (the port of Antioch) to Brundisium in 27 days (*Att.*, xi, 20).

[6] *Op. cit.*, pp. 304–5.   [7] *B. G.*, viii, 55, 1.

[8] *B. C.*, ii, 31, 121–2. Cf. Plut., *Pomp.*, 59, 1.

[9] xl, 64, 4 ; 66, 1.   [10] *Op. cit.*, p. 310.   [11] See p. 255.

[12] *B. C.*, i, 15, 3. Cf. 16, 1.   [13] Feb. 2, 705 = Dec. 13, 50 B. C.

Matisco, and the 12th legion marched from Matisco to Firmum. The distance from Rome to Matisco was about 750 Roman miles, from Matisco to Auximum about 650. Sanford, assuming that the couriers did not travel unusually fast, allows 15 days for their journey and 41 or 42 days for the march ; if the legion overtook Caesar just before he reached Firmum, he would allow 43 or 44. Accordingly he concludes that the courier left Rome not later than December 3, and that Pompey was commissioned not later than December 2. I have only to observe that the legions probably marched rather slower ; but Sanford's conclusion seems to me sound. At all events, as he shows,[1] O. E. Schmidt[2] is wrong in dating Pompey's commission on December 13. Schmidt, disregarding the evidence of Appian,[3] maintains that Marcellus met Pompey not outside Rome, but at Naples, and that Curio left Rome not immediately after the end of his period of office, but on December 21. His theory, which is based upon a forced interpretation of *Att.* vii, 5, 4, would compel him to assume that the couriers travelled considerably over 100 Roman miles a day (although he himself maintains[4] that their usual speed was not more than 50), and that the 12th legion made the incredible average of 26 or 27 miles.[5]

Supposing provisionally that Pompey received his commission on December 2, and that Hirtius meant that Caesar heard of it immediately after he reached Cisalpine Gaul, Sanford[6] infers that he probably did not gét there before the 12th ; for the distance from Rome to the north-western border of the province is more than 500 Roman miles. He thinks, however, that there is reason for believing that Caesar arrived considerably earlier.[7] Remarking that, according to Appian,[8] Marcellus commissioned Pompey in consequence of a rumour that Caesar was about to march on Rome, he conjectures that the rumour was occasioned by his arrival, and accordingly argues that he entered the province by November 20 or 21. Indeed he is inclined to think that he arrived as early as the 14th or 15th, and that Pompey was commissioned before December 2 —probably as early as November 25.[9] Hirtius arrived in Rome on

---

[1] *Op. cit.*, pp. 311–4. Cf. *Klio*, iv, 1904, pp. 334–5, and *Hermes*, xlv, 1910, p. 339.

[2] *Op. cit.*, pp. 94, 100.   [3] ii, 31, 121.   [4] *Op. cit.*, pp. 201–5, 378–9.

[5] Schmidt, supposing that Caesar's messenger travelled from Ravenna to Matisco—nearly 540 Roman miles—in five days (!) and that the legions started on the following day (January 1), reduces the distance from Matisco to Firmum from 690 to 'about 600' miles and holds that the legion reached Firmum on February 3. Even so and allowing only four days for rest, he could not bring down the average day's march to less than 21½ miles.

[6] *Op. cit.*, pp. 314–5.

[7] This, Sanford remarks (pp. 315–6), would compel us to take (quo) *cum venisset*, (cognoscit . . . legiones duas ab se missas . . . Pompeio traditas) (*B. G.*, viii, 55, 1) as equivalent to *postquam venit*, that is in a purely temporal sense.

[8] ii, 31, 120.

[9] *Op. cit.*, pp. 318–9. One objection to Sanford's view is that (in accordance with an old custom) Marcellus, who commissioned Pompey, being the junior consul, presumably held the *fasces* (in other words, took the lead in public affairs) in December (see p. 309). P. Willems (*Le sénat*, &c., ii, 1883, pp. 126–8) and Mommsen (*Röm. Staatsr.*, i³, 1887, pp. 39–41), to whom Sanford appeals,

December 6 and started to rejoin Caesar that night.[1] Sanford argues on the assumption that Caesar had sent Hirtius to Rome because he had received news of Pompey's commission and desired ' to obtain a . . . further account of the situation '. Supposing that Caesar arrived about November 14, and that the rumour which impelled Marcellus to commission Pompey was due to his arrival, the date of the commission would have been about November 25 ; Caesar would have heard of it, say at Mutina or Bononia, by December 1, and Hirtius would have had time to reach Rome by December 6. Granted the professor's somewhat rash assumptions,[2] his argument is sound enough ; but it is safer to rest content with the certain conclusion that, as Curio left Rome on December 10 and found Caesar at Ravenna,[3] Caesar reached Ravenna not later than December 13 or 14, and therefore must have arrived in the province several days before.

Let us now investigate the date of the augural election. Sanford admits that *Fam.*, viii, 14, was one of the letters which Acastus, leaving Rome on September 23, conveyed to Cicero ; nevertheless he proves that it was actually written in August. In *Fam.*, viii, 12, 4, Caelius says, ' I am much vexed by the delay of the slave who took the letters to you ; after he received the earlier one he remained [in town] more than forty days ' (*Conturbat me mora servi huius qui tibi litteras attulit ; nam acceptis prioribus litteris amplius ⟨dies⟩ quadraginta mansit*). Sanford observes that *prioribus litteris* means *Fam.*, viii, 14, and that, if ' more than forty days ' means 41 days, ' the latest date at which Acastus can have received *Fam.*, viii, 14, is August 12 '. But the earliest possible date of the election was July 20, and it was followed by the trial of Sextus Peducaeus, which Caelius mentioned in § 1, and which must have lasted at least 11 days.[4] Sanford argues that the election occurred about July 20 or 22. We shall be safe in concluding that it was held before the end of July.[5]

I have stated in my narrative [6] without direct evidence that when Caesar returned from Cisalpine Gaul to Nemetocenna he left Labienus in charge of that province. Hirtius, immediately after saying that

hold that in the Ciceronian age the consuls no longer held the *fasces* in alternate months ; but Tyrrell and Purser (*The Correspondence of Cicero*, iii[2], 1914, p. lxviii, n. ‡) nevertheless assume, citing Suetonius (*Div. Iul.*, 20, 1), that the old practice remained ' at least in . . . the more important matters when the two consuls were in sharp opposition '.

[1] Cic., *Att.*, vii, 4, 2.
[2] Remember the baseless rumours about Pompey's intended invasion of Spain in 49 B.C. (Caes., *B. C.*, i, 39, 3 ; Cic., *Att.*, x, 9, 1).
[3] App., ii, 32, 124–5.
[4] *Op. cit.*, p. 307.
[5] Sanford points out (p. 326) that ' the comitial days in July after the 20th were the 22nd and the 26th to the 31st inclusive '. In a later passage (pp. 334–6) Sanford observes that Caesar, in order to influence the electors of Cisalpine Gaul in Antony's favour, ought to have arrived by July 1, or even earlier, but did not actually arrive till a month later. He suggests that Antony, when he sent to ask Caesar for help, had reason to believe that the election might not be held till late in August.
[6] p. 252.

Caesar returned and then reviewed his legions in the country of the Treveri, tells us that he placed Labienus in authority over Cisalpine Gaul in order to further his own candidature for the consulship.[1] Sanford,[2] who infers from this passage that Labienus was not appointed until the review was over, remarks that ' it was not till after this appointment, to judge from Hirtius's account,[3] that Caesar was informed of his enemies' efforts to alienate Labienus '. Arguing that the review was held about the middle of October, and that Caesar started for Cisalpine Gaul by the end of the first week in November,[4] he points out that ' the time necessary for Labienus's journey to Cisalpine Gaul, if he had been present at the review, for the fact of his arrival to become known in Rome, for the discovery of the attempts to undermine his loyalty to Caesar, and for the journeys of couriers to Caesar sent to apprise him of these attempts, would much have exceeded the interval between the review and Caesar's departure for Italy '. Accordingly he concludes that Labienus ' had been in Cisalpine Gaul for a considerable time before he was given charge of the province '. But what was Labienus then doing ? Why should Caesar have left him idle ? It seems to me reasonable to suppose that Labienus had accompanied Caesar to Cisalpine Gaul, and that, although Hirtius, who was sometimes loose in chronology,[5] seems to imply that his appointment followed the review, he was really *left* in charge by Caesar.

THE AFFAIR OF SCAPTIUS

Much learning and ingenuity have been expended in endeavouring to ascertain the sum which the Salaminians borrowed, ostensibly from Scaptius, really from Brutus, in 56 B. C. ; but the problem, which does not concern this history, is insoluble. The question, however, arises whether, when Cicero first proposed to allow no more than 12 per cent. interest, he intended to make his rule retrospective —in other words, to sanction that rate and no more from the time when the loan was negotiated—or merely to enforce it for the period which had elapsed since the date—apparently before he had assumed office and probably in February,[6] 52—when the Salaminians had given their ' last note of hand ' (*proxima syngrapha*) [7] to Scaptius. In February, 50, Cicero wrote (let us assume provisionally that the MSS. are correct), ' I had arranged that they should pay with interest for six years at the rate of 12 per cent., added yearly to the capital sum ' (*Confeceram ut solverent centesimis sexennii ductis cum renovatione singulorum annorum*).[8] Taken by itself, this would show that Cicero's edict was retrospective. But in a later letter [9] he says,

---

[1] *B. G.*, viii, 52, 2.   [2] *Op. cit.*, pp. 336–7.   [3] *B. G.*, viii, 52, 3.
[4] *Op. cit.*, pp. 314–9.   [5] *Ib.*, pp. 323, 331–2.
[6] February, as Dr. Purser reminds us (*The Correspondence of Cicero*, iii[2], 1914, p. 339), was ' the month for the reception of provincial embassies by the senate ; and it was probably at that time of the year 56 B.C. that the Salaminian envoys . . . contracted the original loan '.
[7] *Att.*, vi, 2, 7.   [8] *Ib.*, 1, 5,   [9] *Ib.*, 2, 7.

' I have induced the Salaminians to consent to pay the whole amount to Scaptius, with interest calculated at 12 per cent. *from the date of the last note of hand,* and not at simple, but at compound interest ' (*Salaminios . . . adduxi ut totum nomen Scaptio vellent solvere, sed centesimis ductis a* p r o x i m a   q u i d e m   s y n g r a p h a, *nec perpetuis, sed renovatis quotannis*). Dr. Purser,[1] remarking that ' Cicero could only adjudicate on the last " renewal ",' and that ' therefore *sexenni* must be wrong ', says, ' The difficulty is solved by the genius of Sternkopf. He reads *bienni* . . . comparing Livy xliv. 15. 9, *bimensus* for *vi. mensum,*' &c. Why could Cicero ' only adjudicate on the last " renewal " ' ? He intended to set aside the renewal, which, as he says,[2] guaranteed the continued payment of interest at 48 per cent. If he could quash the renewal, which, on Purser's own showing, had preceded his assumption of office, why should he have respected previous renewals ? L. Gurlitt,[3] reviewing the literature of the question, refuses to be spell-bound by the genius of his compatriot. Cicero, he maintains,[4] *originally* intended to let the Salaminians off with the payment of 12 per cent. from the time when their debt was contracted, that is from 56 B. C., and he denies[5] that the two letters are inconsistent ; for he supposes that in the two months or so which elapsed between them Cicero changed his mind and that the Salaminians agreed to compromise. I could not at first acquiesce in this explanation, for whoever studies the three letters in which Scaptius and the Salaminians are mentioned will see that Cicero repeats the same statements again and again ; but I have a reason for believing that *sexenni* must be right : if Cicero had written *bienni*, he would not, I think, have added (cum renovatione) *singulorum annorum*, but *utriusque anni*. It seems to me probable, then, that when Cicero learned that the real creditor was Brutus, he weakly tried to meet him half-way.[6]

POMPEY'S ALLEGED PLAN OF CAMPAIGN FOR 705 (50–49 B. C.)

Colonel G. Veith in his maiden work[7] assured us that Pompey's original plan of campaign (for any account of which the reader will search the original authorities in vain) was ' simple, and in a military

---

[1] *Op. cit.*, p. 343.   [2] *Att.*, v, 21, 11 ; vi, 2, 7.
[3] *Berl. philol. Woch.*, 17 Nov., 1900, col. 1418–23.
[4] *Ib.*, col. 1420.   [5] *Ib.*, 1421–2.
[6] As Gurlitt remarks (*ib.*, 1419, 1423), Sternkopf wrongly holds that the two sums—106 and 200 talents—calculated by the Salaminians and by Scaptius respectively (*Att.*, v, 21, 12) were those on which interest had still to be paid from the date of the last note of hand. Self-evidently they were the final amounts, including interest accumulated since the last note of hand, which respectively the Salaminians offered and Scaptius demanded, to close the transaction.
It may be worth while to point out that Tyrrell's original explanation of *bono nomine* (*Att.*, v, 21, 12) remains unaltered in the 2nd edition, though it is stultified by Purser's appendix (pp. 339–41), to which he refers.
[7] *Gesch. d. Feldzüge C. J. Caesars*, 1906, p. 233.

sense decidedly correct '. Pompey, he explains, being convinced
that Caesar would be obliged to concentrate his entire army and had
no intention of beginning the war before the end of winter, intended
to use the interval for mobilizing his troops in Italy, and in the spring
to invade Cisalpine Gaul with 10 legions, while his Spanish army,
comprising 7 legions, crossed the Pyrenees, assailed Caesar's rear in
Gaul, and thus ensured his overthrow !

The colonel in his preface emphasized the necessity of reading the
Commentaries between the lines. Nobody will question the wisdom
of this instruction, provided that one is careful to avoid reading
what is not there. Cicero had two long conversations with Pompey
shortly before Caesar crossed the Rubicon. He gathered from the
first that Pompey had no hope of maintaining peace :[1] reporting
the second to Atticus, he wrote, ' Pompey thinks that when Caesar
hears that preparations are being made energetically to resist him,
he will abandon the consulship for this year and prefer retaining his
army and his province. . . . What most makes him hesitate, I fancy,
is that it would be undignified to abandon the city.'[2] Evidently
Pompey already realized that in the event of war he would be compelled to leave Rome and to arm the East against his adversary. His
plan, as conceived by the colonel, was undeniably simple, as simple
as the child's plan for catching a bird by putting salt upon its tail :
it might well succeed—if only Caesar were simple enough to sit still
while Pompey was putting it into execution. Even Cicero[3] had the
wit to prophesy that Caesar would be master of the situation.

THE CREDIBILITY OF CAESAR'S REPORT OF THE EVENTS OF JANUARY 1–7, 705

We may assume that Caesar derived his knowledge of the events
that followed the delivery of his ultimatum from the tribunes,
Antony and Cassius, from Curio and Caelius, who accompanied them
in their flight, and probably later from his father-in-law, Piso,[4] Marcus
Calidius,[5] Roscius,[6] and other senators. His information came from
eye-witnesses. Did he use it honestly ? The only way of answering
this question is to compare his narrative, sentence by sentence, with
the other authorities.

Calidius, alluding on the 2nd of January to the two legions which
had been withdrawn from Gaul, said that Caesar was afraid that
Pompey was keeping them ' near the city ' (*ad urbem*) in order to
act against him.[7] This phrase is misleading, for the two legions
were at that time in Capua,[8] if, indeed, they had not already been
transferred to Apulia, where, as Caesar says in a later passage,[9]

<hr>

[1] *Att.*, vii, 4, 2.   [2] *Ib.*, 8, 4–5.   [3] *Ib.* 3, 5 ; 6, 2 ; 9, 2.
[4] See *B. C.*, i, 3, 6.   [5] *Ib.*, 2, 3.   [6] *Ib.*, 3, 6.
[7] *Ib.*, 2, 3.   [8] App., *B. C.*, ii, 29, 115 ; 31, 120.
[9] i, 14, 3. The two legions, except some cohorts in Campania, were apparently
in Apulia, as we learn from one of Cicero's letters (*Att.*, vii, 12, 2), before
January 22.

Pompey quartered them for the winter. On the other hand, the violent language of Lentulus, which Caesar records,[1] is also attested by Plutarch;[2] and Caesar's statement that most of the senators were overawed by the troops which Pompey had outside the city is supported both by Dio[3] and Appian.[4] Caesar[5] says that a majority voted for Scipio's resolution that Caesar should disband his army before 'the fixed day'; Dio[6] that every one voted for it, except Caelius and Curio. What Caesar[7] tells us about the motives of Lentulus, Scipio, and Pompey is amply confirmed.[8]

Caesar says that before the Senate passed the 'ultimate decree' the tribunes, Antony and Cassius, were not permitted to use their reserve weapon, the right of veto, which Sulla had left to them (*neque etiam extremi iuris intercessionis retinendi, quod L. Sulla reliquerat, facultas tribuitur*)[9]; and in the speech which he addressed to the 13th legion at Ravenna he remarked that 'Sulla, though he completely stripped the tribunes of their powers, nevertheless left them free to exercise the veto' (*Sullam nudata omnibus rebus tribunicia potestate tamen intercessionem liberam reliquisse*).[10] 'One cannot believe', says Professor Reid,[11] 'that Sulla would have allowed validity to the use of the *intercessio* which those tribunes attempted'. It would seem that in principle Sulla had left the right of veto unimpaired, but that he had greatly weakened it.[12] When, however, Caesar[13] says that the tribunes were compelled by threats to take thought for their own safety, he is supported by Dio,[14] Appian,[15] and Plutarch;[16] and the complaint which he makes about the ultimate decree is not unreasonable. He insists that it had never before been passed except when the country was in extreme peril,[17] whereupon Mr. Peskett observes that 'it had been issued in 52 and in 63, as well as on other occasions, when the

[1] i, 2, 6.
[2] *Caes.*, 30, 3. Plutarch (*l. c.* Cf. *Ant.*, 5, 3) says that after Scipio had moved that Caesar should resign, the consuls put two questions to the Senate,—(1) should Caesar disband his army? (2) Should Pompey disband his? Nearly all the senators, he says, replied affirmatively to the first question, and a few to the latter. Thereupon Antony proposed that both Caesar and Pompey should dismiss their armies, and every one assented. Lentulus, however, exclaimed that arms, not votes, were needed against a malefactor, and the meeting broke up without having come to a decision.

'Every one' is perhaps an exaggeration; but the reader will remember that a few weeks earlier a majority of 370 to 22 had voted for the disarmament of both Caesar and Pompey (Plut., *Pomp.*, 58, 4; App., ii, 30, 119). I see no reason for accepting the view of E. Meyer (*Caesars Monarchie*[2], 1919, p. 284, n. 1) that Plutarch confounded the last-named division with the one which he says was made on the questions put by the consuls.

[3] xli, 2, 1.   [4] ii, 33, 132.   [5] i, 2, 6.
[6] xli, 2, 1.   [7] i, 4, 2–4.   [8] See p. 269, nn. 1–2.
[9] *B. C.*, i, 5, 1.   [10] *Ib.*, 7, 3.
[11] See Mr. A. G. Peskett's edition of *Bell. Civ.*, i, p. 55, and *Journ. Rom. Studies*, i, 1911, p. 99.
[12] See Cic., *Verr.*, i, 60, 155; *De leg.*, iii, 9, 22; Gell., x, 20, 10; Vell., ii, 30, 4; and cf. Th. Mommsen, *Röm. Staatsr.*, ii[3], 1887, p. 308.
[13] *B. C.*, i, 5, 2. Cf. 7, 2.   [14] xli, 3, 2.   [15] ii, 33, 131.
[16] *Caes.*, 31, 2.   [17] Cf. *Klio*, xiii, 1913, p. 380.

position of affairs was hardly more critical than in this year 49.
Caesar ', he concludes, ' is probably trying to mislead his readers '.
When a man is pleading his own cause you cannot expect from him
the impartiality of a judicial historian ; but Caesar's contemporary
readers remembered the events of 63 and 52, and those of them
who were capable of forming a sound judgement may have reflected
that while the Senate, having decided to resist Caesar's demands,
naturally took steps to protect themselves against the consequences,
' the position of affairs ' when Catiline was engaged in a criminal
conspiracy was very different from that in which Caesar, who, as
it has been truly said,[1] had exhausted all constitutional means,
was striving to avert ' political annihilation '.

I conclude that Caesar's narrative is on the whole trustworthy
and as free from exaggeration as we can reasonably expect.

ON PLUTARCH, *CAES.*, 31, 1

Plutarch, after relating that when Lentulus insisted that arms,
not votes, were needed against a malefactor, the Senate broke up
and adopted mourning,[2] says that a second letter from Caesar was
delivered, in which he offered to resign everything except Cisalpine
Gaul, Illyricum, and two legions, which he should retain until he
stood for his second consulship, whereupon Cicero induced Pompey
to relent, and he agreed to let Caesar keep the two provinces, but
not the troops.   Finally, says Plutarch, Cicero persuaded Caesar's
friends to agree to his retaining the two provinces with 6,000 men.
Pompey consented ; but Lentulus and his party demurred, and
expelled Antony and Curio from the Senate.[3]   According to Appian,[4]
Caesar made this offer before the 1st of January, 705 (50 B. C.) ;
Pompey agreed, but the consuls objected, and Caesar accordingly
wrote the letter, containing his ultimatum, which Curio handed
to the consuls.   Velleius,[5] who says that Caesar would have been
content to retain one legion and the mere ' name of a province '
and offered to stand for the consulship as a private individual,
but that all his proposals were rejected, leaves the question of
date uncertain.   Suetonius,[6] according to whom Caesar offered to
give up Transalpine Gaul and eight legions, provided that he might
retain two legions and Cisalpine Gaul or even one legion and Illyricum until he became consul (*quoad consul fieret*),[7] implies that he
made the offer before he came to Ravenna, that is, before the end
of 704.

---

[1] *Journ. of Philol.*, xxxiv, 1918, p. 221.   [2] Cf. Dio, xli, 3, 1.
[3] *Caes.*, 30, 2–3 ; 31. Cf. Zonaras, x, 7. Plutarch tells the same story more
briefly and with variations, which, however, are not necessarily inconsistent
with the version which I have quoted, in *Pomp.*, 59, 3 and *Ant.*, 5. 3. Cf. *Cic.*,
37, 1.
[4] *B. C.*, ii, 32, 126.   [5] ii, 49, 5.   [6] *Div. Iul.*, 29.
[7] Groebe (W. Drumann's *Gesch. Roms*, iii², 1906, p. 360, n. 1) maintains that
Caesar meant ' until he should be *elected* consul ' ; but, although Appian,
with whom Plutarch substantially agrees, expressly says so, Caesar would have

The question whether the offer was made before the debate of January 1 or, as Plutarch means, on or immediately before the 7th, is not of great historical importance ; but as I have written a detailed narrative, I must justify it. Nissen [1] infers from Plutarch's narrative that the letter containing the offer was delivered in the Senate on January 6, which, he says, would have been quite possible if a courier had left Rome on the evening of the 1st to inform Caesar that his ultimatum had been rejected. Moreover, he argues, Plutarch's account is confirmed by the letter,[2] written on January 12, in which Cicero told Tiro that on arriving outside Rome on the 4th he had desired to heal the discord which he found prevailing, but had been prevented by the factious spirit of interested individuals.

Now a courier who left Rome on the evening of January 1 could hardly have reached Ravenna before the 4th,[3] and even if he had received instructions from Caesar instantly and started on his return journey within an hour after his arrival, he could not have reached Rome in time to deliver the letter on the morning of the 6th. Holzapfel [4] more reasonably supposes that he returned on the 7th, and even then the whole errand would have been performed within five days and a half. But I can afford to waive this objection. For not only am I unable to discover in Cicero's letter the confirmation which Nissen imagines, but his words appear to me absolutely inconsistent with Plutarch's statement. Cicero only alludes to one letter of Caesar. ' To put the matter in a nutshell ', he says, ' our friend Caesar sent a hard threatening letter to the Senate : even now he has the impudence to retain his army and his province despite the Senate, and my friend Curio is egging him on ' (*Omnino et ipse Caesar, amicus noster, minaces ad senatum et acerbas litteras miserat et erat adhuc impudens qui exercitum et provinciam invito senatu teneret, et Curio meus illum incitabat*).[5] Obviously the letter to which Cicero referred was the ultimatum delivered in the Senate on the 1st of January. Is it credible that if a second letter, in which Caesar asked only to be allowed to retain one legion and Illyricum, had been received on the 7th, Cicero would have said nothing about it ? If so, he committed a gross *suppressio veri*. Surely it is more probable that Plutarch made a mistake. All students of Roman history must have noticed how he distorted the order of events in the sixty-second chapter of his life of Pompey [6] and the fifty-first

gained nothing by such an offer ; and I take the words of Suetonius to mean ' until he should become consul '. [Dr. Hardy, who agrees with me (*Journ. of Philol.*, xxxiv, 1918, pp. 211, 218, n. 2), ignores the statements of Plutarch and Appian, which were probably based on some ambiguous phrase like that of Suetonius.]   [1] *Hist. Zeitschr.*, xlvi, 1881, p. 84, n. 1.

[2] *Fam.*, xvi, 11. The following letters have also been cited,—*Att.*, ix, 11 A, 2 ; *Fam.*, iv, 1, 1 ; viii, 17, 1 ; vii, 3, 2 ; vi, 6, 6 ; iv, 14, 2.   Except *Att.*, ix, 11 A and *Fam.*, iv, 1, these probably refer to later efforts which Cicero made in the cause of peace ; and the two exceptions prove no more than *Fam.*, xvi, 11.

[3] See vol. iii, pp. 375-6.   [4] *Klio*, iii, 1903, p. 216, n. 2.
[5] *Fam.*, xvi, 11, 2.   [6] §§ 1-2.

of his life of Cato.[1] One can conceive that Curio, Antony, or Quintus
Cassius may have made a last attempt, on the 7th of January or
earlier, to procure a settlement by suggesting that Caesar's irre-
ducible minimum, offered some weeks before, should be accepted ;
and this hypothesis would explain Plutarch's blunder. But there
is another reason for rejecting his statement. Is it likely that if
Caesar had sent this supposed second letter, he would have omitted
to justify himself by recording the almost incredibly moderate offer
which it is said to have contained ?

[After revising the above article I find that E. Schwartz,[2] while
he agrees with me that the date which Plutarch assigned to the
discussion of Caesar's alleged second offer is ' chronologically as good
as impossible ', and that the letter to which Cicero referred was the
ultimatum delivered in the Senate on the 1st of January, nevertheless holds with Nissen that the date given by Appian is wrong,
and accordingly is forced to identify the offer with that which
Caesar made in reply to Pompey's message, delivered by Roscius
and Lucius Caesar,[3] and which was handed to Pompey at Teanum
on January 23 ![4] This, I need hardly say, has nothing to do with
the proposal which Appian and Plutarch describe. E. Kornemann,
who clings to Nissen's chronologically preposterous theory, points
out Schwartz's mistake.[5] As Schwartz rightly corrects Nissen, and
Kornemann with equal justice corrects Schwartz, I regard their
mutually destructive criticism as confirming my own view.]

THE INTERVIEW OF CAELIUS WITH CICERO
ON JANUARY 7, 705

According to the MSS., Caelius in the letter [6] in which he reminded
Cicero of his visit wrote (cum ad te proficiscens) *Arimini* (noctu
venissem) ; but Cicero was not at that time in Northern Italy.
On the 7th of January he went from Rome to join Caesar, with or
near whom he remained until he was sent to Intimelii (Ventimiglia),
whence he accompanied him to Spain.[7] The required emendation
is obviously that which W. Sternkopf suggested,—*Ariminum*.[8]

[1] § 3.   [2] *Paulys Real-Ency.*, ii, 227–8.
[3] *B. C.*, i, 8. 2–10. 1.   [4] Cic., *Att.*, vii, 14, 1.
[5] *Jahrb. f. class. Philol.*, 22. Suppl., 1896, p. 574.
[6] Cic., *Fam.*, viii, 17.
[7] Cic., *Att.*, vii, 17, 3 ; *Fam.*, viii, 15 ; 16.
[8] E. Meyer (*Caesars Monarchie*[2], 1919, p. 294, n. 1) thinks it 'evident' that
Caelius did not visit Cicero on Jan. 7, but on Jan. 13 or 14, having been
dispatched by Caesar for the purpose. But Caelius and Cicero were both in
Rome on Jan. 7 (*Fam.*, xvi, 11, 2 ; Dio, xli, 2, 1 ; 3, 2), and it seems to me
evident that Caelius did not go to Ariminum and back before visiting Cicero.

DID CAESAR MEET THE TRIBUNES, ANTONY AND CASSIUS, BEFORE OR AFTER HE CROSSED THE RUBICON ?

Professor Tenney Frank remarks that Caesar's ' statement that he met the tribunes only after crossing the Rubicon [1] . . . does not accord with the story as told by Plutarch [2] and Appian [3] ', who emphasize ' the fact that Caesar exhibited the tribunes upon their arrival to his army, thus stirring the soldiers to action. Plutarch and Appian ', says the professor, ' are evidently following Pollio, who was with Caesar on the day of crossing.[4] . . . The only objection against adopting this conclusion is that it seems to assume that Caesar has falsified to his own disadvantage. Why should Caesar . . . make his own case worse than it actually was by stating that he had begun the civil war before the tribunes offered him a plausible excuse ? ' The professor answers his own question by assuming that Antony, ' who after Caesar's death probably had Caesar's manuscript in his possession, inserted the troublesome words : *ibique* [i.e. at Ariminum] *tribunos plebis . . . convenit.* . . . Antony, who took such liberties in changing the other papers [of Caesar] and in forging new ones, would hardly permit the publication of any statement in the *Bellum Civile* that would prove derogatory to himself. During this very time Cicero [5] was abusing him as the cause of the civil war, for by making his theatrical escape to Caesar he had furnished his master [with] a fair excuse for invading Italy. It was an easy matter for Antony to make Caesar's own book refute Cicero '.[6]

Professor Frank then proceeds to argue in favour of the probability of Caesar's having met the tribunes at Ravenna. ' It is now ', he says, ' usually believed that Caesar crossed the Rubicon on the night of January the tenth.[7] It could not have been difficult for Antony and Curio to reach Ravenna by the morning of that day. . . . Again the probability that Antony came to Ravenna is strengthened by the fact that the five cohorts over which he was placed marched [as O. E. Schmidt argues] from Ravenna and not from Ariminum as Caesar implies, and must have set out on the tenth. The strongest argument, however, lies in the unanimous testimony that Caesar

---

[1] *B. C.*, i, 8, 1.   [2] *Caes.*, 31–2 ; *Ant.*, 5, 3.   [3] *B. C.*, ii, 33, 133.
[4] Plut., *Caes.*, 32, 3.   [5] *Phil.*, ii, 22, 53. 55.
[6] *Class. Quart.*, i, 1907, pp. 223–4.
[7] O. E. Schmidt (*D. Briefwechsel d. M. T. Cicero*, 1893, p. 104) and Stoffel (*Hist. de J. César*, i, 1887, p. 203) affirm without any evidence that a courier left Rome on January 7 to inform Caesar of what had happened in the Senate on that day. If they are right, the messenger must have been dispatched by Caesar's champions, Antony, Cassius, Caelius, and Curio ; and as they went the same night to join their chief, I am not convinced that they would have incurred the expense of hiring a carriage for a courier. If, however, as I hold, they met Caesar not at Ravenna but at Ariminum, and had not dispatched a courier from Rome, they must have sent one from Ariminum to Ravenna

addressed his soldiers at the beginning of his campaign, and that the speech . . . would have little excuse or point unless made at Ravenna and in the presence of the tribunes '.[1]

As this is ' the strongest argument ', the professor evidently regards the one which he keeps to the last as less strong. Caesar, he says, was ' not ready to meet Pompey at once ', for he had only one legion with him, while Pompey had four, besides the Italian garrisons. Evidently therefore he crossed the Rubicon ' on a sudden decision before he was prepared to advance '. The motive of this decision was the arrival of the tribunes : he ' suddenly saw in their apparent dishonour a pretext for the daring move, and, though not yet ready, he felt that he could not afford to let so fair a chance slip '. If, the professor concludes, we assume that the tribunes stopped at Ariminum, we must face several embarrassing questions:— ' why should Caesar have been in such haste to cross a day before he could make the best of his exhibit when he knew he must move slowly for several weeks to come ? Or what would be the point of haranguing the soldiers after the vital step was taken ? Or what would be the use of exhibiting the tattered tribunes on the day after the invasion ? '[2]

Let me ask Professor Frank one question :—why does he ignore the testimony of Lucan[3] and of Dio,[4] who (like Suetonius[5]) confirm the statement of Caesar ? The statements of Plutarch and Appian are not inconsistent with the statement of Caesar : both were notoriously careless about chronology, and, not unnaturally, they mentioned ' the fact that Caesar exhibited the tribunes ' immediately after recording their arrival. Neither of them says that the tribunes came to Ravenna : Caesar and Dio expressly say, Lucan and Suetonius imply, that they stopped at Ariminum. Caesar does not say that he ' had begun the civil war before the tribunes offered him a plausible excuse ' : he says that after he learned that the tribunes had been treated with contumely and had fled to join him he harangued the 13th legion,[6] and that he then marched to Ariminum.[7]

When Professor Frank insists that Antony and Curio could without difficulty have reached Ravenna by the morning of January 10, he apparently forgets that they did not leave Rome until the night of the 7th.[8] So far as we know, the shortest time in which the distance—385 kilometres, or 240 English miles—was ever covered was 3 days :[9] what right has the professor to assume that Curio covered it in two days and a half ? Schmidt's theory, which Professor Frank omits to explain, but which I shall examine in a later article, was that when Caesar[10] said that he ' sent Mark Antony with five cohorts from Ariminum to Arretium ' he made a misleading statement ; that the cohorts had already been pushed forward from Ravenna towards Arretium ; and that, as they were not to

[1] Op. cit., p. 224.   [2] Ib., pp. 224–5   [3] i, 231–95.
[4] xli, 4, 1.   [5] Div. Iul., 33.
[6] Cf. B. C., i, 5, 5 with 7, 1, and see Meusel's note on the latter.
[7] Ib., 8, 1.   [8] Ib. 5, 4–5 ; App., ii, 33, 133.
[9] Ib., 32, 127.   [10] B. C., i, 11, 4.

pass through Ariminum, Antony was sent from Ariminum to join them. Suppose that Schmidt is right: how does his theory strengthen 'the probability that Antony came [from Rome] to Ravenna'? Why should Caesar's speech, made 'at the beginning of the campaign', have had no point unless it was 'made in the presence of the tribunes'? Its object was to stimulate the soldiers to vindicate the rights of their commander; and he told them that the tribunes had been wronged. Was there no point in that?

It remains only to answer the three questions which Professor Frank propounds. I do not find them in the least embarrassing. To the first I reply that Caesar crossed the Rubicon immediately after he heard of the flight of the tribunes because it was important to secure Ariminum and other strategical points as soon as possible; that to 'make the most of his exhibit' was a matter of minor importance, since the troops already knew that the tribunes had been wronged and would be just as much impressed by seeing them at Ariminum as at Ravenna;[1] and that since Caesar occupied Ariminum, Pisaurum, Fanum, Arretium, and Iguvium in 8 or 9 days, besides holding a levy and negotiating, it can hardly be said that he moved slowly.[2] To the second question I reply that there would be no point in haranguing the soldiers for the first time 'after the vital step was taken', but that Caesar harangued them before. He harangued them at Ravenna before he crossed the Rubicon: Dio[3] and Orosius[4] may or may not be right in saying that he did so in the presence of the tribunes at Ariminum; but that he should there have made a second speech is perfectly credible. To the third question I reply that to exhibit the tribunes was in any case less important than to let the soldiers know that the tribunes had been wronged, but that to exhibit them on the second day of the war would have been just as useful as on the first, and would have confirmed the resolution of the soldiers if it needed confirmation. And if to exhibit the tribunes was so important, why does Caesar, in giving the substance of his speech, say nothing about them? Are we to understand that in the seventh chapter of his *First Commentary*

---

[1] H. Nissen (*Hist. Zeitschr.*, xlvi, 1881, p. 97, n. 1) says that Caesar, in disagreement with all the other authorities, stated, in order to conceal the violence of his action, that he harangued the troops at Ravenna. There is no disagreement: Dio and Orosius, who alone say that he made a speech at Ariminum, do not deny that he had made one at Ravenna.

Schmidt (*op. cit.*, p. 105, n. 1), who agrees with Nissen that Caesar addressed the troops not at Ravenna, but at Ariminum, and therefore evidently supposes that the cohorts which he believes to have been pushed forward from Ravenna were not addressed at all, thinks it natural that Caesar should not have disclosed his purpose to the men until after he had crossed the frontier! Dr. Purser (*The Correspondence of Cicero*, iii², 1914, p. civ, n. †) takes the same view as Nissen on the ground that 'Caesar's whole plan would have been endangered if the people of Ariminum had got information of his intention and had refused him entrance'. As if they did not know that his troops were approaching!

[2] The distance from Ravenna to Iguvium is 182 kilometres, or 113 statute miles.

[3] xli, 4, 2   [4] vi, 15, 3.

he did describe the exhibition, but that Antony deleted the description?

To sum up, it seems to me that Professor Frank's conjectures are unsupported by evidence, and that we shall do well to follow the authorities who tell us where Caesar and the tribunes met. And in conclusion I will ask the professor one question, which I do not mean to be embarrassing, but only to smooth the way for his graceful recantation : how would he explain away the fact that Caelius, who accompanied the tribunes from Rome on the night of January 7, reminded Cicero in 48 B.C. that his destination had been, not Ravenna but, Ariminum ? [1]

[1] Cic., *Fam.*, viii, 17, 1. Cf. p. 333.

ADDENDA

PAGE 19. ' Leaving Labienus . . . Mont Genèvre.' Why had not Caesar raised the two legions mentioned in this passage and moved them into Gaul before ? Camille Jullian (*Hist. de la Gaule*, iii, 197) conjectures that he kept them in Northern Italy because he had originally planned a war of conquest in the valley of the Danube. I am inclined to believe that the movement of the Helvetii took him by surprise.

PAGE 34. In *Caesar's Conquest of Gaul* [2] (p. 652) I argued that Procillus, whom I there (p. 64), not without some authority, called Trouoillus, was identical with Caesar's interpreter, Troucillus (p. 23, *supra*). See, however, H. Meusel's edition of *B.G.*, vol. i, 1913, p. 353.

PAGE 39, note 2. To the article there cited I should add that it is probable that the principal road from Durocortorum (Reims) to the northern part of the Belgic territory crossed the Aisne at Berry-au-Bac. Cf. *Caesar's Conquest of Gaul* [2], p. 665, n. 5, with C. Jullian's *Hist. de la Gaule*, iii, 253, n. 2.—In *Caesar's Conquest of Gaul*, p. 662, l. 10, *for* Roman (line) *read* Belgic.

PAGE 294, note 2. F. Münzer (*Klio*, xviii, 1922, pp. 200–1), supporting my view that the 10 *legati* assigned to Caesar in 56 B.C. were lieutenant-generals, not a senatorial commission, quotes from H. Usener's edition of scholia on Lucan (p. 167) *Labienus X annis cum Caesare militavit et in Galliis inter decem legatos primus habitus est.*

PAGE 324. ' Sanford rightly holds . . . Aedui.' Caesar (*B. C.*, i, 8, 1) wrongly says that he summoned the 8th and the 12th legion from their winter quarters after he harangued the 13th at Ravenna (see p. 270). Cf. vol. iii, pp. 382–3.

CORRIGENDUM

PAGE 285, line 14. *For* 60 *read* 33.

DUE DATE

FEB 1 8 1991			
NOV 2 4 1996			
MAR 1998			
1991			
1998			
	201-6503		Printed in USA

WS - #0049 - 201124 - C0 - 229/152/20 [22] - CB - 9780265967669 - Gloss Lamination